The Other Dickens

LILLIAN NAYDER

The Other Dickens

A LIFE OF CATHERINE HOGARTH

Mayall Photo.   London

CORNELL UNIVERSITY PRESS *Ithaca & London*

First published 2011 by Cornell University Press
First printing, Cornell Paperbacks, 2012

Printed in the United States of America

Library of Congress Cataloging-in-Publication Data

Nayder, Lillian.
   The other Dickens : a life of Catherine Hogarth / Lillian Nayder.
      p. cm.
   Includes bibliographical references and index.
   ISBN 978-0-8014-4787-7 (cloth : alk. paper)
   ISBN 978-0-8014-7794-2 (pbk. : alk. paper)
   1. Dickens, Catherine, 1815–1879.   2. Authors' spouses—
Great Britain—Biography.   I. Title.
   PR4582.N39 2011
   823'.8 — dc22
   [B]   2010022625

Cornell University Press strives to use environmentally responsible suppliers
and materials to the fullest extent possible in the publishing of its books. Such materials
include vegetable-based, low-VOC inks and acid-free papers that are recycled, totally
chlorine-free, or partly composed of nonwood fibers. For further information,
visit our website at www.cornellpress.cornell.edu.

Cloth printing   10 9 8 7 6 5 4 3 2
Paperback printing   10 9 8 7 6 5 4 3 2 1

FRONTISPIECE
Catherine Dickens (ca. 1863–1865), photograph by John J. E. Mayall, H1201,
Gimbel Collection, Beineke Rare Book and Manuscript Library, Yale University.

Conten[ts]

To the memory of
Helen Roney (1833–1890),
and to Margaret Koski-Kent,
Diane Selinger, Carol Grumbach,
Kelly Ann Johnson and Beverly Johnson,
"For there is no friend like a sister"
or cousin

Acknowledgments

Dozens of people in several countries have supported my work on *The Other Dickens* for the past ten years, generously offering their time, resources, and insight. I owe many, many thanks to family members, friends, colleagues, Dickens scholars, archivists, librarians, and descendants of Catherine Dickens and those in her circle. Among the first to believe it might be a good idea to write this book was Anne Thompson, chair of the Bates College English Department in the 1990s. Thanks go to her and to Michael Slater of Birkbeck College, University of London, whose pioneering work on *Dickens and Women* informs my own and who has kindly shared his ideas and material with me. In the earliest stages of my research, Andrew Xavier of the Charles Dickens Museum provided me with crucial and much appreciated help. Lucy Gent and Malcolm Turner welcomed me to 70 Gloucester Crescent, Regent's Park, the home of Catherine Dickens from 1858 to 1879, providing an unexpected visitor with a tour of the premises and tea in the garden. Several members of the Japan Dickens Fellowship supported this project from the outset, inviting me to speak about Catherine Dickens with their students. For their warm welcome and interest, I thank Eiichi Hara of Tokyo Woman's Christian University, Toru Sasaki of Kyoto University, and Kensuke Ueki of Hiroshima University. I am grateful to Grace Moore for helping to host my visit to the University of Exeter when she was a graduate student, and for her enthusiasm about the project. In Lewiston and in London, my colleague Cristina Malcolmson has provided me with a host of useful suggestions for the book and helped me define its aims.

Many librarians and archivists have contributed to *The Other Dickens* by arranging research visits, answering questions, and making available the primary sources on which I draw. Those to whom I owe thanks include Robert Bearman, Shakespeare Birthplace Trust; Iain G. Brown, Sheila Mackenzie, and Robin Smith, National Library of Scotland; Kathleen Cann, Cambridge University Library; Becky Cape, Lilly Library, Indiana University; Brian Carpenter, Devon Record Office; Revinder Chahal, Victoria and Albert Museum; Philip N. Cronenwett, Special Collections, Dartmouth College Library; Bernard R. Crystal, Rare Book and Manuscript Library, Columbia University; Howard Doble, London Metropolitan Archives; Tracey Earl and Isobel Long, Coutts Bank archive; Corrina S. Flanagan, Eva Guggemos and Naomi Saito, Beinecke Rare Book and Manuscripts Library, Yale University; Imogene Gibbon, Nicola Kalinsky, Susanna Kerr, Kim Macpherson, and Helen Watson, Scottish National Portrait Gallery; Elizabeth Gow, John

A portion of
erine in 184[
chapter 4 as
Rue," *The V*
Vescovi, Lu
early format
ens and Her
Widowhood
I thank the e

I would li
from the lett
Ouvry Paper
edited and c
Dickens, pub
the direction
thankful to t
to the follow
draw on mat
Yale Univer
Charles Dicl
Library, Loi
College Libr
Special Coll
Ransom Hu
Huntington
ety of Penns
Kelvin Smitl
College, Uni
cord Office;
Museum, Nt
National Ma
London Col
Harvard Uni
versity; Rose
Archive; Uni
leigh Memoi
Library, Uni
Albert A. Be
sion of the N

INTRODUCTION
Constructing Catherine Dickens

The daughter and granddaughter of cultured Scotsmen and women—intellectuals, writers, and musicians who highly valued family life—Catherine Hogarth was an animated and well-read nineteen-year-old, and a devoted sister and cousin, when she met Charles Dickens in 1835. For forty-two of her sixty-four years, she lived apart from the famous man who has come to define her, spending her first two decades as Miss Hogarth and her last two as the estranged wife and widow of "the Inimitable." Yet we know her solely as "Mrs. Charles Dickens." Recognized by the one relationship that brought her into the public eye, for better and for worse, she is "understood" by most of those who claim to know her story as a helpmeet gone bad, a figure best characterized by her rejection at Dickens's hands, her star eclipsed in 1858 by that of a much younger woman, Ellen Ternan, or, years earlier, by the attractions of her own sisters Mary and Georgina—justifiably eclipsed, the story goes, her own incompetence to blame.

This plotline is largely the creation of Charles Dickens, and a self-serving fiction at best. But it has proved nearly as powerful and timeless as the tales of Scrooge, Oliver Twist, and Little Nell. *The Other Dickens* debunks this tale in the retelling, exposing its mythic elements and the unspoken functions they serve. Wresting away from her husband the power to shape Catherine's biography, this book forces him to the margins, giving voice to a spectrum of Victorians instead.

Catherine Dickens's life story cannot be told apart from the story of her marriage to Charles Dickens. Yet her relationship to Dickens need not be what scholars have claimed it is: the rationale for any consideration of her experiences. Since 1870, critics and biographers have assumed that Catherine's life has meaning only insofar as it illuminates that of Dickens, and that unless she is defined in relation to him, her story is no story at all. Among its varied aims, this book challenges that assumption, dislodging Dickens from the center of Catherine's story and replacing him with a range of figures whose lives illuminated, and were illuminated by, hers. Undermining the logic of coverture, the principle that governed a woman's subordination to her husband in Catherine's day, it reworks the standard chronology of her life by defining significant events and turning points without using their relevance to Dickens as a necessary measure, and by extending the boundaries of her existence to include the decades that preceded and followed her time with him. Despite the challenge of doing so, the book keeps Dickens from center stage, resisting his mesmerizing powers, his tendency to seize control of narratives, and his uncanny ability to make biographers speak for him from beyond the grave. It focuses on Catherine's own writings, experiences, and needs, and reconceives the plotline of her life so that her separation from Dickens is not its defining and final moment. Although it refers to its subject as Catherine Dickens rather than Catherine Hogarth after her marriage, it follows Catherine herself in doing so, and foregrounds the limits of any one such definition. A somebody rather than a nobody, whatever her title, Catherine becomes a figure with her own claims to significance and agency.

Among those claims, Catherine's complex response to gender inequities is perhaps the most important. The eldest child in a lively family of four girls and five boys, whose parents were highly literate yet often pressed for money, Catherine was a well-spoken teenager when the Hogarths moved from Edinburgh to London in the early 1830s. With her younger sister Mary and a Scottish cousin, she had formed an irreverent coterie of young women by the time she became engaged. Seeking a partnership in marriage, she learned the virtue of willing submission from her husband in a union that proved surprisingly restrictive and from which she was only reluctantly and partially released in 1858. Her embrace of the role that constrained her, her attempts to question and resist those constraints, and the physical and emotional costs of accepting social confines are crucial elements of her story.

So, too, are her varied relations with her sisters—Mary, Georgina, and Helen, in their order of birth—whose sororal ties have been devalued and obscured by Dickens's own claims to (and about) these women. Reclaiming Mary and Georgina Hogarth for Catherine—acknowledging as primary their ties to their sister rather than their "brother"—I punctuate eight chronologically ordered chapters with three "interludes," each examining Catherine's relationship to the sister who was particularly important to her at that stage of her life, and doing so from their perspectives and in their words. While Catherine's separation from Dickens in 1858 and his death in 1870 are crucial turning points in the chapters that follow, changes in Catherine's sisterhood prove equally important signposts: Mary's death in 1837; Georgina's incorporation into the Dickens household in 1843 and her decision to remain with her brother-in-law rather than with her sister at the time of their separation; Helen's staunch advocacy of Catherine in 1858 and her grief over Catherine's death in 1879.

The lives that emerge from this retelling are substantially different from the representations bequeathed to us by Dickens. Among the most striking changes is the role performed here by the woman Dickens cast as his villainess during and after 1858. Insofar as this book has a heroine, Helen Hogarth (Mrs. Richard Roney), the "serpent" in Dickens's account of the Fall of his marriage, assumes that role. Catherine's advocate, companion, and chief mourner, Helen enables us to see Catherine anew, and *The Other Dickens* is dedicated to her memory.

GAPS AND SILENCES

Captured in a painting by Sir Henry Raeburn (1756–1823), Katherine Thomson, the maternal grandmother of Catherine Hogarth, looks straight at the viewer from the canvas, seeming to connect our lives with hers. Her face is soft and partly shadowed, her expression thoughtful, conveying a sense of her intelligence at work. Unlike Raeburn's usual female subjects, represented in domestic settings and in clothes that emphasize their femininity, Mrs. Thomson is dressed for the public realm, a person who goes out into the world.[1] Wearing a plumed hat and a dark coat with fur lapels, her collared blouse loosely tied with a silk scarf, she appears an attractive and genteel figure, ladylike without being modest or demure (fig. 1).

The directness of her gaze proves misleading, as does the public persona that Raeburn creates for her. Despite her apparent willingness to meet our eye, Mrs. Thomson is largely elusive, a woman about whom we can gather information only at second or third hand. Anyone interested in seeing her Raeburn portrait must rest satisfied with a magazine reproduction of the original that is on file at the Scottish National Portrait Gallery, since the painting's whereabouts are now unknown. And those wishing to hear Mrs. Thomson's voice must reconstruct it as best they can on the basis of what was said *to* her—not through her own letters, none of which survive, but through those she received from her husband while he was away from home, dozens of which are preserved at the National Library of Scotland. The mediated quality of Mrs. Thomson's voice reflects, more generally, that of her identity as a member of the "second sex." Whether known as Katherine Miller of Kelso or, after her marriage in 1781, as Mrs. George Thomson of Edinburgh, she is described in terms of her ties to male relations and never in her own right: she is the daughter of a lieutenant in the Fiftieth Regiment and the wife of George Thomson, clerk to

---

1. I am indebted to Rebecca Corrie of Bates College for this insight.

FIGURE 1. *Sir Henry Raeburn, portrait of Mrs. Thomson (ca. 1805), collection unknown, Scottish National Portrait Gallery Reference Section.*

the Board of Trustees for Encouragement of Art and Manufactures in Scotland. In the available sources her own mother is never named.[2]

2. See, for example, J. Cuthbert Hadden, *George Thomson: The Friend of Burns* (London: John C. Nimmo, 1898), 11; and John Christie, *The Ancestry of Catherine Thomson Hogarth, the Wife of Charles Dickens, Novelist* (Edinburgh: William J. Hay, 1912), 10. As Dickens

These lines of identification are familiar to those who investigate nineteenth-century women's history, and consistently grapple with the silences, gaps, and omissions created by the workings of a patriarchal culture. That culture sometimes idealized motherhood and women's domestic roles yet privileged men and male experience, reinforcing the sexual double standard in most political, economic, and legal practices, and discouraging women from entering public life. Most historians have characterized the nineteenth century as a period of increasingly divided gender roles in Britain, as economic developments separated work from home and reduced employment opportunities for women. Some describe a virtual quarantine separating public from private life, charting women's gradual "engulfment" in the private sphere over the course of the 1800s.[3] In increasing numbers, scholars now question the extent to which nineteenth-century Britons were divided into "separate spheres" and warn against confusing gender ideals with the realities of lived experience at the time.[4] But among the Thomsons and the Hogarths, Catherine's families of origin—and, later, among the Dickenses—a gender divide in the concerns and activities of family members is clear. Although Catherine Dickens's sister Helen proved an exception, the women in these families generally did no paid work and focused on domestic matters. By contrast, their fathers, husbands, and brothers led more divided lives as public men who valued family life and actively participated in it while also pursuing their professional careers.

The association of middle-class women with the private and domestic helps to explain why they are not as well represented as their male relations in traditional archival holdings, which often consist of government documents, business contracts, and the papers of well-known public figures. Yet the problem of locating or reconstructing primary source materials is less acute in Catherine Dickens's case

---

himself described Catherine's grandmother in an epitaph he composed in November 1841, she was "For Sixty Years / The dear Wife / of / George Thomson / Of Edinburgh," and her death closed "A life / of affectionate devotion / And domestic excellence." Pilgrim edition of *The Letters of Charles Dickens,* ed. Madeline House, Graham Storey, and Kathleen Tillotson, 12 vols. (Oxford: Clarendon, 1965–2002), 2:432 n. 2. Subsequent references to the Pilgrim edition of Dickens's letters are cited parenthetically as Pilgrim with volume and page.

3. Leonore Davidoff and Catherine Hall, *Family Fortunes: Men and Women of the English Middle Class, 1780–1850* (Chicago: University of Chicago Press, 1987), 321.

4. Amanda Vickery, *The Gentleman's Daughter: Women's Lives in Georgian England* (New Haven: Yale University Press, 1998), 7. Working class women particularly had no choice but to operate in *both* spheres, while some women from the middle classes entered public life through philanthropic and religious missions. For a general overview of the debate over the "separate spheres," see Robert B. Shoemaker, *Gender in English Society, 1650–1850: The Emergence of Separate Spheres?* (London: Longman, 1998), 6–10.

than it is in her grandmother's. Researchers have never found a contract for the cookbook Catherine wrote and published with Bradbury and Evans, her husband's publishers, in 1851, which suggests that the agreement may have been an informal one or, if formally documented, considered too ephemeral to preserve. Catherine Dickens's letters, however, unlike those of her grandmother, survive in the dozens, held in archives from New York to New Zealand.

Ranging from brief social notes and messages conveyed on behalf of her husband to more substantial accounts of her experiences as a mother, grandmother, friend, and mistress of households large and small, these letters provide a sense of the multiple roles Catherine Dickens played and the range of voices in which she spoke. "I am requested by Mr. Dickens to thank you very much for the basket of game you had the kindness to send," Catherine tells one correspondent in 1841, explaining that her husband is ill. "Finding it no very easy matter to use his pen...he...deputes his correspondence to me," she notes.[5] "I wrote to you some time ago...to ask [that] if you should happen to have any vacancy in your female staff, you would kindly employ a very respectable woman who was formerly in my service," she reminds Benjamin Webster, the owner of the renovated Adelphi Theatre, in 1859, following up on her attempt to find a job for one Mrs. Gale. "I should be so glad if she could get regular employment in your new Theatre. I can conscientiously give her an excellent character for honesty, sobriety, etc., and she is also a good needle-woman, if you should require her services in the wardrobe department," Catherine assures him.[6] "I ought long before this to have thanked you for sending me my dear little godson's portrait...and have put it in my Book, next to yours," she informs the novelist Annie Thomas in 1872. "What a darling he must be! I want to see him very much and hope...that I shall have that pleasure next spring."[7]

Unfortunately, crucial portions of Catherine's letters have disappeared—most significantly those she wrote to Dickens over the course of three decades, destroyed by him after their separation. In the "unbalanced conversation" that Dickens has bequeathed to us, Margaret Darby notes, such was the fate of virtually all the correspondence he received.[8] Thus one of Catherine's most intimate voices, that in which she wrote to her fiancé and husband, can be reconstructed only from the

5. Autograph letter signed (hereafter ALS) Catherine Dickens to C. Hunton, Esquire, 21 October 1841, Chicago Historical Society.

6. ALS Catherine Dickens to Mr. Webster, 27 February 1859, private collection.

7. ALS Catherine Dickens to Annie [Thomas] Cudlip, 27 July 1872, Fales Library & Special Collections, New York University.

8. Margaret Flanders Darby, "Dickens and Women's Stories: 1845–1848 (Part Two)," *Dickens Quarterly* 17 (September 2000): 135.

letters she received from him, just as her grandmother's voice must be reconstructed from George Thomson's correspondence.

Whereas Dickens burned Catherine's letters, Catherine preserved those she received from him. Yet even those narrowly escaped destruction. Their rescue marked changing conceptions of gender relations toward the end of the nineteenth century and a new valuation of women's experiences. In 1878 or 1879 Catherine gave her letters from Dickens to her daughter Katey Perugini, requesting that Katey take them to the British Museum after her death. In Catherine's view, they would prove that her husband had loved her, despite his assertion to the contrary after their separation. Wishing to defend her mother yet believing that the letters supported her father's claim, Katey planned to burn them, hoping to spare her mother the humiliating (if posthumous) revelation that she was unloved.[9]

Fortunately, Katey consulted her friend George Bernard Shaw first. It was left to Shaw to convince Katey that the letters were worth saving. Before reading them, Shaw told Katey that her mother, even if unloved by Dickens, was a figure more deserving of sympathy than her famous husband. While Katey saw Dickens as "a man of genius imbedded in a large family of perfectly commonplace persons," Shaw recounts, he explained to her "that the sentimental sympathy of the nineteenth century with the man of genius tied to a commonplace wife had been rudely upset by a writer named Ibsen." In Shaw's view, "posterity might sympathize much more with the woman who was sacrificed to the genius's uxoriousness to the appalling extent of having had to bear eleven children [ten, actually] in sixteen years than with a grievance which, after all, amounted only to the fact that she was not a female Charles Dickens." After reading Dickens's letters to his wife, furthermore, Shaw concluded that Catherine was right about them: "They prove with ridiculous obviousness that Dickens was quite as much in love when he married as nine hundred and ninety-nine out of every thousand British bridegrooms," Shaw asserts, "and that this normal state of things outlasted even the eleven [sic] pregnancies."[10]

Shaw's association between Catherine Dickens and the heroines in Henrik Ibsen's plays is compelling, if only because it reminds us of unrealized plotlines for Catherine's life story. In such plays as *A Doll's House* (1879), first produced in the year of Catherine's death, and *Hedda Gabler* (1890), Ibsen depicts the prison house of Victorian marriage for women while also envisioning their growing ability to resist a husband's authority, speak for themselves, and make their escape, whether by

9. Lucinda Hawksley discusses Katey's handling of Catherine's letters and, more generally, her attitude toward her parents in *Katey: The Life and Loves of Dickens's Artist Daughter* (London: Doubleday, 2006).

10. "A Letter from Bernard Shaw," *Time and Tide*, 27 July 1935, 1111.

To Thomas her present
Respects Drake.

Mrs Charles Dickens
presents her
compliments to
Mr Mason —
She is extremely
obliged by his
kindness in
sending the
Picture for her
to see, & begs

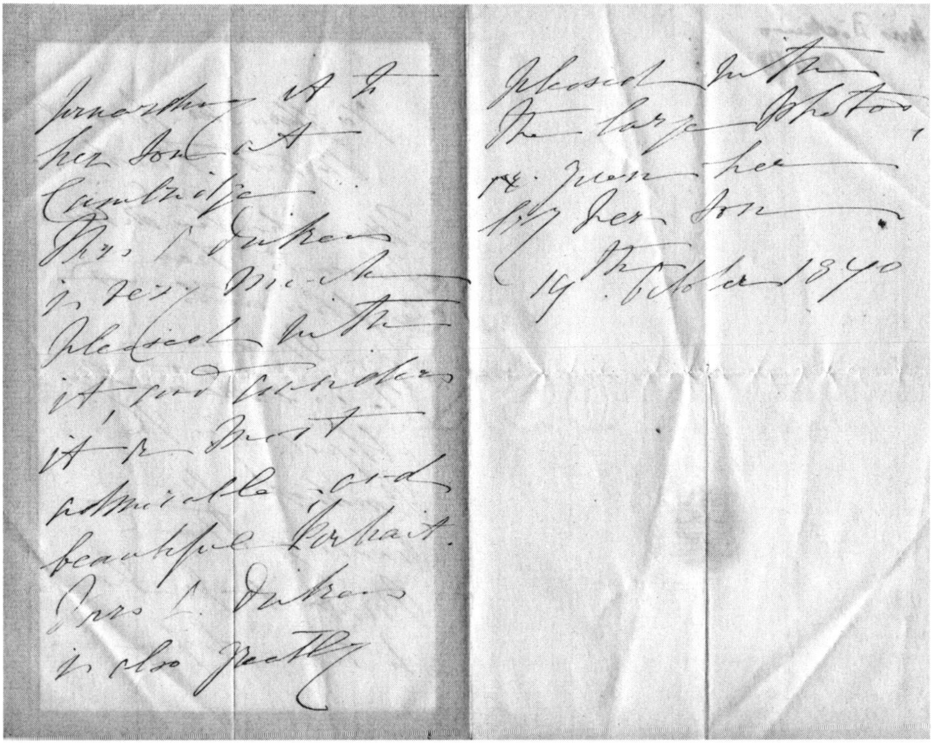

FIGURE 2. *Autograph letter, Catherine Dickens to Mr. Mason, 17 October 1870, private collection.*

leaving their home or, tragically, by committing suicide. Catherine's twelve years of marital separation and, in particular, her nine years of widowhood gave her more autonomy than she had enjoyed while living with her husband. Yet Catherine did not choose that independence for herself, nor was it an alternative that she preferred to marriage. Self-described as "Mrs. Charles Dickens" in many of the letters she wrote during this period (fig. 2), Catherine continued to think of herself in relation to her husband long after she stopped living with him. And as her use of Dickens's letters suggests, she sought to exonerate herself from his charges by means of *his* voice more often than hers. From the earliest years of her marriage, Catherine gave precedence to Dickens's words over her own, a habit that proved difficult to break even after their estrangement.

Catherine's sense of her limited "powers of description"[11] was a product of her marriage to a man of remarkable descriptive powers and sometimes inhibited her in her writing, a problem compounded by her reluctance to address a number of

11. Catherine Dickens to Fanny Burnett, 30 January 1842, in Frederic G. Kitton, *Charles Dickens by Pen and Pencil* (London: Frank T. Sabin, 1890), 39, reprinted in Pilgrim 3:629.

subjects vital to her story. In effect she creates gaps of her own in the biographical record, though in a less literal sense than her husband did by burning her letters. Catherine's silence on certain subjects is unsurprising: like many of her contemporaries, she describes neither her sexual life nor her erotic feelings. Although we can read between the lines, we can't be certain if she found sex to be more a duty than a pleasure, or if her feelings about it changed as a result of her recurring pregnancies. "The plain truth is that we are never likely to know much about the sexual lives of Victorian couples," John Tosh observes, "because they alluded to it so little themselves. The evidence is so patchy and contradictory that a case can be made with equal confidence for fulfilment or frustration as the norm."[12]

Less typical, however, is Catherine's silence on the subject of her marital troubles—what she clearly perceived as the wrongs she suffered at her husband's hands. Unlike her acquaintance Caroline Norton, who used her experiences of marital injustice as the grounds for an effective campaign to reform the laws governing child custody and married women's property rights, Catherine embraced an ideal of ladylike propriety and made no public mention or use of her personal sufferings. Although few Victorian wives were as outspoken as Rosina Bulwer Lytton, who publicly attacked and ridiculed her estranged husband, Sir Edward Bulwer Lytton, at political gatherings and in such novels as *Cheveley, or the Man of Honour* (1839), few remained as mum as Catherine Dickens.

UNDER COVER

Ironically, the primary reason why so many of Catherine's letters survive today—because she was the wife of Charles Dickens—has blinded biographers and critics to the multiplicity of her roles and identities, which those very letters reveal. Over the course of her sixty-four years, Catherine defined herself in various ways and adopted varied personae in writing to correspondents. A member of female communities, she tells other women of childbirths, marriages, and engagements; a faithful Christian, she offers condolences and prayers, and resigns herself to God's will; mistress of a middle-class household, she expresses concern for the welfare of former servants, recommending them for jobs and offering advice. Writing as a Hogarth, Catherine commiserates with her father's niece about her sister Mary's death and, as a Thomson, describes her life at Gloucester Crescent to her mother's sister. Yet most of the critics, biographers, novelists, and playwrights who represent or refer to her conceive of her as a figure brought into being by Dickens's attentions and annihilated by their withdrawal. Whether hostile or sympathetic to Catherine,

12. John Tosh, *A Man's Place: Masculinity and the Middle-Class Home in Victorian England* (New Haven: Yale University Press, 1999), 59.

they reinforce the logic of coverture, which denied a married woman her own legal identity under English common law by "suspending" it—merging it with her husband's and causing her to vanish as a person in her own right.[13] In most representations of Catherine Dickens, a suspension or loss of her being is painfully clear.

Catherine's disappearance under the "cover" of her husband's identity is most pernicious in the two-volume Dickens biography long considered definitive: Edgar Johnson's *Charles Dickens: His Tragedy and Triumph,* first published in 1952. Allowing Dickens to speak for his wife, Johnson promotes the misrepresentations of Catherine that Dickens began to circulate, privately and publicly, in 1858 in an attempt to justify his own behavior during their separation. Thus Johnson emphasizes what he takes to be evidence of Catherine's social and maternal ineptitude and depicts her as difficult and unstable, a constant source of irritation to her long-suffering husband. He calls attention to her fall on a theater stage in 1850 and another during the 1842 American tour, attributing what he terms her "lack of physical control" to an underlying "nervous disturbance" and lending credence to Dickens's false charge that his wife suffered from a mental illness.[14] Whether referring to Catherine's "practical incapacities" as a household manager, her presumably irrational jealousies of other women, or her alleged failings as a mother, Johnson draws almost exclusively from Dickens's own account of events during and after the separation, and he amplifies comical remarks Dickens made about Catherine in the 1840s in letters full of affection and praise for his wife.[15] Following Johnson's lead, generations of students and critics "learned" what Dickens wished them to: that Catherine was an incompetent wife and mother, unloved by her children; that she was psychologically unfit to perform her domestic duties; and that her union, though for many years a successful one by Victorian standards, was ill-fated from the start.

Catherine is made to disappear most completely in the one biography that insists on her presence, at least in a *physical* sense, using that very physicality to disparage and dismiss her: *Georgina Hogarth and the Dickens Circle,* Arthur A. Adrian's life of Catherine's sister, published in 1957. Echoing Dickens's complaints about his wife's fertility, Adrian develops a cutting counterpoint between Catherine's maternal "productivity" and the "literary output" of the male genius, blaming Catherine for burdening her husband with ten children while eliding Dickens's role in their

13. Sir William Blackstone, *Commentaries on the Laws of England,* quoted in Lee Holcombe, *Wives and Property: Reform of the Married Women's Property Law in Nineteenth-Century England* (Toronto: University of Toronto Press, 1983), 25.

14. Edgar Johnson, *Charles Dickens: His Tragedy and Triumph,* 2 vols. (New York: Simon and Schuster, 1952), 2:721.

15. Ibid., 2:906, 909, 906–7.

conception.[16] Although Dickens was himself one of eight children and his mother one of ten, Adrian treats the fertility of the couple as a legacy from Catherine's mother, whom she "rival[ed]" in childbearing and whose "record" she eventually tied, Adrian writes.[17] Valorizing Georgina as the brainy and chaste Hogarth, the one who remained faithful to Dickens despite his separation from her sister, Adrian reduces Catherine to an unthinking female body, cumbersome in its materiality and ungoverned in its "fecundity."[18] Without the insight and sympathy of George Bernard Shaw, who underscored Catherine's physical "sacrifice" to Dickens, Adrian depicts her as "refractory clay" of which "there was literally too much" for her "trim and agile husband."[19] Justifying visually Dickens's decision to separate from his wife and pursue "slight, graceful" Ellen Ternan, the young actress who became Dickens's mistress, Adrian places their photos on the page facing his description of Catherine's "fat and florid" body, as if such images speak for themselves and make his case (fig. 3).[20]

Dickens's ability to "cover" Catherine posthumously, controlling her image and speaking for his wife, persists in such works as *The Friendly Dickens* (1998), which states that "the famed Dickensian fertility apparently came from the Hogarth side,"[21] and in Peter Ackroyd's acclaimed biography, *Dickens,* published in 1990. Although Ackroyd is more theoretically minded and self-aware than most Dickens biographers and draws from a range of sources in characterizing Catherine, his conception of her seems all too familiar. Identifying Catherine as a wholly static figure— "at nineteen . . . what she would always be"—he defines her and her "tangible" (that is, bodily) presence against that of her "spiritual" sister Mary, echoes Dickens in remarking facetiously on her pregnancies, and refers to her "general nervous anxiety," conjecturing that "perhaps she never was completely well."[22] Ackroyd appears to give Catherine the last word, since he brings his massive study to a close with the image of the widow attending a theatrical adaptation of *Dombey and Son* in 1873. Yet he reworks his source material for this scene in a way that effectively silences her. Instead of the survivor described by actor William Farren, who spoke with

16. Arthur A. Adrian, *Georgina Hogarth and the Dickens Circle* (London: Oxford University Press, 1957), 10.

17. Ibid., 22, 33.

18. Ibid., 22.

19. Ibid., 50.

20. Ibid., 46, 50.

21. Norrie Epstein, *The Friendly Dickens: Being a Good-Natured Guide to the Art and Adventures of the Man Who Invented Scrooge* (New York: Viking, 1998), 43.

22. Peter Ackroyd, *Dickens* (New York: HarperCollins, 1990), 165, 163, 213.

ELLEN TERNAN
Enthoven Theatre Collection, Victoria and Albert Museum

CATHERINE DICKENS   CHARLES DICKENS
Henry E. Huntington Library and Art Gallery

FIGURE 3. *"Ellen Ternan, Catherine Dickens, Charles Dickens," from Arthur Adrian, Georgina Hogarth and the Dickens Circle (1957). Studio portrait of Miss E. Ternan, Guy Little Theatrical Photograph, V & A Theatre Collections, Victoria and Albert Museum. Photographs of Charles and Catherine Dickens courtesy of the Huntington Library, San Marino, California. Reproduced by kind permission.*

Catherine and her sister Helen at the Globe Theatre during intermission and was struck by the pride the widow expressed in her husband, Ackroyd suppresses the presence of Helen and the sisterly bond she embodied and renders Catherine mute. An isolated and self-immolating figure in Ackroyd's "Postscript," she cannot even *watch* the play in her grief, much less *speak* about it.[23]

Ackroyd's representations of Catherine are surprising as well as disappointing because they follow by nearly a decade Michael Slater's *Dickens and Women* (1983), which largely discredits such images and allows Catherine to emerge from under her husband's distorting cover. Noting that Dickens was "a supreme dramatizer of his own past, adept at organizing its incidents into a coherent plot," Slater points to the ways in which biographers misrepresent the evidence and mistake Dickens's fictions for facts.[24] He calls attention to Dickens's many affectionate accounts of his wife and draws on some of Catherine's own writings, among other long-neglected sources. Providing a striking counterpoint to Johnson, Slater emphasizes Dickens's affection for Catherine, her helpful suggestions about his work, and their "bond of humor."[25] He introduces us to Catherine's appealing traits: her sense of humor, her charm, and her diplomacy during the American tour. Instead of holding Catherine responsible for the breakdown of the marriage, Slater treats it as a "symptom" of Dickens's own "disturbed state" in the 1850s, the consequence of a mid-life crisis in which Dickens held Catherine responsible for his discontent.[26] "For upwards of seventeen years, Catherine Dickens satisfied a very important part of her genius-husband's nature, played a vital role in his domestic and social existence, and participated fully in many of the enjoyments of his life," Slater concludes. "She deserves better of Dickens scholarship than to be dismissed as a colourless and futile nonentity, a mere drag on his triumphal chariot."[27]

23. According to William Farren, who "sat beside [Catherine] and her sister [Helen], then Mrs. Roney," on the opening night, "Mrs. Dickens was greatly moved and the tears were falling. During the intervals she told me of the greatness of her husband, and one could see how great was her pride in him" (*Daily Mail,* 12 September 1928). According to Ackroyd, by contrast, "Catherine Dickens attended the first performance of *Dombey and Son* at the Globe Theatre in London. But she could not watch it. She broke down and wept" (*Dickens,* 1083).

24. Michael Slater, *Dickens and Women* (London: J. M. Dent, 1983), 113.

25. Ibid., 133.

26. Ibid., 138.

27. Ibid., 162. Slater recognizes Catherine's merits once again in his excellent biography *Charles Dickens* (New Haven: Yale University Press, 2009) but focuses on Dickens's writing life and does not examine at length the novelist's tie to Catherine or their marital dynamic,

Recognizing Catherine as a purposeful entity, Slater challenges the assumptions of coverture and breaks with a long-standing tradition among Dickens scholars of scapegoating Catherine. But because Slater primarily aims to illuminate Dickens's life and fiction, he uses Dickens's relationships with Catherine and other women as a "starting-point," and his remedial effort goes only so far.[28] Foregrounding Dickens's perceptions and representations of women rather than the perceptions and representations of the women themselves, Slater defends Catherine by noting that she satisfied *Dickens's* nature, played a crucial role in *his* existence, and shared in *his* enjoyments. Her own are not the focus.

Those few works that actually center on Catherine Dickens also give primacy to her husband's perceptions in telling her story. Jean Elliott's moving play *My Dearest Kate* is a significant example. First performed in Edinburgh in 1983, it represents Catherine at turning points in her life: during Dickens's courtship, at her marriage, at the birth of her first child, at the death of her sister Mary, and on through her unhappy separation from her children and her husband, and the news of Dickens's death. Intended to tell Catherine's side of the story, it wins sympathy for "dearest Kate" at her husband's expense. "Charlie Was Not Always a Darling" is a representative headline from the reviews.[29]

But as Elliott's title suggests, the play wins sympathy for Catherine by drawing on Dickens's letters to her and calling attention to the gap between what he *says* to his wife and what he actually *does*. Dickens's letters make up a substantial portion of Elliott's text and give the play its chronological backbone, with "dearest Kate" reading from Dickens's fiction, his public statements, and more than a dozen of his letters while quoting from only a handful of her own. This disproportion is due in part to the relative obscurity of Catherine's writings, few of which have been published. But it also supports the central theme of Elliott's play—Catherine's voicelessness—the sign of her disempowerment as a Victorian wife and mother. Elliott ends *My Dearest Kate* with a gesture of vindication—when the dying Catherine tells Katey to bring her letters from Dickens to the British Museum "so that the world may *know*, he loved me . . . once."[30] This triumph is double-edged, however, as Catherine remains at best the object of her husband's affectionate letters rather than the subject of her own history. Throughout the play, "Charles says" serves

---

citing "the absence of much knowledge of how the relationship between husband and wife actually worked, or failed to work" (365).

28. Slater, *Dickens and Women*, xi.

29. *Islington News*, 13 October 1983.

30. Jean Elliott, *My Dearest Kate: The Marriage of Mrs. Charles Dickens*, typescript, 21. Elliott wrote and performed her play under the pen name "Ellie Dickens."

as Catherine's refrain, signaling her deference and subjection to her husband's authority.[31] "What can I say?" Catherine asks after reading from one of her husband's published statements about their separation—an account in which he alleges that she has a "mental disorder" and accuses her of having "thrown all the children on someone else."[32] "May I not publish a statement? Who would believe me? He is the great writer, the friend of the poor, the Inimitable Boz. He is Charles Dickens. I am only Mrs. Dickens. Nobody."[33]

Imagining Catherine Dickens as a woman with pen in hand in *Girl in a Blue Dress* (2008), the novelist Gaynor Arnold breaks down the division between wife and author. By means of Dorothea (Dodo) Gibson, widow of the celebrated writer Alfred Gibson, Arnold responds to what she, like Elliott, considers the "voiceless" Catherine, using Dodo to correct the problem.[34] Ultimately the widowed Dorothea begins to write the missing portion of *Ambrose Boniface,* the work left unfinished at her husband's death. Yet as an author, Dodo promises to "echo" Alfred—to do so would be "a great honour," she asserts—and she feels as if she has his blood circulating in her veins when she starts to write.[35] Indeed Arnold's heroine seems entirely transfused with Charles Dickens—created largely from his statements and the scholarship of those who echo him—and Dodo's deference to Alfred as well as her jealousy of her sister-rivals conform to *Dickens's* version of history, not Catherine's.[36]

In their evocative and sympathetic representations, writers such as Arnold challenge those who scapegoat Catherine Dickens yet share a common assumption with them: that Catherine's significance and that of her sisters lie solely in their relationships with Dickens. Describing his work on Georgina, Adrian explicitly tells us what more recent and recuperative accounts of the Hogarths imply: "If this work seems to devote a disproportionate amount of space to Dickens...it is because [Georgina's] relationship with [him] was not only the mainspring of her life, but also the chief justification for a biography of her."[37]

31. Ibid., 8.

32. Ibid., 19; Charles Dickens to Arthur Smith, 25 May 1858, in Pilgrim 8:740.

33. Elliott, *My Dearest Kate*, 19.

34. Gaynor Arnold, *Girl in a Blue Dress* (Birmingham: Tindal Street Press, 2008), 440.

35. Ibid., 434, 438.

36. Like Ackroyd in *his* vision of Catherine's widowhood, Arnold fails to acknowledge the existence of Helen Roney, the third Hogarth sister and Catherine's chief ally, representing only the two sisters whom Dickens valued: Mary ("Alice" in the novel) and Georgina ("Sissy").

37. Adrian, *Georgina Hogarth and the Dickens Circle,* ix.

Disputing such assumptions, this book retells Catherine Dickens's story to the ends of truth and equity. Yet it does not discover for readers her "real" self; the work of postmodern theorists and biographers casts doubt on such claims. Influenced by deconstruction and semiotics, theoretically minded critics now question the notion of selfhood as "a unified, knowable, and recoverable entity"—as something essential or authentic—and urge biographers to admit to their own artfulness when they unveil their subjects in that way. "If the self is considered decentered, multiple, unknowable, how can any genre purport to give us the 'presence,' 'essence,' or meaning of a self?" Sharon O'Brien asks in an essay considering the possibilities for postmodern biography.[38] Rather than search for an "essential" Catherine Dickens, this book considers how she presented herself to the world, constructing and reconstructing her own identity while also being constructed by others. It looks at her from an array of vantage points, acknowledging discrepancies rather than seeking to obscure them, and approaching selfhood as a largely relational phenomenon.

Catherine's story helps us understand the workings of her culture and ours. For all its notoriety, her situation as Dickens's estranged wife merely publicized the potential vulnerabilities of *all* Victorian wives, legally denied property and custody rights well into the nineteenth century, many of whom struggled to embrace submission and service as womanly duties, as Catherine long did. Catherine's connections to, and differences from, such famously misused wives as Caroline Norton and Rosina Bulwer Lytton reveal a surprising range of responses to gender inequities among well-to-do Victorian women—of possibilities for expression and compensation that were seized by some but refused by others. Simultaneously, Catherine's close relationships with her female servants, some of whom struggled to find work after leaving her service, point to the relative privilege of middle-class wives estranged from their husbands.

The cultural distance separating us from Catherine Dickens and the ideals she questioned and embraced seems readily apparent, revealed in part by our very interest in figures like her, in the seemingly ordinary wives of extraordinary men. Shaw gauged that distance when he told Katey Perugini that her mother had been sacrificed to Dickens and that modernists like himself and Ibsen no longer accepted such sacrifices uncritically. Yet we may be closer to the Victorians than we think. The persistent willingness of women to see themselves as subordinate and

38. Sharon O'Brien, "Feminist Theory and Literary Biography," in *Contesting the Subject: Essays in the Postmodern Theory and Practice of Biography and Biographical Criticism*, ed. William H. Epstein (West Lafayette: Purdue University Press, 1991), 125.

commonplace, and the varied ways in which they are encouraged to do so in our culture, suggest our proximity to Catherine and her contemporaries.

Our continued sentimental embrace of Dickens as a cultural icon does so as well. For nearly three decades a diverse group of scholars have focused attention on "the other Dickens": the writer who not only created Tiny Tim but also advocated harsh social discipline and the extermination of "savages"; who kept a mistress his daughter Katey's age and treated his wife unkindly while commemorating hearth and home. Nonetheless, he is still revered as the champion of the oppressed by readers and critics willing to accept and venerate his word.[39] Recapturing Catherine Dickens's voice as well as acknowledging her silences, this book avoids—and exposes—that trap.

39. Myron Magnet coined the phrase "the other Dickens" in *Dickens and the Social Order* (Philadelphia: University of Pennsylvania Press, 1985), 1.

CHAPTER 1

"The Mind of Woman Occasionally Asserts Its Powers"

CATHERINE HOGARTH AMONG ENLIGHTENED

PATRIARCHS, 1815–1835

A printer's widow in Germany, while a new edition of the Bible was printing at her house, one night took an opportunity of going into the office to alter that sentence of subjection to her husband pronounced upon Eve in Genesis, chap. 3, v. 16. She took out the two first letters of the word Herr, and substituted Na in their place, thus altering the sentence from 'and he shall be thy Lord' (Herr), to 'and he shall be thy fool' (Narr). It is said her life paid for this intentional erratum; and that some secreted copies of this edition have been bought up at enormous prices.
—"Varieties," *Western Luminary,*
edited by George Hogarth, 29 November 1831

SCRIPTS AND POSTSCRIPTS

"Kate & Mary Hogarth to tea."[1] With this brief and mundane entry for 30 August 1832 in the journal of Mrs. William Ayrton, Catherine Dickens enters the archival record, a seventeen-year-old girl paying a social call at 4 James Street, Buckingham Gate, London, with her thirteen-year-old sister in tow. More than two years pass before Kate's own voice is heard—in her two earliest extant letters, which she wrote to her cousin Mary Scott Hogarth of Scremerston, near Berwick, in 1835. At nineteen Catherine Hogarth sounds much like Catherine Morland, the teenage protagonist of Jane Austen's *Northanger Abbey* (1818), who is "in training for

1. Journal of Marianne Ayrton, 30 August 1832, British Library, Add. 52351, f. 104.

a heroine."[2] Well read in sentimental and Gothic fiction, Miss Morland indulges in exaggerated professions of feeling for her false friend Isabella Thorpe. Similarly, Miss Hogarth waxes sentimental in telling her cousin Mary how much she has missed her since her recent visit to London: "I have thought about you almost constantly ever since you left. You can have no idea how much I miss you and how often I long for you to be here again—but there is no use dwelling on this (to me) painful topic."[3] Constant (or at least "almost" constant) thought since a loved one's departure; longings that exceed conceptualization; topics that pain one's sensibility: such is the stuff of the novels that Catherine Hogarth read as a girl.

Unlike writers who cultivate sensibility, however, and make a vulnerability to tender feeling heroic, Catherine refers to herself and her feelings equivocally. Her self-reference—"this (to me) painful topic"—points two ways. A parenthetical aside, it both foregrounds and undermines her importance. If Catherine Hogarth recalls Catherine Morland, she is also less naïve than Austen's heroine-in-training, particularly in her self-knowledge. She fixes her affections wisely, since the cousin whose absence pains her is deserving while Catherine Morland's friend is not; but she also understands that professions of sentiment ring false even when they are meant truly—all the more so when they are used by young women whose experiences are limited and everyday.

Like Austen herself, Catherine Hogarth gives an ironic inflection to sentimental language, acknowledging that its tendency to magnify female experience and give women's lives dramatic intensity is overblown. Her humor emerges in a second letter to her cousin, when she describes the fate of a female friend, the niece of Stephen Frampton, a schoolmaster who lives next door: "The lovely Miss Frampton is thrown upon the wide world or her Uncle."[4] Catherine imagines the possibility of female adventure and peril only to deny it. Admitting the existence of a male guardian ("or her Uncle"), she deflates her own heightened language ("thrown upon the wide world") and recognizes the limits of experience for young women in her time and place. She then reinforces the point by characterizing her own domestic concerns as nearly unmemorable: "I had almost forgotten to tell you that Georgie and

2. Jane Austen, *Northanger Abbey*, ed. James Kinsley and John Davie (1818; Oxford: Oxford University Press, 2003), 7.

3. ALS Catherine Hogarth to Mary Scott Hogarth, 11 February 1835, D. Jacques Benoliel Collection of the Letters of Charles Dickens, 86-2739, Rare Book Department, Free Library of Philadelphia.

4. ALS Catherine Hogarth to Mary Scott Hogarth, [4 July 1835], D. Jacques Benoliel Collection of the Letters of Charles Dickens, Rare Book Department, Free Library of Philadelphia.

the dear twins have had the measles. They are perfectly well again. They had them very mildly."[5]

The trivial nature of female concerns becomes the explicit theme of this letter when Catherine turns over its authorship to her fiancé, Charles Dickens, leaving him a "morsel of paper" on which to write to her cousin. "My dear Miss Hogarth," Dickens begins in the half-page "P.S." he appends to Catherine's letter:

> I have been requested by Catharine [sic] (upon my word I don't know why) to communicate the singularly interesting intelligence that I have got two black eyes—naturally and not artificially acquired. I am also requested to ask a question in which you will readily believe I am deeply interested—Is William Dove married? Catharine says she forgot to enquire, and as I have no distinct recollection of ever having heard that gentleman's name, whoever he may happen to be, before this moment; I hope you will answer the question by return of post.[6]

Catherine herself concedes that she "almost forgot...to tell" her domestic news as she relays it, diminishing its importance while also treating it as noteworthy. But Dickens subjects "female matters" to a more thoroughgoing irony. Performing Catherine's "requests" in his postscript, Dickens mocks the urgency and importance of the women's concerns—what he suggests is their inexplicable interest in the eye color of fiancés and in news of marriages—representing their preoccupations with manly facetiousness. What becomes in Dickens's hands the theme of this letter—the comic insignificance of Catherine's concerns—takes actual form in its partially destroyed manuscript as well as in the "definitive" version of the text published in the Pilgrim edition of *The Letters of Charles Dickens.*

The letter was originally a double sheet on which Catherine wrote the first page and a half and Dickens composed his "P.S." on the "morsel" (the final half page) left to him by his fiancée. The Free Library of Philadelphia, however, has only the surviving second page, the "valuable" portion clipped from the first page of Catherine's writing at the top edge, with her text consequently beginning in mid-sentence (fig. 4). Though in a less literal sense, the editors of the Pilgrim *Letters* take this clipping process further. As published in volume one, Dickens's "morsel" of writing has completely lost its status as postscript, instead appearing as *the* script, as if Dickens's address to "dear Miss Hogarth" opened the letter rather than bringing it to its close. Conversely, Catherine's *script* is reduced to less than a postscript—now

5. Ibid.
6. ALS Charles Dickens to Mary Scott Hogarth, [4 July 1835], D. Jacques Benoliel Collection of the Letters of Charles Dickens, Rare Book Department, Free Library of Philadelphia.

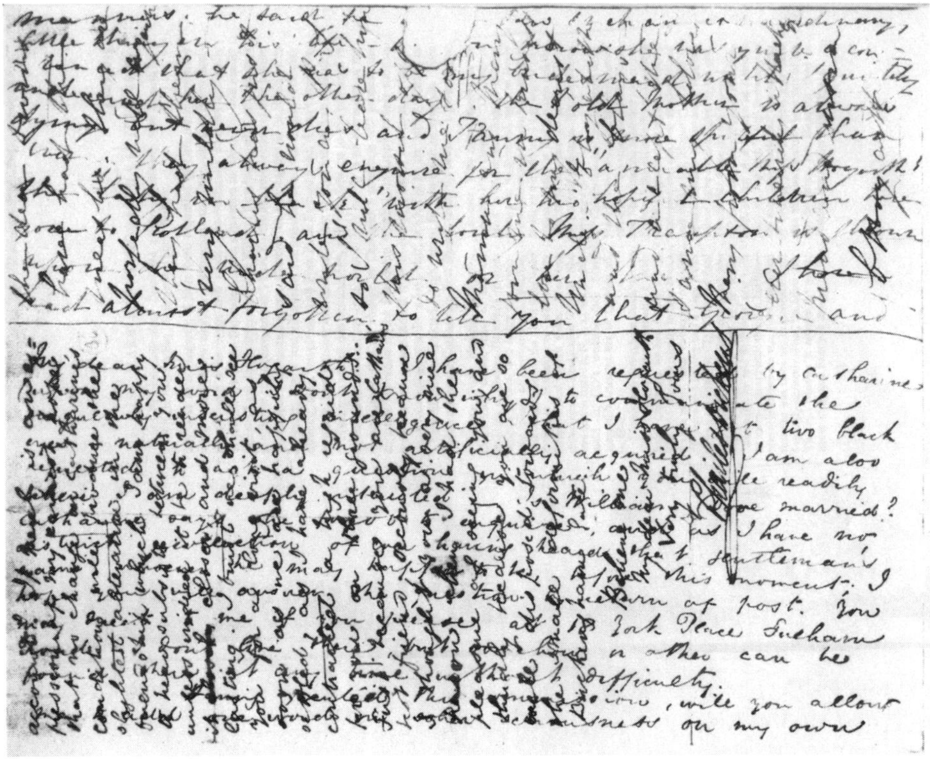

FIGURE 4. *Autograph letter signed Catherine Hogarth and Charles Dickens to Mary Hogarth of Scremerston [4 July 1835], D. Jacques Benoliel Collection of the Letters of Charles Dickens. Used by permission of the Rare Book Department, Free Library of Philadelphia.*

a portion of the second footnote to Dickens's "letter" to Miss Hogarth (fig. 5). As Catherine describes their composition to her cousin, "Charles has just said he would write you a P.S. so I will leave him this morsel of pa[per]." But as the Pilgrim editors describe it, "C[harles] D[ickens]'s letter is written beneath a letter from Catherine to her cousin Mary" (Pilgrim 1:68 n. 2). Seeming to elide questions of agency by using the passive voice ("is written beneath") while exercising agency themselves, they place *her* text beneath *his,* reprinting the original script within a footnote, in reduced font.

This inversion of script and postscript may seem inevitable in a volume devoted to Dickens's letters. Nonetheless, it misrepresents what were originally the relative positions of the two texts and undermines, through editorial means, Catherine's humorous attempt to retain authorship of her letter, leaving her fiancé only a "morsel" on which to write. Such editorial practices reenact, on a small, textual scale, the social and legal processes through which Catherine passed as a married woman, her

To MISS MARY SCOTT HOGARTH,[1] [4 JULY 1835]

MS Benoliel Collection. *Date:* PM 4 July 35. *Address:* Miss Hogarth | Robert Hogarth Esq | Scremerston | near Berwick.

My dear Miss Hogarth. I have been requested by Catharine[2] (upon my word I don't know why) to communicate the singularly interesting intelligence that I have got two black eyes—naturally and not artificially acquired. I am also requested to ask a question in which you will readily believe I am deeply interested—Is William Dove[3] married? Catharine says she forgot to enquire, and as I have no distinct recollection of ever having heard that gentleman's name, whoever he may happen to be, before this moment; I hope you will answer the question by return of post. You may direct to me if you please at 18 York Place Fulham Road. I don't live there, but somehow or other can be found there at any time without difficulty.

Having executed this commission, will you allow me to add one word in sober seriousness on my own account? It merely is an expression of my earnest hope, that no change in Catharine's condition will produce the slightest alteration in the friendship which I am happy to hear subsists between you, unless indeed it be to render it closer, and more lasting. I trust we shall see you for a long visit, as soon as we are happily settled, as I have already contracted a high regard for you on three grounds. First because you are Catharine's best friend; secondly because I thought you

[1] Mary Scott Hogarth (1813–76), Catherine's cousin, one of the six children of George Hogarth's younger brother Robert. Her father was originally tenant of Newton Farm, Bedrule, Roxburghshire; in the 1830s they were living at Scremerston, where Mary Hogarth had visited them. She died unmarried at Berwick-on-Tweed. She was not, as stated in N, I, 44 *n*, a bridesmaid at CD's wedding (see Mary Hogarth's letter to her of 15 May 36, p. 689).

[2] Spelt thus throughout this letter.— CD's letter is written beneath a letter from Catherine to her cousin Mary. The MS seems originally to have been a double sheet, with Catherine covering 1½ pages and leaving half a page ("this morsel of paper") to CD. Only the final page, clipped at the top edge, has survived. Catherine's half of it reads: "manners; he said he [never] saw such an extraordinary little thing in his life—h[eave]n knows she was quite convinced that she was to be my bridesmaid until I quickly undeceived her, the other day. The old Mother is always dying but never dies, and Fanny is more spiteful

than ever. They always enquire for the 'amiable Miss Hogarth'. The 'lady in black' with her two hopeful children have gone to Scotland, and the lovely Miss Frampton is thrown upon the wide world or her Uncle. I had almost forgotten to tell you that Georgie and the dear twins have had the measles. They are perfectly well again. They had them very mildly.

"Charles has just said he would write you a P.S. so I will leave him this morsel of pa[per]. Do write me so[on]. Mama and Mary join me in kindest love to my dearest Uncle. Elizabeth and the Clays —and accept the warmest love & believe me your ever sincerely attached friend and cousin | C. Hogarth". [Words in square brackets conjecturally supplied where paper has been torn by the seal. For further notes see pp. 689–90.]

[3] Possibly William Dove, of Huddersfield, author of *A Treatise on Penmanship; or, the Lady's Self-Instructor, in the most fashionable and admired styles of writing*, 1836. Catherine may have met him (and perhaps been one of his pupils) when the Hogarths lived at Halifax, seven miles away, 1832–4.

---

a very nice person when I had the pleasure of seeing you; and thirdly because you are so well disposed towards the small deformities of Buckingham Gate.[1]

Believe me
My dear Miss Hogarth
Very truly Yours
CHARLES DICKENS

To MISS CATHERINE HOGARTH, [9 JULY 1835]

MS British Museum. *Date:* On 10 July CD returned proof sheets of her uncle's book (see next); Miss Drummond's miniature of CD is inscribed on the back "Painted by Rose Emma Drummond, 8 Soho Square, 9th July 1835".

Selwood Place | Thursday Morning 4 o'Clock

My Dearest Kate.

I was unconsciously three quarters of an hour too late last night; I had not finished at the office until eleven, and had to go on again at one.[2] I had therefore nothing to do, but sit down and look over your uncle's[3] slips,[4] and curse the cross accidents which keep me from you—the latter ceremony I assure you I performed with heartfelt energy.

As I was disappointed in seeing you again last night, I shall *fully expect*[5] you and Mary to breakfast with me this morning—not later than 11 and rather before than after, as we have to call on Miss Drummond[6] & I want to write a few pages if possible first. Mind you are punctual my dear, and recollect I take *no denial on any pretence*.

I am very tired my dearest, and can only add the—I hope—most unnecessary assurance that I am.

Yours most truly & affecy.
CHARLES DICKENS

[1] Perhaps a reference to the family of William Ayrton (see *To* Ayrton, 3 Dec 36, *fn*), who lived in Buckingham Gate and were friendly with the Hogarths. One of the two daughters was evidently very small (see Catherine's letter); Mrs Ayrton was probably the "old Mother" mentioned as "always dying" by Catherine, and the "poor old lady [who] was very ill before she died" of Mary Hogarth's letter of 15 May 36.

[2] The Commons sat until 1.30 a.m.

[3] William Thomson (1790–1876), Catherine's maternal uncle, second son of George Thomson. Appointed Deputy Assistant Commissary General to the Forces 1813, aged 23. Served in Portugal 1827, West Indies 1836, and Canada. In Audit Office *c.* 1844–6; Deputy Commissary General 1846.

Married Barbara Sinclair, heiress of Freswick, Caithness, in 1843, and changed his name to Thomson-Sinclair. Left £30,000.

[4] The proofs of Thomson's *Two Journeys through Italy and Switzerland*, published by Macrone in August.

[5] Underlined 3 times.

[6] Rose Emma Drummond, miniaturist, daughter of Samuel Drummond, ARA, of 14 Church Street, Soho. She exhibited 31 portraits at RA 1815–35, many of well-known actresses. Awarded silver medal by the Society of Arts 1823. According to Kitton (*CD by Pen & Pencil*, I, 15), her miniature of CD on ivory was commissioned by CD and given to Catherine to mark their engagement.

FIGURE 5. *"To Miss Mary Scott Hogarth [4 July 1835]," from* Pilgrim Edition of the Letters of Charles Dickens, *vol. 1.* With the kind permission of the Pilgrim Trust.

---

desires compromised and her expression contained, at times surrendering the sense of self that she acknowledged, though parenthetically—("to me")—as a teenager.

In fact Catherine's sense of self was strongest before her marriage, largely owing to the values and behavior of her parents and maternal grandparents. Although they were not advocates of gender equity in the modern sense and generally organized their homes along traditional lines, they openly discussed gender roles as well as instances of their subversion, believing that girls and women were unduly limited both by convention and by the education deemed proper for them. While praising "feminine" behavior, they also recognized and promoted the intellectual and artistic powers of women and defended those who sought professional careers.

When John Ruskin visited the city of Catherine's birth to lecture on architecture in 1853, he thought that the citizens of Edinburgh had much to learn. England's leading art and culture critic, Ruskin had recently published *The Stones of Venice* (1851–1853), a defense of the Gothic style and its irregularities, which he associated with individual freedom and expression. Now focusing on Edinburgh's New Town, a prestigious series of neighborhoods planned and developed between the 1760s and the 1820s, Ruskin praised its location on a ridge but condemned its architectural monotony. Built entirely of local sandstone, its neoclassical terraces laid out in straight rows, New Town struck Ruskin as oppressive in its elegant symmetry. He had counted 678 windows of the same size and shape as he walked down Queen Street to the lecture hall that morning, one example of the "dulness" that typified New Town in his view. "Walk round your Edinburgh buildings, and look at . . . what you will get from them," he advised his audience. "Nothing but square-cut stone—square-cut stone—a wilderness of square-cut stone for ever and for ever; so that your houses look like prisons, and truly are so; for the worst feature of Greek architecture is, indeed, not its costliness, but its tyranny. These square stones are not prisons of the body, but graves of the soul."[7]

In one of these sandstone houses—at 8 Hart Street, New Town—Catherine Hogarth was born on 19 May 1815. A short side street connecting Forth Street and Broughton Place, Hart Street slopes downhill, and thus its rooflines are more varied than most. But on Hart Street, as on Nelson and Albany streets, where Catherine lived later in her childhood, architectural similarities prevail. Each two-story tenement has a slate-roofed addition that makes a third floor, and the pattern of sandstone blocks repeats from one building to the next, all the windows divided into twelve panes and all the front doors reached by five steps passing over a basement area. Cast iron railings run in front of the houses, up and down the street. To modern eyes, as to Ruskin's, Hart Street looks monotonous and dull, particularly on overcast days.

Yet to Catherine in the 1820s the neighborhood had a very different appearance, though the buildings were virtually the same. When Catherine was born, Hart Street was just seven years old. Far from dull and dreary, it was part of a fashionable and elegant district in which neoclassical regularities marked the Enlightenment values of its designers and residents. Rather than suggesting cultural "tyranny," its square-cut stones and repeating architectural features offered visible signs that Edinburgh was "the Athens of the North."

7. John Ruskin, *Lectures on Architecture and Painting, Delivered at Edinburgh in November 1853,* 2nd ed. (London: Smith, Elder, 1855), 6–7, 9, 76.

The seat of the Scottish Enlightenment from the mid-eighteenth century into the nineteenth, Edinburgh was home to an intellectual elite of philosophers, historians, economists, and artists, among them David Hume, Adam Smith, Sir Henry Raeburn, and William Robertson. Robert Burns and Sir Walter Scott were both connected to Edinburgh, as were a number of women writers, among them Joanna Baillie, Eliza Fletcher, and Anne Grant. A decade before Catherine's birth, Francis Jeffrey, who would become a friend of the Dickenses in the 1840s, helped establish the *Edinburgh Review,* an influential monthly aligned with the Whig Party. When Catherine was a toddler, William Blackwood established *Blackwood's Magazine,* the famous periodical that supported Tory opinion and to which her father contributed. Blackwood's editorial team included John Wilson (writing as "Christopher North"), James Hogg, and J. G. Lockhart, the son-in-law of Scott. Alongside Edinburgh's print medium, the oral tradition of Scottish ballad singing flourished, and Catherine's mother and aunts as well as her grandfather were accomplished in this art.

When Catherine was a child, Edinburgh was a hub of literary and artistic activity, and her family belonged to its cultured and intellectual community. Although her grandmothers are largely absent from the public record, her grandfathers are well represented there, particularly her mother's father, to whom Catherine was close. Her paternal grandfather, Robert Hogarth, was a Scottish farmer who lived in the countryside southeast of Edinburgh. Her maternal grandfather, George Thomson, was well known in Edinburgh's literary and musical circles. Born in 1757, Thomson moved with his parents from his birthplace, Banff, to Edinburgh in 1774. His mother, Anne Stirling, is an obscure figure; his father, Robert, was a schoolmaster and notary public who taught his son the classical languages. From 1780 until 1839 George Thomson served as clerk to the Board of Trustees for the Encouragement of Art and Manufacturers in Scotland. An amateur vocalist and violinist, he became one of the directors of the first Edinburgh Music Festival when his granddaughter Catherine was five months old. For nearly fifty years he dedicated himself to his collection *Select Scottish Airs,* published in six volumes between 1793 and 1841, initially collaborating with Robert Burns and soliciting musical contributions from Beethoven, Haydn, Hummel, and Pleyel, among other European composers.

In December 1781 Thomson married Katherine Miller of Kelso. Their first daughter, Catherine, was born in 1783, and a second was born and died in 1785. Six more children followed: Robert (b. 1786), Margaret (b. 1787), Anne (b. 1788), William (b. 1790), Georgina (b. 1793), and Helen (b. 1795). Catherine Hogarth's mother, Georgina, was thus the sixth of seven surviving children and the fourth of five girls.

When Georgina Thomson was born, her family was living on Blair Street, Old Town, but she spent much of her childhood in New Town. Although relatively little is known about her early years, several telling details illuminate the values and priorities of her parents. When Georgina was a child, for example, they chose to have her inoculated against smallpox. Members of the Church of Scotland sometimes objected to the practice on religious grounds, but the Thomsons subscribed to an Enlightenment theology that welcomed scientific and medical advances.[8] "Let us be thankful for rational Episcopacy or Presbyterianism," Thomson characteristically remarked in 1819, writing his wife from Paris after attending Catholic mass at Notre Dame and witnessing what he considered its superstitious "mummery."[9] Georgina's inoculation suggests the value her parents placed on reason and medical science. Because the wealthy and educated in Scotland were generally the ones who accepted the procedure in the 1790s, it also marks their relative social privilege.[10]

So too does the record of George Thomson's run-in with the police when Georgina was in her early teens. In 1807 Georgina and her sisters invited their dancing school friends to their New Town home for tea and a dance, annoying John Balvaird, their downstairs neighbor. When their father refused to stop the dancing, Balvaird summoned the police, who demanded that the Thomsons end their party. Their father again refused, having promised the "young people" that they could continue until half-past ten and insisting that he was not breaking the law. The altercation made its way into print, with Balvaird publishing a four-page tract on the subject and Thomson a pamphlet defending his conduct and criticizing police interference in private affairs.[11] As this episode reveals, Georgina and her sisters were raised by a man who was eager to promote their happiness and to keep his word to them. Intellectual and cultured as well as indulgent, Thomson saw to it that parties and dancing lessons for his daughters were balanced with schooling, musical and voice training, and a love for Burns.

8. Deborah Brunton, "Smallpox Inoculation and Demographic Trends in Eighteenth-Century Scotland," *Medical History* 36 (1992): 415.

9. ALS George Thomson to Katherine Thomson, 23 August 1819, MS 7198, ff. 29–30, National Library of Scotland.

10. Brunton, "Smallpox Inoculation," 407, 415.

11. Drawing on Thomson's "Statement and Review of a recent decision of the Judge of Police in Edinburgh, authorising his officers to make domiciliary visits in private to stop dancing," published under the pen name "Civis," J. Cuthbert Hadden discusses this confrontation in *George Thomson: The Friend of Burns; His Life and Correspondence* (London: John C. Nimmo, 1898), 40–43.

It is unclear how Georgina Thomson first met George Hogarth, but it may have been his musical interests that first brought him together with her family. Like George Thomson, George Hogarth was an amateur musician—a cellist and composer—who had come to Edinburgh as a young man. Born in 1783 in Channelkirk, Berwickshire, he was the son of Mary Scott and Robert Hogarth; his father was known for innovations in farming and land management. Choosing law rather than farming for his profession, Hogarth was apprenticed to James Alexander Higgins of Newck, Stirlingshire, W.S. (Writer to the Signet), in Edinburgh. He first appears in the Edinburgh Post Office directory in 1806 as a "writer" (or solicitor in training). In 1807 he moved from Sellers' Close, Old Town, to South Charlotte Street, New Town, and remained in that part of the city until he and his family left for England in 1831. By that time he had been a solicitor in Scotland for twenty years, having finished his training and become a W.S. on 22 June 1810.

In his legal practice Hogarth was primarily concerned with trusts and estates and with real estate transactions; he advised Sir Walter Scott after Scott's disastrous financial failure, spending some weekends at Abbotsford, Scott's home, in 1826 and 1827. But Hogarth's real interests lay in music and literature. He contributed to a multitude of periodicals, often on musical subjects, and helped organize the Edinburgh Music Festival in its earliest years.

Georgina Thomson married George Hogarth, ten years her senior, on 1 June 1814, according to the rites of the Presbyterian Church of Scotland. That summer the newlyweds visited friends in Glasgow and Helensborough, west of Edinburgh, sometimes accompanied by Georgina's sister Anne and by George Thomson. "Today Mr. Hogarth and I have been in Glasgow and have walked ourselves as tired as greyhounds after a chace," Thomson told his wife in August 1814.[12] By that time Georgina Hogarth was pregnant with Catherine. Other children followed in rapid succession. She gave birth to Robert in 1816, and to a second daughter, Mary Scott, in 1817 or 1818. Mary died in infancy, and the Hogarths gave another daughter, born in 1819, her name. They had six more children, four born before their departure from Edinburgh: George (b. 1821), William (b. 1823), James (b. 1825), and Georgina (b. 1827). The last of the Hogarth children, twins Helen and Edward, were born in Halifax in 1833, eighteen years after their sister Catherine.

Until the Hogarths left Edinburgh in 1831, they spent much of their leisure time with the Thomsons. When he was away from home, George Thomson wrote for news of the Hogarths, concerned in one instance about Georgina's impending

12. ALS George Thomson to Katherine Thomson, [August 1814], MA 7198, ff. 17–18, National Library of Scotland.

childbirth, her fifth in six years.[13] Devoted to his extended "family circle," he often helped organize gatherings in which the Hogarths and Thomsons combined their talents and in which Catherine's father and her unmarried aunts played leading roles: "Tell the spinsters and Mr. Hogarth that I have pick'd up some new trios... for our petites concerts, & that I have heard nothing [on the continent] which will in the least prevent my enjoyment of our own excellent performances!" he writes his wife in 1819.[14] Returning to the same subject two years later, he asks Katherine to "let Mr. Hogarth know that I have got the music he wanted, and two or three pretty things for the Piano Forte, Violin & Violoncello, which I hope we shall enjoy all together in a short time. No concerts of 100 performers are to be compared to our own little domestic parties!!!"[15]

Yet the domestic realm had its trials as well as its pleasures, particularly for Katherine Thomson and Georgina Hogarth. Like her mother, Georgina gave birth four times in the first five years of her marriage, and most of her energy was devoted to child rearing. She organized the household, cooked and cleaned with a servant's aid, and helped educate her children. Cultured and capable, she sometimes felt burdened by the demands placed on her by virtue of her sex and did not hide her feelings. Writing to William Ayrton in 1833, six months before Georgina give birth to the twins, George Hogarth described his wife as "fatigued and harassed,"[16] and Dickens's reference to a domestic "flare" during his courtship of Catherine suggests a marital disagreement of some sort (Pilgrim 1:92).

A woman willing to assert herself and voice her opinions, even when they were unwelcome, Mrs. Hogarth is generally derided by Dickens scholars, who characterize her, at best, as "an excitable, not to say somewhat hysterical, lady."[17] Such is the price she has paid for defying certain gender expectations and making trouble for men, her famous son-in-law in particular. In the early years of Catherine's marriage Mrs. Hogarth sometimes bristled at the psychological counsel Dickens offered her when she was in mourning. While house-sitting for the Dickenses, she did not try

13. "Pray do not fail to write concerning Georgina," Thomson tells his wife in 1821. "I hope and pray she may get well through her confinement." ALS George Thomson to Katherine Thomson, 26 April 1821, MS 7198, ff. 43–44, National Library of Scotland.

14. ALS George Thomson to Katherine Thomson, 13 August 1819, MS 7198, ff. 29–30, National Library of Scotland.

15. ALS George Thomson to Katherine Thomson, 26 April 1821, MS 7198, ff. 43–44, National Library of Scotland.

16. ALS George Hogarth to William Ayrton, 13 March 1833, British Library, Add. 52338, f. 90.

17. Michael Slater, *Dickens and Women* (London: J. M. Dent, 1983), 104.

to meet her son-in-law's rigid housekeeping standards, leading him to remonstrate with her (Pilgrim 7:764). To his annoyance, she sought to insure her life in 1854, a proceeding usually reserved for male providers (Pilgrim 7:376). And in 1858, believing that her daughter had been wronged by Dickens, Mrs. Hogarth openly criticized him, earning Dickens's enmity. Mrs. Hogarth's outspokenness was a crucial element of her frank and forthright character and marked her strong sense of self. But it also tied her to a cultural tradition in which Scotswomen famously disregarded men in positions of authority, ignoring the directives of ministers and government officials and instead turning a "semi-sarcastic humour" against them.[18]

"RINNING ABOOT A GAIRDEN STAIRK NAKED 'ATING GREEN APPLES"

Despite her own unwillingness to speak out against her husband and what she privately termed his "hard" usage in 1858,[19] Catherine enjoyed telling stories about Scotswomen who openly questioned or defied male authority. That much is clear from her son Henry's accounts of Catherine's favorite joke, which centered on such a figure and conveyed "a Scotch woman's views with regard to the Garden of Eden": "Someone had been expatiating to her on its beauties when she retorted, in broad Scotch, 'Eh mon, it would be nae temptation to me to gae rinning aboot a gairden stairk naked 'ating green apples.'"[20] Catherine's joke works to the disadvantage of the Scotswoman, whose ignorance of the Genesis story is comical in itself. But Catherine's humor, like the "Scotch woman's," is also aimed at the ministerial "mon" (man) who holds forth about the Garden and its perfections in a failed attempt to convey to her a sense of our loss through Eve's transgression. Unimpressed by his sermonizing, the Scotswoman in Catherine's joke suggests instead that Paradise is overrated and that no apple would ever tempt a woman to fall.

In the nineteenth century, the biblical story of Eve's fall and the idea of women's innate moral weakness continued to fuel misogynist arguments about the inevitable limitations of the sex. Ironically enough, idealizations of womanhood proved equally

18. E. B. Ramsay, *Reminiscences of Scottish Life and Character,* 7th ed. (Boston: Ticknor and Fields, 1863), 98. See also Henry Cockburn on "Scotch Old Ladies," in *Memorials of His Time,* ed. Karl F. C. Miller (1856; reprint, Chicago: University of Chicago Press, 1974), 52–62.

19. ALS Catherine Dickens to Angela Burdett Coutts, 19 May 1858, MA 1352, the Morgan Library & Museum, New York.

20. Henry Dickens, *The Recollections of Sir Henry Dickens, K.C.* (London: William Heinemann, 1934), 19. The same joke, recalled by Katey Perugini as well as Henry Dickens, is recounted in Gladys Storey, *Dickens and Daughter* (London: Frederick Muller, 1939), 103.

constraining. Whether fallen or angelic, women were set apart from men by nature, it was widely claimed, and their education and range of action were restricted accordingly. In 1835 Catherine Hogarth became engaged to a man who believed that the nature of women differed markedly and intrinsically from that of men, a view that would mold her experiences as an adult. But her father and grandfather held a less polarized view of gender relations, one shaped by Enlightenment values and the assumption that women were intellectual partners who shared the power of reason with men.[21]

During Catherine's girlhood, well-educated Edinburgh men were divided on the subject of women's nature and intellectual capabilities and the consequences of providing them with academic instruction.[22] According to the conservative view expressed by John Wilson in *Blackwood's Magazine,* women's knowledge is "intuitive" and endowed by nature: "The woman who never saw a book may be infinitely superior, even in all those matters of which books treat, to the woman who has read, and read intelligently, 10,000 volumes[,] . . . and one single smile from an infant at its mother's breast may make that mother wiser in love than even all the philosophy of Plato and the poetry of Wordsworth." Granting women a denigrating type of superiority, Wilson, speaking for himself and his associates at *Blackwood's,* argued against their formal education, claiming that their "ignorance of all that is written in books" makes them "delight[ful]" and that learning would divert them from "the path of duty."[23]

While often agreeing that women's proper place was in the home, more liberal-minded Edinburgh men argued that their daughters and wives required intellectual training and knowledge to perform their proper roles most effectively—to be "ra-

21. Influenced by Enlightenment perspectives in nineteenth-century Edinburgh, "a growing number of individuals . . . argued for women's absolute right to education," Lindy Moore notes, although "views on what constituted woman's sphere and what education this necessitated, continued to be more influential." See Lindy Moore, "Educating for the 'Woman's Sphere': Domestic Training versus Intellectual Discipline," in *Out of Bounds: Women in Scottish Society, 1800–1945,* ed. Esther Breitenbach and Eleanor Gordon (Edinburgh: Edinburgh University Press, 1992), 10.

22. Jane Rendall discusses this "contested . . . terrain" in early-nineteenth-century Edinburgh and the views of writers for *Blackwood's* and the *Edinburgh Review* in "'Women that would plague me with rational conversation': Aspiring Women and Scottish Whigs, c. 1790–1830," in *Women, Gender, and Enlightenment,* ed. Sarah Knott and Barbara Taylor (New York: Palgrave, 2005), 326–47 (quotation 337).

23. Christopher North [John Wilson], *Noctes Ambrosianae,* no. 12, *Blackwood's Magazine* 14 (October 1823): 493.

tional as well as sensitive and virtuous companions."[24] Writing on "Female Education" for the *Edinburgh Review* five years before Catherine's birth, Sydney Smith asserted that with "half the talent in the universe," women ought to have a better chance to cultivate that talent. Improving their educational opportunities would also improve public morals, the education of children, and the quality of married life.[25]

In his *Lectures on Education*, published when Catherine was in her teens, George Combe, an old friend of her father's, supported the idea of separate spheres while also expanding the boundaries of the private. "The great business of female life [is] the nurture and rearing of children, and the due management of the domestic circle," Combe argued, "occupations...equally important to women as professions are to men."[26] Yet to conduct their business well, women needed to study anatomy and physiology in addition to chemistry, natural history, and natural philosophy. Just as "the natural proportions of the female figure are destroyed by stays," Combe contended, so the female mind is "cribbed and cabined by custom and fashion." Women should learn music, drawing, and manners—the "elegant and refined accomplishments" that "throw over the domestic circle a charm which cannot be too highly prized." But they should also study fields of knowledge mistakenly considered too "shocking and indelicate" for them.[27] Even while viewing women's minds as analogous to their bodies—as possessing "natural proportions"—Combe grants reasoning power to both sexes. In the process he reveals the equalizing effect of Enlightenment values on women's prospects.

The two men with whom Catherine was closest as a girl both held the abilities of women in high esteem and recognized their conventional domestic roles as unduly constraining while also praising "feminine" characteristics and behavior. Although her grandmother's letters do not survive, those Katherine Thomson received from her husband suggest the happy reciprocity of their union and reveal what George Thomson valued in his wife and kinswomen. In a letter of 30 April 1821, for example, he outlines his understanding of female excellence when writing to Katherine of their daughter-in-law Harriet Thomson, married to their eldest son. Noting "how few mothers devote themselves as Harriet has done to the education of her children," Thomson tells his wife, "'tis impossible to praise her too much. She is

24. Moore, "Educating for the 'Woman's Sphere,'" 10.

25. Sydney Smith, "Female Education," *Edinburgh Review* 15 (January 1810): 310–11, quoted in Rendall, "'Women that would plague me,'" 337.

26. George Combe, *Lectures on Popular Education; Delivered to the Edinburgh Association for Procuring Instruction in Useful and Entertaining Science, in April and November, 1833* (Boston: Marsh, Capen & Lyon, 1834), "Lecture III," 84.

27. Ibid., 96, 94, 87.

cheerful, acute, graceful in every thing she does or says, and has much good sense &
I think the greatest evenness of temper. So Robert has really drawn a valuable prize
in the matrimonial lottery."[28] A matrimonial "prize," Harriet is the wife defined as
helpmeet; her intellect complements her obliging nature and feminine grace.

In other letters written to his wife, however, Thomson acknowledges that wom-
en's capacities, both physical and intellectual, exceed what the domestic ideal re-
quires. Recounting his arrival in Havre de Grace in August 1819, he tells his wife
that on "entering the harbour the first person who laid hold of a rope thrown from
the packet was a woman who handled it as cleverly as any main-top-man could
have done, for in this country one sees that the fair sex take their full share of labour
both within & without doors, much more than my fair country women."[29] Three
weeks later, still preoccupied with this theme, he writes to Katherine from France
that "the women in this country seem to take a most active concern in business of all
kinds.... The Parisian women do not appear to me to have that winning sweetness &
beauty of features which one finds in the English women, but in general their eyes
are darker & express more of character & intelligence."[30] Contrasting the "sweetness & beauty" of women whose occupations keep them "within...doors" with
the "character & intelligence" of those who also "labour...without," "cleverly"
performing the work of men, Thomson conveys his idea of the benefits and losses
entailed when women leave the domestic sphere. The feminine ideal embraced
by George Thomson in praising Catherine's aunt Harriet—that of the unwaged
helpmeet—had an economic rationale: it discouraged women from competing with
men for jobs in what was often a tight marketplace. But Thomson generally supported women with professional talents and ambitions. For his collection of Welsh
airs, he solicited contributions from a number of women authors, Joanna Baillie
and her aunt, Anne Home Hunter, among them. At the turn of the nineteenth century, when his acquaintance Anne Grant was widowed with several young children to support and felt "scorn[ed]" as a women writer by some of "the Edinburgh
Literati,"[31] Thomson helped launch her literary career, negotiating with printers

28. ALS George Thomson to Katherine Thomson, 30 April 1821, MS 7198, ff. 45–46,
National Library of Scotland.

29. ALS George Thomson to Katherine Thomson, 6 August 1819, MS 7198, f. 27, National Library of Scotland.

30. ALS George Thomson to Katherine Thomson, 27 August 1819, MS 7198, ff. 31–32,
National Library of Scotland.

31. Anne Grant to John Hatsell, 14 December 1806, in *Memoir and Correspondence of Mrs.
Grant of Laggan,* ed. J. P. Grant, 3 vols. (London: Longman, Brown, Green, and Longmans,
1844), 1:81.

and subscribers on her behalf and helping to edit her work. Decades later Thomson argued that middle-class women should be better trained for employment as music teachers. "Unless more thoroughly instructed in the best classical music," he told Catherine's father, they "cannot stand their ground as Teachers of their own Sex, in comparison with the talented German professors who are attracted to this country by its ability to pay them well."[32] But it was one thing for his countrywomen to compete with German professors and another for them to compete with himself. Thus Thomson characterized the Scotswomen who compiled and published their own bowdlerized collection of Scottish airs as "canting old maids" who had "castrated all the songs ancient and modern in which the dangerous word 'kiss' occurs."[33] Thomson's objection to the censorship of Burns seems justifiable, but his metaphor for that process—castration—suggests his sense of the sexual threat posed by women who had intruded into his professional domain and whose music collection was outselling his own.

With this one exception, Thomson encouraged ambitious or financially pressed women who sought training, education, and employment. Indeed the economic vulnerability of his own unmarried daughters ("the spinsters"), who remained dependent on him until his death, made him all the more aware of the need for middle-class girls to become self-supporting. While he idealized family life and "acute" yet domestic women, Thomson understood that women were capable of much more than their conventional roles allowed.

So too did George Hogarth. A cultured and thoughtful man—"quiet, intellectual, unobtrusive," as one acquaintance described him[34]—Catherine's father believed in the importance of "free discussion" and the dispassionate search for truth.[35] He was happy to discover "the highest intellectual power" among women.[36] Unlike his father-in-law, however, he believed that such power need not make a woman "unfeminine." Characterizing the pioneering woman scientist Mary Somerville in

32. George Thomson to George Hogarth, 1846, quoted in William J. Carlton, "George Hogarth—A Link with Scott and Dickens," *Dickensian* 59 (May 1963): 85.

33. George Thomson to Allan Cunningham, December 1823, quoted in Hadden, *George Thomson,* 70.

34. Henry Burnett, "Mr. Henry Burnett's Reminiscences," in Frederic G. Kitton, *Charles Dickens by Pen and Pencil* (London: Frank T. Sabin, 1890), 138.

35. ALS George Hogarth to George Combe, 11 June 1829, MS 7223, f. 132, National Library of Scotland.

36. [George Hogarth], review of *The Connexion of the Physical Sciences* by Mary Somerville, *Halifax Guardian,* 19 April 1834, 292.

his 1834 review of her *Connexion of the Physical Sciences* for the *Halifax Guardian,* Hogarth outlines his position:

> The mind of woman has, in all ages, occasionally asserted its claims to the highest intellectual power; but the comparative narrowness of female education has rendered the attainment of great distinction in learning or science a rare occurrence; and this rarity has had the effect of communicating to the gifted few certain foibles of character which have made a learned lady, or a *bluestocking,* be looked upon, in society, as something pedantic, stiff, and unfeminine. In this respect, however, a great change has taken place; and our most distinguished authoresses form the grace and ornament of the society in which they move. This is very remarkably the case with the lady whose latest work is before us;—a lady who, while she exhibits a mind of the most masculine depth and vigour, preserves all the softest features of the female character.[37]

Hogarth's attitude toward women and their powers appears curiously mixed here. Like men, presumably, women possess "the highest intellectual power" only on occasion; there are never more than a few geniuses of *either* sex in a given age. Yet in "assert[ing] its claims" to "the highest . . . power," the female mind seems strident, claiming its rights as a feminist would. Like George Combe, who sees the female mind as unfortunately "cribbed . . . by custom and fashion," Hogarth views women as hindered by their "narrow" education, which fails to cultivate their natural abilities. But by its very scarcity, education weakens those women who become learned by giving them "foibles of character." Those "foibles" may be largely imagined, Hogarth suggests—a matter of how the women are "looked upon" and misperceived. Lending credence to these misperceptions, however, he praises the "great change" that has occurred among "learned ladies." The "stiff," "pedantic," and "unfeminine" bluestocking has become a graceful and ornamental lady whose "soft" female features are preserved despite the masculine "depth and vigour" of her mind.

Without challenging the conventional association of women with grace, beauty, and softness, Hogarth believes them capable of "masculine" thought but too often constrained by their "female education." Unfortunately, little is known of his approach to educating his own daughters. Yet their likely course of instruction can be inferred from various sources. Before Catherine's birth, at least one school for middle-class girls was established in New Town—the Edinburgh Ladies' College,

37. Ibid.

known as "Queen Street" for its location.[38] But what we know of the practice of schooling daughters within Catherine's extended family and of George Hogarth's capacities as a tutor, coupled with his growing financial difficulties, suggests that Catherine and her sisters were educated by their parents at home.

When Catherine was six years old, her grandfather described the education of her female cousins, the daughters of Robert and Harriet Thomson. The girls were schooled by their parents, who "taught them to read, write, cast accounts, geography etc.," Thomson reported, their lessons supplemented by the instruction of "a French dancing master" under whom they were "making great progress in the acquisition of grace and agility."[39] Catherine's education probably took a similar form. To supplement his income as a newspaper editor in the early 1830s, George Hogarth advertised for pupils, proposing to give "private lessons in the classics, mathematics, arithmetic, belles lettres, and the practice of English composition,"[40] and it seems reasonable that the Hogarth girls as well as children from other families benefited from his tuition. Like her mother and aunts a generation earlier and her Thomson cousins, Catherine would have received dancing lessons in addition to instruction in academic subjects.

By her teens Catherine had become an avid reader. Her grandparents were highly literate and sometimes compared people they met to characters from their favorite novels.[41] Her father, as a critic and newspaper editor, received the latest literary works to review. Thus Catherine had ready access to each issue of *Blackwood's Magazine* and a host of other periodicals and annuals. Fluent in French, she readily composed letters to Parisian correspondents as an adult and was most likely taught the language by her multilingual father. Scottish Presbyterians, the Hogarths had their first child baptized at Greyfriars Church when she was two months old, and they attended to her religious education. Mrs. Hogarth's prayer book was among Catherine's most prized possessions, left to her at her mother's death in 1863. In turn Catherine bequeathed it to her sister Helen.

Catherine's parents considered her musical training to be essential and saw to it themselves. As her father put it, music had importance "as a branch of polite knowledge, as a powerful aid in the exercises of devotion, and as a rational and

38. David Daiches, *Edinburgh* (London: Hamish Hamilton, 1978), 165.

39. ALS George Thomson to Katherine Thomson, 30 April 1821, MS 7198, ff. 45–46, National Library of Scotland.

40. *Halifax Guardian*, 7 December 1833.

41. Writing to his wife in 1819, for example, George Thomson describes a French postilion as "the identical La Fleur of Sterne to a tittle," referring to *A Sentimental Journey;* quoted in Hadden, *George Thomson*, 53.

elegant recreation in social and domestic life."[42] In his view, an understanding of music and its history was "indispensable to every person of liberal attainments," and both he and George Thomson objected to what they saw as the "superficial [musical] instruction of our young Ladies in the middle rank of life."[43] Catherine's abilities as a pianist and vocalist were not simply feminine ornaments that would attract men but the mark of her liberal education. As a girl Catherine participated in the "petites concerts" put on by her extended family, and she attended public concerts with her father, the music critic for the *Edinburgh Courant.* The musical interests and enterprises of her family members brought her into contact with some of the most famous composers and performers of the day. Catherine was fourteen when she met Felix Mendelssohn, a guest of the Hogarths "for some days" during his first visit to Scotland in 1829.[44]

Although George Hogarth recognized women's intellectual powers and believed that girls were held back by the "comparative narrowness" of their education, his everyday practices as a father sometimes proved inconsistent with his theories. Finding himself in economic difficulties, he adopted a sexual double standard in educating his children, privileging the boys over the girls. When Catherine's brothers William and James were thirteen and eleven, respectively, he sent them to a school in Hamburg, feeling that "a thorough knowledge of the German and French languages w[ould] be of so much use to them" in their future careers, Mary Hogarth told their cousin. "We shall of course be very sorry to part with them," she went on, "but it will do them a great deal of good."[45] With his family on a very limited budget, Hogarth saw foreign schooling as a male prerogative, since the boys would necessarily become self-supporting and enter professions, while the girls most likely would not. As Mary's tone suggests, the sisters understood and accepted that distinction. Like their mother, they were home-centered to an extent that their father and brothers were not. Yet there remained common

42. George Hogarth, *Musical History, Biography, and Criticism* (1835; reprint, New York: Da Capo Press, 1969), v.

43. Ibid.; George Thomson to George Hogarth, 1846, quoted in Carlton, "George Hogarth," 85.

44. "Mendelssohn was my guest in Edinburgh for some days during his first visit to this country," Hogarth told a correspondent in 1843, "and it was the hearing the great annual competition of Highland bagpipes (to which I took him) that suggested many of the ideas in this symphony [Mendelssohn's Scottish Symphony], as he told me last time he was here." ALS George Hogarth to V. Neville, 28 July [1843], National Library of Scotland, Acc. 9089.

45. ALS Mary Hogarth to Mary Scott Hogarth, 15 May [1836], Charles Dickens Museum, London.

ground in what the Hogarth children learned, regardless of their sex. George and Georgina Hogarth expected their daughters as well as their sons to be rational, cultured, and knowledgeable people, and boys and girls alike were taught a common set of values—in particular, the importance of ideas and the arts over profit and financial success.

"PROFIT . . . IS AN INFERIOR CONSIDERATION"

For both the Hogarths and the Thomsons, intellectual and cultural life took precedence over material considerations—a fact to which the financial difficulties of both Catherine's father and her grandfather attest. George Thomson was well paid as clerk to the Board of Trustees for the Encouragement of Arts and Manufactures in Scotland. From £40 in 1780, his annual salary rose to £150 in 1797, to £300 by 1824, and to £420 in the 1830s, placing him well within the middle class. Nonetheless, he found himself in financial difficulties in 1814, the year before Catherine's birth. Recovering from that crisis, he eventually purchased a home in Leith for £650 but lost most of the savings he hoped to leave to his unmarried daughters by investing more than £1,300 in shares of the ill-fated Caledonian Railway. While Thomson was upset over his losses "for the sake of the woman-kind that [were] to survive [him],"[40] economic success had never been his priority. Over several decades he devoted much of his time and energy to his collection of Scottish airs, although that project barely paid its own costs. His collections of Welsh and Irish airs, which sold poorly, cost him hundreds of pounds. From Thomson's point of view, what mattered was the cultural value of his enterprises, which bore little or no relation to their market value, and he continued to lay out money on them, despite their drain on his resources.

For George Hogarth, too, cultural and intellectual endeavors were considerably more important than money making. To become a Writer to the Signet, Hogarth worked as an apprentice for five years and took two years of classes at the University of Edinburgh. His decision to train for and practice law marked his ambition as a farmer's son. As a solicitor he held a respectable position in Edinburgh society, yet he found more satisfaction in his amateur musical and literary undertakings than in his legal practice. As early as 1812 he was trying to drum up interest among his fellow solicitors and advocates in a new periodical, its contents to be written by the members of the legal profession. "I have agreed to become a partner in this concern," Hogarth told the Edinburgh advocate John Borthwick, "and several young men of our profession have also done so. . . . There may be an eventual profit, though

---

46. George Thomson to Robert Chambers, 1847, quoted in Hadden, *George Thomson,* 99.

this is an inferior consideration: and at any rate we should have a stimulus to literary exertion, which we at present want."[47]

Hogarth's discounting of financial profit as a primary goal of his exertions neatly captures his attitude toward business matters and helps to explain his growing financial problems and his turn from law to journalism when Catherine was in her teens. To judge from appearances in the 1820s, Catherine's father was doing well professionally. From their lodgings on Hart Street, Hogarth moved his family to larger accommodations at 2 Nelson Street by 1820. A two-story flat, or "double upper," their apartment fronted Abercromby Place, the first curved street in the neighborhood, and two rows of windows gave an expansive view of New Town and, most immediately, Lady Blair's Field (now Queen Street Gardens). From Nelson Street the Hogarths moved two blocks east, to 19 Albany Street, in 1828, a few doors away from Christian and James Ballantyne, Catherine's aunt and uncle, the latter Sir Walter Scott's printer and editor. With the birth of Georgina the year before, the nine Hogarths needed more room. This move, their last in Edinburgh, seemed to signal their upward mobility, since their new home was spacious and elegant. Its three stories included ample servants' quarters and kitchen, dining room, parlor, and study, a large drawing room, and bedrooms of varying sizes. A fan-lit front door led to an entrance hall and the hall to an oval stairway illuminated by a large domed skylight. With its broad bay windows, its high ceilings framed by floral moldings, and its other symmetrical and stately details, 19 Albany Street exemplified the neoclassical style of New Town and conveyed its feeling of affluence.

Nonetheless, Hogarth's legal practice was not in a flourishing state, and he and his family were headed for what he later termed his "evil days."[48] Within two years of moving to Albany Street, he was forced "to stop payment, and lay [his] affairs before [his] creditors."[49] Writing to William Blackwood at the end of August 1830, Hogarth refers to the crisis in his finances, promising to repay a debt of £30, perhaps by performing "some service . . . in a literary way." Four years earlier Hogarth had been able to lend Blackwood £300; now he found himself thanking the Edinburgh publisher for the latter's "friendly behavior."[50] To George Combe, Hogarth expressed his "deep feeling" for Combe's "kind behavior in [these] unfortunate

47. ALS George Hogarth to John Borthwick, 24 December 1812, MS 10371, f. 184, National Library of Scotland.

48. ALS George Hogarth to William Ayrton, 13 March 1833, British Library, Add. 52338, f. 89.

49. ALS George Hogarth to William Blackwood, 31 August 1830, MS 4027, f. 177, National Library of Scotland.

50. Ibid.

matters," which he would "never forget."[51] Writing to Sir Walter Scott, who was struggling to pay off his own burdensome debts, Hogarth asked for a brief letter of recommendation, explaining his circumstances and his career prospects:

> You may perhaps have heard that I have been unfortunate in business; and having failed of success in a profession which I have carried on for so many years, I have no prospect now of being able to continue it with better fortune. Indeed, my want of capital has always prevented my doing business to advantage, or competing with the other members of a profession so much overstocked. I take the liberty of saying all this, to shew you (who have often expressed a kind interest in my affairs) that it is not without reason that I wish to do something for my family in another way.
>
> Hearing that the Editorship of the [London] Courier was vacant, James Ballantyne wrote to Mr. Rees, enquiring as to this and mentioning it as an object which I considered desirable. He has just received an answer from Mr. Rees, in which that gentleman advises me immediately to come to London, as he says the newspaper proprietors are now forming their arrangements for the next season; and he offers, in the kindest manner, to use his good offices in my behalf.[52]

Hogarth's "want of capital" may have placed him at a disadvantage in a competitive legal marketplace, as he tells Scott. Yet he seems to have been ready if not eager for a career change and had been drifting toward journalism since his early days in law. With James Ballantyne, he invested in the *Edinburgh Weekly Journal* in 1817, contributing reviews to its columns, and he wrote for the *Edinburgh Courant,* the *Harmonicon,* and *Blackwood's Magazine* before giving up his legal practice. Thus Hogarth's financial failure was liberating in its way, providing him with a rationale for shifting to journalism full-time.

For Catherine, her father's financial crisis was unsettling, forcing her and her family to economize and leaving them uncertain about what the future would hold. She had been taught to value the arts and the intellect more highly than material goods and prosperity, but at fifteen, she knew that her social status and prospects largely depended on her father's ability to provide for his family, and she had seen firsthand the difficulties that could face middle-class women left to fend for themselves. In 1815, when James Ballantyne proposed to Catherine's aunt, Robert

51. ALS George Hogarth to George Combe, 10 December 1830, MS 7225, f. 119, National Library of Scotland.

52. ALS George Hogarth to Sir Walter Scott, 30 September 1830, MS 3914, f. 93, National Library of Scotland.

Hogarth required proof that Christian's suitor was debt-free before allowing the marriage.[53] Although Christian suffered through her husband's financial vicissitudes, she proved less vulnerable to economic hardship than her sister-in-law Hermione. When John Ballantyne died in June 1821, *his* wife was left with nothing but a small sum provided by a friend and, in George Thomson's words, was forced to practice "a rigid economy and much self-denial" in her struggle to survive.[54]

From popular fiction as well as the lives of women around her, Catherine learned of daughters and wives imperiled by the business failure or death of male providers and confronted with the prospect of governessing "slavery," as Austen puts it in *Emma* (1816).[55] In recurring tales about governesses and their plight, nineteenth-century writers registered commonly held anxieties about the humiliating loss of position endured by middle-class women forced by necessity into employment by their own social peers. Within five years of her father's bankruptcy, however, Catherine could joke about Miss Frampton being "thrown upon the wide world," suggesting that fantasies of adventure and autonomy counterbalanced the anxieties created by the failure of her father's legal practice in 1830.

Animated by his hope of becoming a newspaper editor and by Mr. Rees's promise of assistance, George Hogarth traveled to London in December 1830. Whatever the reason, he did not secure the position he sought there. But from January until July 1831 the Hogarths were staying in London, at least periodically, their presence recorded in Marianne Ayrton's journal for that year.[56] Having dined with the Ayrtons at James Street on 10 July, they moved from London to Exeter the following week. Through the influence of his friend Lockhart, Hogarth had obtained the editorship of a weekly Exeter newspaper, the *Western Luminary*. Writing to Blackwood from Exeter on 18 July, Hogarth described the *Luminary* as a paper of "long standing" and "strong Tory principles," one "firmly established among the clergy and Tory Gentry of Devonshire, Cornwall, and Somersetshire." The paper had "been lamely conducted for some time," Hogarth noted, but he hoped "to infuse

53. "The Ballantyne Brothers," Walter Scott Digital Archive, Edinburgh University Library, *http://www.walterscott.lib.ed.ac.uk/biography/ballant.html* (accessed 21 January 2007).

54. George Thomson to Robert Chambers, 14 May 1844, quoted in Hadden, *George Thomson*, 91.

55. Jane Austen, *Emma,* ed. James Kinsley (1816; Oxford: Oxford University Press, 1995), 271.

56. Mrs. Ayrton hosted one or both of Catherine's parents in January, May, and July 1831.

more life & vigor into it" and "to give [it] a decidedly literary character."[57] From Blackwood he requested advance copies of new publications to review.

"AMONG STRANGERS"

With an estimated population of 28,000, one fifth that of Edinburgh, Exeter was not intimidating to the Hogarths, although they found themselves "entirely among strangers," as Catherine's father told Blackwood.[58] Their relocation posed challenges for the family, particularly Mrs. Hogarth, separated from friends and relations and managing a household of seven children in unfamiliar surroundings, on all too limited means. However, the Hogarths soon befriended the Franklins, a prosperous family with ten children. Their coach building and saddlery business was located on High Street and run by son George. His brother Henry was a music teacher, and Catherine found a companion in their musical sister Eliza, two years her senior. In a portrait commissioned before her marriage to John Trix in 1843, Eliza appears with stylish ringlets, in a lace-trimmed dress, holding a musical score. When she visited Catherine and her husband in 1840, George Hogarth took her to a Handel oratorio at Exeter Hall.[59]

With its news items and its advertisements and reviews of literary works and performances, the *Western Luminary* provides an index to the activities and concerns of the Hogarths during their brief time in Exeter. The publications sent to Hogarth for review and circulated among family members included the 1831 edition of *Frankenstein* and a number of literary annuals and magazines, *Fraser's*, *Blackwood's*, and the *Metropolitan* among them. The Hogarths read the *Harmonicon* and studied new pieces for the pianoforte. When a new five-volume edition of George Thomson's *Melodies of Scotland* was published, his son-in-law praised it as "a great and splendid literary, as well as musical work."[60] In November 1831 the Hogarths heard the twenty-five-member Russian Horn Band, each musician playing two horns and producing the effect of "a powerful full toned organ." Before the end of the year, Paganini followed the Russians to Exeter, impressing his audi-

57. ALS George Hogarth to William Blackwood, 18 July 1831, MS 4029, ff. 247–48, National Library of Scotland.

58. Ibid.

59. David Parker, Anno Wilson, and Roger Wilson discuss Eliza Franklin and her tie to the Hogarths and Charles Dickens in "Letters of a Guest at Devonshire Terrace," *Dickensian* 92 (1999): 51–60. I thank Anno and Roger Wilson for a photograph of Eliza Franklin's oil portrait.

60. [George Hogarth], review of *The Melodies of Scotland* by George Thomson, *Western Luminary*, 10 January 1832, 4.

ence with his own Sonata Militaire, played "entirely on one string (the Fourth)."[61] In showrooms on High Street, Catherine and Mary saw the latest London fashions, comparing them to those described in columns on "Female Fashions" in their father's paper.

In the midst of these entertainments, Catherine and her family discussed more weighty and sensational matters, such as "Burking," the "horrible crime" that supplied anatomists with bodies, named for Edinburgh's own William Burke; and instances of wife-selling at Smithfield Market and in Carlyle, described in the *Western Luminary* as "disgraceful transactions which are most unaccountably allowed to take place publicly in this country."[62] Most important, the Hogarths followed the debate surrounding the first Reform Bill, passed into law by Parliament in 1832 and covered in great detail by Hogarth's paper. The Reform Act eliminated the so-called "rotten boroughs," making government more fully representative of heavily populated industrial areas, and it extended the franchise to include most middle-class men. Intended in part to defuse the threat of social revolution, the act sharply limited aristocratic and landed power while also "safeguarding" against democracy by instituting substantial property qualifications for voters.

While growing up in Edinburgh, Catherine had been aware of the often sharp boundaries separating social classes, boundaries given physical form through urban planning. With the creation of New Town, as Robert Chambers noted in 1823, Edinburgh was made into a "double city" that divided "the high from the low, the intelligent from the ignorant." North of Old Town, that "ancient and picturesque hill-built [city], occupied chiefly by the humbler classes," there was now "an elegant modern one, of much regularity of aspect, and possessed almost as exclusively by the more refined portion of society."[63] Establishing his social status, Catherine's father had moved from the Old Town to the New in 1807, the year after he first paid for a listing in the Edinburgh Post Office directory and eight years before his first child was born.

Despite separating themselves from the poor and the working classes by relocating to New Town, both George Thomson and George Hogarth remained keenly aware of the struggles of those less educated and affluent than themselves. In 1819, during a time of political reaction against class unrest in Britain, Thomson criticized the violent suppression of working-class demonstrators in Manchester, where ten protesters were killed and hundreds wounded at what came to be known as

61. *Western Luminary,* 15 November 1831, 5; ibid., 20 December 1831, 5.

62. Ibid., 15 November 1831, 3; ibid., 1 May 1832, 4; ibid., 28 February 1832, 4.

63. Robert Chambers, *Traditions of Edinburgh,* new ed. (1823; London: W. & R. Chambers, 1868), 18–19.

the "Peterloo Massacre": "How lamentable, & what heart burning discontent will be the consequence of so many deaths," he told his wife.[64] Concerned with the well-being of factory workers, he proposed that mill owners hold dances to provide employees with entertainment and exercise, having seen "the happiness [dancing] produces among the peasantry and the other working classes in France and Belgium," where the people conducted themselves with "perfect decorum."[65] In an article he submitted to Robert Chambers's *Edinburgh Journal* in 1835, he argued that members of the working classes should be allowed to study music as well,[66] a view that Catherine's father shared.

In his own article on the subject, Hogarth noted that workers benefited from that "refined and intellectual pursuit" and contended that their musical instruction and recreation provided an antidote to "the demoralizing effects of a crowded population, fluctuating employment, and pauperism." While respecting class divisions, Hogarth defended "the spirit of industrious independence" among workers, shown in part through their formation of choral societies and orchestras. He envisioned "mechanics and work people . . . mingl[ing] with their employers and their families" in church oratorios,[67] an ideal of harmonious class relations that his eldest daughter embraced. As mistress of her own household, Catherine would form close ties with women she or her husband hired, exchanging gifts and letters with them, writing recommendations on their behalf after they left her service, and naming them in her will.

In Exeter, George Hogarth edited a paper devoted to Tory interests and supported the party platform, which was aligned with landed as opposed to mercantile interests and wary of representative government. Hogarth had obtained the editorship of the *Western Luminary,* at least in part, because of his affiliations with Edinburgh's "Anti-Reformers," about whom he reported at second hand.[68] Thus many of the editorials he published in 1831 and 1832 criticized reform, associating it with the "anarchy" of the French Revolution rather than with social harmony. "The circumstances which deluged France with blood may find a counterpart in

64. ALS George Thomson to Katherine Thomson, 23 August 1819, MS 7198, ff. 31–32, National Library of Scotland.

65. George Thomson to Robert Chambers, October 1835, quoted in Hadden, *George Thomson,* 43.

66. Ibid., 44.

67. Hogarth, *Musical History,* 173.

68. *Western Luminary,* 6 December 1831, 4.

this country if our present headlong career toward revolution is not arrested," one editorial warned.[69]

But Hogarth's conservatism was more a matter of regional habit and expediency than of deep personal conviction,[70] and the political views expressed in the paper he edited were inconsistent. The paper urged carpenters and farmers to remember their "proper business," place their political faith in the wisdom of their betters, and drop their demand for the vote, yet it also praised the "bookish farmers" of Scotland, well educated, capable of making scientific improvements—and, by implication, wise enough to elect their own political representatives.[71] As Hogarth remarked to William Ayrton in 1833 after accepting the editorship of the *Halifax Guardian,* another Tory weekly, whatever his own private opinions might be, he was required by virtue of his position to "advocate the views of [his] party, not in a lukewarm, indifferent tone . . . but, though earnestly, yet temperately and dispassionately. . . . That I succeed, *in this respect,* is apparent from the circumstance, that while I satisfy the warmest of my political supporters, I have made no enemies among the opposite party, among whom, I hear, I am always spoken of with respect."[72] By the mid-1830s, in fact, Hogarth had entirely abandoned his Tory views and joined "the opposite party," working in London for the *Morning Chronicle,* one of the "Reforming Journals" criticized by the *Western Luminary* during his brief tenure there.

Whatever their views of political reform, the Hogarths faced another and more pressing danger than the impending "deluge" of democracy in 1832: the outbreak of Asiatic cholera, which reached Exeter in July. The disease had been spreading through England since the close of 1831. In February it reached London; on 19 July the first cases were reported in Exeter, which was declared an infected port on the twenty-third. City leaders and medical men did what they thought proper to curtail the contagion but were unaware that cholera bacteria were spread through contaminated water supplies. The disease ran its course among the population, with 1,200 cases reported between July and November, more than a third of which proved fatal. In the business district on Fore Street, where Hogarth's office was

69. Ibid., 8 November 1831, 4.

70. "Of . . . those who came to the [Scottish] Bar between 1790 and 1804," Henry Cockburn notes, the "overwhelming numerical majority" were Tories, and the Whigs "saw themselves excluded from everything that power could keep from them" (*Memorials of His Time,* 134–36).

71. *Western Luminary,* 29 November 1831, 5; [George Hogarth], review of the *Quarterly Journal of Agriculture; and the Prize Essays of the Highland Society of Scotland* 15 (November 1831), *Western Luminary,* 8 November 1831, 2.

72. ALS George Hogarth to William Ayrton, 21 October 1833, British Library, Add. 52338, f. 91v.

located, a young compositor at a rival paper sickened and died in a single day.[73] Within weeks of the outbreak, Exeter's streets were unusually empty and the air was filled with the acrid smell of burning disinfectants.[74] Riots and other disturbances broke out in burial grounds and homes when people felt that medical authorities were disposing of bodies too quickly and without due respect. The alarming and painful symptoms of the disease contributed to the prevailing sense of anxiety, as did its swift course. Death would occur within two days and often much sooner—in some cases as little as two hours after the onset of symptoms.

In July 1831 George Hogarth told William Blackwood that his position at the *Western Luminary* seemed "advantageous and agreeable."[75] Within a year he had changed his mind. By the end of August 1832 the Hogarths had moved back to London, within walking distance of the Ayrtons. If their departure from Exeter was triggered by the cholera outbreak, it was also driven by Hogarth's dissatisfaction with the newspaper, which he was unable to shape as he wished. He had wanted to give the *Luminary* "a decidedly literary character," and its weekly discussion of literature and the arts was in fact expanded during his year-long editorship. Yet he had to answer to its proprietor, J. S. Dewdney, who bought out the weekly *Exeter Alfred* in 1831 to "enlarge [his] command" of local news,[76] but who had little interest in changing a well-established and successful newspaper formula.

Back in London, Catherine and Mary entered into a round of social engagements with the Ayrtons, hosting the Ayrton daughters Fanny and Matilda and visiting at James Street, often several times a week. Walking to the Hogarths, Fanny and her sister were sometimes joined by their mother or their brother Scrope. The growing intimacy between the two families reflected their common interests. William Ayrton was a former music critic at the *Morning Chronicle* and a founding member of the Philharmonic Society; for years he had edited one of George Hogarth's favorite periodicals, the *Harmonicon*. Mrs. Ayrton, the former Marianne Arnold, was the daughter of a composer and organist at Westminster Abbey. Though suffering from tuberculosis, to which she succumbed in 1836, she entertained guests and managed the household despite her debilitating symptoms and her difficulties with an alcoholic housemaid. Married in 1803, the Ayrtons had lost three of

73. Richard S. Lambert, *The Cobbett of the West: A Study of Thomas Latimer and the Struggle between Pulpit and Press at Exeter* (London: Nicholson and Watson, 1939), 54.

74. Thomas Shapter, M.D., *The History of Cholera in Exeter* (London: John Churchill, 1849), 178.

75. ALS George Hogarth to William Blackwood, 18 July 1831, MS 4029, ff. 247–48, National Library of Scotland.

76. *Western Luminary*, 22 November 1831, 4.

six children. When Catherine and Mary became fast friends with their daughters, Fanny was in her early twenties and Matilda in her late teens. Matilda died young, in 1842, and was fondly eulogized by her father for her "solid good sense" and "gentle temper."[77] Fanny seems to have been a less placid figure.

By mid-November 1832 George Hogarth had secured a new position, in Yorkshire, as editor of the *Halifax Guardian*. Leaving his wife and children in London, he moved to Halifax on 22 November. Within a month the family had joined him. They called on the Ayrtons one last time, on 15 January 1833, then left for Halifax the next day. Mrs. Hogarth was two or three months pregnant at the time.

The *Guardian* was "a new conservative paper," and as before, Hogarth secured his position through the influence of his friend J. G. Lockhart. "I was very slow in listening to this proposal, after finding that my experiment at Exeter did not answer my expectations," Hogarth told Blackwood on 1 December, "and I did not agree to it until I was convinced of its eligibility. The terms offered me, both in amount & permanence, are much more advantageous than ordinary in country papers. There is an excellent field here, the great majority of the gentry and better classes being conservatives—a large capital is subscribed for supporting it, and a great body of the first people in the West Riding are shareholders."[78] With his newspaper "promis[ing] to get on exceedingly well," and declaring himself "much pleased" with Halifax,[79] Hogarth and his family settled into their home at 8 Clare Place, Ward's End. They soon faced a family crisis when Mrs. Hogarth became "very ill" with smallpox, which she contracted despite her childhood inoculation against the disease. "Recovered, but still weak,"[80] the forty-year-old mother of seven gave birth for the last time on 8 July 1833—to twins Helen and Edward, who were baptized on 28 October in the parish church. Catherine was now the eldest of nine. Mrs. Ayrton wrote to her for news of Mrs. Hogarth and the babies, to whom Catherine became devoted. In Halifax the Hogarths carried on a steady correspondence with the Ayrtons and entertained friends from London; publisher John William Parker

77. William Ayrton, annotated abstracts from memoranda of Frances (Fanny) Ayrton, 1836–1847, British Library, Add. 60373, f. 41.

78. ALS George Hogarth to William Blackwood, 1 December 1832, MS 4033, f. 115, National Library of Scotland.

79. ALS George Hogarth to William Blackwood, 31 December 1832, MS 4033, f. 117, National Library of Scotland.

80. ALS George Hogarth to William Ayrton, 13 March 1833, British Library, Add. 52338, f. 90.

"enjoy[ed] himself at [their] little fireside" in the fall of 1833.[81] The Hogarths be-friended several Yorkshire families, and Catherine's father provided their sons with letters of introduction when they left for Edinburgh University. According to local tradition, Catherine and Mary attended private school in Halifax;[82] but no records of such schooling exist, and George Hogarth's continual efforts to supplement his newspaper income make it seem unlikely.

Whatever their financial constraints, the Hogarths continued their cultural pur-suits in Halifax. George Hogarth helped establish the local Orchestral Society. He found the city's residents "musical to a degree [he] had no idea of" and ready to sing "the most difficult madrigals...in 5 & 6 parts...with little preparation."[83] In October 1833, when Edward Taylor, future professor of music at Gresham College, visited the Hogarths during a lecture tour on English vocal harmony, there was "a performance...of the *Deluge,* one evening, by about 40 voices & instruments with-out any preparation at all," Hogarth told William Ayrton. "Mr. Taylor conducted it, and was quite astonished at the way in which it was done."[84]

In the spring of 1833 Hogarth found his work to be going on "smoothly," with "perfect satisfaction," the paper "increas[ing] in circulation, slowly but steadily."[85] But in the winter of 1834 he fell out with the *Guardian's* proprietors and resigned his editorship. Offered the position of musical and dramatic editor at the *Morning Chronicle,* he took the job, which marked a significant shift in his career: he would be working no longer for conservative provincial weeklies but for one of the most influential and liberal of the London dailies, second only to the *Times* in circula-tion. The change substantially altered the lives of his dependents as well. It brought them back to London for good and introduced them to a promising young parlia-mentary reporter and writer at the *Morning Chronicle,* Charles Dickens.

"MR. DICKENS IMPROVES VERY MUCH ON ACQUAINTANCE"
George Hogarth was living in London by mid-February 1834 and his family followed in mid-June, moving to 18 York Place, Queen's Elm, Brompton, on the south side of Fulham Road. Their house was one in a row, each fronted by its own small garden.

---

81. ALS George Hogarth to William Ayrton, 21 October 1833, British Library, Add. 52338, f. 91.

82. Arthur A. Adrian, *Georgina Hogarth and the Dickens Circle* (London: Oxford Univer-sity Press, 1957), 9.

83. ALS George Hogarth to William Ayrton, 13 March 1833, British Library, Add. 52338, f. 89; ALS George Hogarth to William Ayrton, 21 October 1833, British Library, Add. 52338, f. 92.

84. ALS George Hogarth to William Ayrton, 21 October 1833, British Library, Add. 52338, f. 92.

85. ALS George Hogarth to William Ayrton, 13 March 1833, British Library, Add. 52338, f. 90.

Now a crowded section of southwest London, Brompton had a rural flavor in the 1830s, and the Hogarths' home stood opposite "orchards and gardens extending as far as the eye could reach."[86] At 19 York Place their neighbor Dr. Frampton ran his academy for boys; his niece became a friend of Catherine and Mary. While the two eldest girls helped with household matters and took their turns with "the dear twins," who called Mary "Ma" and seemed, to Catherine, "more engaging every day,"[87] they also went to the Olympic and Drury Lane theaters and to concerts, and Catherine began to receive, in earnest, the attentions of eligible men, Dickens among them.

Despite her father's financial struggles, which left the Hogarth girls without a settlement of any kind, Catherine possessed her own attractions for young men already making their way in the world or determined to do so. Cultured and intelligent, happy among her siblings and accustomed to caring for them, she was physically attractive as well, with large blue eyes, a nose that turned up slightly, and a well-developed figure. Her penchant for humor made her appreciate those with a comic streak. And for Dickens particularly, Catherine held another attraction: she was the daughter of George Hogarth.

Dickens met Hogarth at the *Morning Chronicle* in the fall of 1834 and described himself as "acting under" Catherine's father there (Pilgrim 1:55). When John Easthope, the newspaper's proprietor, appointed Hogarth co-editor of the new *Evening Chronicle* in January 1835, Hogarth invited Dickens to write a story for its first number. Nine of Dickens's sketches had already appeared in the *Morning Chronicle*. "Acknowledging the numerous kindnesses [he had] already received at [Hogarth's] hands," Dickens proposed writing a series of sketches for the *Evening Chronicle,* for which he hoped to receive "*some* additional remuneration" (Pilgrim 1:55). Hogarth eagerly accepted this offer, and Dickens's weekly salary rose from five to seven guineas. His twenty "Sketches of London" appeared in the *Evening Chronicle* from 31 January to 20 August. Catherine's earliest description of Dickens recounts their meeting on 7 February 1835 at his twenty-third birthday party, one week after the first of his *Evening Chronicle* sketches was published. The two were already acquainted by that time.

Dickens's developing relationship with Catherine enabled the ambitious young writer to enter a literary network in which professional ties between men were often reinforced by marriage. In marrying Sir Walter Scott's associate, James Ballantyne, Christian Hogarth had strengthened her brother George's working relationships with her husband and Scott, just as Scott's daughter Sophia, by marrying J. G. Lockhart, had brought her father and his future biographer into close affiliation.

86. Burnett, "Reminiscences," 138.

87. ALS Catherine Hogarth to Mary Scott Hogarth, 11 February 1835, D. Jacques Benoliel Collection of the Letters of Charles Dickens, 86-2739, Rare Book Department, Free Library of Philadelphia.

"At this delicate stage of his fortunes," Ian Duncan observes, "Dickens would boast that his prospective father-in-law had been 'the most intimate friend and companion of Sir Walter Scott, and one of the most eminent of the literati of Edinburgh.'"[88] So Dickens told his uncle Thomas Culliford Barrow shortly before his wedding, using George Hogarth's connections to gain status in the eyes of an affluent relation.

Like Dickens, Catherine considered herself to be "her father's daughter," at least in part. But this phrase meant something different to her than it did to him. As the daughter of George Hogarth, Catherine was a link to Scott in Dickens's eyes, and to literary tradition and renown. While she possessed her own attractions for Dickens, he defined her and her value in terms of her relation to well-placed literary men, especially when writing to those he wished to impress. For Catherine, however, being George Hogarth's daughter meant possessing worth in and of herself. Although Hogarth benefited from the male network Duncan describes, both he and his father-in-law had long recognized and argued for women's agency, not their objectification, and he gave his daughters a strong sense of their own intrinsic value. Despite the gendered division of labor in their home, the Hogarth girls were raised as individuals capable of intellectual and cultural engagement as well as young women prepared for marriage and womanly self-sacrifice. From her father Catherine learned that the interests, talents, and accomplishments of those she met were more important than their status, position, and gender. Having found "Mr. Dickens" to "improve . . . very much on acquaintance," she emphasized his character rather than his connections in writing to her cousin in February 1835, describing him as "very gentlemanly and pleasant." Insofar as she positions Dickens in relation to others, she does so without regard to social status. He is the brother of "a very pretty girl who sings beautifully" and who seems as talented and attractive as himself.[89]

Given the dire financial straits of his own father, Dickens benefited from the Hogarths' system of values, which enabled them to quickly recognize and appreciate his remarkable qualities. An avid reader, Catherine prized his striking literary talents as much as her father did. She also found Dickens affectionate, entertaining, and energetic. Only three years older than herself, he was physically attractive, with his slim figure, wavy brown hair, and expressive features. They both enjoyed books, the theater, and family life. Catherine soon found herself in training for the role of Mrs. Charles Dickens, under the firm guidance of a loving but determined fiancé eager to teach his future wife her proper place.

88. Ian Duncan, *Modern Romance and Transformations of the Novel: The Gothic, Scott, Dickens* (Cambridge: Cambridge University Press, 1992), 189.

89. ALS Catherine Hogarth to Mary Scott Hogarth, 11 February 1835, D. Jacques Benoliel Collection of the Letters of Charles Dickens, 86-2739, Rare Book Department, Free Library of Philadelphia.

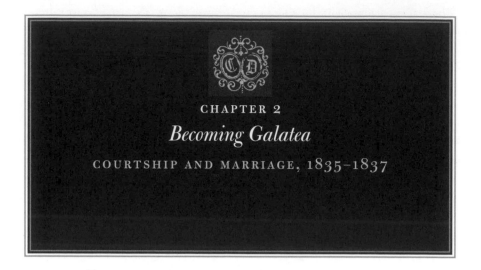

CHAPTER 2

Becoming Galatea

COURTSHIP AND MARRIAGE, 1835–1837

> Liza: Freddy's not a fool. And if hes weak and poor and wants me, may
> be hed make me happier than my betters that bully me and dont
> want me.
>
> Higgins: Can he make anything of you? Thats the point.
>
> Liza: Perhaps I could make something of him.
>
> —George Bernard Shaw, *Pygmalion*, act 5

RULES OF ENGAGEMENT

The quest of the male artist to create a perfect female subject—and often a perfect wife—is a familiar cultural motif, one that dates from ancient Greece and the myth of Pygmalion and Galatea. Disgusted by the faults of womankind and resolving to live unmarried, Pygmalion sculpts his perfect female out of ivory and falls in love with her, hopelessly it seems. Fortunately for the artist, Aphrodite ultimately unites him with his beloved Galatea by bringing the female sculpture to life. But nineteenth-century versions of this myth often end less happily than the ancient one, particularly for the Galatea figure. In Nathaniel Hawthorne's tale "The Birthmark" (1843), the husband perfects his beautiful wife by eliminating her one flaw, killing her in the process. And in Mary Shelley's *Frankenstein* (1818), the eponymous hero constructs an Eve for his Adam, only to destroy his handiwork when she is "half-finished," fearing that she will have a mind of her own and "refuse to comply" with the demands of her creator and her mate.[1]

---

1. Mary Shelley, *Frankenstein*, ed. Johanna M. Smith (New York: Bedford Books, 1992), pp. 144, 140.

These fears are realized, to a feminist end, in George Bernard Shaw's *Pygmalion* (1913), a modernist reworking of the classical myth. An advocate for Catherine Dickens and, more generally, the "commonplace" wives of men of genius, Shaw believed that "Galatea never does quite like Pygmalion: his relation to her is too godlike to be altogether agreeable."[2] Revisiting the myth from Galatea's perspective, Shaw shows that the ability to sculpt one's spouse need not be a male prerogative. His heroine, Eliza Doolittle, decides "not to marry her Pygmalion," who transforms her from a lowly flower girl into a seeming duchess, because he is unwilling to be transformed himself. She chooses the pliable Freddy Eynsford Hill over the domineering and inflexible Henry Higgins, although the linguist claims that she is his "masterpiece" and is not to be "thrown away" on the other man. Eliza balks at her objectification and answers Higgins's skeptical question about Freddy—"Can he make anything of you?"—by suggesting that *she* might "make something of him." In this way Shaw's Galatea figure proves as much an artist as a "masterpiece" and rejects "the foolish romantic tradition that all women love to be mastered, if not actually bullied and beaten," the playwright notes.[3]

Both Catherine Hogarth and Charles Dickens were familiar with myths in which male artists shape and perfect female subjects. Catherine read Mary Shelley's novel as a teenager, and her husband jokingly adapted the story in a comical love song he wrote for Mrs. David Colden (née Frances Wilkes) while he and Catherine were touring America in 1842:

—Poor Frankenstein, that Prince of fools
Why grim male monster made he,
When with the self-same clay and tools
He might have built a Lady!
(Pilgrim 3:220)

Hoping to realize her own variation of the story in 1835, at the outset of her engagement to Dickens, Catherine attempted to shape the behavior of her fiancé and mold his priorities to fit her own. She was quickly thwarted. If she wished to marry Dickens, she learned, she would have to acknowledge his sole claim to such artistry and allow him to author the terms of their union. Although Catherine was "not actually bullied and beaten," to use Shaw's phrase, she was mastered. Under Dickens's tutelage, she came to embrace the "romantic tradition" that Shaw derides and, along with it, the virtue of willing submission.

2. George Bernard Shaw, *Pygmalion,* in *George Bernard Shaw's Plays,* 2nd ed., ed. Sandie Byrne (New York: Norton, 2002), 360.

3. Ibid., 352, 349, 348, 353.

When Catherine accepted Dickens's marriage proposal in the spring of 1835, she had known him for less than a year and probably closer to six months. In February 1835 she attended his "delightful" birthday party,[4] and fourteen months later they married. Their timing was apt by Victorian standards; middle-class advice manuals discouraged prolonged engagements. If a couple could not afford to marry within two years, writers warned, the relationship would likely be marred by frustration or by changing affections and expectations.[5]

Before marrying, a middle-class man was expected to be earning enough money to support himself and his wife "comfortably" and to employ at least one servant, a maid-of-all-work; this standard of living required an annual salary in the range of £300.[6] Dickens was already earning that amount by the summer of 1835, since his weekly salary at the *Morning Chronicle* was raised from five to seven guineas between January and August—that is, to nearly £400 per year (Pilgrim 1:55 n. 2). While Catherine's parents were concerned about where the young couple would live, they were satisfied with Dickens's decision to remain in modest rented chambers at Furnivals Inn, moving from number 13 to number 15 to better accommodate their daughter: "a very nice and prudent way of beginning," as Mary put it.[7] And neither Catherine nor the Hogarths could have any doubt about Dickens's determination to succeed in life. "All that any one can do to raise himself by his own exertions and unceasing assiduity I have done, and will do," Dickens wrote with truth to his first love, Maria Beadnell, in 1833 (Pilgrim 1:29).

Emotionally as well as financially, Catherine and her fiancé felt ready for marriage in 1835. The Thomsons and the Hogarths tended to idealize domestic affections and pleasures, and Catherine had a happy family life, surrounded by younger brothers and sisters. Having turned twenty, she could now achieve the same domestic happiness in her own household. Her engagement marked her success in a competitive circle of young women concerned with their appearance and their appeal to men and measuring themselves against one another when they gathered to dress for concerts and balls. Catherine's earliest letters are those of a young woman actively interested in the marriage prospects of her friends and in eligible bachelors,

4. ALS Catherine Hogarth to Mary Scott Hogarth, 11 February 1835, D. Jacques Benoliel Collection of the Letters of Charles Dickens, 86-2739, Rare Book Department, Free Library of Philadelphia.

5. See Ginger Frost, *Promises Broken: Courtship, Class, and Gender in Victorian England* (Charlottesville: University Press of Virginia, 1995), 85–86.

6. John Tosh, *A Man's Place* (New Haven: Yale University Press, 1999), 12, 19.

7. ALS Mary Hogarth to Mary Scott Hogarth, 15 May [1836], Charles Dickens Museum, London.

and convinced that the task of caring for young children was rewarding. She was prepared to pass on the title "Miss Hogarth" to Mary, the next-eldest daughter of the family, and to have children of her own. Both Catherine and Mary treated their eligibility for marriage with humor rather than anxiety, but neither one intended to remain single.

Although the right to propose was his as a bachelor and time was on his side, Dickens was even more eager to find a suitable marriage partner than Catherine in 1835, having already suffered through a frustrating and unsuccessful courtship and now making a name for himself as a journalist and author. In 1830 he had met Maria Beadnell, the daughter of a London bank clerk, and by 1831 he had become her suitor, encouraged by her behavior and permitted to visit by her parents. By 1832, however, the Beadnells had changed their minds, most likely alarmed by the chronic financial woes of Dickens's father. They sent Maria to a Parisian finishing school, and by the time she returned, she had lost interest in Dickens. "Our meetings of late have been little more than so many displays of heartless indifference on the one hand while on the other they have never failed to prove a fertile source of wretchedness and misery," he wrote her in March 1833 (Pilgrim 1:17). He briefly renewed his attentions in May. "I never have loved and I never can love any human creature breathing but yourself," he confessed (Pilgrim 1:29). But his attempt was rebuffed, and the "heartless" Maria married Henry Louis Winter in 1845.

Unlike Dickens, Catherine did not have another love interest before she became engaged, although the references to young bachelors in her early letters suggest the presence of other suitors. Scrope Ayrton, the brother of Fanny and Matilda, who was making his way in the legal profession, saw Catherine frequently in the early 1830s, and her father approved of him as "one of those young men who are sure of success," for "talent & industry, combined with a love of the profession, never fails," George Hogarth told Scrope's father.[8] But it was Dickens—entertaining, clever, and physically attractive—who caught Catherine's eye, as she did his, seeming to Dickens in 1835 a more fitting choice than Maria. The daughter of his editor at the *Chronicle* and an indirect link to Sir Walter Scott, Miss Hogarth was herself a product of Edinburgh's artistic and highly literate society. Sharing the cultural interests that formed the basis of companionate marriage, they easily moved beyond the superficial flirtations that characterized Dickens's relationship with Maria.

Like most young Victorian couples, Catherine and Charles went out walking during their courtship, usually accompanied by Mary Hogarth or by Dickens's younger brother Fred. They exchanged and discussed books as well as Dickens's writing,

8. ALS George Hogarth to William Ayrton, 21 October 1833, British Library, MS. 52338, f. 91v.

and spent evenings at the English Opera House and the West End theaters, to which Dickens was sometimes sent for work. With her mother and Mary, Catherine went to stay with Dickens's parents in their London lodgings, while Dickens gave lessons in shorthand to Catherine's brother Robert and checked the page proofs of her uncle William Thomson's forthcoming travel book, *Two Journeys through Italy and Switzerland* (1835). Together they called on Rose Drummond, a well-known miniaturist whom Dickens commissioned to paint his portrait for Catherine. When Catherine was sick, Dickens urged her to take Camphor Julep and calomel pills and sat by her bed; when he was ill, she expressed "so much anxiety" on his behalf that he sent Fred to assure her that he was feeling much better (Pilgrim 1:79). To be closer to Catherine, Dickens temporarily moved to 11 Selwood Terrace, less than a quarter mile from her parents' home, and they enjoyed some quiet days together (Pilgrim 1:72). Despite Dickens's claim that he could "never love any human creature" but Maria, he had fallen in love a second time, and now his affection was warmly returned. Catherine told Charles that she "could be happy anywhere" with him; he told her that his love was one "which nothing [could] lessen" (Pilgrim 1:65, 63).

With each offering such assurances to the other, the two formed a tie that was reciprocal in its affection and remained so for years to come. Yet this reciprocity of feeling was at odds with the power imbalance in the relationship, in which Dickens insisted on wielding the upper hand. Catherine entered into her engagement assuming that she would be able to influence her fiancé and enjoy her fair share of control. As a young and unattached woman, she had taken pleasure in putting down the presumption of men who assumed rights to which they were not entitled, ridiculing, for instance, an "insufferable" fellow for whom a female friend had only "a *little* liking" and whose attempts to "appear…at his ease" were thus "rather surprising."[9] But as Catherine discovered, the courtship period was notorious for its shifting balances of power and the growing subordination of women once they became engaged.

At the beginning of a courtship, Victorian suitors often assumed the subordinate role, since women could choose to accept or reject their advances. Yet "the closer the courtship came to an actual marriage," one social historian observes, "the more the power shifted to the future husband's benefit."[10] Having accepted a proposal, a woman became dependent on her fiancé, sometimes giving up paid employment in anticipation of her marriage and, if sexually precipitate, relying on her fiancé

9. ALS Catherine Hogarth to Mary Scott Hogarth, 11 February 1835, D. Jacques Benoliel Collection of the Letters of Charles Dickens, 86-2739, Rare Book Department, Free Library of Philadelphia.

10. Frost, *Promises Broken*, 67.

to safeguard her reputation. Catherine Hogarth was not vulnerable in these ways, but she found her power negligible once she and Dickens were engaged. Her submission and compliance were all the more important to Dickens because of what he felt he had already suffered from female caprices during his first, unsuccessful romance and the prolonged and frustrating sense of powerlessness he had endured.

Although two years had passed since Dickens's final break with Maria Beadnell when Catherine accepted his proposal, her fiancé's experience as a spurned suitor largely determined the way in which he conducted their courtship. Dickens loved Catherine, but he would not allow her to toy with his affections, as he saw it—to show him "kindness and encouragement one day and a total change of conduct the next," as Maria had (Pilgrim 1:17). Women were said to have "a Thousand minds," as Dickens put it in his comic verses on *Frankenstein* (Pilgrim 3:220). Catherine had accepted his suit, and if she showed such changeable behavior, he would reprove her. If she persisted, she would have to seek a husband elsewhere.

So Catherine realized in May 1835, three weeks into her engagement, after having tried to set the terms of the courtship herself and alter Dickens's behavior by changing her own. Early that month she had received a letter to "dearest Kate" from Dickens, who was distressed by his "unavoidable detention in town" and concerned about a minor illness from which she was suffering (Pilgrim 1:60). But his tone shifted dramatically in the next letter she received, addressed more formally to "dear Catherine" and written after she had twice treated him with "coldness," withdrawing from him.

"It is with the greatest pain that I sit down, before I go to bed to-night, to say one word which can bear the appearance of unkindness or reproach," Dickens begins, "but I owe a duty to myself as well as to you, and as I was wild enough to think that an engagement of even three weeks might pass without any such display as you have favored me with twice already, I am the more strongly induced to discharge it" (Pilgrim 1:61). Opening his letter to Catherine with cutting sarcasm, Dickens both conveys and masks his anger, "pained" by the duty of reprimanding her. His "wild" thoughts are reasonable enough, he makes clear, while her "favors" are wholly unwelcome—"displays" both impulsive and stubborn:

> The sudden and uncalled-for coldness with which you treated me just before I left last night, both surprised and deeply hurt me—surprised, because I could not have believed that such sullen and inflexible obstinacy could exist in the breast of any girl in whose heart love had found a place; and hurt me, because I feel for you far more than I have ever professed, and feel a slight from you more than I care to tell. My object in writing to you is this. If a *hasty* temper produce this strange behaviour, acknowledge it when I give you

the opportunity—not once or twice, but again and again. If a feeling of you know not what—a capricious restlessness of you can't tell what, and a desire to teaze, you don't know why, give rise to it—overcome it; it will never make you more amiable, I more fond, or either of us, more happy. If three weeks or three months of my society has wearied you, do not trifle with me, using me like any other toy as suits your humour for the moment; but make the acknowledgment to me frankly at once—I shall not forget you lightly, but you will need no second warning. Depend upon it, whatever be the cause of your unkindness—whatever give rise to these wayward fancies—that what you do not take the trouble to conceal from a Lover's eyes, will be frequently acted before those of a husband. (Pilgrim 1:61)

Hurt and surprised by Catherine's "strange behaviour," Dickens enumerates the female failings it suggests to him: artfulness ("display"), obstinacy, capriciousness, and coyness ("a desire to teaze"). He uses his power properly, he claims, while she abuses hers, "toying" and "trifling" with him.

Describing her as "wayward," he exhibits and justifies his authority over her even as he goes on to disclaim it:

I know as well, as if I were by your side at this moment, that your present impulse on reading this note is one of anger—pride perhaps, or to use a word more current with your sex—"spirit." My dear girl, I have not the most remote intention of awakening any such feeling, and I implore you, not to entertain it for an instant. I am very little your superior in years; in no other respect can I lay claim to the title, but I venture nevertheless to give you this advice first, because I cannot turn coolly away and forget a slight from you as I might from any other girl to whom I was not warmly and deeply attached; and secondly, because if you really love me I would have you do justice to yourself, and shew me that your love for me, like mine for you, is above the ordinary trickery, and frivolous absurdity which debases the name, and renders it ludicrous. (Pilgrim 1:62)

While assuring Catherine that he is "very little [her] superior in years" and "in no other respect can ... lay claim to the title," Dickens establishes his superiority over her by invoking familiar stereotypes of gender difference, disparaging her "sex," and threatening to break their engagement promptly if she fails to heed him. As if to bridge this difference, Dickens uses a syntax of equivalence to teach Catherine her proper place. "Your love for me, like mine for you, is above the ordinary trickery" of women, he tells her, and "a desire to teaze ... will never make you more amiable, I more fond, or either of us more happy." He thus conveys his message in carefully balanced clauses that appeal to Catherine's desire for equity even as their substance refuses to satisfy it. Despite his balanced syntax, the difference is clear: it is her role to be "amiable," his to be "fond," his job to outline her faults, hers to "overcome" them. Representing himself as loving yet stern, Dickens does his manly duty by Catherine in correcting her. "What you do not take the trouble to conceal from a Lover's eyes, will be frequently acted before those of a husband," he warns. Although Dickens sounds less like Pygmalion than like a conduct book author, his aim is to mold and perfect his Galatea before marrying her.[11]

Ironically, what Dickens perceived to be Catherine's imperfection in treating him coldly was, in effect, her own attempt to perfect *him*—to alter and improve *his* behavior by withdrawing her warmth and affection. In analyzing Catherine's "coldness," Dickens attributes it to various causes, all of which suggest her unthinking and unexamined state: "you know not what...you can't tell what...you don't know why." Yet Catherine acted as she did purposefully, to protest Dickens's overdedication to work and professional success and his consequent neglect of her and their relationship—and to discourage his chronic "detention[s] in town." With its unspoken and indirect expression of anger and disapproval, her behavior might seem underhanded or unduly manipulative. But it was an adaptation of a feminine ideal celebrated among Victorians: the ladylike "influence" with which women were to achieve the moral improvement of their male relations while withholding criticism or remark. Dickens unwittingly reveals the limits imposed on Catherine's range of expression when he promises to "give [her] the opportunity" to speak— and tells her, too, what he expects to hear, "again and again": remorse over her "strange behaviour." According to the terms of his letter, in fact, an "acknowledgment" made "frankly" would lead to Catherine's dismissal. Faced with such constraints, expectations, and guidelines, Catherine offered her criticism nonverbally, but her meaning and aim were clear: what she sought in trying to change Dickens's behavior through her emotional withdrawal was a partnership or equivalence with her husband that her position as an unwaged middle-class wife would preclude.

From this, her initial disagreement with Dickens, Catherine got her first glimpse of what friends and acquaintances would later term Dickens's "dominating power."[12]

11. In *Dickens and Women* (London: J. M. Dent, 1983), Michael Slater reads Dickens's letter differently: "It is very much the letter of a young man on his dignity," yet its "Johnsonian cadences...betray not...any chilly sense of superiority but an effort...to impress upon Catherine the gravity, the desperate importance for them both, of what he is talking about" (107–8).

12. George Hodder, *Memories of My Time* (1870), quoted in *Dickens: Interviews and Recollections*, 2 vols., ed. Philip Collins (London: Macmillan, 1981), 1:100.

More generally, she was discovering what the gendered division of labor would mean for her as a married woman: that her husband would have a professional life in which she could participate only at second hand, and that his need to support her and their family financially would give him sources of fulfillment and pleasure that lay outside their home. As Dickens himself put it in justifying his work schedule to Catherine in November 1835, he was playing a professional game open solely to men and in which Catherine was, in effect, part of his winnings: "I will not do you the injustice to suppose that knowing my reason and my *motive* for exertion, *you* of all people will blame me one instant for my self-denial. You may be disappointed:—I would rather you would—at not seeing me; but you cannot feel vexed at my doing my best with the stake I have to play for—you and a home for both of us" (Pilgrim 1:97). From her fiancé Catherine continually heard that the stark divide between male agency and female objectification was a matter of course and served her best interests.

Because Dickens destroyed all of the correspondence he received from Catherine, we have no way of knowing precisely what she said to him in response to his reproof of May 1835, although she clearly did *not* make the frank acknowledgment that he warned would end the engagement. Despite the loss of her letters, however, her reactions to some of his reprimands and corrections can be pieced together by means of his letters to her, which often repeat fragments of her speech and writing. These letters reveal that Catherine was sometimes cowed or persuaded by his reproaches; submitting to them in one instance, she asked him to love her "once more" (Pilgrim 1:104). But she was not always willing to recognize his authority or accept his point of view, and she remained angry ("coss," as she more playfully put it [Pilgrim 1:110]) about his ambition, insisting that desire rather than necessity kept him at his desk. As Dickens acknowledged to Catherine, men and women often call things by different names: what he imagines as her "anger—pride perhaps" on reading his early reproof would instead be termed "spirit," he says, by members of her sex. These divergent languages were nowhere more apparent than in their respective representations of Dickens's professional labors. In this case what Dickens termed "necessity," "self-denial," and "duty" Catherine considered his "pleasure." Despite Dickens's efforts to correct Catherine's "obstinacy" in this regard, she proved less malleable than he wished—as did *he* from her point of view.

"Necessity and necessity alone, induces me to forego the pleasure of your companionship," Dickens told Catherine in November 1835.

You will never do me the justice of believing it however, and all I can do until [*Sketches by Boz*] is finished will be to reflect that I shall have (God willing) many opportunities of shewing you for years to come how unjust you used to be, and of convincing you then of what I would fain convince you now—that my pursuits and labours such as they are are not more selfish than my pleasures, and that your future advancement and happiness is the main-spring of them all. (Pilgrim 1:95)

"Don't say you are angry to receive a letter from me, or that I could come to you if I would," Dickens wrote in December. "I am obliged to determine with the most unfeigned reluctance, that I *must not* leave home to-day" (Pilgrim 1:111). As late as February 1836, less than two months before their marriage, the couple continued to argue the point. "You must not be 'coss' with what I cannot help," he instructed her. "If the representations I have so often made to you, about my working as a duty, and not as a pleasure, be not sufficient to keep you in good humour, which you, of all people in the World should preserve—why then, my dear, you must be out of temper, and there is no help for it" (Pilgrim 1:133).

"TO MINISTER, AND NOT TO BE MINISTERED TO"

From our vantage point, it may seem difficult to take seriously Catherine's dissatisfaction, since her desires appear insignificant when weighed against the productions of her husband's genius. Dickens was, in fact, on the verge of literary celebrity during their engagement. In February 1836 he accepted a proposal from Chapman and Hall to write the new monthly publication that became *The Pickwick Papers*, its first number appearing two days before he and Catherine were married. "The work will be no joke," he told her, "but the emolument is too tempting to resist" (Pilgrim 1:128–29). Few readers of *Pickwick* would wish he had resisted professional temptation in order to spend more time with his bride.

Yet in complaining of Dickens's dedication to his writing and his pursuit of professional success, Catherine was responding to traits that would later prove damaging to herself and their children: Dickens's willingness to put his work before his family; his refusal to compromise; his tremendous drive to succeed; and, in particular, his ability to represent and justify the things he enjoyed doing as acts of self-sacrifice that benefited others. More generally, Catherine's dissatisfied insistence on the pleasures Dickens derived from his professional labors conveys her sense of what Jane Austen termed the "poverty" of a lady's solely domestic life—its lack of intellectual rigor, economic productivity, and political relevance, despite its privilege and affluence.[13] Dickens was, in truth, working for Catherine, at least in part, for his labors would enable him to support her and their household at the same time that they established his own fame. Yet this "sacrifice" on his side

13. Jane Austen, *Sense and Sensibility*, ed. James Kinsley (1811; Oxford: Oxford University Press, 1990), 204.

required a corresponding one on hers, although it went largely unacknowledged in her circle—that of intelligent middle-class women whose only experience of professional success was vicarious. "I inclose such notices [of *Sketches*] as I have by me," Dickens wrote his publisher John Macrone in March 1836, shortly before he and Catherine wed, sending a number of favorable reviews. "Be good enough to preserve them for me, when you have made your Extracts.—Mrs. D takes some pride out of them" (Pilgrim 1:140).

There was, of course, another route to success open to Catherine—that of the capable housewife and domestic manager—and this was the role for which she went into training in 1835 under the supervision of her fiancé. As her parents' eldest daughter, Catherine knew at first hand what this role entailed, all the more so because the Hogarths, eleven in number, could afford to employ only one female servant and thus did much of the cooking and cleaning themselves. But Catherine would now be the mistress of her own household, responsible for its management and for meeting her husband's needs, and Dickens wanted her to practice being a wife before she actually became one. Catherine's domestic training under Dickens's tutelage shows how fully the sexual double standard informed their relationship—perhaps most notably in Dickens's assumption that *she* rather than *he* needed to be trained for marriage.

"Will you indulge me by making breakfast for me this Morning?" Dickens asked Catherine early in their engagement. "It will give me pleasure; I hope it will give you no trouble; and I am sure will be excellent practice" (Pilgrim 1:64). "I should like to see you *here* early. You can surely come to breakfast at half past ten. . . . I hope to be awakened by *your* tapping at my door in the morning and I look forward on making my appearance in the sitting room, to find you heading my breakfast table" (Pilgrim 1:65–66). "I shall *fully expect* you and Mary to breakfast with me this morning—not later than 11 and rather before than after. . . . Mind you are punctual my dear, and recollect I take *no denial on any pretense*" (Pilgrim 1:69).

In addition to these underlined requests and commands from her fiancé, Catherine also received books outlining models of proper feminine behavior and wifely compliance. Dickens marked specific passages for her consideration and told her to read them "attentively" (Pilgrim 1:85). In the fall of 1835, for example, Catherine opened a package containing Catharine Sedgwick's novel *The Linwoods*, which begins by defining "the destiny of woman": "Thou art born to love, to suffer, to obey,—to minister, and not to be ministered to."[14] Soon afterwards she received Samuel Johnson's *Life of Mr. Richard Savage*, a biography that reinforces

14. Catharine Maria Sedgwick, *The Linwoods; or, "Sixty Years Since" in America,* ed. Maria Karafilis (1835; Hanover: University Press of New England, 2002), 7.

Sedgwick's theme by illustrating the destructive effects of poor mothering on an artist son, a subject Dickens took to heart, believing himself a victim of maternal callousness and neglect.[15] After more than twenty years of marriage, Catherine would find herself inserted into a similar plotline by Dickens and unjustly represented as a heartless and neglectful mother.

In the early weeks of their engagement Catherine had tried to shape her fiancé and his priorities, only to find the role of creator claimed exclusively by him. Insofar as Dickens was being trained for marriage, he was performing that function himself, learning to exert his authority as a husband. His underlined commands were punctuated by expressions of love and affection—with "God bless you my more than life" and "10,000 kisses" (Pilgrim 1:77, 106), his numbers containing so many zeroes that they sometimes run the width of the page—and by playful nicknames for Catherine, among them "dearest Mouse," "Darling Tatie," and "darling Pig" (Pilgrim 1:139, 81, 119). Nonetheless, Dickens's letters show him authoring the terms of their marriage, which he intended to be hierarchical as well as companionate, with Catherine ministering to him as an angel of the hearth: "How eagerly I long for your society this evening. . . . [H]ow much delight it would afford me to be able to turn round to you at our own fireside when my work is done, and see in your kind looks and gentle manner the recreation and happiness which the moping solitude of chambers can never afford" (Pilgrim 1:95).

In managing Catherine's moral instruction, Dickens repeatedly invoked an ideal that he identified "as" Catherine even as he encouraged her to attain it: the "self" to whom she was to "do justice," according to his earliest reproof. He endowed her with an authentic self that conformed to his desires and needs—one that was kind, gentle, and (paradoxically) selfless. Cultivating that persona in his dealings with Catherine, he reproved her "coldness" and commended what he considered her "amiable and excellent feeling," especially the warmhearted "anxiety" and "solicitude" she expressed on his behalf when he was ill (Pilgrim 1:104, 79). "Above all, write like yourself," he urged her, "or in other words just such a note as you sent me last night. It was faultless" (Pilgrim 1:86).

Catherine clearly had other selves than the one writing "faultless" notes that, for Dickens, captured her essence. In December 1835, less than four months before their wedding, Catherine was still objecting to Dickens's long hours and Dickens complaining that she had "not yet subdued one part of [her] disposition—[her]

15. As Slater notes, Dickens identified with Savage, an illegitimate child whose artistic ambitions were thwarted by "maternal rejection and cruelty," since Dickens himself had been forced into what he considered degrading manual labor by his parents, his mother particularly, as a boy (*Dickens and Women*, 13, 106).

distrustful feelings and want of confidence," which "would have annoyed [him] greatly" in anyone he loved less (Pilgrim 1:110). His scattered references to Catherine's objections and "coss"ness during their engagement, like his insistence that he would "take *no denial*" when asking her to make him breakfast, suggest that she was capable of ignoring his wishes and declining his requests. In the mid-1840s Catherine's "distrustful" self would reemerge. But for now the mixture of reproofs, corrections, and commendations Dickens offered his fiancée, combined with his evident affection for her, had their effect, shaping her sense of herself, her expectations, and her position. By the time they married, Catherine's "faultless" self was ascendant; as Mrs. Charles Dickens, she took pleasure in pleasing her husband, putting his needs and desires before her own.

"A MOST CAPITAL HOUSEKEEPER"

Catherine Hogarth married Charles Dickens on 2 April 1836 at St. Luke's Church, Chelsea. Four days earlier her fiancé and her father had obtained the marriage license. Because Catherine was not yet twenty-one, George Hogarth needed to give his official consent to the union. The wedding itself was "altogether a very quiet piece of business," Dickens's best man, Thomas Beard, recalled.[16] In addition to Beard, only family members and Dickens's publisher John Macrone attended the ceremony, although Fanny Ayrton and her sister may have come to the wedding breakfast. "Miss Hogarth married to Mr. C. Dickens," Fanny noted in her journal entry for 2 April.[17] The bride and groom, both sets of parents, and Beard signed the marriage register, along with the curate who performed the service. Henry Burnett, later married to Fanny Dickens, remembered Catherine as "a bright, pleasant bride, dressed in the simplest and neatest manner," and the wedding breakfast as happy, with no show or pretension. "A few common, pleasant things were said, healths drunk with very few words said by either party—yet all things passed off very pleasantly, and all seemed happy, not the least so Dickens and his young girlish wife. . . . I can see [Dickens] now helping his young wife out of the carriage after the wedding, and taking her up the steps of the house of. . . Mr. Hogarth in the Fulham Road."[18] Among her wedding gifts, Catherine received a six-volume set of Milton's *Poetical Works* from Macrone, its publisher, and an ivory-fitted sewing box from her husband, an apt symbol of her new position.

16. Quoted in Frederic G. Kitton, ed., *Charles Dickens by Pen and Pencil* (London: Frank T. Sabin, 1890), 10.

17. William Ayrton, annotated abstracts from memoranda of Frances (Fanny) Ayrton, 1836–1847, British Library, Add. 60373, f. 27.

18. Quoted in Kitton, *Dickens by Pen and Pencil*, 11, 138.

After a honeymoon in Chalk, near Gravesend, the couple established themselves at 15 Furnivals Inn, their home for the first year of their marriage. Leased for £50 annually, their chambers consisted of a bedroom, dining room, and drawing room on the third floor, all facing south and opening one into another, a kitchen and cellar room in the basement, and a lumber room on the roof. The rooms were furnished "most tastefully and elegantly" in Mary Hogarth's view, the drawing room in rosewood and the dining room in mahogany,[19] and the couple had the occasional help of a young maid-of-all-work (Pilgrim 1:138). Writing to their cousin in May 1836, after spending a month "with dearest Catherine in her own house," Mary reported that her sister "makes a most capital housekeeper and is as happy as the day is long," adding of the newlyweds, "I think they are more devoted than ever since their Marriage if that be possible" (Pilgrim 1:689).

Mary's use of such a hackneyed phrase to describe her sister's joy ("as happy as the day is long") might suggest that her account was idealized and inauthentic. Yet the accounts provided by the couple themselves support Mary's portrait of Catherine as a capable young housewife devoted to her husband and happy with her lot. In a letter written to George Thomson in July 1836, Dickens describes Catherine's "high and mighty satisfaction" in a supper she arranged, her first as a married woman (Pilgrim 1:159). And in her only extant letter from 1837, Catherine conveys her marital contentment when inviting her cousin to visit her in London. "What pleasure it would give me to see you in my own house, and how proud I shall be to make you acquainted with Charles. The fame of his talents are [*sic*] now known over all the world, but his kind affectionate heart is dearer to me than all."[20]

Catherine's letter shows that by 1837, a sense of pride and pleasure had largely replaced the "distrustful feelings" and anger that plagued her during her engagement. The devotion to work that she resented in her fiancé she more readily accepted in her husband. The public might celebrate Dickens's talents, but she knew and privileged the private man, with his kindness and affection. Her love for Dickens and her prenuptial training reconciled her to this divide, as did her new sense that her home "belonged" to her—that she would be welcoming her cousin to her own house. Twenty years later Catherine would realize that "her" house was not actually hers, and the qualified sense in which she possessed it was evident much

19. ALS Mary Hogarth to Mary Scott Hogarth, 15 May [1836], Charles Dickens Museum, London.

20. ALS Catherine Dickens to Mary Scott Hogarth, 30 May [1837], D. Jacques Benoliel Collection of the Letters of Charles Dickens, 86-2740, Rare Book Department, Free Library of Philadelphia.

earlier. But in 1837 it seemed that she could lay claim to a realm of her own, one equivalent to, if separate from, that of Dickens the professional writer.

Catherine's belief that the home and its duties could empower her was one widely accepted by Victorians. As Isabella Beeton put it in her *Book of Household Management* (1861), the middle-class housewife resembled "the commander of an army, or the leader of any enterprise," for "her spirit will be seen through the whole establishment, and just in proportion as she performs her duty intelligently and thoroughly, so will her domestics follow in her path."[21] Catherine may not have seen herself as a "commander" of domestic troops, but she considered the household and its management her own province, and its borders were expanding; in March 1837 Dickens leased 48 Doughty Street for three years, at £80 annually, and they moved there soon after their first anniversary. With five stories, including a basement and a garret, their new home was much more spacious and elegant than their lodgings at Furnivals. They had a large dining room and a morning room on the ground floor, a front-facing drawing room on the first, and bedrooms, dressing rooms, and a study on the first and second floors, with a stillroom and kitchen in the basement. Located on a private road gated at each end, with a uniformed porter for security, 48 Doughty Street offered a measure of Dickens's success—and of Catherine's by proxy. From *The Pickwick Papers* alone her husband earned £2,000. Between November 1836 and March 1837 he negotiated contracts with Richard Bentley to edit *Bentley's Miscellany* at a monthly salary of £20, in addition to twenty guineas per month for the work that would become *Oliver Twist*, a sum that Dickens soon deemed grossly beneath his market value.

At Doughty Street, Catherine supervised a cook, a maid, and, with the birth of each child, a wet nurse, while a manservant answered more exclusively to her husband. In November 1837 Dickens opened a bank account at Coutts; the first checks he wrote specifying "housemaid's wages" and "cook's wages" date from July and November 1838, respectively,[22] though he and Catherine likely employed these servants beginning in the spring of 1837. In addition to managing the household and, after January 1837, caring for her first child, Catherine organized frequent dinner and evening parties for her husband's professional associates as well as family

21. Isabella Beeton, *The Book of Household Management,* facsimile ed. (1861; reprint, East Sussex: Southover Press, 1998), 1.

22. Charles Dickens, Esq., Account Ledger, Coutts & Co., London. M. Veronica Stokes discusses the ledger and its significance in "Charles Dickens: A Customer of Coutts & Co.," *Dickensian* 68 (January 1972): 17–30, but makes substantial errors, mistaking payments to George Hogarth for payments to Catherine's sister Georgina, for example (22–23).

friends and relations, large entertainments, sometimes several each month, which grew more lavish as her husband's fame and income increased.

Dickens's description of his wife's satisfaction in her first dinner party and her reign ("high and mighty") over the domestic sphere (Pilgrim 1:159), like Catherine's reference to her own house, draws on what the historian John Tosh terms the "conventional wisdom...that home was the wife's domain." Yet this widely held belief conflicted with social and legal realities, since the wife was herself subject to her husband's authority: "The contradiction was obscured when work or pleasure kept the husband away for most of the time. It became potentially explosive when he was constantly at home, even when he strove to be a 'good' husband and father," since he then had "more scope to assert [his] mastery over the household."[23]

As a professional writer, Dickens generally worked at home, and as a result was more of a presence in his "wife's domain" than many of his peers were in theirs. But even by the standards of work-at-home men, Dickens played an unusually active part in household matters. In middle-class Victorian households, wives usually controlled the finances. This was in fact so much the norm that in legal proceedings between spouses, a husband who prohibited his wife from managing the family accounts was seen to damage his case.[24] But in the Dickens household, the husband was the money manager and, before he and Catherine had been married for two years, the primary consumer for household goods as well. During her engagement Catherine learned from her fiancé of his various household purchases. Dickens prided himself on his ability to discover the best butchers and fishmongers with whom to do business.[25] By the 1850s he was notorious for "tak[ing] on himself all possible trouble as regards his domestic affairs," as Nathaniel Hawthorne wrote in his *English Notebooks*, "making bargains at butchers and bakers, and doing, as far as he could, whatever duty pertains to an English wife."[26]

In the first eighteen months of their marriage, Catherine generally performed these wifely duties. She was the primary household consumer between 27 November and 31 December 1837, the first five weeks after Dickens opened his bank account, during which period he wrote nine checks out of twenty-four to his wife and none to himself. Catherine was responsible for nearly one third of their total expenditures, all those not covered by checks made out to specific merchants and

23. Tosh, *A Man's Place,* 63–64.

24. Ibid., 63.

25. For Dickens's comic description of shopping for venison at "Mr. Groves of Charing Cross" in 1842 and his pleasure in such transactions, see Pilgrim 3:276.

26. Nathaniel Hawthorne, *Nathaniel Hawthorne's English Notebooks,* ed. R. Stewart (1941), quoted in Slater, *Dickens and Women,* 128.

tradesmen. By June 1838, however, Catherine had been supplanted in this role by her husband. Between January 1838 and June 1839, the cash earmarked for Dickens's use exceeded the sum provided to Catherine by a ratio greater than two to one. Of a total household expenditure of £228 from 30 January to 3 March 1838, £41—less than one fifth—passed through Catherine's hands. Of the £305 that the Dickenses spent from 25 October to 3 December 1838, Catherine had charge of only £37: £20 for winter dresses, £3.3 for the housemaid's wages, £1.17 for household expenses, and £12 for unspecified costs. In this period she spent less than one eighth of the household total.[27]

Dickens was not only the primary consumer but also the one who disciplined the servants, and usually it was he who paid them their wages; he more often than Catherine decided with whom to do business and how the household furniture would be arranged. "Keep things in their places," he wrote her when he was away from home, referring to *his* placement of things. "I can't bear to picture them otherwise" (Pilgrim 4:216). Thus the home and its management were Catherine's in a more limited sense than for wives in many socially comparable households.

Dickens took on these duties not because Catherine was an unwilling, uninterested, or incapable housekeeper but because he was a micromanager who wanted to control the details of their lives.[28] Commenting on what he termed his friend's "domestic nature," which he found essential to Dickens's character, John Forster noted that Dickens was "personally interested in every detail... of the four walls within which [he] live[d]" and exhibited "the kind of interest in a house which is commonly confined to women," observing: "There was not an additional hook put up wherever he inhabited, without his knowledge, or otherwise than as part of some small ingenuity of his own. Nothing was too minute for his personal superintendence."[29] Despite Forster's characterization, Dickens's "interest" in the house was not a "womanly" one. Rather it was a prerogative Dickens exercised

27. Charles Dickens, Esq., Account Ledger, Coutts & Co., London.

28. In *Dickens and Women,* Slater draws from a range of sources to illustrate Catherine's competence as a domestic manager and hostess (126–29), as does Susan M. Rossi-Wilcox in *Dinner for Dickens: The Culinary History of Mrs. Charles Dickens's Menu Books* (Totnes: Prospect Books, 2005), her study of Catherine's 1851 menu book. Both Slater and Peter Ackroyd discuss Dickens's micromanagement of the household and his unwillingness to delegate power to others. See Slater, *Dickens and Women,* 128–29; and Peter Ackroyd, *Dickens* (New York: HarperCollins, 1990), 223.

29. John Forster, *The Life of Charles Dickens,* ed. J. W. T. Ley (New York: Doubleday, Doran and Co., 1928), 835.

as a husband, one that effectively trumped Catherine's domestic management and signaled his ultimate superintendence and control.

Catherine did not perform her husband's duties or encroach on his domain. When Dickens was ill and unable to hold a pen for extended periods of time, she served as his amanuensis and wrote from his dictation; the preface to Dickens's third novel, *Barnaby Rudge* (1841), is in her hand. On one occasion during their engagement, Dickens adopted an idea of Catherine's for a work in progress, the comic burletta *The Village Coquettes,* opening its second act, he told her, "with a Scene founded on your suggestion" (Pilgrim 1:119). But generally Catherine was his first reader—not an author or collaborator but a proud witness and auditor whose reactions gave Dickens his first sense of a work's success. Before their marriage Dickens told Catherine of his "extraordinary idea for a story"—"The Black Veil"— promising to "shew it to [her] the moment it is finished" (Pilgrim 1:98), and three years later, when bringing *Oliver Twist* to its close, he did the same. "Nancy is no more," he informed Forster, referring to Sikes's brutal murder of the prostitute. "I shewed what I have done to Kate last night who was in an unspeakable '*state,*' from which and my own impressions I augur well" (Pilgrim 1:439). These acts of reading on Catherine's part, like her writing from dictation, were forms of wifely service. Like Dickens's domestic management, they did nothing to lessen the gender divide between them. In the first years of their marriage, in fact, that divide only widened—in part because Catherine's recurring pregnancies and confinements seemed to define her psychological and physical makeup as essentially different from her husband's.

"KEEPING THE HORIZONTAL POSITION"

How much the virginal Catherine knew about sex before marriage, and how much pleasure, if any, she derived from it, remain matters of educated guesswork. Medical theories of the day were divided on the subject of female sexual desire and fulfillment, with some physicians arguing that a woman needed to experience an orgasm to conceive and others insisting that spontaneous ovulation meant that women were sexually passive beings.[30] Whether or not Catherine expected to enjoy sex, she probably understood at the time of her marriage how babies were conceived. Mrs. Hogarth was unlikely to have sheltered her from that knowledge; and Catherine was eighteen years old when her mother gave birth to the twins and may have been present at their delivery.

30. See Michael Mason, *The Making of Victorian Sexuality* (Oxford: Oxford University Press, 1994), 177, 195–205; and Robert B. Shoemaker, *Gender in English Society, 1650–1850* (London: Longman, 1998) 62–63.

It is unclear how much sexual experience Dickens brought to their marriage; his comments about the masculine norm point in opposing directions. In 1848 Dickens told Ralph Waldo Emerson "that if his own son were particularly chaste, he should be alarmed," suspecting ill health, since "chastity in the male sex was as good as gone," his word choice implying regret at a change in mores from his own youth, before sexual "incontinence" became "so much the rule in England," as he put it.[31] But Dickens himself sought sexually explicit material in the early 1830s, when his reading at the British Library included Francis Foster's *Profligacy of Our Women and Its Causes* (1779), "a treatise about female sexuality and the threats to female sexual continence," John Bowen explains, with an explicit discussion of "digitation" and "the Nature of the Clitoris."[32] Furthermore, Dickens defended the poet Samuel Rogers against the allegation that Rogers had exploited a prostitute decades earlier, telling a correspondent in 1840 that prostitutes were "willing and consenting part[ies]" and exclaiming, "Good God if such sins were to be visited upon all of us and to hunt us down through life, what man would escape!" (Pilgrim 2:141). Suggesting Dickens's own "sinfulness" in this regard, his letter of August 1841 to Daniel Maclise urges the artist to join him and his family in Broadstairs, a seaside resort, and promises "conveniences of *all kinds* at Margate (do you take me?) and I know where they live" (Pilgrim 7:831). As Claire Tomalin notes, "unless Dickens meant the ponies on the sands, living conveniences could mean one thing only in this context."[33]

Like most of their contemporaries, the Dickenses did not record their thoughts about their sexual experiences. But the evidence suggests that their sex life was fulfilling, at least in the first few years of their marriage, and probably as active in the late 1840s as it was in the late 1830s (see chapter 5). Their union was quickly consummated, since Catherine was pregnant within two weeks of the wedding,[34] and Dickens's joking allusion to sexual abstinence during the final days of her fifth pregnancy implies that the couple only stopped having intercourse during her third trimesters (Pilgrim 4:3). Some of the letters Catherine received from her husband while he was away from London express the warmth and longing that are, in one historian's view,

31. Ralph Waldo Emerson, *The Journals and Miscellaneous Notebooks of Ralph Waldo Emerson,* ed. William H. Gilman, 16 vols. (Cambridge: Harvard University Press, 1960–1982), 10:550–51.

32. John Bowen, "Dickens and Digitation," *Dickensian* 100 (2004): 121–22.

33. Claire Tomalin, *The Invisible Woman: The Story of Nelly Ternan and Charles Dickens* (New York: Knopf, 1991), 84.

34. I base my calculations of Catherine's conception dates on an average full-term gestation of thirty-eight weeks.

our best evidence of sexual fulfillment in Victorian marriage.[35] "God bless you my darling—I long to be back with you again, and to see the sweet Babs—Your faithful and most affectionate Husband," Dickens wrote Catherine in November 1838, eight months after the birth of their second child (Pilgrim 1:448). If Catherine had been sexually aloof or unresponsive, Dickens would not have written in this way.

Several methods of birth control, of varying degrees of reliability, were available to Victorians: among them coitus interruptus, the sponge, and the douche. Charles Knowlton's *Fruits of Philosophy or, the Private Companion of Young Married People* (1832), reprinted in London two years before the Dickenses married, detailed contraceptive techniques and recommended the douche method in combination with the sponge for family planning.[36] But as social historians note, advocates of contraception were "a tiny and precarious minority" in the first half of the nineteenth century,[37] and their efforts ran against religious teachings as well as prevailing medical opinion.[38] Thomas Malthus's warnings about the dangers of overpopulation cast new doubt on the tie between fertility and health. But Dickens was notoriously critical of Malthus, putting his words into the mouth of the unreformed Scrooge. Coming from large families themselves—she was the eldest of nine surviving children and he the second of eight, six of whom reached adulthood— Charles and Catherine expected to have several children and viewed a series of closely spaced pregnancies as the norm.

The Dickenses' marriage eventually suffered as a consequence of their burgeoning family, with Catherine burdened by pregnancies that stretched over a sixteen-year period and her husband increasingly annoyed by what he perceived as a population explosion within his own home and for which he unfairly held Catherine responsible. But these problems did not become notable until well into the 1840s. In their first decade together, if not as clearly in their second, their experience of parenthood strengthened their mutual attachment. When her husband was away from home, Catherine wrote to him about the activities and health of the children (Pilgrim 1:447), and he answered in kind. "To say how much I miss

35. Tosh, *A Man's Place*, 58.

36. See Angus McLaren, *Birth Control in Nineteenth-Century England* (New York: Holmes & Meier, 1978).

37. Roy Porter and Lesley Hall, *The Facts of Life: The Creation of Sexual Knowledge in Britain, 1650–1950* (New Haven: Yale University Press, 1995), 104.

38. Joan Perkin, *Victorian Women* (New York: New York University Press, 1993), 68–69. In Slater's view, Dickens did not consider using birth control because "the intrusion of prudential considerations into the intimate expression of connubial love" seemed inappropriate to him (*Dickens and Women*, 121).

you, would be ridiculous," he told her in March 1839, soon after their third child was conceived. "I miss the children in the morning too and their dear little voices which have sounds for you and me that we shall never forget. I have not forgotten the Mouse's [Mamie's] birthday to-morrow, and shall keep it though after a lonely fashion. If you will drink her health at six o'Clock exactly, I will do the same as if we were together" (Pilgrim 1:523).

But if parenthood united the pair in certain respects, it divided them in others, since the customs surrounding pregnancy, childbirth, and child rearing were governed by and in turn reinforced ideas of sexual difference. Sometimes treated as a condition to be concealed among middle-class Victorians, pregnancy drove women into varying degrees of retirement.[39] Even Queen Victoria, who enjoyed many privileges denied to other women, complained that she could not "travel about or go about" with Prince Albert as usual when she was expecting.[40] Some families considered it unseemly for a visibly pregnant woman to be seen at all outside her home, although this was not the case in Catherine's circle. But with pregnancy, Catherine's sphere of activity gradually narrowed, as did the companionship she could offer her husband. Thus she was described by him as "a great stay-at-home" in November 1836, when she was eight months pregnant with her first child (Pilgrim 1:200). Six months pregnant with her second in December 1837, she curtailed her social calls because of her "delicate health," Dickens wrote (Pilgrim 1:338). The unexpected end of a pregnancy could be even more restricting than pregnancy itself, Catherine found. When she suffered her first miscarriage in May 1837, between her first and second full-term pregnancies, she was "obliged to keep very quiet," she told her cousin.[41]

The restrictions to which Catherine was subject as an expectant mother were given a physiological rationale by Victorian medical men, who considered the performance of "fatiguing" domestic tasks as well as walking to be physically injurious toward the end of a pregnancy, and "every kind of agitating exercise" throughout.[42] When Catherine stayed in Brighton during her second pregnancy, she was

39. See Judith Flanders, *Inside the Victorian Home: A Portrait of Domestic Life in Victorian England* (New York: W. W. Norton, 2004), 51–52.

40. Queen Victoria, *Dearest Child: Letters between Queen Victoria and the Princess Royal, 1858–1861,* ed. Roger Fulford (London: Evans Brothers, 1964), 77–78, quoted ibid., 52.

41. ALS Catherine Dickens to Mary Scott Hogarth, 30 May [1837], D. Jacques Benoliel Collection of the Letters of Charles Dickens, 86-2740, Rare Book Department, Free Library of Philadelphia.

42. Thomas Bull, *Hints to Mothers, for the Management of Health during the Period of Pregnancy, and in the Lying-in-Room* (1837; New York: Wiley and Putnam, 1842), 27–28.

"scarcely able to peep out of doors," Dickens told Forster, so unless he was "joined by some male companion," his impressions of the town would be "limited to the Pavillion, the chain Pier, and the Sea" (Pilgrim 1:328). Although Catherine wanted to attend Joseph Stirling Coyne's *Valsha, or the Slave Queen* at the Adelphi Theatre soon afterwards, she was wary of the heat and crowds, Dickens told manager Frederick Yates, asking for the use of his private box. "You pack your other boxes so closely that although I have ventured to brave the heat, Mrs. D being in delicate health is afraid" (Pilgrim 1:348). Catherine's "fears," however, were generated at least as much by social expectations or convention as by physical weakness or vulnerability; a feminine foil to Dickens's male "bravery," they were also more a matter of *his* perception than *hers.* In female company, in fact, Catherine lost some if not all of her alleged apprehensions, abandoning her "delicacy" as a pregnant woman. Thus, accompanied by Eliza Franklin in 1840, six months into her fourth pregnancy, Catherine and her friend got out of their carriage and went "galloping"—on foot—up the Strand.[43]

Catherine did not challenge or reject the "necessary" restrictions placed on women during and following pregnancy and childbirth, but she was less mindful of them than her husband was. "Take care of Mrs. Macrone," Dickens instructed his publisher in October 1836, nearly three weeks after Eliza Macrone had given birth and three months before Catherine's first delivery. "How could you let her come down to dinner so soon? Catherine is all anxiety to hear of her getting better" (Pilgrim 1:183). Asking Macrone to Sunday dinner two days later, Dickens explained the logic of his invitation: "If you are out, you will deprive Mrs. M of any temptation to come downstairs again" (Pilgrim 1:184).

Dickens's sense of Macrone's permissiveness in letting Eliza "come downstairs" reflected the standard view that extended rest and "quietude" were necessary for new mothers.[44] As the physician-accoucheur Thomas Bull advised in *Hints to Mothers,* first published in 1837, a woman was to remain in bed for four days postpartum, after which she might be removed to a nearby sofa; but "on no account" must she "give the *slightest assistance* in her removal, and when on the sofa must strictly keep *the horizontal position.* Indeed, for *three weeks* after delivery an almost constant compliance with the latter direction is highly important," Bull emphasized. "Among the poorer classes of society, who get up very soon after delivery, and undergo much fatigue, *'the falling down of the womb'* is a very common and

43. Eliza Franklin to George Franklin, [26 October 1840], reprinted in David Parker, Anno Wilson, and Roger Wilson, "Letters of a Guest at Devonshire Terrace," *Dickensian* 95 (1999): 59.

44. Bull, *Hints to Mothers,* 165–66.

distressing complaint[,] . . . the effect, simply, of their not being able to keep the re-cumbent posture long enough." Warned against walking from one room to another and prohibited from entering passageways or going up or down stairs, the new mother was told that it was "never safe for her to join her family before the expira-tion of the third week" or to "resume . . . her accustomed domestic duties" before the end of a month.[45]

The women in Catherine's circle did not voice dissatisfaction with these re-strictions; in her letters about childbirth Catherine uses the standard term "con-finement" without any ironic inflection. But the behavior of the women tells a somewhat different story. Subjected to postpartum limitations, Catherine some-times ignored them or expressed, indirectly, her unhappiness with them. While Eliza Macrone succumbed to "temptation" in going downstairs prematurely, Catherine lapsed into postpartum depressions after her first two deliveries, recov-ering almost immediately after her confinements ended.

"After a day and night" of labor (Pilgrim 1:221), Catherine gave birth to a healthy boy at six o'clock Friday evening, 6 January 1837. Her mother and her mother-in-law, Elizabeth, were at Furnivals to help with the delivery of Charley. Francis Pickthorn, the medical man who would assist at the birth of Mamie the following year, may also have been present. Dickens had been waiting and watching with anxiety but once the baby had safely arrived, he announced that "Mrs. Dickens had . . . presented [him] with a son and heir" (Pilgrim 1:221). His feelings of satisfaction soon waned. For the first week or so Catherine and the baby did well, with Mary Hogarth there to help during her sister's confinement. By the second week, however, Catherine was "not quite so well" (Pilgrim 1:223), and by the third she was often crying and was unwilling to eat. Writing to Richard Bentley on 24 January, Dickens referred to "the anxieties of [his] private affairs," disclosing that Catherine "has been for some days past, in a very low and alarming state" and that he "was obliged to be constantly with her, being the only person who can prevail upon her to take ordinary nourishment" (Pilgrim 1:226–27). Dickens was so concerned about Catherine's "low" state, in fact, that he had arranged for a medical consultation at six o'clock that day.

Writing to their cousin two days later, Mary elaborated on Catherine's condi-tion, explaining that her sister had "not gone on so well as her first week made us hope she would." She continues:

After we thought she was getting quite well and strong it was discovered she was not able to nurse her Baby so she was obliged with great reluctance as you may suppose to give him up to a stranger. Poor Kate! it has been a dreadful

45. Ibid., 166–67.

trial for her.... They are going into the Country whenever she is able to be moved, and I am in great hopes the change of scene may do much for her. Every time she sees her Baby she has a fit of crying and keeps constantly saying she is sure he will not care for her now she is not able to nurse him.... She has got a very nice Nurse for him but poor Kate looks upon her now with very jealous eyes.[46]

In Mary's view, Catherine's postpartum distress was triggered by her inability to breast-feed; the implication is that an unexpected physiological problem, whether a breast defect or a deficiency of milk, was the cause. This failure would be a source of anxiety for any young mother, since a new emphasis had been placed on the "natural duty" of maternal breast-feeding by medical and moral authorities in the nineteenth century. Breast-feeding was seen to benefit the mother's health as well as the baby's and to promote the bond between mother and child,[47] and Mrs. Hogarth had nursed all of *her* babies. In failing to nurse Charley, Catherine felt that she was failing as a mother. Her inability to breast-feed also meant that she would need the services of a wet nurse. Not only would her newborn have a surrogate mother, an object of jealousy in Catherine's eyes; his physical well-being would depend on a servant and "stranger."

For all her sensitivity to Catherine, Mary seems not to have fully understood her sister's crisis. The pairing of Catherine's inability to breast-feed with her unwillingness to eat and her generally "low" state indicates that she was suffering from postpartum depression, and that her failure to nurse Charley was likely a symptom, not a cause.[48] In the 1830s and 1840s "puerperal insanity," as it was known, was

46. ALS Mary Hogarth to Mary Scott Hogarth, 26 January 1837, D. Jacques Benoliel Collection of the Letters of Charles Dickens, 83-1842, Rare Book Department, Free Library of Philadelphia.

47. See Amanda Vickery, *The Gentleman's Daughter: Women's Lives in Georgian England* (New Haven: Yale University Press, 1998), 107; Valerie A. Fildes, *Breasts, Bottles, and Babies: A History of Infant Feeding* (Edinburgh: Edinburgh University Press, 1986), 81–133; and Lynda Nead, *Myths of Sexuality: Representations of Women in Victorian Britain* (Oxford: Basil Blackwell, 1988), 27.

48. The inability to breast-feed is taken as a sign of postpartum depression by some medical researchers, as are "fits of crying" and the refusal to eat. See, for example, T. Tamminen, "The Impact of Mother's Depression on Her Nursing Experience and Attitudes during Breastfeeding," *Acta Paediatrica Scandinavica,* suppl. no. 344, 77 (1988): 87–94. In "Postpartum Depression in the Breastfeeding Mother," *NAACOG's Clinical Issues in Perinatal and Women's Health Nursing* 3, no. 1 (1990): 375–84, Kathleen G. Auerbach and Angela M. Jacobi conclude that "the literature on postpartum depression and the literature on lactation intersect

thought to result from excitation of the "cerebro-spinal system," since the uterus, "disturbed and excited" from the delivery, would "exert...sympathetic action" on the brain.[49] The physician John Conolly, who knew Dickens in the 1850s, noted in 1830 that "women are liable to temporary insanity after confinement," their condition arising "partly perhaps from an undue circulation in the brain, and partly from a morbid state of the brain itself, explained by its sympathy with the states of the uterus."[50] As the physician James Reid put it in 1848, "any unusual excitement or irritability of the uterine organs...furnished cases for the lunatic asylum."[51]

Despite their emphasis on the weaknesses of female physiology, Victorian physicians acknowledged that "moral causes" as well as uterine "derangements" triggered postpartum depression—that the social circumstances in which women found themselves could produce the illness as easily and as powerfully as any physiological cause.[52] Thus Reid found that unmarried mothers, especially those "of a superior class" who were "obliged...to hide their shame," were particularly liable to postpartum depression. Among his most severe cases were women "highly educated, of sensitive dispositions, and compelled by the cruel desertion of their seducers, and neglect of their friends, to seek for admission into a public hospital."[53] Although their understanding of the illness and of women's bodies differs from Reid's, psychologists now emphasize the social as well as the physiological causes of postpartum depression. They point to the "losses" that childbirth entails (the loss of "physical integrity," autonomy, and adult companionship, for example) and attribute feelings of sadness and failure to the conflict between cultural ideals of motherhood and "the reality of mothers' lives."[54] According to this view, postpartum depression is as much a product of circumstance and social pressures as it is of steep reductions in progesterone and estradiol levels.[55]

so infrequently" that it is impossible to identify clearly "the relationship between the two elements and/or which influences the other" (383).

49. James Reid, "On the Causes, Symptoms, and Treatment of Puerperal Insanity," *Journal of Psychological Medicine and Mental Pathology* 1 (1848): 128–29, 131, 134.

50. John Conolly, M.D., *An Inquiry Concerning the Indications of Insanity, with Suggestions for the Better Protection and Care of the Insane* (1830; reprint, London: Dawsons of Pall Mall, 1964), 234, 424.

51. Reid, "On the Causes, Symptoms, and Treatment of Puerperal Insanity," 143.

52. Ibid., 146.

53. Ibid.

54. Paula Nicolson, *Post-natal Depression: Psychology, Science and the Transition to Motherhood* (London: Routledge, 1998), 4, 6.

55. See Rosalind R. Unterman, Norman A. Posner, and Karen N. Williams, "Postpartum Depressive Disorders: Changing Trends," *Birth* 17, no. 3 (September 1990): 132.

Several factors may have combined to produce Catherine's postpartum depression, including the physiological changes associated with childbirth and the changes in her social circumstances—most immediately the demand that she remain upstairs in bed. For Catherine, this restriction was compounded by the contrast between her situation and that of Mary, staying at Furnivals to help her. On the day Catherine gave birth, Mary went out shopping with Dickens; although the two were looking for a bedside table for Catherine, Mary was enjoying the companionship and activity prohibited to her sister for a month. In Mary's letter to their cousin, her kindness to Catherine is clear, as is that of Dickens. Yet under the circumstances, this kindness was disabling; it allowed Catherine a reprieve from domestic duties but also kept her inactive and dependent. Once Catherine was allowed downstairs four weeks after Charley's birth and traveled with her husband for a month in Chalk, with Mary and the baby for company while Dickens worked, she quickly recovered. Less than two weeks after her confinement ended, Dickens reported that Catherine was "very well" (Pilgrim 1:234), and by the end of February, she, her husband, and Mary were enjoying outings from Chalk to Chatham and eating dinner at the local pub.

Catherine's experiences with her next three deliveries—on 6 March 1838 (Mamie), 29 October 1839 (Katey), and 8 February 1841 (Walter)—lend force to the idea that postpartum restrictions were largely responsible for her depression. After the birth of Mamie, Catherine's confinement and consequent depression followed virtually the same pattern as they did after Charley's delivery. Three weeks postpartum she was "alarmingly ill" (Pilgrim 1:392), and a medical consultation was deemed necessary. At Richmond for her convalescence, she recovered rapidly. But when her confinements were abbreviated following her third and fourth deliveries, she suffered no postpartum depression at all. Two weeks after Katey's birth, Dickens could report that Catherine "progresses splendidly" (Pilgrim 1:601), and the same was true after the birth of Walter. With Charley, Catherine had remained in her room for weeks on end, but with Walter, she was out of her bedroom and "up to dinner" within a week, joining company in the drawing room a few days later (Pilgrim 2:211). Once her husband recognized that extended postpartum restrictions were a matter of custom and not medical necessity, Catherine's experience of childbearing improved. Writing to a correspondent eleven days after Walter's birth, Dickens noted that "Kate . . . is in a brilliant state, and is rather sitting in the drawing room up stairs as a matter of form, than for anything that prevents her coming down here" (Pilgrim 2:216).

As Mary had hoped when writing to her cousin in January 1837, "change of scene" did do much for Catherine after Charley's birth. Back in London from Chalk, Catherine helped with the move to Doughty Street, cared for the baby, and, with Mary often there to assist, began a new round of entertainments and dinner parties. With her sister and her husband, Catherine went to the theater to see Dickens's own burletta *The Strange Gentleman,* among other productions. Enjoying motherhood, she wrote glowingly of her baby to her cousin: "My darling boy grows sweeter and lovelier every day. Although he is my own I must say I never saw a dearer child."[56]

A mother as well as a wife, Catherine was gaining a more complex sense of herself, her duties, and her allegiances even as her roles were being defined for her by her husband and their culture. Catherine's connection with Charley, who would choose to live with his mother rather than his father after their separation in 1858, provided her with a crucial counterpoint to her relationship with Dickens and became one of the strongest and most important in her life. But at nearly the same time that Catherine became a mother, forging her tie to her son, she lost her first and closest friendship and with it the less restricted sense of self it had fostered. On the morning of 7 May 1837, four months after Charley's birth, her sister Mary died suddenly of heart failure at Doughty Street. For Catherine, Mary's death marked a significant shift in the character of her female community and narrowed her range of experience and expression, focusing her attention more exclusively on Dickens and his world.

56. ALS Catherine Dickens to Mary Scott Hogarth, 30 May [1837], D. Jacques Benoliel Collection of the Letters of Charles Dickens, 86-2740, Rare Book Department, Free Library of Philadelphia.

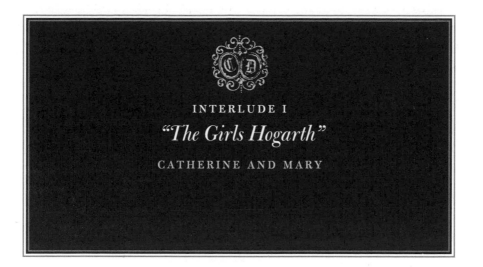

Laura would call the little ones...
Would tell them how her sister stood
In deadly peril to do her good,
And win the fiery antidote:
Then joining hands to little hands
Would bid them cling together,
 "For there is no friend like a sister
In calm or stormy weather;
To cheer one on the tedious way,
To fetch one if one goes astray,
To lift one if one totters down,
To strengthen whilst one stands."
— Christina Rossetti, "Goblin Market"
   (1862)

"WHAT HAS BEEN GOING ON IN THIS HOUSE?"
Variously interpreted as a simple moral tale for children, a complex narrative of
Christian sacrifice and rebirth, and a homoerotic celebration of women's love,
Christina Rossetti's poem about Laura, Lizzie, and the redemptive quality of their
sisterhood reveals the perceived attractions and dangers of that relationship for Victorians. Drawing on idealized conceptions of womanhood, Rossetti's selfless and
virginal Lizzie purposely seeks the seductive goblin merchants in a nearby glen,
hoping to purchase their "fruit forbidden" for the fallen and dying sister who has

consumed it. When Lizzie refuses to eat with the men or "open lip from lip," they pelt her with their goods and cover her with fruit juice as, "mauled and mocked," she defeats them through her suffering. Running home to give Laura the necessary "antidote," however, Lizzie caps her sacrificial act with a homoerotic one; she offers herself and "[her] juices" to her sister as part of the cure, whereupon Laura "kissed and kissed her with a hungry mouth," paradoxically regaining her lost purity through sexual communion with Lizzie. Norms appear to be restored in Rossetti's conclusion, when Lizzie and Laura, now wives, tell their "little ones" about the importance of sisterhood in conventional, if not hackneyed, terms. Yet their tidy moral fails to acknowledge or address the subversive quality of their union and the alternative to marriage that it provides, for although they are described as wives, their husbands are nowhere to be found.[1]

The Hogarth sisterhood, like the one imagined by Rossetti, is often perceived as a source of transgressive feeling and behavior—not because of the intimacy between or among the sisters but because of their alleged intimacy with Dickens. Responding to Dickens's posthumous idolatry of Mary in the days following her death—his claims that "so perfect a creature never breathed" and that "she had not a fault" (Pilgrim 1:259), praise he would repeat in the months and years ahead—critics read backwards from the events of 1858 and argue that the novelist married the wrong Hogarth sister, that Dickens was romantically attached to Mary, with an affection that she returned.[2] This argument underlies Gaynor Arnold's *Girl in a Blue Dress,* in which Dorothea Gibson is painfully jealous of her sister Alice Millar, and their mother suspects that Alice has been seduced by Dorothea's husband. "No married man has the right to be *inconsolable* over his sister-in-law," Mrs. Millar asserts. "What has been going on in this house?"[3] This question receives its most sensational and explicit answer in an earlier novel, Peter Carey's *Jack Maggs* (1998), in which Lizzie Warriner, Carey's Mary Hogarth figure, dies from a double dose of

1. Christina Rossetti, "Goblin Market" (1862), in *The Norton Anthology of English Literature,* 5th ed., ed. M. H. Abrams, 2 vols. (New York: W. W. Norton, 1986), 2:1508–20, ll. 479, 431, 429, 559, 468, 492, 548.

2. "The *ménage* in three small rooms appears to have been a happy one, but with obvious dangers," critic Albert Guerard argues in discussing what he terms Dickens's "fondest forbidden game," an "imagined marriage with an idealized virgin all the more forbidden because she might be . . . sister-in-law." Albert J. Guerard, *The Triumph of the Novel: Dickens, Dostoevsky, Faulkner* (New York: Oxford University Press, 1976), 71. With variations, Guerard's argument is reiterated by others writing on the subject. See, for example, Karen Chase and Michael Levenson, *The Spectacle of Intimacy: A Public Life for the Victorian Family* (Princeton: Princeton University Press, 2000), 105–20.

3. Gaynor Arnold, *Girl in a Blue Dress* (Birmingham: Tindal Street Press, 2008), 122.

an abortifacient. One dose is handed to her by her brother-in-law, author Tobias Oates, who has seduced and impregnated her, and the other surreptitiously administered by her outraged sister Mary, Carey's Catherine figure. As Carey depicts the family's dynamics, Lizzie Warriner not only commits adultery but also betrays her sister, as Mary Oates betrays Lizzie in turn. Looking at the blood-soaked sheets on which Lizzie lies dying, Mary imagines being sent to prison for her crime. "Soon all of England would know how she had put poison in her sister's tea," she worries.[4]

In his fictional representation of Catherine and Mary as women who turn against each other, Carey takes to an extreme the standard Dickens-centered view of the Hogarth sisterhood. In exaggerated form, his novel reveals the consequence of approaching the Hogarth women in relation to Dickens rather than in relation to each other, mistakenly casting them as competitors and seeing them exclusively through Dickens's eyes. By focusing on *their* writings and *their* perspectives instead of his, we can reclaim Mary for Catherine and Catherine for Mary, and see that their tie, while neither homoerotic nor particularly self-sacrificing, more closely resembles the allegiance of Laura and Lizzie in "Goblin Market" than it does the antagonism of Lizzie Warriner and Mary Oates in *Jack Maggs*. Fifteen years old at the time of Catherine's engagement, Mary was akin to her older sister in intelligence and humor, making for camaraderie between them. Unlike Carey's Warriners, neither measured herself against the other. Their sisterhood allowed them an escape from the competition often produced among young women by the marriage market, enabled them to temporarily circumvent and mock the privileges of men even as they prepared to recognize those privileges as wives and mothers, and gave Catherine a more equitable form of companionship than her marriage did.

"C & M"

Born on 26 October 1819, Mary was four years younger than Catherine, with brother Robert (b. 1818) intervening. Although there were two other daughters in the family, both of whom eventually played important roles in Catherine's life, Georgina was a little girl and Helen yet unborn when the Hogarths first arrived in London and Catherine and Mary were teenagers making their way around it. The earliest surviving reference to them as individuals, in Mrs. Ayrton's journal for 30 August 1832, records their arrival for tea.[5] In what both sisters later referred to as their "intimacy" with the Ayrtons,[6] Catherine twice slept over at James Street without Mary,

4. Peter Carey, *Jack Maggs* (New York: Knopf, 1998), 294.

5. Journal of Marianne Ayrton, 30 August 1832, British Library, Add. 52351, f. 104.

6. ALS Mary Hogarth to Mary Scott Hogarth, 15 May [1836], Charles Dickens Museum, London; ALS Catherine Hogarth to Mary Scott Hogarth, 11 February 1835, D. Jacques

and after Catherine's engagement to Dickens, Mary alone was sometimes "fetched" by Matilda.[7] More commonly, though, the two eldest sisters were a visiting pair— "the girls Hogarth" or "C & M," as Mrs. Ayrton referred to them[8]—and whether dressing for balls and concerts, drinking tea, or eating lunch and dinner with their friends, doing so together.

Setting aside Dickens's own writings about Mary Hogarth, long regarded as the definitive source of information about her, the extant primary material with bearing on her character and her tie to Catherine is relatively scarce. It includes Mrs. Ayrton's scattered journal references to the pair, brief accounts provided by various friends and acquaintances, and records of material objects associated with Mary: among them an inscribed fruit knife and traveling inkwell she gave her brother-in-law before his marriage, a portrait of her made from memory by Hablot Knight Browne at Dickens's request, a wide bracelet with gold snaps made from her hair, and an 1837 sketch of her that belonged to her mother. But the most valuable resource for constructing "the girls Hogarth" are their own surviving letters from 1835–1837, five in number, all written to Mary Scott Hogarth, the cousin in Scremerston who shared Mary's name. While illuminating the sisters' relationship, these letters also dispel some of the myths that Dickens generated after Mary's death and that critics and biographers often promote: that Mary perceived the same defects in her sister that he later did, and that she centered her concern and affections on her brother-in-law rather than on Catherine and the Hogarths.

Catherine writes the first of the five-letter sequence in the absence of her "dear Mary," who is staying at Brighton with their aunt Anne (Thomson) Fisher at the time. Denied Mary's companionship, Catherine makes the nature of their friendships with other women particularly clear. Relaying news of Miss Frampton and Miss Ayrton in the midst of her talk about the marriage market—the visits and doings of eligible bachelors, some hardworking and "pleasant," others not—nineteen-year-old Catherine represents these women as competitors as much as companions. While Mary is away, Catherine dresses for a ball with Miss Frampton. But in recounting the event, she compliments her friend only to criticize her: "Her dress really looked well—but instead of a wreath she stuck a great vulgar white flower with her usual taste on the front of her bow which quite spoilt [it]." Mary's absence also gives Catherine a welcome reason to avoid the Ayrtons, with whom she and Mary

Benoliel Collection of the Letters of Charles Dickens, 86-2739, Rare Book Department, Free Library of Philadelphia.

7. Journal of Marianne Ayrton, 30 July 1835, British Library, Add. 52351, f. 177v.

8. Journal of Marianne Ayrton, 28 July and 16 August 1834, British Library, Add. 52351, ff. 149v, 150v.

have quarreled, Fanny being "as dictatorial as ever," as she puts it. "I very seldom see them as I have a good excuse—no one to come with," she explains.[9]

Catherine's complaint about the "dictatorial" Fanny Ayrton—"more spiteful than ever," she tells her cousin in her next letter[10]—suggests that the Hogarth sisters were allied in a power struggle among young women, all vying for the position and status that marriage brings. Thus Catherine rather unkindly lords it over Matilda Ayrton—at least in her account to her cousin—by curtly informing her friend that she would *not* be a bridesmaid at her wedding.[11] Defining herself against and above other women in her circle, Catherine attempted to recoup what power she could in a culture that recognized and rewarded heterosexual unions while treating female friendships as second best. Yet both Catherine and Mary clearly understood where the *real* power lay in this dynamic: with the men whose privileges effectively set unmarried women at odds. Feeling relatively secure in their ability to attract men despite their father's precarious financial position, and taking advantage of their unmarried status, "the girls Hogarth" encouraged each other to exercise their power over those who paid court to them, an attitude captured in letters they sometimes discussed with each other before sending to their cousin and read to each other when they could, occasionally composing them together: "my (or rather our) letter," as Mary put it in one.[12] With their cousin, they formed a cohort of young women joking about male presumption among themselves and encouraging one another to put men in their place.[13]

9. ALS Catherine Hogarth to Mary Scott Hogarth, 11 February 1835, D. Jacques Benoliel Collection of the Letters of Charles Dickens, 86-2739, Rare Book Department, Free Library of Philadelphia.

10. ALS Catherine Hogarth to Mary Scott Hogarth, [4 July 1835], D. Jacques Benoliel Collection of the Letters of Charles Dickens, Rare Book Department, Free Library of Philadelphia.

11. Ibid.

12. ALS Mary Hogarth to Mary Scott Hogarth, 15 May [1836], Charles Dickens Museum, London. Mary discussed both of her extant letters with Catherine; she conveys messages for her sister in them and tells their cousin when Kate will next write.

13. Other unmarried cousins may have belonged to this cohort as well, although their correspondence does not survive. In her letter of 26 January 1837 Mary gives cousin Mary news of their other cousins "Jane and Teenie [Ballantyne]," noting that she "wrote to Jane the other day and gave her your message" (D. Jacques Benoliel Collection of the Letters of Charles Dickens, 83-1842, Rare Book Department, Free Library of Philadelphia). Attending school in London, Jane and Teenie had last seen Mary in October; they were in Brighton when Mary wrote to Jane.

In her first letter, for example, Catherine puts down a young man who "talks...nonsense" and has forgotten his subordinate position as a suitor, and in her second she limits her fiancé—an aspiring professional writer—to the "morsel" she leaves him for his message to her cousin.[14] In a similar strain, Mary criticizes "a Mr. Henry Johnstone" for "reporting" her "behaviour" to her Scremerston connections,[15] and she turns the tables on the men who patronized her even as they praised her, using their own condescending language against them. "How does [Dickens's] pretty little sister-in-law get on," John Strang asks John Macrone in January 1837 after meeting Mary at a party, wondering that "some *two-legged* monster does not carry her off," for "she is a sweet interesting creature."[16] "I am sure you would be delighted with [Charles] if you knew him," Mary tells her cousin in the first of her two letters, before going on to describe him with the same term he and Strang used to describe her: "He is such a nice creature and so clever."[17] Enjoying the manner in which both Catherine and Mary are writing and clearly amused by the powers they assume, their cousin eggs them on in her replies. "You ask me if [I] carry my new title with dignity," Mary reminds her correspondent in a postscript, referring to the position she has gained as "Miss Hogarth" now that her older sister is married. "If you saw me I am sure you would be perfectly satisfied."[18] Although Strang uses a series of diminutives to describe Mary—among them "pretty," "little," and "sweet"—men also noted her archness, her propensity to challenge pertly and talk back, conflating flirtation with aggression. Thus the poet Robert Story, who visited the Hogarths in 1836, memorialized Mary as "the fairest flower of spring" but also compared her glances to those of a falcon.[19]

14. ALS Catherine Hogarth to Mary Scott Hogarth, 11 February 1835 and [4 July 1835], D. Jacques Benoliel Collection of the Letters of Charles Dickens, 86-2739, Rare Book Department, Free Library of Philadelphia.

15. ALS Mary Hogarth to Mary Scott Hogarth, 26 January 1837, D. Jacques Benoliel Collection of the Letters of Charles Dickens, 83-1842, Rare Book Department, Free Library of Philadelphia.

16. John Strang to John Macrone, 2 January 1837, Charles Dickens Museum, London, quoted in Pilgrim 1:65 n. 3.

17. ALS Mary Hogarth to Mary Scott Hogarth, 15 May [1836], Charles Dickens Museum, London. Here the term "creature" conveys both the affection and the "shade of patronage" noted in the *Oxford English Dictionary*.

18. Ibid.

19. Robert Story, *Love and Literature; Being the Reminiscences, Literary Opinions, and Fugitive Pieces of a Poet in Humble Life* (London: Longman, Brown, Green, and Longmans, 1842), 217–18.

In 1835 Dickens was training Catherine for marriage, complaining of her "obsti-nacy" and what he found the "distrustful" elements of her character (Pilgrim 1:110) while also praising what he imagined to be her "faultless," selfless self. At least to some degree he was also training Mary to play a supporting role in their household, although her compliance would be wholly voluntary. While a falcon is a bird of prey, to use Story's image for Mary, it hunts in the service of a master, and Richard Bentley's account of Mary's part in deferring his departure from a party in 1837 suggests that Dickens could use her in this way: "Toward midnight...I rose to leave, but D. stopped [me] & pressed me to take another glass of Brandy & water. This I wd. Gladly have avoided, but he begged Miss Hogarth to give it me. At the hand of the fair Hebe I did not decline it."[20] In this account Bentley seems to recog-nize Mary's own power—as Hebe, goddess of youth—as does Dickens in the act of "begging." Yet Mary serves Bentley here, as Hebe poured nectar for the gods, and does so at Dickens's behest, appearing less an agent with power in her own right than a deputy for her brother-in-law and an object exchanged between men.

Between themselves, however, Mary and Catherine, in combination with their cousin, cultivated a very different idea of gender relations, one that was irreverent toward men, that mocked male presumption and that emphasized, with comic self-consciousness, their own power, not their power by proxy. Once Catherine had accepted his proposal, Dickens drew a distinction between her obligation to serve him and Mary's voluntary compliance with his requests. "Tell [Mary] I rely on her characteristic kind-heartedness and good nature to accompany you," he wrote Catherine early in their engagement, *and mind on your own behalf that I fully and entirely expect you*" (Pilgrim 1:65). To the sisters themselves, though, such distinc-tions were moot, and after Catherine's marriage, Mary continued to think of her as an autonomous and capable being—"Catherine in her own house," the successful housekeeper as well as the devoted and loving wife.[21] Particularly when the sisters were alone together after the marriage—at Furnivals, for example, when Dickens was out of town on a journalistic assignment—Catherine could think of herself in a different way than she did in the company of her husband and talk to a best friend who was also a peer, with neither the right nor the desire to control or amend her. As Mary herself suggested in writing to her cousin, the women behaved more freely

20. Journal of Richard Bentley, The Henry W. and Albert A. Berg Collection of English and American Literature, New York Public Library, quoted in Pilgrim 1:253 n. 2.

21. ALS Mary Hogarth to Mary Scott Hogarth, 15 May [1836], Charles Dickens Museum, London.

around each other than they did when men were present and forcing them to mind their "Ps and Qs."[22]

Mary's perspective on her sister's household and her idea of her own purpose within it differed markedly from those of her brother-in-law. To Mary's thinking, Catherine's marriage was one in which the husband ("a nice creature") was there to serve the wife and not the reverse—in which Catherine's desires and needs were to be the first consulted. Unlike men of her acquaintance who thought "*promising* quite enough without taking any further trouble about *fulfilling*," as Mary describes one of her brother Robert's friends, Dickens is there to provide for her sister and does so ably, "so clever he is courted and made up to by all the literary Gentleman [*sic*], and has more to do in that way than he can well manage."[23] When Catherine underwent her "dreadful trial" after the birth of Charley, her husband was "constantly studying her comfort in every thing," Mary noted approvingly, as she was herself: she has been "with dear Catherine" since last writing to their cousin, she reports, "so taken up with her and her Baby" that she has "not been able to think of any thing else."[24]

On Charley's first birthday, Dickens looked back to Mary's three-week stay at Furnivals following Catherine's confinement and remembered her keeping house for *him* at the time (Pilgrim 1:630). But as Mary understood it, she had been "staying with *her*"—that is, with *Catherine*—"since her confinement,"[25] primarily concerned with her sister and her nephew and not with her sister's husband. After Mary's death, Catherine told their cousin that Dickens had loved Mary as much as she did: "We have both lost a dear and most affectionate sister . . . and now every thing about us, brings her before our eyes."[26] But as her own letters reveal, Mary thought of her brother-in-law in relation to Cathcrine, not in relation to herself. While Mary praised Charles and his professional success, her praise marked her pleasure in her sister's good marriage, not her own delight in her "clever" brother-

22. ALS Mary Hogarth to Mary Scott Hogarth, 26 January 1837, D. Jacques Benoliel Collection of the Letters of Charles Dickens, 83-1842, Rare Book Department, Free Library of Philadelphia.

23. ALS Mary Hogarth to Mary Scott Hogarth, 15 May [1836], Charles Dickens Museum, London.

24. ALS Mary Hogarth to Mary Scott Hogarth, 26 January 1837, D. Jacques Benoliel Collection of the Letters of Charles Dickens, 83-1842, Rare Book Department, Free Library of Philadelphia.

25. Ibid.

26. ALS Catherine Dickens to Mary Scott Hogarth, 30 May [1837], D. Jacques Benoliel Collection of the Letters of Charles Dickens, 86-2740, Rare Book Department, Free Library of Philadelphia.

in-law. As Michael Slater notes, Mary reported on Dickens in an amused tone, not a reverential or dazzled one,[27] and she placed much less importance on her tie to him than he did after her death. Dickens transformed the dead Mary into his "better angel" (Pilgrim 3:409), dreamed of her recurrently at certain times in his life, and called her to his defense in 1858, telling Angela Burdett Coutts that Mary perceived Catherine's inadequacies "in the first months" of their marriage (Pilgrim 8:560). Yet Mary herself had only praise for her older sister, and while she esteemed her brother-in-law, she neither dreamed of nor worshiped him.[28] Even after Catherine proved unable to nurse Charley, Mary described her as a loving mother eager to care for her firstborn herself, a view antithetical to the one Dickens later adopted.

"STANDING PROXY"

Free from obligation to a husband, often irreverent or arch in her dealings with men and full of admiration for and fellow feeling with her older sister, Mary gave Catherine a sense of herself that was difficult to sustain after Mary's death. Writing to their cousin three weeks into her mourning period, having suffered a miscarriage in her "heart rending" distress, Catherine invites the other Mary Hogarth to "spend a few months" with her at Doughty Street and asks her cousin to serve as Charley's godmother in Mary's stead. "My poor departed sister was to have been Godmother to my dear little boy," she tells her cousin. "Will you take her place? . . . I shall stand proxy in your name. Do not say no as you are the only person I could bear to put in her place." While offering to "stand proxy" for her cousin at Charley's christening, Catherine is really struggling to find a proxy for her sister, all the while aware that Mary cannot be replaced. She conveys that awareness through her reference to her cousin's *approximation* to her sister (she will have to "bear" with substituting her cousin for Mary), her use of the double negative ("do not say no") instead of the affirmative ("say yes"), and her desire to see her cousin so that the two can "talk of the time when we were *all* together."[29]

Catherine lost Mary at a time when the English were preoccupied with the idea of female surrogacy and the possibility that one sister might stand proxy for another—not in sisterhoods or in female communities but in marital relations. In the decades-long debate over the Deceased Wife's Sister Bill, the question facing

27. Michael Slater, *Dickens and Women* (London: J. M. Dent, 1983), 80.

28. As Slater notes, it was Dickens's own memory that cast Mary as a woman who adored him, not Mary herself. See Slater's chapter on Mary Hogarth, ibid., 77–102.

29. ALS Catherine Dickens to Mary Scott Hogarth, 30 May [1837], D. Jacques Benoliel Collection of the Letters of Charles Dickens, 86-2740, Rare Book Department, Free Library of Philadelphia.

members of Parliament was whether or not, with the death of a married woman, her sister would be able to marry the bereaved brother-in-law and take her dead sister's place, a union legally prohibited with the passage of Lord Lyndhurst's Act in 1835 but quickly contested.[30] As Elizabeth Gruner points out in discussing this debate, "the significance of [a woman's] originary, defining relationship to her sister [was] lost in the shuffle—as [were] her desire . . . and her voice."[31] The controversy thus enacted on a large scale Dickens's appropriation of the Hogarth sisters, and that of Dickens scholarship as well. Although Catherine, not Mary, was the survivor in 1837, critics use this parliamentary debate to illuminate the relations among Dickens, Catherine, and her sisters and, without regard for *their* thoughts on the issue, to argue that the Hogarth women were virtually interchangeable in his thinking.[32] In so doing they cite the remarks Dickens made to Mrs. Hogarth on the sixth anniversary of Mary's death, after Georgina had become a member of his household:

> I trace in many respects a strong resemblance between [Mary's] mental features and Georgina's—so strange a one, at times, that when she and Kate and I are sitting together, I seem to think that what has happened is a melancholy dream from which I am just awakening. The perfect like of what she was, will never be again, but so much of her spirit shines out in this sister, that the old time comes back again at some seasons, and I can hardly separate it from the present. (Pilgrim 3:483)

In fact Dickens, like Catherine, felt that Mary could not be replaced, as his comments to Mrs. Hogarth reveal; to his mind, as to Catherine's, anyone resembling Mary could offer at best an imperfect approximation of her. But because husband and wife perceived Mary and her "spirit" in very different ways—increasingly so over time—Dickens "traced" her likeness in a different Hogarth than Catherine did. Whereas Dickens discovered Mary's proxy in Georgina, who became the devoted

---

30. For discussions of the Deceased Wife's Sister Bill and the cultural controversy that surrounded it, see Nancy F. Anderson, "The 'Marriage with a Deceased Wife's Sister Bill' Controversy: Incest Anxiety and the Defense of Family Purity in Victorian England," *Journal of British Studies* 21, no. 2 (Spring 1982): 67–86; Elizabeth Gruner, "Born and Made: Sisters, Brothers, and the Deceased Wife's Sister Bill," *Signs* 24, no. 2 (Winter 1999): 423–47; and Margaret Gullette, "The Puzzling Case of the Deceased Wife's Sister: Nineteenth-Century England Deals with a Second-Chance Plot," *Representations* 31 (September 1990): 142–66.

31. Gruner, "Born and Made," 425.

32. According to Chase and Levenson, for example, Dickens shared the "controlling fantasy" of his culture: "that a husband will always have a second choice, a second sister, waiting nearby in domestic reserve" (*The Spectacle of Intimacy,* 106, 117).

and worshipful sister-in-law he imagined Mary to be, Catherine first sought it in her cousin Mary Hogarth, only to find it, much later, in her own sister Helen. Resisting and defying Dickens in 1858 as neither Georgina nor Catherine would, Helen supplied Catherine with the sisterly "antidote" she needed after her "fall"—not only anger at Dickens but also allegiance and companionship from that time onward—playing the part of Lizzie to Catherine's Laura, to use Rossetti's formulation, the two Hogarth sisters, like those in "Goblin Market," destined to be wives and mothers yet to live without husbands. Aptly, it was Helen and not Georgina whom Catherine identified as Mary's true heir, bequeathing to the youngest of the Hogarth girls the mementoes most closely associated with their dead sister.

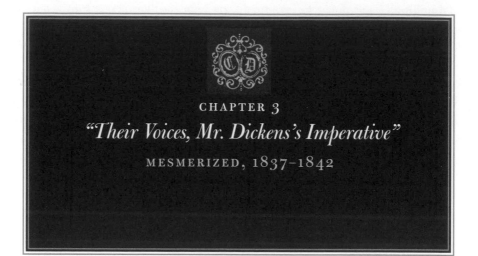

Have and hold, then and there,
Her, from head to foot,
Breathing and mute,
Passive and yet aware,
In the grasp of my steady stare.
—Robert Browning, "Mesmerism"
(1855)

"I DID NOT QUITE LIKE IT"

En route from Siena to La Scala, Italy, in late January 1845, Catherine sat beside her husband on the box of their carriage. They had been living in Genoa since July and were expanding their Italian vocabulary during the ride, with Dickens teaching Catherine some new words. After a few minutes of silence Catherine dropped her muff, and her husband looked her way. What he saw surprised him. Catherine had lost consciousness but had neither fainted nor fallen asleep. "Her eyelids quivering in a convulsive manner" and "her senses numbed," she had unexpectedly entered "the Mesmeric trance," he reported. Roused "with some difficulty" by Dickens, who asked her what was wrong, a trembling and discomposed Catherine explained that she "had been magnetized" (Pilgrim 4:253–54). She was unaware that her husband, sitting silent beside her, had been attempting to mesmerize, long distance, someone else—Augusta de la Rue, whom he had been treating "magnetically" for a host of debilitating symptoms at her home in Genoa during the past month.

Unwittingly, Catherine had fallen into a trance her husband intended for another woman, in another place.[1]

We have only one primary source for this episode in Catherine's history—a letter Dickens composed later that day to Émile de la Rue, the husband of the woman he termed his "patient." Of the half dozen or so surviving letters that Catherine wrote in 1845, none mentions either a mesmeric trance or her husband's magnetic powers. Relying solely on Dickens's account for our knowledge of Catherine's loss of consciousness and reawakening at his hands, we run the risk of falling under his powers ourselves—of being unduly influenced by his construction of events and his representations of himself and his wife—and need to be on our guard.

In the 1840s a number of those in Dickens's circle resisted his "magnetic" influence, among them the famous actor William Macready, who "did not quite like it" but agreed to submit to Dickens's powers at first. Following Macready, we might "reason . . . [ourselves] out of it," as the actor did when Dickens made "a trial on [him],"[2] and instead of serving as Dickens's willing subjects, challenge his authority by trusting to our own skeptical conjectures: surmising that Catherine simply fell asleep on the ride to La Scala, for example; or that in claiming to be entranced, if in fact she did, she echoed an explanation her husband provided; or that she "succumbed" to his powers consciously, in staged fashion, hoping to rival Madame de la Rue and regain his diverted attention. As Dickens himself acknowledged in relating the incident to Émile de la Rue, readers would find it "stupendous[ly] difficult" to credit his statement were it to appear in print. "Will you believe me?" he asked his correspondent. "*Can* you believe me?" (Pilgrim 4:253–54).

There seems little doubt, however, that Catherine believed herself to be entranced by her husband during his experiments with mesmerism and proved highly suggestible to him, at times surrendering her will to his. We have at least three

1. Fred Kaplan briefly discusses this episode in *Dickens and Mesmerism* (Princeton: Princeton University Press, 1975), 83–84, a detailed study of Dickens's fascination with the phenomenon, his literary use of it, and its place in Victorian culture. Michael Slater notes Dickens's interest in mesmerism and Catherine's unhappiness with his treatment of Madame de la Rue in *Dickens and Women* (London: J. M. Dent, 1983), 122–24, while Margaret Darby sees Dickens's magnetic pursuits as a displaced expression of his "autobiographical impulse" as well as a means of extracting stories from women for his own purposes. Margaret Flanders Darby, "Dickens and Women's Stories: 1845–1848 (Part One)," *Dickens Quarterly* 17 (2000): 68. All three consider the sexual implications of the mesmerist's power.

2. William Macready, *The Diaries of William Charles Macready, 1833–1851,* ed. William Toynbee, 2 vols. (London: Chapman and Hall, 1912), 2:180.

more records of Catherine succumbing to her husband's mesmeric powers—two from Dickens but the third from Macready, all in 1842—and several of their contemporaries witnessed and described Dickens's mesmeric "trials" on and treatment of various subjects. "He did it completely," Christiana Thompson noted in April 1850, when Dickens mesmerized her ailing sister Anna, the wife of Dickens's brother Fred.[3] Whether or not we place any faith in mesmerism—a prototype of modern-day hypnotism—those who knew Dickens accepted that he possessed that power and that he exercised it on Catherine and others.

While Dickens described his magnetic influence over his wife as extraordinary, particularly when he was not even directing it her way, the image of Mrs. Dickens in a trance induced by her husband is strangely familiar. It gives literal form to what we have seen of his influence over her during their courtship and first year of marriage, an influence that strengthened steadily in the five years that followed. In fact the mesmeric state might be seen as a fitting emblem for Catherine's experience of coverture during that period, as Browning suggests it could be for Victorian wives generally, when the narrator of his poem "Mesmerism" seeks to "have and hold" his beloved subject with his "steady stare."

In Catherine's day, coverture signified a woman's dependence on and subordination to her husband as well as his obligation to protect or "cover" her. More specifically, it stipulated that a woman's legal selfhood was subsumed by that of her husband upon marriage, when they became "one person." Mesmerism, too, was understood by Victorians to involve a union or merger of two people, most often a male operator and his female subject, whose "extreme intimacy and 'oneness'" required a suspension of will and agency on the subject's part.[4] Under coverture, the legal identity of a married woman was suspended indefinitely, and she lost the autonomy she had exercised when single, no longer able to own property or sign binding contracts. In mesmerism, the entranced subject became "depersonalized,"

3. Christiana Thompson, 1850 diary, MS Meynell Family Papers, Greatham. Alison Winter approaches Dickens's public readings as an adaptation of his magnetic powers in *Mesmerized: Powers of Mind in Victorian Britain* (Chicago: University of Chicago Press, 1998), 321–22.

4. Winter, *Mesmerized*, 239. While some women acted as mesmerists in Victorian London, they were a small minority and "did not give public demonstrations, perhaps because the role of mesmerist . . . was too overt a display of power" (ibid., 138). Dickens's conception of mesmerism and Catherine's experience of it involved a gender dynamic in which magnetic powers were exercised solely by men whose subjects were usually women. Dickens always refused to be mesmerized, telling Chauncy Hare Townshend in 1841, for example, that he "dare not"; since he was hard at work on *Barnaby Rudge*, "even a day's head ache would be a serious thing" (Pilgrim 2:342).

with "no intentions of [her] own." Entering what was considered a "community of sensation," she ceased to experience her own sensory perceptions, instead sensing those of the mesmerist; a "living marionette," she would "speak his thoughts, taste the food in his mouth, move her limbs in a physical echo of his."[5] For Catherine Dickens, whose husband was also her mesmerist, the inequitable intimacies of the magnetized state mirrored and reinforced those of the matrimonial.

To resist Dickens's influence properly, then, we need not doubt that Catherine sometimes occupied a trancelike state but keep from entering one ourselves, in part by considering Catherine's mesmerized subjectivity in relation to other, more conventional forms of self-abnegation that she embraced in her marriage, and by recognizing her wifely selflessness as an ordinary rather than an extraordinary condition. Among the demands it placed on her, this selflessness required Catherine to adopt Dickens's allegiances at the cost of some of her own and to negotiate among her various selves in a way that best suited her husband, subordinating her identity and duties as a mother to those belonging more strictly to Dickens's wife when asked to do so.

"SELF-DENYING SAINTS"

Little more than a year after Catherine's marriage, on 13 May 1837, Mary Hogarth was buried at Kensal Green cemetery. Drawing on her religious training and her faith in God, Catherine resigned herself to the loss of her sister as best she could. "Is it not dreadful to think she has left us for ever?" Catherine asked her cousin Mary, "although it is a blessed change for her, for if ever there was an angel she is one."[6] Despite such consolations, it was "a melancholy . . . time" for Catherine; she spent her first week or two of mourning with her husband and baby in Chalk, recovering, too, from the miscarriage triggered by the "*awful* shock."[7] Proud of Dickens, happy in his love, and delighted with their baby, Catherine had nonetheless suffered an irreparable loss even as she attempted the impossible task of replacing her dead sister with the cousin of whom Mary had always spoken "with the greatest affection."[8]

With the loss of Mary, Catherine lost a tangible hold on her younger, more assertive self as well as the intimate relationship that had provided her with an alternative

5. Winter, *Mesmerized*, 83, 77, 3.
6. ALS Catherine Dickens to Mary Scott Hogarth, 30 May [1837], D. Jacques Benoliel Collection of the Letters of Charles Dickens, 86-2740, Rare Book Department, Free Library of Philadelphia.
7. Ibid.
8. Ibid.

to marriage, its duties and restrictions. Their cousin was separated from her London relations by hundreds of miles, her life centered in Scremerston, and could not become the surrogate that Catherine desired, even if she had been able to accept the invitation to stay at Doughty Street for several months. As for Catherine's remaining sisters, Georgina was nine and Helen three in the spring of 1837—her surrogate children, not her peers—and Mrs. Hogarth, distraught over Mary's death, could not supply the female camaraderie her married daughter wanted. Shortly after Mary's death, in fact, the two women were purposely kept apart while Catherine recovered from her miscarriage, since she needed calm and quiet. "We almost feared for her reason," Catherine told her cousin, describing Mrs. Hogarth's response to losing Mary, "but she is now more resigned. I have not seen her for nearly ten days."[9]

Although they were soon reunited, the distance separating Catherine from her mother became a theme of her married life. From the time of Mary's death, Catherine earned praise from her husband by behaving unlike Mrs. Hogarth. Stoically serving others rather than indulging in grief, Catherine embodied a feminine ideal that her mother rejected. As Macready "theor[ized]" in one of his diary entries for September 1845, it was virtually impossible for most middle-class women to become "great or good tragic actress[es]" because "all they are taught for their own particular role" in real life "goes to extinguish the materials out of which an actress is formed—acquaintance with *the passions*—the feelings common to all, and indulged and expressed with comparative freedom in a poorer condition of life, but subjugated, restrained and concealed by high-bred persons."[10]

Mourning Mary's death, Mrs. Hogarth revealed her "acquaintance with *the passions*," while Catherine restrained her own. "Mrs. Dickens still continues to bear her trial with more fortitude than could possibly have been expected," Dickens wrote Edward Chapman on 9 May 1837, but "Mrs. Hogarth has relapsed into a worse state than ever. It is only by force that she can be kept from the room where poor Mary lies in her coffin" (Pilgrim 7:784). While "Mrs. Hogarth has suffered and still continues to suffer most deep and bitter anguish," he told Thomas Beard nearly two weeks later, "Kate, I am glad to say, made such strong efforts to console her, that she unconsciously summoned up all her fortitude at the same time, and brought it to her own assistance" (Pilgrim 1:260). In "sooth[ing] the sufferings of her bereaved mother" rather than focusing on "her own affliction," Catherine proved self-sacrificing as well as ladylike and restrained, assisting herself by serving others. "She has borne up through her severe trial like what she is—a fine-hearted noble-minded girl" (Pilgrim 1:263–64).

9. Ibid.
10. Macready, *Diaries,* 2:303.

Dickens wrote to his mother-in-law at intervals in 1837, telling her it was "really time [she] made the effort" to become more cheerful and describing the "pleasure" and "relief" it would give him to find her "calm upon this sad subject" (Pilgrim 1:275, 323). Such an end—that of pleasing Dickens—proved considerably more effective in shaping Catherine's behavior than that of her mother. Having received, at the start of 1838, yet another letter from her son-in-law "imploring her . . . not to give way to unavailing grief" for the sake of her remaining family members, Mrs. Hogarth replied, "protesting that in all useful respects she [was] the same as ever" (Pilgrim 1:629). In her view, women could give rein to their emotions and yet still perform the duties expected of them.

Set apart from her mother by her husband and deprived of Mary's companionship, Catherine found her circle largely defined by Dickens's professional connections and interests and his own family ties and composed of women who earned his approval. While Catherine's friendships with Eliza Franklin and the Ayrton sisters survived into the 1840s, the ties she had formed in her teens weakened with her marriage. Eliza stayed with the Dickenses in October 1840 only to drop from sight. Fanny and Matilda Ayrton celebrated New Year's Eve at Devonshire Terrace that year, Matilda having "stood as godmother" to ten-month-old Katey in August.[11] But Matilda died in September 1842, and while Catherine saw Fanny in 1844 and again in 1847, the two had become acquaintances rather than remaining close friends. The women most important to Catherine in her first years as Mrs. Charles Dickens were her sister-in-law Fanny, who married Henry Burnett in September 1837; Catherine ("Kitty") Atkins Macready, married to the actor William Macready since 1824; and Elizabeth Smithson and Milly Thompson, the sisters of T. J. Thompson, a member of Dickens's circle. Elizabeth was the wife of Charles Smithson, the law partner of Dickens's old friend Thomas Mitton. The membership of Catherine's cohort and its surprising conventionality were thus largely determined by the values and preferences of her husband. Although the details are fragmentary, the example of Martha Ball provides a case in point.

In her extant writings Catherine never mentions or addresses Martha Ball, but Dickens refers to "that dreadful girl" on three occasions in 1840, expressing his animosity in terms that are comic but scathing. "Kate has a girl stopping here, for whom I have conceived a horrible aversion, and whom I *must* fly," he tells Daniel Maclise. "Whither can I turn from this fearful female! She is the Ancient Mariner of young ladies. She 'holds me with her glittering eye', and I cannot turn away. The basilisk . . . is of a prim and icy aspect, her breast tight and smooth like a sugar

11. William Ayrton, annotated abstracts from memoranda of Frances (Fanny) Ayrton, 1836–1847, British Library, Add. 60373, f. 35.

loaf,—she converseth with fluency, and hath deep mental lore." Asking Maclise, in a postscript, if the sculptor Edward Davis is "excitable and ardent," Dickens hopes that the latter "might be got to run away with this tremendous being" who "is remarkable for a lack of development everywhere, and might be useful as a model of a griffin or other fabulous monster" or else transformed as Davis, Pygmalion-like, "make[s] her bust" and shapes her into a properly feminine figure (Pilgrim 2:103-4).

In Coleridge's poem, the Ancient Mariner "hath his will" over his listeners, holding them "spellbound" with his eye; they "cannot choose but hear," Coleridge writes, providing a disturbing example of the mesmeric power that fascinated him.[12] Calling Catherine's guest a "basilisk"—a monster whose looks kill rather than entrance—Dickens nonetheless ascribes to her the powers of a mesmerist, claiming to "*feel*" her through the wall," as those subject to animal magnetism reputedly could (Pilgrim 2:104).[13] But in Catherine's sphere, Dickens was the mesmerist, not the mesmerized; there was no room for assertive women eager to display their powers, whether those of basilisk, mesmerist, or independent-minded spinster. If Dickens did not explicitly prohibit Catherine from having contact with the likes of Martha Ball—as he would prohibit their children from seeing Mrs. Hogarth and Helen from 1858 onward—he could discourage such friendships through ridicule, hostility, and rudeness. That Dickens could make ambitious women feel unwelcome in his home and overrule Catherine's desire to befriend them is clear from the experience of a second unmarried acquaintance, Emma Picken, later Eleanor Christian.

Describing herself as "a young artist struggling into notice," Miss Picken knew T. J. Thompson and his sisters and spent time with the Dickenses at Broadstairs in Kent in the summer of 1840, when the novelist comically flirted with and teased both her and Milly Thompson.[14] But when Catherine took a serious interest in Miss Picken, hoping to promote her fledgling career, Dickens balked. Catherine offered to sit for her portrait and then try to persuade her husband to do the same. When Picken brought her finished work to Devonshire Terrace, Catherine "went straight into the library to Mr. Dickens with [it] in her hand," but her "expostulations" failed to convince him. Picken later described the scene:

> Notwithstanding the closed door, and that I sat far from it at the fire, I could hear the tones of their voices. Mrs. Dickens's expostulatory, Mr. Dickens's

12. Winter, *Mesmerized,* 158.

13. See Kaplan, *Dickens and Mesmerism,* p. 84.

14. [Eleanor Christian], "Reminiscences of Charles Dickens. From a Young Lady's Diary," *Englishwoman's Domestic Magazine* (1871): 342.

imperatively; at last she returned, looking flurried, but trying to put the best face on the matter. She made apologies for him, "That he was not very well, and tired. She hoped I would excuse him not being able to see me."

I faltered out, "Does he not like the portrait?"

"He has not had time to look at it properly. Of course he will think it like. You mustn't mind, dear, but to tell the truth he is a little grumpy just now, but it will be all right presently. You know a man is always cross when he has been kept without his dinner. Won't you stay?" she added, hesitatingly, and in such a tone that I knew she was *afraid* I might. . . . I never crossed his threshold again.[15]

Unable to sway her husband, despite her assurances that, with time, he would come around, Catherine became his messenger, conveying his dismissal to Miss Picken even while ostensibly speaking kindly, for herself. Catherine's "flurried" looks, hesitations, and apologies marked Dickens's "imperative" stance in the household as well as her uneasy acceptance of it.

Among the women Dickens encouraged to "cross . . . his threshold" and form his wife's circle, none were mesmerized by their husbands as Catherine was, although Dickens comically declined to make Mrs. Macready his magnetic subject in 1846, the same year in which Catherine brought an ailing Fanny Burnett to consult John Elliotson, one of the best-known proponents of mesmerism and the Dickenses' own doctor at the time. Yet the influence Henry Burnett and William Macready exercised over their wives, and the virtuous self-denial Fanny and Kitty were seen to embody, help to explain why the practice and dynamics of mesmerism could be readily incorporated into Catherine's married life.

Two years older than her brother Charles, Fanny became an award-winning pupil at the Royal Academy of Music, where she enrolled in 1823. Studying piano with Ignaz Moscheles and singing with Domenico Crivelli, she began giving lessons there four years later to defray her tuition costs. Her career as a public performer, launched in 1835, earned her praise in the London *Times* as one of "the most eminent professors which the Royal Academy of Music has produced."[16] John Hullah described her as "an excellent musician, *one who knew the sound of what she saw, and could reproduce it by voice or hand readily and correctly.*"[17]

15. Ibid.

16. Quoted in William J. Carlton, "Fanny Dickens: Pianist and Vocalist," *Dickensian* 53 (1957): 139.

17. [Frances R. Hullah], *Life of John Hullah, LL.D., by His Wife* (London: Longmans, Green, and Co., 1886), 13. Here Hullah's second wife quotes from his autobiographical narrative.

Given the expectations of the day, it is not surprising that, having married tenor Henry Burnett in 1837 and given birth to the first of their two sons in 1839, Fanny should devote herself to domestic duties instead of her career. Such was the experience of her friend and fellow performer Caroline Foster, who married Hullah in 1838 and "found...that domestic cares, the bringing up of a rather numerous family, keeping close accounts of expenditure, and the management of social life generally, filled up her time, leaving none for money earning."[18] In Fanny's case, however, it was her husband's increasingly prescriptive views as a Protestant dissenter, not her domestic responsibilities, that put an end to her public performances. Henry Burnett confided to James Griffin, their minister in Manchester, that Fanny "had never shown any particular interest in Divine worship" before he renounced theatrical life and its worldly pleasures and they moved away from London in 1841.[19] Fanny's insistence, in October 1839, that her husband would not be leaving the stage suggests that her plans ran counter to his (Pilgrim 1:592). Nonetheless, Fanny submitted to her husband's wishes. Attending Griffin's Sunday services with him, she entered "a state of mind altogether new to [her]," she wrote, "as if...entering a new world," declaring herself "anxious to be spiritually-minded" and perform "the service of Christ."[20] "Thank God she [was] not behind [him]" in her spiritual awakening, Henry Burnett told Griffin, "more especially as we have children whose young minds are generally more under the guidance of mother than father."[21] A devoted mother to her "dear little ones," as Catherine termed Fanny's two boys,[22] particularly her crippled Harry, who survived her by only four months, Fanny died of tuberculosis in September 1848, aged thirty-eight, "a self-denying saint, if ever one existed," a Manchester acquaintance remarked.[23]

While Fanny's spiritual awakening echoed that of her husband, the influence William Macready exercised over his wife was more formative and profound. The daughter of a Scottish scene painter, Kitty Atkins met Macready in 1815, when he was a rising theatrical star of twenty-two and she was nine years old, a

18. Ibid., 23.

19. James Griffin, *Memories of the Past. Records of Ministerial Life* (London: Hamilton, Adams & Co., 1883), 171–72.

20. Quoted ibid., 172, 178.

21. Quoted ibid., 181.

22. Catherine Dickens to Fanny Burnett, 30 January 1842, in Frederic G. Kitton, *Charles Dickens by Pen and Pencil* (London: Frank T. Sabin, 1890), 39, reprinted in Pilgrim 3:629.

23. Sir E. W. Watkin, *Alderman Cobden of Manchester: Letters and Reminiscences of Richard Cobden* (London: Ward, Lock, Bowden & Co., n.d.), 123.

"beautiful light-haired little Scotch girl in [a] plaid frock."[24] When Macready saw her again in 1820, Kitty was playing Virginia to his Virginius in the work by James Sheridan Knowles. The actor found her "*remarkably clever*" and predicted that she would "stand high in her profession."[25] But having accepted his proposal of marriage in 1822, she agreed to leave the stage and receive a yearlong, prenuptial education from him and his sister Letitia. With her unmarried sister-in-law, she kept house at Elm Place, a nine-acre farm in Elstree, north of London, and at 5 Clarence Place, Regent's Park. By the time she met Catherine Dickens in 1838, she had given birth to six children in eight years. Before her death from tuberculosis in 1852, she bore four more children. Most of the ten eventually succumbed to the same disease.

Married at eighteen, and thirteen years her husband's junior, Catherine Macready earned his praise for her docility as well as "her wonderful aptness for improvement."[26] As Macready put it, "The studies [his] Catherine had taken up with so much earnestness before [their] union she continued . . . throughout her after life, and she never entirely relinquished the character of pupil."[27] He not only supervised her reading but also gave her detailed instructions for her household management, her behavior, and her modes of expression, including the entries she wrote in her private diary.[28] After her death, Macready told his sister that his love for his wife resembled "the love of Dante for Beatrice."[29] Yet Jane Carlyle's assessment seems more apt. In her view, she told Macready, his wife was "that dear, sweet, loving woman, for whom you were a sort of Divinity on Earth."[30]

Years before he "reasoned [him]self out" of Dickens's magnetic influence, Macready expressed skepticism about the phenomenon. In 1836 John Elliotson became Macready's family doctor, and the actor "liked him very much."[31] But in 1838, when Macready saw Elliotson's "very extraordinary" exhibition of mesmerized epileptics at North London Hospital, he could "not help thinking that they [were] partly

24. Lady Pollock, *Macready As I Knew Him* (London: Remington and Co., 1884), 69.

25. William Macready to William McCready (father), 1820, quoted in Alan S. Downer, *The Eminent Tragedian: William Charles Macready* (Cambridge: Harvard University Press, 1966), 83.

26. [William Charles Macready], *Macready's Reminiscences*, ed. Sir Frederick Pollock (New York: Macmillan and Co., 1875), 219.

27. Ibid., 229.

28. See Downer, *Eminent Tragedian*, 118–19.

29. Lady Pollock, *Macready As I Knew Him*, 69.

30. Jane Carlyle to William Macready, 11 August 1853, quoted in Downer, *Eminent Tragedian*, 119.

31. [Macready], *Reminiscences*, 404.

under a morbid influence, and partly len[t] themselves to a delusion."[32] Nonetheless, Macready shared Elliotson's ability to influence the members of an audience powerfully: "to pass into the[ir] hearts," as one theater critic put it, and make them cry against their will, "possess[ing] in the highest degree the secret of speaking to the soul," another wrote.[33] Understanding Macready's powers of influence, both in the theater and in the home,[34] Dickens asked his friend to bring them to bear on his own wife in the fall of 1841, half a year before he first tried his hand at mesmerism, and at a time when Catherine felt particularly divided in her allegiances. To his dismay, she had objected to his plan to tour North America with her for several months, leaving their four young children behind.

WHICH SELF?

By the time Macready counseled Catherine Dickens on the virtues of wifely self-abnegation, she had various selves to suppress—a range of self-definitions that corresponded to her developing roles and responsibilities. Catherine Hogarth, the daughter of her Scottish parents and, after Mary's death, the sister of seven, was also Mrs. Charles Dickens, the helpmeet and "deputy" of the famous writer, her 1838 portrait by Samuel Laurence the counterpart of his (fig. 6). She was the hostess of their frequent social gatherings, the mistress of a substantial middle-class household, the mother of four young children.

In mid-December 1839 the Dickenses moved from 48 Doughty Street to 1 Devonshire Terrace, York Gate, Regent's Park, which remained their home until 1851. Dickens paid £800 for the eleven-year lease in addition to an annual rent of £160, double that of Doughty Street. To John Forster, Dickens joked about the "excessive splendour" of their new home, its "great promise (and great premium)" (Pilgrim 1:598), a change that reflected his professional success and better accommodated his growing family. In April 1838, a month after Mamie's birth, fifty thousand copies of the first number of *Nicholas Nickleby* had been sold, and Dickens received £3,000 from publishers Edward Chapman and William Hall for its twenty-month serialization. In 1839 they agreed to publish a weekly serial, *Master Humphrey's*

32. Ibid., 447.

33. Quoted in Downer, *Eminent Tragedian*, 114, 116.

34. Recalling Macready from her girlhood, Mrs. E. M. Ward claimed that "in public he electrified his audience with extraordinary power. In domestic life he overawed and terrified his household as an autocrat." Mrs. E. M. Ward, *Memories of Ninety Years,* 2nd ed., ed. Isabel G. McAllister (New York: Henry Holt, 1925), 97.

FIGURE 6. *Samuel Laurence, portraits of Charles Dickens (1837) and Catherine Dickens (1838), Charles Dickens Museum, London.*

Clock, paying all expenses and sharing equally in the profits; the following year they agreed to pay £3,000 for *Barnaby Rudge.*[35]

With its large garden, its entrance hall, and more than a dozen rooms, 1 Devonshire Terrace was yet another step up for the Dickenses. They now had a library as well as dining and drawing rooms and, in addition to several bedrooms, two nurseries, one for daytime use and one for night. Even with the birth of Katey in October 1839 and Walter in February 1841, all the children could sleep in the night nursery; it held two cribs and two beds and was adjacent to the bedroom assigned to the women servants.

Before relocating their household to Genoa for a year in the summer of 1844, Catherine and her husband took a detailed inventory of the contents of 1 Devonshire Terrace. Along with the surviving record of Catherine's invitations to christenings, birthday parties, and other gatherings and accounts written by guests, their list of material possessions—among thousands of items, a "Mahogany Dining table with 5 leaves" and a "Best Dinner Set" with a service for twenty (Pilgrim 4:705,

35. Robert Patten discusses Dickens's income and his complex and sometimes contentious negotiations with his publishers in *Charles Dickens and His Publishers* (Oxford: Clarendon Press, 1978).

710)—conveys a sense of what her role as hostess entailed.[36] Catherine's first year at Devonshire Terrace began with a dinner party on New Year's Day, with Daniel Maclise and John and Caroline Hullah among nine guests; it ended with the New Year's Eve party at which the Ayrton sisters joined members of Dickens's circle—J. P. Harley, W. Harrison Ainsworth, George and Mary Ann Cruikshank, George and Clarissa Cattermole, and others—playing charades and forfeits after dinner. Her year included a dinner celebration for those involved with *Master Humphrey's Clock,* at which Eliza Franklin, visiting in October, happened to be a guest, although Macready failed to note her presence or that of their hostess in his diary. "Dined with Dickens," the actor wrote for 20 October: "Met his artists, Cattermole and Browne; publishers Chapman & Hall; printers, Bradbury & Evans; also Egan, Harley, Talfourd, Forster, T. Hill, Maclise. A very cheerful day."[37] In a letter to her brother, Eliza was more effusive about the "splendid affair," writing: "'The dinner' I told of went off in style 16 guests. . . . I was quite grand & feel assured I was honoured to move among *the great.* After dinner we retired, [Dickens] had the folding doors, in the dining room, closed & we heard the speaker. Sergeant T[alfourd] is a tremendous speaker. I enjoyed this dinner very much 'twas as you may imagine very stylish 4 men waiting beside their own."[38]

As Eliza's tally ("4 men waiting beside their own") makes clear, the class system shaped the social interactions of the Dickenses as it did Catherine's sense of self, even though the members of their set were relatively informal. Their cook prepared the meals that other servants placed on their table, in a dining room their housemaid cleaned. Eager to make his mark socially, Dickens spent his income freely, on services as well as goods. At Doughty Street two or three female servants were employed. At Devonshire Terrace there were four women on the household staff: a nursery maid and a lady's maid as well as a cook and a housemaid. The 1841 census return for the household includes Elizabeth Stockhausen, Anne Brown, Harriet Pile, and Charlotte Stubbey, all between the ages of twenty and thirty. By contrast, Catherine's parents employed one female servant in 1841, a teenager two years older than their daughter Georgina. Each of the servants at Devonshire Terrace was paid quarterly, their wages typical of the period; in 1840 the housemaid's annual wages

36. Susan M. Rossi-Wilcox explains the significance, for Catherine's domestic management, of some of these items in *Dinner for Dickens: The Culinary History of Mrs. Charles Dickens's Menu Books* (Totnes: Prospect Books, 2005), 166–67, 191–92.

37. Macready, *Diaries,* 2:90.

38. Eliza Franklin to George Franklin, [26 October 1840], in David Parker, Anno Wilson, and Roger Wilson, "Letters of a Guest at Devonshire Terrace," *Dickensian* 95 (1999): 59.

totaled £13, the cook's £14, and the nursery maid's £10.10.[39] Because their services were indispensable, the children's wet nurses, though temporary employees, received wages somewhat higher than the other female servants on the staff, as was the common practice in middle-class Victorian households.

As the mistress of 1 Devonshire Terrace, Catherine was responsible for managing the household and its female servants, at least in theory. But the unusual interest her husband took in household matters and goods at Doughty Street carried over to their new home, limiting her role. By all contemporary accounts, Catherine was a capable household manager; but so was her husband, who liked to arrange for improvements, comforts, and "little conveniences here and there" (Pilgrim 1:600) and enjoyed his purchasing power. He might spend an entire day shopping for one particular item—such as a lamp for his study—or, without consulting his wife, decide on a new decorating scheme to "surprise" her. Discovering his plan before the work started, Catherine prevented the hall and staircase at Devonshire Terrace from being painted "a good green," which she thought "quite out of the question" (Pilgrim 4:297–98, 312).

As Catherine learned, her husband's domestic pleasures were inseparable from his control over their home. The shift that occurred in the financial workings of their household between 1837 and 1838 was even more pronounced from 1838 to 1841, with Catherine exercising less autonomy as a consumer than she did early in her marriage and receiving most of her spending money directly from Dickens instead of a teller at Coutts Bank, to whom she could bring checks made out in her name. In dispensing cash for household expenses to Catherine himself, Dickens might be seen as acting thoughtfully by saving her occasional trips to the Strand. But at the same time he was exercising more control over her spending by handing her specific sums for specific purposes and not allowing her to obtain, allocate, and budget money herself.

In the first two months of 1838, more than one quarter of the checks written by Dickens were made out to Catherine, for a total of £75; in the corresponding periods for 1839 and 1840, this figure had dropped to one twentieth (5 percent), with amounts totaling £12.10 and £46, respectively. In 1838 the total Dickens allocated to himself for unspecified expenditures was £263.15 and for Catherine £166.12 (63 percent of his total); in 1839, £438.10 for himself and £62.10 for her (14 percent of his total); in 1840, £326 for himself and £77 for her (24 percent of his total); and in 1841, £363.2 for himself and £47.10 for her (13 percent of his total).[40] Since Catherine gave birth in 1837, 1838, 1839, and 1841, with a break in 1840, the modest rise in

39. Charles Dickens, Esq., Account Ledger, Coutts & Co., London.
40. Ibid.

her allocation for that year suggests that her childbearing, as well as her husband's micromanagement, was responsible for her diminished role as a household consumer. But while the growing number of their children necessarily shifted the focus of Catherine's attention, she proved capable of making all the necessary purchases for the household (or directing a servant to do so) when her husband was away, and her childbirths and confinements had an inconsistent effect on their financial arrangements. After the birth of Mamie in March 1838, Catherine did not receive a check made out in her name for more than two months. After the birth of Katey in October 1839, however, that lapse of time was less than one month, increasing to seven weeks after Walter's birth in February 1841, even though that fourth delivery posed as few problems for Catherine as the third. The fact that Georgina— commended by Dickens for her organization and efficiency—had significantly less autonomy as a household consumer than Catherine did during the period in which all three lived together points to Dickens's desire for control rather than Catherine's childbearing or alleged incapacity as the primary reason for his prominence in household budgeting and spending.

In financial matters, as in her domestic management generally, Catherine derived her authority from her husband, "depute[d]" by "Mr. Dickens" to act in his name.[41] Her position as deputy and subordinate differed markedly from the partnership that John Stuart Mill claimed for the Victorian wife in representing the social progress of his age. "Among the educated classes," the wife had become, Mill asserted, her husband's "chief associate, his most confidential friend, and often his most trusted adviser."[42] Despite his love for Catherine, Dickens reserved the roles outlined by Mill for his male friends and relations. Deliberating over a detail of his preface to *The Old Curiosity Shop* in September 1840, Dickens asked Catherine for her opinion as well as asking John Forster and Thomas Mitton for theirs. But Forster, not Catherine, was his primary reader and editor, as Mitton was his financial consultant, and when planning his North American tour in September 1841, he confided to his brother Fred that he and his wife would be gone for half a year while withholding that information from Catherine. "Kate and I are going to America for five or six months," he wrote Fred, "but I don't tell her how long" (Pilgrim 2:392).

Rather than reflecting on Catherine and her limitations, Dickens's decision to withhold his full confidence from her reveals his tendency to "manage" his wife: one sign of what he perceived as his responsibility and privilege as a guardian of *all*

41. ALS Catherine Dickens to "Dear Sir," 21 October 1841, Chicago Historical Society.

42. John Stuart Mill, speech to the House of Commons, 20 May 1867, quoted in John Tosh, *A Man's Place: Masculinity and the Middle-Class Home in Victorian England* (New Haven: Yale University Press, 1999), 53.

his female relations. Thus when John Dickens borrowed money in the name of his famous son in February 1841, Charles consulted his brother-in-law Henry Austin and not his own sister Letitia, Henry's wife, just as he conferred with Henry Burnett on such matters instead of his sister Fanny.

Despite their mutual attachment, Catherine's subordination to Dickens extended to their love relationship. Whereas he prided himself on being "the Inimitable," a sense of self derived from his literary genius and dependent on him alone, Catherine was known by her husband and his closest friends as "the Beloved," an identity that acknowledged her worth, but as an object of affection, tracing her value to a source outside herself—her husband's feelings and perceptions. In his 1847 portrait of Catherine (fig. 7), which he first conceived and sketched in 1842, Daniel Maclise conveys her status as "the Beloved" as well as the objectification associated with that identity. As fixed a figure as the flowers placed beside her, in a painting that seems more like a human still life than a portrait, Catherine holds her work instead of producing it, as much an object of beauty and admiration as the roses and the embroidery themselves. Using his color scheme and composition to link the natural objects with the artful and the human ones, Maclise levels the differences among them, capturing the loss of agency that admiration and love sometimes entail. As David Parker insightfully observes, Dickens's identity as "the Inimitable" allowed for "almost any kind of behavior," but "'the Beloved' is a constraining sobriquet, prescribing a narrow range of behavior, and revocable at Dickens's will."[43]

In Parker's view, Catherine was happy as Dickens's beloved, but her happiness came "at a cost," one she herself paid "in the surrender of her will" to her husband's and "the narrowing of personality Dickens's vision of the ideal marriage demanded."[44] Yet Catherine was more than the wife of Charles Dickens, narrowed to fit his marital ideal. To identify her narrowly—solely as Dickens's beloved wife—is to accept the logic of coverture and grant her husband the power to revoke her selfhood by withdrawing his affections from her. While Catherine "was" Mrs. Charles Dickens, that identity did not erase or subsume Catherine Hogarth, a person defined by her relationships with parents, grandparents, siblings, and a network of aunts, uncles, and cousins. In the summer of 1841, Catherine was brought to consider the relationship between her identity as a married woman and her "original" self when she returned to Edinburgh for the first time since her family had left it ten years earlier.

43. David Parker, *The Doughty Street Novels: Pickwick Papers, Oliver Twist, Nicholas Nickleby, Barnaby Rudge* (New York: AMS Press, 2002), 62.
44. Ibid.

FIGURE 7. *Daniel Maclise, portrait of Catherine Dickens (1847),
Charles Dickens Museum, London.*

She traveled to Scotland as the consort of the famous writer, whose most recent novel, *The Old Curiosity Shop,* had reached sales of 100,000 copies, and who had been invited to Edinburgh to receive its honors. Those honors would be bestowed by members of the "Edinburgh literati," among whom George Hogarth had been eminent, as Dickens proudly told his uncle five years earlier. Dickens conceived of the trip as a way to thank his northern public and see the land of Sir Walter Scott, whom he considered his literary father. He planned a ten-day tour of the Highlands to follow his visit to Edinburgh. But Catherine conceived of the trip quite differently than her husband did—as an exciting chance to revisit scenes of her childhood and adolescence and to capture as best she could an idea of what she had been in the past. Her interest was piqued by the arrival in London that spring of her grandparents, "transplant[ed] from Edinburgh" to a "new abode" in Brompton, near the Hogarths, where they were visited in May by the Edinburgh judge and literary critic Francis Jeffrey, on a "pilgrimage" to see "old George Thomson, whom [he] found marvellously entire."[45] As a somewhat dismissive Dickens explained to Angus Fletcher, who was to tour with the couple through the Highlands, "Kate will be mad to see the house she was born in, and all the rest of it" (Pilgrim 2:299). Indeed the morning after their arrival, as her husband toured Edinburgh with the historical painter William Allen, Catherine went on a tour of her own with Allen's niece, stopping at 8 Hart Street, among other places important to the Hogarths in the 1810s and 1820s—"the house she was born in, &c," as Dickens again put it (Pilgrim 2:309).

Although Catherine's tour of her past was merely an abbreviation in her husband's letter, it figured largely in her experience of Edinburgh, where she and Dickens dined with some of her father's former associates, and her connection to the city was often acknowledged by their hosts. Sending his regards to Catherine in a letter to Dickens after the couple visited his home, Jeffrey hoped that her "nationality...ha[d] lost nothing of its ardor, by this little peep of her native land—or the proofs it had given of its sympathy of choice with her—as to the being it most delights to honor."[46] At the grand dinner for Dickens at the Waterloo Rooms in Edinburgh, Fletcher claimed that in fact the honor was Catherine's rather than her husband's when, toasting the women present, he declared that the novelist "owed much of his distinction to his having selected as a partner for life a Scottish lady."[47] Thus while Dickens celebrated

45. Francis Jeffrey to Henry Cockburn, 4 May 1841, in *Life of Lord Jeffrey, with a Selection from His Correspondence,* ed. Lord Cockburn, 2 vols. (Edinburgh: Adam and Charles Black, 1852), 2:338.

46. ALS Francis Jeffrey to Charles Dickens, 20 July 1841, HM 18524, Huntington Library, quoted in Pilgrim 2:320–21 n. 2.

47. *Caledonian Mercury,* 26 June 1841, quoted in Pilgrim 2:311 n. 2.

his literary succession, with the mantle of fame passing down from Scott to himself as literary heir,[48] he was brought to recognize Edinburgh as the birthplace of his wife and to acknowledge, implicitly, the importance of mothers as well as literary fathers, telling his audience, in response to Fletcher's toast, that "he had always looked with pleasure upon his children as half bred English and Scotch."[49]

During his speech at the dinner, Dickens compared his "fictitious creatures" to "real" beings that he "conceived," and he sometimes spoke of his real children as "volumes" he authored.[50] But if they were "half" Scottish, Catherine could be considered his coauthor. On their tour of Scotland, Dickens joked that the precocious Charley "takes arter his father, he does," as if to claim sole authorship of their firstborn (Pilgrim 2:313). But Catherine also considered Charley to be *hers* ("my own," she called him),[51] despite her initial fear that, without her nursing, he would "not care for her,"[52] and by the time Walter was born, Catherine could refer to wet nurses and weanings as a matter of course, not a cause for sorrow, feeling that she had done right by her "darlings,"[53] and secure in their attachment to her. Like other middle-class Victorian mothers, Catherine cared for her young children with the help of live-in servants, but she did not think of the nurses as her surrogates. While their work supplemented hers and enabled her to manage the household and pay and receive social calls, Catherine played with the children as she had with her youngest siblings and as she would with her grandchildren in the 1860s and 1870s,[54] and she saw to their needs, tending them when they were sick and taking pleasure in their enjoyments.

48. Ian Duncan, *Modern Romance and Transformations of the Novel* (Cambridge: Cambridge University Press, 1992), 189.

49. *Caledonian Mercury,* 26 June 1841, quoted in Pilgrim 2:311 n. 2.

50. Charles Dickens, *Speeches of Charles Dickens,* ed. K. J. Fielding (Oxford: Clarendon Press, 1960), 9. "I shall hope to have an early opportunity of presenting you to Mrs. Dickens and my six live volumes now in private circulation," Dickens wrote Amédée Pichot in 1846 (Pilgrim 4:687).

51. ALS Catherine Dickens to Mary Scott Hogarth, 30 May [1837], D. Jacques Benoliel Collection of the Letters of Charles Dickens, 86-2740, Rare Book Department, Free Library of Philadelphia.

52. ALS Mary Hogarth to Mary Scott Hogarth, 26 January 1837, D. Jacques Benoliel Collection of the Letters of Charles Dickens, 83-1842, Rare Book Department, Free Library of Philadelphia.

53. ALS Catherine Dickens to Frederick Dickens, [22 March 1842], The Henry W. and Albert A. Berg Collection of English and American Literature, New York Public Library.

54. One acquaintance recalls Catherine playing with Charley's children at Gad's Hill in the 1870s: "The youngsters had got Gran'ma in a swing, and the more she begged of them to

"Mrs. Dickens adored Charles and the children," a family friend recalled. "In the early days she used to say what a good husband he made, and speak of his passionate love for his children from their babyhood."[55] Indeed Dickens was a loving father when his children were young but often saw very little of them—so little he sometimes made a point of dining early to try to remedy matters. "I have been out every day this week, and have scarcely seen the children," he told Mitton in May 1841, when Walter was a baby of three months and Charley four years old. "If we dine so late as 6, it is their bedtime when the cloth is removed—and I don't like to deprive them of the opportunity of coming down" (Pilgrim 2:282). Dickens organized special events for the children—exhibiting a magic lantern at Charley's sixth birthday party, releasing balloons for their entertainment in the summertime, and performing remarkable feats as a conjuror—yet Catherine was the one immersed in their daily lives. In August and September, when they took lodgings outside London, most often in Broadstairs on the Kentish coast, Dickens continued to work on his books—*Old Curiosity Shop* in 1840, *Barnaby Rudge* in 1841, *American Notes* in 1842, and *Martin Chuzzlewit* in 1843—while Catherine focused her attention on the children and their "seaside amusements."[56]

As the mother of their four young children, Catherine came closer to achieving parity with Dickens than she did as his wife—not because they cared for the children together but because the care of infants and toddlers largely fell to her, in a sphere that was uncontested. From her children Catherine gained a sense of herself that was independent from Dickens even as her intimacy with him made it possible. Acquired "naturally" rather than by proxy or contract, motherhood could never be revoked, whatever her husband and the laws of custody might suggest to the contrary. Nonetheless, its demands and satisfactions could be superseded by a call to duty on Catherine as Dickens's wife and by her need to give precedence to the selfless self that defined her position under coverture.

"THE FACE SHE PUTS UPON IT"

At the time of their move to Devonshire Terrace, with his fame growing, Dickens felt certain that he could afford to live in "splendour." Yet the profitability of his works did not always match their popularity—and their popularity could waver. After the weekly serialization of *Old Curiosity Shop* in *Master Humphrey's Clock*,

---

stop it, the more they did nothing of the sort." J. Gibbs, "How I First Met Charles Dickens," *Press News*, December 1905, 28, quoted in Slater, *Dickens and Women*, 411 n. 73.

55. Ward, *Memories of Ninety Years*, 86.

56. ALS Catherine Dickens to Mrs. Felton, 2 September 1843, Charles Dickens Museum, London.

sales of *Barnaby Rudge* declined as low as thirty thousand copies. And since *Master Humphrey's Clock* was expensive to produce, its profits were disappointing. For its eighty-eight weekly numbers, Dickens earned approximately £5,469, much less than he had anticipated.[57] Because of a falling-out with Richard Bentley, he borrowed from Chapman and Hall to buy out Bentley's rights to his early works. In June 1840 his new publishers advanced him more than £2,000 for that purpose. Furthermore, his parents were in continual financial difficulties and needed support, as did the Hogarths on occasion. Thus Dickens's financial position in 1841 could be seen as somewhat precarious.[58] Dickens's dinners were "rather too sumptuous...for a man with a family, and only beginning to be rich," Francis Jeffrey noted to Henry Cockburn in May 1841.[59] "Do not spend your money as you get it," Jeffrey advised Dickens directly, "but secure as near as you can, a full *independence.*"[60]

Under these circumstances, Dickens decided, in September 1841, to travel to North America, proposing to write the book that became *American Notes,* which Chapman and Hall agreed to subsidize by providing him with £150 monthly in 1842. They would then pay £200 for each monthly installment of his next work as well as a significant percentage of its profits, which he would use to pay back the subsidy. The difficulty, Dickens told Forster, William Hall, and Macready, in turn, was Catherine's aversion to the project. "I am still haunted by visions of America, night and day," he confessed to Forster. "To miss this opportunity would be a sad thing. Kate cries dismally if I mention the subject. But, God willing, I think it *must* be managed somehow!" (Pilgrim 2:380–81).

Dickens weighed his options: he could tour North America by himself or with Catherine, or he could bring his family along. But he did not want to travel through America with the children and thought of leaving them in New York. For Catherine, however, divided between her marital and her maternal concerns, each of her husband's proposals was distressing. "I can't persuade Mrs. Dickens to go, and leave the children at home; or to let me go alone," Dickens told Hall (Pilgrim 2:383). To Macready, Dickens formulated Catherine's dilemma somewhat differently: she did not want to travel to North America *without* the children, nor did she want to *bring* them, "fearing sickness might make them ill." "She naturally finds it difficult to contemplate a subject which is so new to her and so startling in any very reasonable light," he added (Pilgrim 2:388).

57. Patten, *Dickens and His Publishers,* 112–13.
58. Ibid., p. 118.
59. Francis Jeffrey to Henry Cockburn, 4 May 1841, in *Life of Lord Jeffrey,* 2:338.
60. ALS Francis Jeffrey to Charles Dickens, 20 July 1841, HM 18524, Huntington Library, quoted in Pilgrim 2:320 n. 2.

With Macready's help, Dickens brought Catherine "to reason," the actor persuading her that she owed her first duty to her husband and that she could and must leave the children behind. Macready was well positioned to intervene on Dickens's behalf: a close friend of the couple, he had traveled to North America in 1826, before his children were born, accompanied by his wife and sister; he was the father of a large family; he was skilled at directing and controlling his own wife; and he was decisive, claiming to know, "on the instant," the "best course to be pursued" in the case.[61] Traveling to London from Broadstairs on 23 September, Dickens consulted with Macready and engaged the actor to counsel Catherine on his behalf. "He spoke of Mrs. Dickens's reluctance and regret, and wished me to write to her and state my views, putting them strongly before her," Macready noted in his diary. "When he was gone, I wrote to her, enclosing the note to him."[62]

A note within a note, Macready's advice to Catherine, however sincere or heartfelt, constituted a strategy on his part and that of her husband. In effect it was a tool that Macready placed in Dickens's hands. In his enclosure Macready told Catherine "of what *is a duty* and *must be a source of happiness to her*," reminding her of her obligations as a wife and the pleasure she "must" take in meeting them. Assuaging her maternal anxieties, he promised that he and his wife would help supervise the four Dickens children while their parents were away. Outlining his strategy in his cover letter to Dickens, Macready explained his approach. He had invoked the selfless ideal in writing to Catherine, knowing it would prove more persuasive than the "selfish . . . argument" could be—the argument that would emphasize "the great delight and enjoyment that [lay] before her in that grand country." Fearing, nonetheless, that he was not "sufficiently impressive" in what he "urged upon her," Macready encouraged Dickens to reiterate "forcibly" his views on the subject; the actor was "very anxious she should view this matter in its proper light, and . . . make all so much happier by the face she puts upon it."[63]

As events proved, there was no need for Dickens to push the point, although he imagined himself "wr[inging] a reluctant consent" from Catherine (Pilgrim 2:391). As Macready knew, the selfless argument was a powerful one with a "good little" woman, as he termed Catherine later that month,[64] and Dickens, "in great delight

61. Macready, *Diaries,* 2:143.

62. Ibid.

63. ALS William Macready to Charles Dickens, 23 September 1841, HM 18553, Huntington Library, quoted in Pilgrim 2:390–91 n. 4; Macready, *Diaries,* 2:144.

64. ALS William Macready to Charles Dickens, 28 September 1841, HM 18554, Huntington Library, quoted in Pilgrim 2:398 n. 5.

at the effect of [Macready's] letter to his wife,"[65] considered himself indebted to the actor. Yet Macready's success also belonged to Dickens; since first courting Miss Hogarth in 1835, he had laid the groundwork for everything his friend urged on her. Within the past six months, in fact, Dickens had shared with Catherine an unpublished manuscript, sent to him by Basil Hall, that captured a wife's selfless devotion to her husband in a way he found particularly "powerful and affecting"— "beautiful and tender" (Pilgrim 2:235)—and that brought Catherine to tears: Lady de Lancey's account of her husband's sufferings and death after he was wounded at the Battle of Waterloo.

Lady de Lancey's account conveyed her heroics as a bride who traveled from Antwerp to the French front to nurse her husband in a rustic cottage during his final six days, suppressing her own anxieties to better serve him. "I was so grateful for seeing him once more, that I valued each hour as it passed," she wrote, "and as I had too much reason to fear that I should very soon have nothing left of happiness but what my reflections would afford me, I endeavoured, by suppressing feelings that would have made him miserable, and myself unfit to serve him, to lay up no store of regret."[66] In Dickens's eyes, such devotion was "sacred" and the path Lady de Lancey traveled was "holy ground." As for Catherine, she showed her appreciation for Lady de Lancey by "sobbing over" the manuscript, Dickens told Basil Hall, and retiring "in an agony of grief" (Pilgrim 2:236).

Urged by Macready to perform her duty by Dickens, trained by her husband to do so, and inspired by celebrated examples of selflessly heroic wives, Catherine replied to the actor's letter with "a very fervent and grateful letter" of her own, "acquiescing in all" he recommended.[67] "Pray tell your good wife, that she made me very happy in the very sweet & amiable letter she sent me," Macready wrote Dickens, "and that she cannot gratify me more than by calling, and believing me her true friend."[68] "Macready's note to Kate was received and acted upon with a perfect response," Dickens told Forster on 26 September. "She talks about [the tour] quite gaily, and is satisfied to have nobody in the house [in their absence] but Fred, of whom, as you know, [the children] are all fond" (Pilgrim 2:393). To cut his expenses, Dickens arranged to sublet 1 Devonshire Terrace to Sir John Wilson while he and Catherine were abroad, moving the children to lodgings at

65. Macready, *Diaries,* 2:144.

66. Lady de Lancey, *A Week at Waterloo in 1815: Lady de Lancey's Narrative,* ed. Major B. R. Ward (London: John Murray, 1906), 69.

67. Macready, *Diaries,* 2:144.

68. ALS William Macready to Charles Dickens, 28 September 1841, HM 18554, Huntington Library, quoted in Pilgrim 2:398 n. 5.

25 Osnaburgh Street, where they would live with the servants and their uncle until their parents returned, with supervision from the Macreadys. In his willingness to stay with his nieces and nephews, Fred helped reconcile Catherine to the trip, as did her maid Anne Brown, who consented to accompany the Dickenses to North America.

Within a month of agreeing to join her husband on his American tour, Catherine was reminded that her allegiances were varied and that the Hogarths and Thomsons had their claims on her as well. After Dickens underwent surgery to remove a fistula on 8 October, Catherine acted as his nurse and secretary, writing his letters from dictation and signing them in his name. Five days later, still tending to Dickens on the sofa, she learned that her grandmother had died; in her new Brompton home, Katherine Thomson had been ailing since September. On 24 October, less than two weeks after her grandmother's death, Catherine's brother George died suddenly in London; only twenty years old, he had been a particularly hardworking and promising young man, commended by his employer and rewarded with a raise. The Hogarths were distraught, particularly Catherine's mother, who had lost her own mother and her son within eleven days. George was buried at Kensal Green, next to Mary Hogarth and Katherine Thomson, on 28 October. While Catherine grieved for her grandmother and her brother and did what she could to console her mother, Dickens encouraged Mrs. Hogarth to "bear [her loss] well, for the love of [her] remaining children," yet himself mourned for Mary, whom he felt he was "losing . . . a second time" (Pilgrim 2:408, 410). When Dickens was ordered to Windsor by his surgeon for a two-week convalescence in November, Catherine accompanied him but brought along her teenage sister Georgina, now one of six siblings left to her.

In the time that remained before her departure for North America, Catherine prepared for another loss—her six-month separation from the children. She had been away from them before—for as long as a month, during her trip to Scotland. This time, however, she would be traveling on the other side of the Atlantic and would be gone for half a year. Scheduled to leave for Boston on the S.S. *Britannia* on 4 January 1842, she would miss Charley's fifth birthday on 6 January, Walter's first birthday on 8 February, and Mamie's fourth birthday on 6 March. But before she left, she would see Walter christened, a ceremony she planned for early December, all the more anxious to have it performed because of her renewed sense of life's uncertainty. She arranged to bring a sketch of the children with her on the tour as well, writing to Daniel Maclise before Walter was baptized for that purpose. "*With all my heart.* I will do what you wish," he replied. "Embrace Charley and May and Katy, and hang me if I believe you have named the younger yet—but kiss the little unknown too—we must include him in our projected group if it is only three dots and a line."[69] Leaving the children with Fred on 2 January, Catherine, her husband, and Anne Brown departed for Liverpool, where Fanny Burnett spent their last day with them and saw them embark on the fourth, as did John Forster and Angus Fletcher.

Their ship was a wooden paddle steamer designed for 115 passengers. The Dickenses slept in a tiny cabin while Anne had a bed in a larger but less private room for women. They arrived in Boston on 22 January after a dangerous passage across the Atlantic and what Catherine described as "all the horrors of a storm at Sea."[70] They spent two weeks in Boston and then traveled through Connecticut to New York City for a three-week stay. They proceeded to Philadelphia, Washington, D.C., Richmond, Baltimore, Harrisburg, and Pittsburgh, arriving in Cincinnati on 4 April. After visiting Louisville and St. Louis, they returned to Cincinnati and then went on to Columbus, Buffalo, and Niagara Falls. Entering Canada on 4 May, they saw Queenstown, Toronto, Kingston, Montreal, and Quebec before returning to New York at the beginning of June for a short excursion up the Hudson. They embarked for Liverpool from New York on the *George Washington* on 7 June, arriving back in London on the twenty-ninth.

In more than four months in North America, the couple attended dozens of balls and dinners in their honor and shook hands with thousands of strangers. They were bitten by fleas and hounded by intruders who had no regard for their privacy. Accompanied by George Putnam, hired in Boston as Dickens's secretary, they traveled by rail, steam, and canal boat, and by carriage, sometimes across rough "corduroy" roads. "We are constantly out two or three times in the evening," Catherine wrote Fanny from Boston. "The people are most hospitable, and we shall both be killed with kindness. . . . Sometimes we are quite knocked up, and long most ardently for dear Devonshire Terrace."[71]

In persuading Catherine to accompany her husband, Macready had purposely avoided the "selfish argument," though he was sure that many pleasures awaited her in "that grand country" and that she "*must* make herself happy in the thought of being able to *make such a tour in such a way!!*"[72]—that is, without the children. Indeed Catherine took pleasure in the tour, noting the sights and sounds that were new to her in writing home. "I daresay you can hardly realize (a favourite expression

---

69. ALS Daniel Maclise to Catherine Dickens, "Monday" [27 September 1841], MA 104, the Morgan Library & Museum, New York.

70. Catherine Dickens to Fanny Burnett, 30 January 1842, reprinted in Pilgrim 3:629.

71. Ibid.

72. ALS William Macready to Charles Dickens, 23 September 1841, HM 18553, Huntington Library, quoted in Pilgrim 2:391 n. 4.

here) seeing Peach trees in full blossom in March," she told Fred.[73] Honored as the wife of Charles Dickens, she received bouquets and tributes, including a poem written by John Quincy Adams that described his joy in meeting her. While she was disturbed by repeated intrusions on her privacy—by people who stared at her through windows and saw her in bed—she enjoyed more routine types of publicity. She joked to Maclise about her "heavenly portrait" in the *Extra Boz Herald,* which bore no resemblance to her whatsoever,[74] and she made her stage debut in Montreal before an audience of six hundred, acting the part of Amy Templeton alongside her husband in a private amateur production of John Poole's farce *Deaf as a Post.*

Yet from the start of the tour Catherine described herself as "*very* homesick,"[75] and all her enjoyments were tempered by her anxieties about the children and her sense of guilt at having left them behind. She traveled with Maclise's sketch (fig. 8), which she displayed in her hotel rooms or unpacked at night when she and her companions were on the road. Despite her repeated assurances to Fred that she trusted him with her "treasures,"[76] and her reiterated thanks to the Macreadys for overseeing them, she sometimes feared, not unreasonably, that she might never see them again: "You cannot think how our thoughts flew to our precious children . . . during that terrible night," Catherine told Fanny, recounting the storm that nearly wrecked the *Britannia.* "God grant that the darlings are well,—how my heart yearns for them!"[77] Writing to Fred in January, she lamented, "How often I long to have even on[e] look at my beloved darlings," asking him to "tell [her] all about them" when he next wrote.[78] In March she told him, "It is impossible to feel anxious about my darlings, when they have such a kind and anxious friend in you," a point she repeated in April: "How easy and happy we feel about our treasures as we hear from all . . . accounts of their health and happiness." But adding, "God grant it may be so till we return,"[79] Catherine voiced her unease. Her persistent fears were compounded by what she considered her "truancy." As she told the

73. ALS Catherine Dickens to Frederick Dickens, [22 March 1842], The Henry W. and Albert A. Berg Collection of English and American Literature, New York Public Library.

74. ALS Catherine Dickens to Daniel Maclise, 22 March 1842, Charles Dickens Museum, London. Catherine's letter is added to one her husband wrote.

75. Ibid.

76. ALS Catherine Dickens to Frederick Dickens, 4 April 1842, The Henry W. and Albert A. Berg Collection of English and American Literature, New York Public Library.

77. Catherine Dickens to Fanny Burnett, 30 January 1842, reprinted in Pilgrim 3:629.

78. ALS Catherine Dickens to Frederick Dickens, 30 January 1842, The Henry W. and Albert A. Berg Collection of English and American Literature, New York Public Library.

79. ALS Catherine Dickens to Frederick Dickens, 22 March and 4 April 1842, The Henry W. and Albert A. Berg Collection of English and American Literature, New York Public Library.

FIGURE 8. *Daniel Maclise, drawing of Charley, Mamie, Katey, and Walter Dickens (1841), Charles Dickens Museum, London.*

poet Samuel Rogers in March, "You may easily imagine . . . how often we long to see those dear little ones, who I almost fear will have forgotten their truant parents before we get back to them" (Pilgrim 3:163 n. 4).

The pleasures in which Catherine could freely indulge on the tour were not the selfish ones imagined by Macready but those of selflessness, derived from performing her duty to her husband and meeting his needs. Those needs were manifold. Cheering Dickens at the outset of their voyage, she made light of their cramped quarters on the *Britannia,* despite a painful toothache and swollen face, earning Forster's praise: "She deserves to be what you know she is so emphatically called—the Beloved," he told Maclise, describing the couple's departure.[80] Before Dickens hired Putnam, Catherine wrote letters from his dictation; she intercepted "persevering bore[s]" and saw to social niceties with visitors and fellow travelers so that her husband could read and write in relative privacy (Pilgrim 3:177).[81] Knowing that she could "make all so much happier by the face she puts upon it," as Macready told Dickens in September, Catherine impressed her husband with her cheerful endurance of discomfort and exhaustion, proving a "perfectly game" companion. She was uncomplaining even when jolted painfully on backwoods roads, tied to the doors inside the carriage in an effort to minimize bruising. As Dickens told Forster in April:

> [Catherine] really has . . . made a *most admirable* traveller in every respect. She has never screamed or expressed alarm under circumstances that would have fully justified her in doing so, even in my eyes; has never given way to despondency or fatigue, though we have now been travelling incessantly, through a very rough country, for more than a month, and have been at times . . . most thoroughly tired; has always accommodated herself, well and cheerfully, to everything; and has pleased me very much. (Pilgrim 3:204–5)

Accommodating and cheerful, restrained despite alarms, Catherine pleased herself by pleasing Dickens.

In his letters home Dickens sometimes represented Catherine as "a kind of Queen" to his Albert, the pair holding court in "a perpetual Drawing Room" in the United States (Pilgrim 3:154, 151). But if Catherine was a queen, she was so in the sense outlined by John Ruskin in "Of Queens' Gardens" (1865)—a domestic paragon who brought "sweet order" to her realm.[82] Thus when Senator John Calhoun visited the Dickenses in Washington, Catherine "continu[ed] at her needle all the time . . . except when she took part in the conversation," impressing him as

80. ALS John Forster to Daniel Maclise, [3] January 1842, Charles Dickens Museum, London. Forster's letter is appended to that of Dickens to Maclise.

81. As a fellow passenger recalled, while Dickens treated most on the *Britannia* with reserve and "engaged in solitary rambles about the ship," Catherine "was far more socially inclined"; with a "little Scotch lady," she "generally held an informal after-dinner *levee* over a glass of punch or sherry." Pierre Morand, "Reminiscence of Charles Dickens' First Visit to America," reprinted in Noel C. Peyrouton, "Re: Memoir of an *American Notes* Original," *Dickens Studies* 4 (March 1968): 27.

82. John Ruskin, "Of Queens' Gardens," in *Sesame and Lilies,* vol. 18 of *The Works of John Ruskin,* Library Edition, 39 vols. (London: George Allen, 1905), 121–22.

an "amiable and sensible" woman, not a regal one.[83] Dickens's "Queen" proved an unassuming and self-deprecating consort, describing herself as "quite an object" with her face swollen from her toothache in the first days of the trip and deferring to her husband's powers, literary and otherwise. "I will not pretend to give you any account, dear Fan, of the manners and customs, and so on," she wrote her sister-in-law from Boston, "as my powers of description are not great, and you will have it some day or other so much the better from Charles." "The reception Charles has met with is something not to be described. He is perfectly worshipped, and crowds follow him in the streets even." "I . . . don't know what I should have done had it not been for the great kindness and composure of my dear Charles," she told Fanny, recounting her "terror" when the Atlantic storm "broke [their] paddle-boxes and the life-boat to pieces," and suggesting her own worshipful attitude.[84]

THE "INFLUENCE"

Catherine's most pointed expression of her reliance on her husband and her subject position as a wife was a nonverbal one: she allowed herself to be mesmerized by him twice on the American tour, willingly surrendering her will to his. Dickens wrote about the experience on 2 April—their sixth wedding anniversary and also Forster's birthday—a day the three always celebrated together. "The other night at Pittsburgh," he told his friend, "there being present only Mr. [Putnam] and the portrait-painter [George D'Almaine], Kate sat down, laughing, for me to try my hand upon her":

> I had been holding forth upon the subject [of mesmerism] rather luminously, and asserting that I thought I could exercise the influence, but had never tried. In six minutes, I magnetized her into hysterics, and then into the magnetic sleep. I tried again next night, and she fell into the slumber in little more than two minutes. . . . I can wake her with perfect ease; but I confess (not being prepared for anything so sudden and complete), I was on the first occasion rather alarmed. (Pilgrim 3:180)

Although Dickens begins by poking fun at his own bravado as he "hold[s] forth" and "assert[s]" himself, Catherine's response quickly justifies his claim to magnetic power. Implicitly measuring himself—and Catherine—against John Elliotson and *his* subjects at University College Hospital, Dickens underscores his remarkable

83. John Caldwell Calhoun to Mrs. Clemson, "Correspondence of John C. Calhoun," ed. J. F. Jameson, *Annual Report of the American Historical Association* 2 (1899): 506, quoted in Pilgrim 3:133 n. 7.

84. Catherine Dickens to Fanny Burnett, 30 January 1842, reprinted in Pilgrim 3:629.

success. Like Elliotson, whom he watched mesmerize patients in the hospital theater and from whom he learned the mesmerist's techniques, Dickens stages his magnetic "trial," exercising the influence in front of male spectators. But unlike Elliotson, who sometimes failed in attempts to wake the female subjects he displayed, Dickens wakes Catherine with the same "perfect ease" with which he magnetizes her.

At University College Hospital, Elliotson magnetized his best-known subjects, the O'Key sisters, to cure their epilepsy. As a result of their treatment, they seemed to gain unusual abilities. Mesmerism appeared to make them clairvoyant, enabling them to foretell the deaths of fellow patients, although Elliotson argued that in fact it simply heightened their sensory perceptions, allowing them to detect unhealthy bodily emissions that others could not.[85] But while Elliotson's demonstrations ostensibly served the ends of medical science and provided therapy to the young women it empowered, Dickens's demonstrations showcased his power alone, and as an end in itself. Unlike the O'Key sisters, Catherine was neither cured nor empowered when she was magnetized in Pittsburgh. Instead of experiencing heightened perceptions, she lost self-control, becoming hysterical and then unconscious. Her "hysterics" corresponded to the phase of "delirium" or excitement that typically preceded the deep sleep or "trance" of the magnetized state, although Dickens's term also conveys a sense of his subject's emotional weakness and volatility as a woman.

As the timing of Dickens's narration reveals, what Catherine and her husband were demonstrating in Pittsburgh was in effect her selfless submission to him under coverture. His portrait of Catherine's magnetized submission, included in his anniversary letter wishing Forster "many, many happy returns of the day," follows a comic description of marital sparring and insubordination on her part—when he and Catherine argued over whether or not Forster and Maclise would celebrate the day without them: "I say yes, but Kate says no" (Pilgrim 3:178). As Dickens knew, Catherine's very presence on the tour was a mark of her compliance with his wishes. But any nay-saying from her at all was impossible when Dickens tried his "hand upon her," placing her under "the influence," an apt symbol of their marital dynamic for their anniversary, Dickens suggests, and one he hopes will be enduring. Telling Macready of his "extraordinary success in magnetizing Kate," and using the celebratory language of his anniversary letter, Dickens hopes that his friend will "be a witness of that, many, many, many happy times" (Pilgrim 3:175).

Macready would testify to Dickens's success only once, and then at second hand, shortly after the couple returned to London. The relevant entry in Macready's diary reveals not only Dickens's "success in magnetizing Kate" but also his growing sphere of influence at Devonshire Terrace. Unable to dine there on 12 July,

85. Winter, *Mesmerized*, 78.

Macready joined the party in the evening to discover that "Dickens had been mesmerizing his wife and Miss Hogarth."[86] On their return home from North America, Catherine and her husband invited her sister Georgina to join their household and help with the children, who had seen their young aunt with Mrs. Hogarth while their parents were away.

Catherine's intimate circle—and Dickens's sphere of influence—could expand to include Georgina and their marriage remain a happy one. But that expansion had its limits, and Catherine's willing submission to her husband depended on his understanding that fact. If he misunderstood, he would learn what Dr. Elliotson already knew: that even a powerful magnetic operator depended on the cooperation of his subjects, who might appear submissive and insensible but who exercised their own agency in becoming so and who could resist control in numerous ways.

As Alison Winter notes in discussing the Victorian practice of mesmerism, the magnetized subject, presumed to be "rendered powerless" by the operator, did not always prove as passive and mechanical as expected and "sometimes seemed to seize control."[87] She might acquire unusual powers during an experiment, becoming clairvoyant; but she might also exercise a transgressive social license while magnetized, or use her experience to her own ends, challenging the authority of her mesmerist. So Elliotson discovered in 1838, when Elizabeth O'Key publicly mocked him in front of a crowded audience in the hospital theater, proved embarrassingly willful, and was soon exposed as a fraud, discrediting him in the eyes of many of his colleagues.[88] Elliotson's experience—and that of his patient—suggests that we need to look carefully at the dynamics of magnetism from *Catherine's* point of view and, despite her obliging and compliant posture, recognize the element of volition and the possibility for resistance in her submissive and entranced state.

While Catherine did not turn against her mesmerist as Elizabeth O'Key turned on Elliotson, she could resist as well as submit to his powers, rousing herself when she thought they were being misused. Between their first residence on the continent in 1844–45 and their second in 1846–47, Catherine did just that, thwarting Dickens's desires and effectively putting an end to their intimacy with the de la Rues. Revealing the complexities of her position, Catherine broke her marital trance in order to insist that she rather than Madame de la Rue be the primary subject of her husband's magnetic powers.

86. Macready, *Diaries,* 2:179–80.

87. Winter, *Mesmerized,* 23.

88. For a detailed discussion of Elliotson's experiments with Elizabeth and Jane O'Key, see ibid., 79–104.

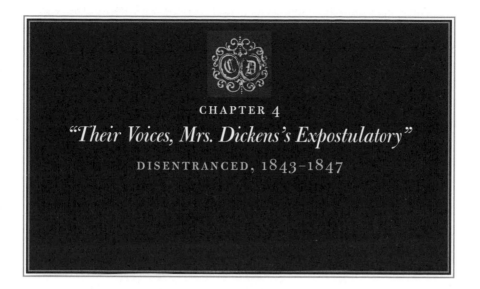

Finally, the task remained of recovering Okey from the state of "delirium,"
in which she had continued throughout the two hours and a half of
experiments; but this proved to be rather difficult of accomplishment....
"Shall you awake of yourself?"—"No."
"How then?"—"You must wake me."
"In what way?"—"By rubbing my neck."
—"University College Hospital: Animal Magnetism," *Lancet*,
26 May 1838

"SHE COLOURED UP, BUT LAUGHED IT OFF"

For Catherine, the process of awakening from a trance varied. Mesmerized by Dickens in Pittsburgh in 1842, she awoke easily, he claimed—most likely by means of the sweeping hand movements or the facial massaging he had seen other mesmerists use for that purpose. When she was en route to La Scala, Italy, in 1845, Catherine's coming to consciousness was more protracted, with Dickens "rousing her, with some difficulty," after she had unwittingly succumbed to his magnetic spell. But her awakening in its broadest sense—as an experience of disentrancement with her husband and with certain aspects of her married life—was an even more difficult process, one initiated without the usual invitation or command from the mesmerist and lacking the familiar sequence of phases. Defying John Elliotson's power during their public demonstration in May 1838, Elizabeth O'Key refused to awaken when he instructed her to do so, instead stipulating to his clerk, Mr. Wood, the conditions under which she would emerge from her trance.[1] In the mid-1840s Catherine, too, challenged the authority of her mesmerist—but by rousing herself rather than remaining entranced. Awakening without the intervention of her husband—indeed, against his will—she objected to his magnetic influence over Augusta de la Rue in Genoa. Faced with the prospect of a second sojourn in Italy and a renewed attempt on Dickens's part to cure his "patient" magnetically, Catherine insisted that he tell the de la Rues of her objections and distance himself from them. He was to consider and explain her "state of mind" rather than alter or control it (Pilgrim 7:224).

Despite this act of self-assertion, the signs that Catherine was emerging from her marital trance were usually more subtle—manifested in anxieties over childbearing, for example, and in her pursuit of friendships with women who valued self-fulfillment and self-expression over self-sacrifice. Seeking out Christiana Thompson, a woman Dickens particularly disliked, Catherine declined to adopt her husband's opinions of her friend. Failing to observe what Dickens did and to echo his disapproval, she dissolved the "community of sensation" that characterized the magnetized state and that achieved "oneness" by replacing the subject's perceptions with her mesmerist's.

Before Catherine sought to end her husband's intimacy with Madame de la Rue, instances in which she "declared" herself (Pilgrim 7:224) in opposition to him were scarce. She was more inclined to *show* than to state her disagreement with his views and her disapproval of his actions: through tears and embarrassed blushes, for example. When Dickens hotly argued with Forster at Doughty Street in August 1840 and suggested that his friend leave the house, both Macready and Catherine criticized him for it—the actor by drawing from Dickens "the admission that he had spoken in passion," Catherine by leaving the painful scene "in tears."[2] When her husband treated *her* rudely, Catherine was as likely to blush as to cry. Having enjoyed reading some stories by Andrew Picken, her friend Emma's deceased father, "a Scottish author of considerable reputation," Catherine recommended them to her husband in Emma's presence. "He looked his distaste at the idea," Picken recalled. "When she pressed him 'just to read one tale, such a beautifully written one, and very short,' he turned and walked off abruptly, muttering—'I hate Scotch stories, and everything else Scotch.' I thought this was very unkind to his wife as well as to me, as she was Scotch too. She coloured up, but laughed it off."[3]

1. Alison Winter, *Mesmerized: Powers of Mind in Victorian Britain* (Chicago: University of Chicago Press, 1998), 75–76.

2. William Macready, *The Diaries of William Charles Macready,* ed. William Toynbee, 2 vols. (London: Chapman and Hall, 1912), 2:74.

3. [Eleanor Christian], "Reminiscences of Charles Dickens. From a Young Lady's Diary," *Englishwoman's Domestic Magazine* (1871): 341.

Despite such rebuffs, Catherine could feel justified in pressing her views, particularly those that concerned the children. Having resisted her months-long separation from them only to be persuaded to accept it, she returned from the American tour to discover that her objections had been well founded—that a half year without their parents was almost too much for some of them to bear. It was not that the children *forgot* their "truant" parents, as Catherine put it to Samuel Rogers, but that they remembered them all too clearly. To her dismay, six-year-old Charley, on first catching sight of his parents, fell into convulsions after telling Catherine that he was "too glad," and both Charles Morgan, a surgeon, and Elliotson were quickly summoned to his aid. "Joy had quite overthrown his system," Elliotson explained once Charley recovered, and "perfectly turned his brain" (Pilgrim 3:295, 302). Although none of the other children showed quite as dramatically how much they had missed their parents, Mamie recalled that they had been "most miserable" in the care of the stern Macreadys and that two-year-old Katey would cry whenever she was being dressed at Clarence Place, "declaring over and over again that she would 'not doe.'"[4] For the future, Catherine would try to balance more equally her obligations as a wife with her duties as a mother.

The illness Charley suffered on his parents' return left Dickens with the affectionate sense that his eldest son was "a very queer fellow" (Pilgrim 3:295), different from and more sensitive than most other children (fig. 9). Over the years, Charley's "difference," as Dickens saw it, became more troubling to him, less endearing than alarming; it also became a subject on which he and Catherine disagreed. Arranging for Charley's schooling in 1845, with Angela Burdett Coutts of the Coutts banking family acting as the boy's sponsor, Dickens suggested that he understood, as Catherine did not, the problem with Charley's character—when he explained why he thought it best for his son to attend nearby King's College School rather than board at Marlborough. "We have no reason to think that Charley has anything but a vigorous constitution," he told Miss Coutts. "But when he is in full school employment, there is a strange kind of *fading* comes over him sometimes: the like of which, I don't think I ever saw. Whether the child is anxious at his book, or excited at his Play, or what, I cannot make out. But I see it occasionally, in a very remarkable degree—more plainly, I think, than his mother does, although I am by no means open to such impressions in general" (Pilgrim 4:442).

In her own exchanges with Miss Coutts, as in her correspondence with others, Catherine represents "little Charley" as an utterly normal boy, as dependable as he

4. Mamie Dickens, *Charles Dickens, by his Eldest Daughter* (London: Cassell, 1911), 68, quoted in Pilgrim 3:302 n. 1.

FIGURE 9. *George Richmond, portrait of Charley Dickens (1852),*
Charles Dickens Museum, London.

is dear, happy in his amusements and eager to play with other children.[5] We might interpret Catherine's not mentioning Charley's "strange…*fading*" as a mark of her fond blindness as a mother—her failure or unwillingness to see what her husband perceived. Yet the problem Dickens saw in Charley might as easily be taken as a sign of the *father's* blindness, not the mother's, particularly if we accept as valid Catherine's hopes for the children, which differed from his. Catherine wanted her children to be happy, playful, and loving; Dickens wanted his sons to be earnest, ambitious, and sharply focused—like their father rather than their mother, he later said. By the time Charley was fourteen, Dickens had redefined the "fading" he had perceived in his seven-year-old as a lack of manly energy and drive, a condition his eldest son inherited from Catherine, he claimed. "[Charley] has less fixed purpose and energy than I could have supposed possible in my son," Dickens told Miss Coutts in 1854. "He is not aspiring, or imaginative in his own behalf. With all the tenderer and better qualities which he inherits from his mother, he inherits an indescribable lassitude of character—a very serious thing in a man" (Pilgrim 7:245). What Charley had failed to become, Dickens proceeds to make clear, was his father at fourteen: "When I told him this morning…that when I was his age, I was teaching myself a very difficult art [shorthand], and walking miles every day to practise it all day long in the Courts of Law; he seemed to think I must have been one of the most unaccountable of youths" (Pilgrim 7:245).

Of course, Dickens *was* "one of the most unaccountable of youths"—unusually driven, energetic, and successful. Despite his brilliance as a novelist, his perception of lassitude and incapacity in those around him shows that his imagination failed him as a husband and father, and with it the sympathetic understanding of others that imagination enables. Where he could not successfully influence and control family members, he judged and criticized, a pattern particularly evident in his marital relations.

Ten months after their return from North America, Catherine conceived their fifth child, Francis, who was born on 15 January 1844. Having conceived Charley in April 1836, Mamie in June 1837, Katey in February 1839, and Walter in May 1840, Catherine was pregnant for part of every year from 1836 through 1841. Until the spring of 1843, however, she had not been pregnant for more than two years, including her six months abroad, a prolonged interval that may have resulted from planning on the Dickenses' part (see chapter 5). While she probably did not believe that her childbearing had ended with Walter, she had been free from its constraints

5. ALS Catherine Dickens to Angela Burdett Coutts, 1 February 1847, MA 1352, the Morgan Library & Museum, New York; Catherine Dickens to Mrs. [Yeats] Brown, [May 1845], reprinted in F. Yeats-Brown, "Dickens in Genoa," *Spectator,* 22 September 1928, 358.

for a time and viewed her fifth pregnancy with a degree of apprehension that perhaps signaled regrets she left otherwise unacknowledged. She perceived the pregnancy as physically difficult and, feeling "not very well" in her third trimester, "[went] out very little," sending her sixteen-year-old sister to social engagements in her place.[6]

While Dickens recognized that Catherine was "not quite as well as usual" toward the end of her pregnancy—"nervous and dull" and "exceedingly depressed and frightened" (Pilgrim 4:3, 27)—he was impatient with his wife, whose anxiety he found self-indulgent. "Her health is perfectly good," he told Harvard professor Cornelius Felton, "and I am sure she might rally, if she would" (Pilgrim 4:3). For Catherine, the birth of a fifth child would significantly change the tenor of life, adding a newborn to the family. The event had fewer immediate consequences for Dickens, and he joked with Felton about one of them—the temporary suspension of sexual activity with Catherine's late-term pregnancy and confinement. "I shall be much relieved when it is well over," he confided to his friend. "In the mean time total abstinence from oysters"—thought to be an aphrodisiac—"seems to be the best thing for me" (Pilgrim 4:3).

With the birth of Frank, Mrs. Hogarth and Elizabeth Dickens arrived at Devonshire Terrace, as did a wet nurse for the baby and a "monthly nurse" for Catherine; typically, middle-class mothers had the aid of their own attendant during the month that followed delivery. Georgina helped with the four older children and assumed some of Catherine's domestic responsibilities, writing letters for Dickens in her stead. Dickens made out his first check to "Miss Hogarth," for £5, two weeks after Catherine gave birth.[7] Catherine herself did not receive a check from her husband for more than six weeks after Frank's birth, although she was sitting in the drawing room within two weeks and was downstairs within three, joining guests to celebrate Dickens's thirty-second birthday. "Both she and Baby . . . are getting on capitally," Georgina told Thomas Beard at the end of January,[8] though Dickens found Catherine's recovery cautious and slow if steady (Pilgrim 4:33, 36). "I was coming to you yesterday, and brought Kate to walk half the way," he told his brother-in-law Henry Austin on 7 March. "She walked so impossibly slowly, that I was benighted at Covent Garden Market, and came back again" (Pilgrim 4:64). At her request, Dickens

6. ALS Catherine Dickens to Miss Holskamp, [?8 January 1844], Fales Library & Special Collections, New York University.

7. Charles Dickens, Esq., Account Ledger, Coutts & Co., London.

8. Georgina Hogarth to Thomas Beard, 31 January 1844, in *Dickens to His Oldest Friend: The Letters of a Lifetime,* ed. Walter Dexter (London: Putnam, 1932), 272.

asked Francis Jeffrey to be the baby's godfather, and the Scotsman was happy to grant "that most flattering wish" of "dear Kate."[9]

By 2 April 1844, her eighth wedding anniversary, Catherine had returned to her usual pace of activity and celebrated the day with her husband, Georgina, Forster, and Maclise in Richmond. But later that week she was reminded of the pitfalls of wifely dependence when Elizabeth Smithson's husband, Charles, thirty-nine years old, was discovered to have died intestate after a month-long illness and to have dropped a life insurance policy worth £3,000, leaving his wife with a one-year-old daughter and uncertain about her financial circumstances. Writing to Catherine on 6 April from Yorkshire, where he had gone for the funeral, Dickens noted that "the estate will not yield more than two or three thousand pounds" but assured her that, with "£330 a year, of her own"—and the same guaranteed to her sister Milly—the two women would undoubtedly have enough to maintain themselves "genteelly" (Pilgrim 4:97).

Along with Dickens and Georgina, Catherine began Italian lessons with Luigi Mariotti to prepare for an extended residence in Italy. Dickens had decided to move their household there for a year, hoping to live more cheaply but also, after disappointing sales of *Martin Chuzzlewit,* to take a break from fiction and instead write a second travel book, along the lines of *American Notes.* Since they would be taking the children with them, Catherine could now enjoy the prospect of living abroad. In addition to Georgina, three servants would join them: Anne Brown, Charlotte Stubbey, and their cook Jane, hired since their return from North America. As their departure date approached, Catherine rescheduled lessons and declined invitations, describing to Mariotti and others her state of "constant bustle." The Dickenses had "very unexpectedly let [their] house to a widow lady" toward the end of May, Catherine told Helen Tagart, whose husband, Edward, was a Unitarian minister, and they had abruptly moved to 9 Osnaburgh Terrace, rented for the few weeks preceding their journey. As her friend could imagine, she and her family "had . . . enough to do," having moved with "only a few days warning."[10]

Nonetheless, Catherine helped introduce the aspiring young pianist Christiana Weller to London audiences before leaving Devonshire Terrace. Ten years younger than Catherine and two years older than Georgina, Christiana was the second of five daughters of T. E. and Betty Weller. Raised in Cheltenham and Liverpool, she was

9. Francis Jeffrey to Charles Dickens, 1 February 1844, in *Life of Lord Jeffrey,* ed. Lord Cockburn, 2 vols. (Edinburgh: Adam and Charles Black, 1852), 2:382.

10. ALS Catherine Dickens to Luigi Mariotti, [26 May 1844], Historical Society of Pennsylvania; ALS Catherine Dickens to Mrs. Tagart, 1 June 1844, Staples B55, Charles Dickens Museum, London.

trained as a concert pianist by her mother and performed with Sigismond Thalberg in Dublin in 1842 before playing for Liverpool and Manchester audiences in 1843 and 1844. Dickens met her three months before Catherine did, in February 1844, when she played a piano solo at the annual "Soirée" of the Mechanics' Institution in Liverpool, where he was speaking. Struck by the "spiritual young creature," for whom he conceived an "incredible feeling" and mistakenly predicted "an early death" (Pilgrim 4:55), Dickens sent her his personal copy of Tennyson's *Poems,* joked about wanting to marry her, and praised her effusively in letters to her father and to T. J. Thompson. Thompson, who had accompanied Dickens to Liverpool, soon declared himself Christiana's admirer and married her in October 1845.[11]

When T. E. Weller asked Dickens for help in launching Christiana in London, Catherine became involved, arranging for her father and William Ayrton to hear the eighteen-year-old play and suggesting possible venues for her London debut. On 23 May, at a large "musical party" the Ayrtons hosted, Christiana was introduced to the 250 guests by Dickens and "played charmingly on the P. F.," William Ayrton noted, "delight[ing] everybody as much by her performance as her great beauty."[12] Neither Catherine nor her parents were struck by any "ethereal" quality in Christiana, as Dickens was. But they admired her and her abilities, and George Hogarth praised "the lightness, rapidity, and brilliance of her fingers" in a *Morning Chronicle* review after her first London performance in June.[13] To Mrs. Hogarth, Christiana resembled her own daughter Mary; Catherine's mother put the young performer "in ecstasies" with the "charming compliment."[14] Struck by the similarity herself, Catherine went on to form an important friendship with Christiana, one that brought her marriage into conjunction with a very different type of union and highlighted the self-abnegation required of her as Dickens's wife.

"UNHAPPY IN THE GENOA TIME"

With their entourage of children and servants, and their courier (or guide) Louis Roche, the Dickenses left London for Genoa on 2 July 1844, traveling in an

---

11. David H. Paroissien provides a detailed discussion of the relationships among the Dickenses and the Wellers in "Charles Dickens and the Weller Family," *Dickens Studies Annual* 2 (1972): 1–38. Rosemary Bodenheimer insightfully analyzes the dynamics of the "Christiana Weller Affair," with its "triangulated desires and rivalries," in *Knowing Dickens* (Ithaca: Cornell University Press, 2007), 101–5.

12. William Ayrton, annotated abstracts from memoranda of Frances (Fanny) Ayrton, 1836–1847, British Library, Add. 60373, f. 48.

13. [George Hogarth], *Morning Chronicle,* 12 June 1844, quoted in Pilgrim 4:143 n. 3.

14. Christiana Weller Thompson, 1845 diary, MS Meynell Family Papers, Greatham.

enormous carriage through Paris and Marseilles. Two weeks later they arrived at the Villa Bagnerello in Albaro, outside Genoa, the home selected for them by Angus Fletcher, who was living in Carrara. Despite its ample space, its view of the Mediterranean, and its vineyard, the villa was an uncomfortable choice and unfit for winter residence. For the first month Katey was sick with a bad throat, and Anne spent part of every evening killing fleas in infested bedrooms. In September, several days into a fortnight's visit, Fred nearly drowned in the bay as the children, with Georgina and Charlotte, shouted for help; he was saved by nearby fishermen.

By the third week in September the family had moved from Albaro to Genoa proper, renting the Palazzo Peschiere, with frescoed walls, a grand *sala,* sea views, fishponds, and beautiful gardens. There they were visited by Edward and Helen Tagart, among other friends from home, while forming a new circle: Timothy Yeats Brown, British consul at Genoa, and his wife, Stuarta; Charles Gibbs, the Dickenses' banker; Mr. and Mrs. Thomas Curry; Sir George and Hester Craufurd; and Émile and Augusta de la Rue. Émile was a Swiss banker resident in Genoa; his wife, an Englishwoman and invalid of sorts, was the former Miss Granet.

With Georgina, Catherine drove through the countryside, her husband sometimes walking the distance they covered. In town they went to the theater and the opera, where they had a private box. From her father-in-law Catherine received word of Fanny Burnett, who was hoping that a summer on the Isle of Man would improve her health. From Christiana Weller, Catherine heard that Bessy Shaw, Christiana's older sister, wanted Dickens to become a godfather to her baby girl. Catherine had news from the Hogarths as well. Despite her father's work as a journalist, the family was again in financial difficulties. Through Forster, Dickens fulfilled some "commissions" for his in-laws, "the main subject" of one of his September letters (Pilgrim 4:194, 196). When Dickens saw Mrs. Hogarth on a December visit to London, he wrote her a check for £6.9.6.[15]

Whatever anxieties she may have harbored about the Hogarths and their necessities, Catherine was soon reminded of her husband's needs—when he repeated to her, not once or twice but "three or four times over," the details of a dream about her sister Mary (Pilgrim 4:196). Catherine knew that her husband had dreamed of Mary before, virtually every night for months after Mary's death. At the time, he hesitated to tell Catherine of the dreams, apparently concerned that he might sharpen her sense of loss. Once he did tell her, however, in February 1838, he stopped dreaming of Mary altogether.[16]

15. Charles Dickens, Esq., Account Ledger, Coutts & Co., London.

16. "As she had been my wife's sister, and had died suddenly in our house," Dickens explained to Dr. Thomas Stone in 1851, "I forbore to allude to these dreams" (Pilgrim 6:277).

But on one of the first mornings at the Peschiere—perhaps after their very first night in their new bedroom—Catherine was urgently awakened at dawn by her husband, who had been weeping. For much of the night he had been kept awake by a pain in his back, a recurring rheumatic ailment. Once asleep, he told her, he had again dreamed of her dead sister, who appeared to him as a spirit, a being he referred to as "it," not "she." Catherine learned that it was clad in blue like the Madonna, its facial features indistinct but its voice recognizable. When her husband reached out and called the spirit "Dear," it recoiled, "not being of [his] gross nature." Apologizing, he explained that "poor living creatures" were limited to such terminology; he believed the spirit understood his feelings. "Cut . . . to the heart" by the apparition, which was "full of compassion and sorrow" for him, Dickens asked for a token of its visit. Told to form a wish—and deciding to form an unselfish one so as to keep the spirit from vanishing—he suppressed his own "hopes and anxieties" in favor of his mother-in-law's. "'Mrs. Hogarth is surrounded with great distresses,'" he told the spirit, not thinking to say "'your mother' as to a mortal creature—'will you extricate her?' 'Yes.' 'And her extrication is to be a certainty to me, that this has really happened?' 'Yes.'" Again delaying the spirit's departure, Dickens asked it to identify "the True religion," suggesting that "'perhaps the Roman Catholic is the best.'" "'For *you*,' said the Spirit, full of such heavenly tenderness for me, that I felt as if my heart would break; 'for *you*, it is the best!'" Awaking in tears, Dickens woke Catherine, recounting to her repeatedly his dream (Pilgrim 4:196).

Our knowledge of *Catherine's* dreams is much more limited than our knowledge of her husband's. In October 1849 she "dreamed all . . . night that Rogers was learning to dance," Dickens told Angela Burdett Coutts (Pilgrim 5:628), and earlier that year he described to Macready her visions under the influence of chloroform. But we do not know if Catherine ever dreamed of Mary, nor do we have a record of her thoughts on Dickens's dreams. At the Peschiere she was asked to bear witness to the spirit vision of her husband, who wanted to remember it as accurately as possible. If the couple discussed its details and meaning, as Dickens and Forster did by letter, her part in that discussion has been lost.

To judge from what we know of the sisters and their relationship, however, it seems likely that Catherine was struck by the difference between Dickens's vision of Mary and her own. Soon after Mary's death, Catherine imagined her sister as "an angel . . . only too good for this world," yet it was as a person of *this* world that Catherine cherished her—arch, vivacious, irreverent, "never look[ing] so lovely" as on

---

Their meaning for Dickens is not my subject, although many critics have discussed them; see, for example, Michael Slater, *Dickens and Women* (London: J. M. Dent, 1983), 86–88.

the day before she died.[17] Catherine did not want to make a saint—or a Madonna—out of her dead sister any more than she wanted to lose her mother to the more distant figure identified to Mary's spirit as "Mrs. Hogarth." That was her husband's vision, not hers. Mary may have been tender and compassionate in life, but those were not her leading traits, and she did not center her affections on her brother-in-law, despite Dickens's wishful imaginings ("for *you* . . . for *you*"). In the months before her death, Mary concerned herself with her sister and infant nephew; their needs, not her brother-in-law's, were primary. But Catherine had long recovered from the postpartum distress that worried her sister, and now Dickens seemed the one in need. Despite his selfless wish on behalf of Mrs. Hogarth, Dickens himself was the object of pity and compassion in his dream, his "hopes and anxieties" acknowledged, if unexpressed. On that morning at the Peschiere, Catherine did what she could to help her husband, listening to his recital as many times as he wished.

If Catherine had any trouble recalling Mary's nature or the irreverent coterie they formed with their like-minded cousin, seventeen-year-old Georgina was there to remind her that the Hogarth women were more likely to be cutting or sarcastic in their humor than pitying or compassionate in their glance. Georgina was in fact causing her brother-in-law some concern in Genoa, in the humor he felt she was misdirecting toward their visitor Susan Atkins, the sister of Kitty Macready. Writing to Catherine from Parma, having embarked on a tour of northern Italy with Roche, Dickens warned her that, in sending comical messages about their guest to Forster, Georgina "does a glaringly foolish and unnecessary silliness, and places huge means of misrepresentation in very willing hands." Catherine, like her sister, was "too easily run away with . . . by the irritation and displeasure of the moment," he told her, reminding her to overlook their guest's "inanities," whatever her "natural dislike" of them. "I should never forgive myself or you," he warned, "if the smallest drop of coldness or misunderstanding were created between me and Macready, by means so monstrously absurd." Unless Susan was properly chaperoned, he refused to permit Catherine and Georgina to leave her to meet him in Milan. Instead they must bring her along, Dickens wrote, twice underlining his command as he sometimes had in letters to Catherine during their courtship: "And observe. *I positively object, and say No, to her going to Rome under the protection of any entire stranger. I cannot allow it to be, until I have seen Macready*" (Pilgrim 4:215).

After Dickens toured the north and briefly met the sisters in Milan, Catherine took charge of their household, Dickens having gone on to London to read his new

17. ALS Catherine Dickens to Mary Scott Hogarth, 30 May [1837], D. Jacques Benoliel Collection of the Letters of Charles Dickens, 86-2740, Rare Book Department, Free Library of Philadelphia.

Christmas story, *The Chimes,* to friends in early December before visiting Paris and the Macreadys, who were staying there. When Catherine received his letter from Parma, the Genoa household had been under her supervision for the first two days of a projected six weeks; for that purpose she had received a portion of the £400 Dickens obtained from his Coutts account in October.[18] But despite his absence, Dickens continued to direct Catherine's actions. Whether writing from Parma, Fribourg, Paris, or London, he made his wishes known to her, entertaining her with reports of his travels while also telling her to keep things as they were. "Don't fail to let me know," he urged, asking for details of the children's lessons, and later commending her for an "excellent" letter that supplied them (Pilgrim 4:229, 234). From London, Dickens described the efforts of others to please and serve him. "With that winning manner" which she knew, he wrote her, he had persuaded his illustrators to rework their designs for his story, one sign of his power to move those around him. "If you had seen Macready last night—undisguisedly sobbing…as I read [*The Chimes*]— you would have felt (as I did) what a thing it is to have Power" (Pilgrim 4:234–35).

In what became his strongest show of "Power" during their year abroad, Dickens set out to cure Augusta de la Rue of her nervous illness in an extended series of magnetic sessions which weakened his influence over his own wife as it strengthened his hold on another's.[19] Considered a victim of "shattered nerves" by Dickens (Pilgrim 4:254), and suffering from *tic douloureaux* (he termed her disorder "tic in the brain" [Pilgrim 12:443]), Madame de la Rue first submitted to his magnetic influence on 23 December, three days after his return to Genoa from London and Paris. By 27 December he had treated her a second time, and for the next three weeks their sessions took place daily. Leaving Catherine for the de la Rues' in the late morning, he would put Augusta into a magnetic sleep and then ask her about her visionary surroundings, encouraging her to confront her fears. He believed that she might eventually go mad if unable to defeat the "bad phantom" that haunted her dreams, an intimidating and demonic male figure who caused her considerable mental anguish but whom he hoped to expose as a "powerless shadow" through mesmerism (Pilgrim 4:264). Before he and Catherine left Genoa with Roche on 19 January for an extended tour of Italy, Dickens arranged for a March reunion with the de la Rues in Rome and, meanwhile, for daily magnetic sessions to be held long distance, at eleven every morning. It was during one of these sessions in

18. Charles Dickens, Esq., Account Ledger, Coutts & Co., London.

19. On Dickens's sessions with Augusta de la Rue, see Margaret Flanders Darby, "Dickens and Women's Stories: 1845–1848 (Part One)," *Dickens Quarterly* 17 (2000): 69, 72; and Fred Kaplan, *Dickens and Mesmerism: The Hidden Springs of Fiction* (Princeton: Princeton University Press, 1975), 74–105.

late January, carried on without Catherine's knowledge, that she was inadvertently mesmerized, as Dickens told Émile.

It is unclear at what point Catherine began to object to her husband's arrangements with the de la Rues and what she perceived as his improper intimacy with another woman. She may have questioned her husband's behavior or that of his "patient" before she and Dickens left Genoa on their travels, since Madame de la Rue "unaccountably" proposed a halt to her treatment in early January, at a gathering where she and Catherine met (Pilgrim 4:259). If Catherine hoped that her husband would lose interest in the case once they headed for Carrara, Pisa, and Rome, she was disappointed. Dickens remained preoccupied with Madame de la Rue and her condition, frequently exchanging detailed letters with her and Émile. Although Catherine may not have seen much, if any, of their correspondence, she saw or heard enough to make her uncomfortable. In his letters, certainly, Dickens described his relationship with Madame de la Rue in terms that suited a romantic or marital bond. Augusta was "yielding" to Dickens, trusting to him, confiding in him; he was agonized by their separation and troubled by his loss of influence over her (Pilgrim 4:249, 259). He "thought continually about her, both awake and asleep," for days on end; "her being [was] somehow a part of [him]" (Pilgrim 4:264).

The union of mesmerist and subject did not suspend the intimacies of husband and wife; Catherine conceived her sixth child, Alfred, in late January or early February, while the Dickenses were on their travels and her husband was attempting to magnetize Madame de la Rue from the road. But Catherine's continued intimacy with her husband did not reconcile her to his magnetic "oneness" with Augusta, whose own husband shared some of Catherine's unease. Once the de la Rues arrived in Rome, Émile called Dickens to his wife's side in the middle of the night, hoping to curtail her sufferings. Yet he feared that Dickens doubted his attachment to Augusta; feeling powerless, he deeply regretted that it was left to another man to mesmerize his wife and "grieved at not being able to exert the influence" over her (Pilgrim 4:263, 323).

Catherine remained a lively companion through the winter, making the most of her travels—climbing the Leaning Tower, throwing sugarplums to crowds during the Roman carnival, attending High Mass at St. Peter's, watching the dancer Fanny Cerrito perform. After Georgina joined them in Naples in mid-February, Catherine and her sister accompanied Dickens on a nighttime ascent of Mount Vesuvius, the volcano then forming a new cone and spewing fire, cinders, and ashes. While Dickens and the guides walked, the two women rode on horses and were carried on litters most of the way up but hiked in the steepest regions and were forced by icy conditions to descend the steep, glazed surface on foot, as part of a human chain. For nearly one week before and after their ascent, Dickens failed to reserve the eleven o'clock hour for Madame de la Rue, as if her case had become less important to him. But that changed with their return to Rome in early March and the de la Rues' arrival there.

Catherine was distressed—so much so that nine years later, when he revisited Italy with Wilkie Collins and artist Augustus Egg, Dickens could still refer to the behavior that "made [her] unhappy in the Genoa time," although he considered her response an unreasonable overreaction and his preoccupation an example of the intensity that helped make him a celebrated writer (Pilgrim 7:224). Whether or not Catherine was correct to criticize her husband's behavior in this instance, the influence he exercised over her was checked. She saw him misjudging and misusing his powers and would not watch silently while he did so. The precise timing of her request is uncertain, but she ultimately "constrained [Dickens] to make [a] painful declaration . . . to the De la Rue's [*sic*]" of her viewpoint (Pilgrim 7:224), although it was probably clear already. The following year Catherine accepted Dickens's suggestion of Lausanne as the site of their next continental residence while refusing to consider Genoa and stipulating that they would not venture south of France.

By April, when they returned to the Peschiere, Catherine's pregnancy had been acknowledged. Her husband "hadn't reckoned on [it]" (Pilgrim 4:301); but the more surprising news was received by Catherine from Jane and Charlotte: neither woman would remain in her service at Devonshire Terrace. On 8 May, Jane told her mistress that she would instead be marrying a Frenchman, the local governor's cook; the couple hoped to settle in Genoa and open a restaurant. Charlotte, too, had become engaged—to a Mr. Johnson, a servant of Sir George Craufurd. In July, Dickens secured a position for him with his publishers Bradbury and Evans.

Against Catherine's objections, Dickens continued to mesmerize Madame de la Rue. As if to turn the tables on his wife and place *her* in the wrong, he threatened to cancel a reading of *A Christmas Carol,* to be hosted by the Yeats Browns in early June, because Catherine hadn't told him of their plan to include strangers in the audience. He was more careful of his privacy than she was, he implied, and wished to avoid any type of "exhibition" (Pilgrim 4:317). While Catherine, with Georgina and the servants, was busy packing for their 9 June departure, Dickens took refuge with the de la Rues, watching the commotion from their window. When Catherine and Georgina, en route to England, went to Antwerp from Brussels for a day with Forster and Maclise, who had joined them, Dickens remained at their hotel; he wished "to write to Madame De la Rue and [Émile], and read [their] letters in peace." Looking forward to another residence in Genoa and another chance to cure Augusta, he told Émile that he "had no heart" to join the others, unable to forget his "Italian wanderings" with the couple (Pilgrim 4:324). Before a year had passed, he was forced to explain that Catherine—"never very well" in Genoa, he claimed—could "not be got to contemplate" a return there and to concede that for now, his influence had failed him in that quarter (Pilgrim 4:534).

To become a magnetic subject meant something different for Madame de la Rue than it did for Catherine Dickens, just as it varied, according to context, for Catherine herself. To willingly surrender her will to her husband had its satisfactions, since it brought the self-abnegating ideal within her reach. But to be magnetized unknowingly and collaterally, without her consent, in an effort aimed at another, was much less satisfying. It was to experience the pitfalls of wifely submission without the pleasures—to submit without getting credit for doing so—and to glimpse the potential for infidelity on Dickens's part.

For Madame de la Rue, mesmerism appears to have been more liberating than it was for Catherine: it promised to free her from the psychic "phantom" that enslaved her and from some of the constraints of marriage and propriety as well, even as it left her "subservient" to a man other than her husband (Pilgrim 4:260). For Christiana Thompson, a significant figure for Catherine in the mid- to late 1840s, mesmerism seems to have offered something else: a stage for her artistic and emotional susceptibilities. Hence her frustration when she experienced "the influence," only to have it abruptly withdrawn. In the winter of 1846, lodged in Genoa for a month, Christiana proved that she "should be an excellent subject for experiment," she noted in her diary, by quickly falling into a magnetic slumber induced by Émile de la Rue, who had apparently turned mesmerist since Dickens's departure. But "the moment [she] went off," she complained, she was "unfortunately . . . roused . . . up" by Émile and her husband, who took less pleasure than Dickens did in the spectacle of his entranced wife.[20]

Five months pregnant on her return to London in July 1845, with her sixth confinement still months away, Catherine was soon engaged with Elizabeth Smithson, Milly Thompson, and their prospective sister-in-law Christiana, with whom she had corresponded in Italy. The two seemed eager to pursue their connection. During Catherine's absence Christiana had moved to London with her parents and befriended the Hogarths. She and her mother opened a pianoforte academy in the spring of 1845, and Christiana was giving concerts as well as lessons, in some cases playing works she herself had composed, among them a "valse fantastique." After various starts and reversals, her courtship with Thompson led to their engagement shortly before the Dickenses returned from Italy, although the

20. Christiana Weller Thompson, 1846 diary, MS Meynell Family Papers, Greatham.

Wellers had qualms about letting their daughter sacrifice her musical training and career to marriage. By the end of July, Christiana, her fiancé, and his sisters had joined Catherine, Georgina, and Dickens on an extended outing to Greenwich, and Christiana had spent the night at Devonshire Terrace, talking "confidentially" with Catherine while Dickens and Georgina were at church.[21] Catherine learned from Christiana about her relationship with Thompson, which differed markedly from that of the Dickenses, in part because the fiancé declined to wield the upper hand.

During her own engagement ten years earlier, Catherine was trained by a man anxious to perform what he considered his "duty" toward her. Her behavior was criticized at times and commended at others, while her attempts to correct what she saw as Dickens's imperfections were rebuffed by him. But Thompson sounded a very different note in his relationship with "darling Christie." Telling her that he "hate[d] preachments," he refused to play the role of her superior and guide. If he "impressed" any view upon her, it was the importance of "being altogether open"—feeling free to correct *him* if he acted in a way she disliked. "I shall never prove obstinate or unreasonable," he assured her, "and it will always be a source of pride to find you in the right, even in opposition to myself."[22]

Although Catherine was not privy to these assurances, she was drawn into the courtship and its dynamics not only by Christiana's confidences but also by the mediating role she played when the engagement was imperiled. In early October, three weeks before the couple planned to marry, a crisis erupted, and "Mr & Mrs Dickens" were asked to intervene, meeting with Christiana's father at Devonshire Terrace.[23] The immediate cause of the trouble was Mr. Weller's sense that the couple had been precipitate in scheduling their wedding. Yet the larger issue of Christiana's sacrifice remained. Christiana's mother had been educated for the music profession and, after *her* marriage, resumed her studies under Pio Cianchetti, becoming "a first class teacher," Mr. Weller noted. Like his wife, his daughter was "educated . . . for the profession" and had "attained an immense celebrity in a very short period of time."[24] What was to become of her talent and celebrity? An affluent

21. Christiana Weller Thompson, 1845 diary, MS Meynell Family Papers, Greatham.

22. T. J. Thompson to Christiana Weller, 31 August 1845, MS Meynell Family Papers, Greatham, reprinted in Paroissien, "Charles Dickens and the Weller Family," 32–34.

23. Christiana Weller Thompson, 1845 diary, MS Meynell Family Papers, Greatham.

24. T. E. Weller to Charles Dickens, 23 March 1854, MS (copy) Meynell Family Papers, Greatham, reprinted in Paroissien, "Charles Dickens and the Weller Family," 35–37, and Pilgrim 7:912–14 (Appendix C).

gentleman, Thompson did not work for a living. Why, then, would his wife? Before the wedding could take place, the Wellers had to stifle their ambitions for their daughter, at least for the time being.

Catherine's position as Christiana's confidante and her mediation in her friend's affairs led her to compare their situations—as wives and, later, as mothers. As both she and Christiana knew, the men around them drew comparisons between them and did so in a less than friendly spirit, defining the Weller sisters against the sisters Hogarth to the advantage of one set. From 1845 well into the 1850s, Dickens and T. E. Weller repeatedly cited the failings of the women in each other's family in defense of their own, inspired to do so by the ill-fated attraction between Dickens's brother Fred and Weller's daughter Anna, who married Fred in 1848 and separated from him ten years later. Discouraging his brother from pursuing Anna in October 1845, when Thompson was about to marry Christiana, Dickens warned him that the Wellers were "feverish, restless, flighty, excitable, uncontrollable, wrong-headed; under no sort of wholesome self-restraint; and bred to think the absence of it a very intellectual and brilliant thing":

I grant [Anna] good looks. I grant her cleverness[,] . . . but I doubt her quiet wisdom in the quiet life to which you must inevitably retreat. I doubt whether that "Soul" of which the family make such frequent mention, may not be something too expansive for a domestic parlor. . . . The world about her seems to be a Great Electrifying Machine, from which she gets all sorts of unaccountable shocks and knocks and starts; and it seems to me to be an open question whether she will ever be shocked and knocked and started into a reasonable woman. (Pilgrim 4:400–401)

Catherine and Georgina might not have "Soul" in the Wellers' sense, but they were "discreet and rational." Able to "govern . . . their sentiments, sympathies, antipathies," they resembled the "reasonable woman" that Anna was unlikely to become (Pilgrim 4:400).

Once Anna was engaged, Mr. Weller took his turn, praising his daughter at Catherine's expense, embittered that Anna and her talents would be wasted on Fred, insulted by Dickens's continued objections to her as a sister-in-law, and convinced of her vast superiority to Dickens's own wife. "*Health* is all [Anna] wants," he told Christiana, "& *then* I calculate she will do herself as much *honor as a pianiste* as the great 'Boz' does *as a writer*—and cut *rather* a higher figure in the *intellectual world* than *Mrs.* Boz! Mrs. F. D. will be a greater personage than *Mrs.* C. D.—which will no doubt be very annoying—Had Anna been an ordinary young Lady all would have been well but she is too talented to be tolerated."[25] Outraged when Dickens, in the spring of 1854, cast doubt on Anna's musical abilities and counseled Fred against allowing his wife to repair their fortunes by teaching piano, Weller wrote Dickens an angry rebuttal, distinguishing his daughter's "high" and "refined" playing from "the musical snuff-box delicacy of the timid adherents of Mrs. Grundy or the soulless manipulations of the dogmatic self styled English classicals."[26] Sending a copy of his letter to Christiana, he glossed it for her benefit, explaining his reference to "soulless manipulations" of the pianoforte as a "hit at the sort of playing old Hogarth's daughters exhibit."[27]

Six months before Weller launched this critique, Dickens had written to "old Hogarth's daughters" of the pitfalls of Christiana's soulfulness, having just visited the Thompsons near Genoa. He found their two young children "in a singularly untidy state," he told Catherine, "one (Heaven knows why) without stockings," and the mistress of the household devoted to the arts rather than domestic matters (Pilgrim 7:178). To Georgina, he mocked Christiana's claims about music and painting and characterized her as a woman who led her husband by the nose (Pilgrim 7:212).

When, in the middle of this decade-long acrimony, Dickens mesmerized the ailing Anna, and Christiana met Catherine and Georgina by the sickbed, Christiana found the Hogarth sisters "stiff" in their demeanor.[28] The friendships the women had enjoyed in the 1840s could not survive the hostilities between the men. But the sparring between Dickens and Mr. Weller and the disdain each showed for the other's female relations were not exhibited by the women themselves. When Christiana referred to Georgina's playing in her 1846 diary, her remarks were never disparaging, and the Weller sisters had only positive things to say of Catherine, whom they found "kind, cordial, affectionate and sincere."[29] Catherine was aware that she and Christiana were very different, but that was a source of attraction, not

25. T. E. Weller to Christiana Weller Thompson, 7 December 1848, MS Meynell Family Papers, Greatham, quoted in Pilgrim 5:401 n. 1.

26. T. E. Weller to Charles Dickens, 23 March 1854, MS (copy) Meynell Family Papers, Greatham, reprinted in Paroissien, "Charles Dickens and the Weller Family," 35–37, and Pilgrim 7:912–14 (Appendix C).

27. T. E. Weller to Christiana Weller Thompson, [27 March 1854], MS Meynell Family Papers, Greatham, reprinted in Paroissien, "Charles Dickens and the Weller Family," 35, and Pilgrim 7:912 n. 1.

28. Christiana Thompson, 1850 diary, MS Meynell Family Papers, Greatham.

29. Bessy Shaw to Christiana Weller, 16 February 1845, typescript, Meynell Family Papers, Greatham.

antagonism or opposition. For Dickens, the Hogarth sisters were reasonable, aptly restrained, and wise in their calm domesticity, while the Wellers were undisciplined, presumptuous, self-indulgent, and unladylike. To Mr. Weller, his daughters appeared exceptionally gifted, intellectual, and refined in their feelings, while the Hogarths were ordinary, conventional, and overly restrained. But for Catherine, Christiana was a talented friend with whom she could discuss people, music, and art, refreshing in her expressiveness and her relative unconcern with social proprieties. Catherine might not envy the more bohemian and equitable relationship Christiana enjoyed with her husband, but neither would she criticize her for having attained it. It reminded her that some men cared far more than others about discipline and domestic order and thus underscored what she had given up in order to meet Dickens's expectations.

"WE SHALL NOT GO ANY FURTHER SOUTH"

What Catherine gave up in October 1845, after helping to negotiate it, was Christiana's wedding, which took place on the twenty-first, one week before Catherine gave birth for the sixth time. By the seventeenth of the month she was "in a most critical condition," Dickens reported, and on the twentieth "in a state of tribulation" (Pilgrim 4:408). She delivered Alfred on the morning of the twenty-eighth, having "suffered very much" (Pilgrim 4:418). "My sister, I fear made her last public appearance for some time, at the theatre the other night," Georgina told Christiana several days before the ceremony, accepting an invitation to serve as a bridesmaid while conveying Catherine's regrets. "She desires me to say how very very sorry [she is] that she shall not see you as a bride, and personally offer[s] you her warmest congratulations in her imagination, though that will be a poor substitute for the pleasure she would have felt in being with you."[30]

Catherine recovered more quickly from her sixth delivery than she had from her fifth but continued to substitute imagined pleasures for real ones for a time. While she was confined in November, Georgina took the children to see the Lord Mayor's Show and attended a benefit performance of *Every Man in His Humour,* managed by Dickens at the St. James Theatre; he and some of his friends were in the cast. Catherine had seen the first performance, at Frances ("Fanny") Kelly's Royalty Theatre, in September, writing many of the invitations herself. Back in circulation in December, she attended a stage version of Dickens's new Christmas story, *The Cricket on the Hearth,* and a benefit performance of a Restoration comedy that he had organized. On 6 January she co-hosted their annual Twelfth Night party at

30. ALS Georgina Hogarth to Christiana Weller, [16 October 1845], MS Meynell Family Papers, Greatham, reprinted in Paroissien, "Charles Dickens and the Weller Family," 38.

Devonshire Terrace, with a dance and supper for the children in celebration of Charley's ninth birthday.

Although Catherine lost sight of Christiana, who left for the continent shortly after her wedding, she befriended another musically gifted young woman in January 1846—the sixteen-year-old American vocalist Abby Hutchinson, who was touring Great Britain with her brothers. Popular singers in New England and active in the abolitionist movement, the Hutchinsons knew George Putnam, who had served as Dickens's secretary on the American tour. They called at Devonshire Terrace on 26 January, two days after arriving in London, and sang for Catherine, Georgina, and several visitors. Impressed, Catherine arranged for them to perform for her father, who lost "the cool air of a Scotch critic" when they did, Abby recalled, "came rapidly across the room, grasping us each and all by the hands, [and] said with emotion—'I never heard such harmony before.'"[31]

At the end of January, Catherine and her husband hosted a party in the Hutchinsons' honor, introducing Abby and her brothers to Macready, Douglas Jerrold, Rogers, and Caroline Norton, among other notables. Those gathered heard them sing Thomas Hood's "Bridge of Sighs," which they "delivered with such feeling that no one could listen to them unmoved," George Hogarth wrote.[32] As struck by their singing as her father, Catherine brought tickets for their first London performance to Kitty Macready, only to find that her friend "had already provided herself."[33] Until the singers left London in April, Abby exchanged visits and letters with Catherine, who collected autographs for her from well-known friends. "I have just received the autograph from Mr. Rogers, which I now enclose," she wrote Abby in March. "Mr. Jerrold . . . says he is going to send [his] in a little book, which I have no doubt he will send me for you—very shortly. Mr. Macready is at present in Scotland. By the time you return to London he will be at home again, and I can then get his." Adding her thanks for a note Abby had sent her, Catherine told the singer that she valued it as much as her friend did the autographs of famous men: "I shall always keep [it] for your sake."[34]

31. "Abby's Account of Meeting Mr. Hogarth the Opera Critique for the London Daily Times, in 1846," n.d., MS Ludlow Patton's Hutchinson Family Scrapbook (Item 122v), Wadleigh Memorial Library, Milford, N.H.

32. George Hogarth, "The American Vocalists," *Daily News*, 11 February 1846.

33. ALS Catherine Dickens to Mr. Hutchinson, 7 February [1846], HM 18482, Huntington Library.

34. ALS Catherine Dickens to Abby Hutchinson, 4 March 1846, H1321, Gimbel Collection, Beinecke Rare Book and Manuscript Library, Yale University.

Drawn to the earnest and expressive American who appeared onstage in a simple dress, Catherine considered herself Abby's "very affectionate friend."[35] The connection she formed with the singer, like her friendship with Christiana, stemmed from her musical background and position as George Hogarth's daughter. But it also reflected her interest in talented young women who were making their own way in the world through artful self-expression and whose lives differed markedly from hers.

After celebrating Dickens's thirty-fourth birthday in Rochester and their tenth anniversary in Richmond, Catherine and her husband started to plan for their upcoming year abroad. In mid-April, Dickens told Forster that he would economize by writing his next novel "in Lausanne and in Genoa," as he would be "living in Switzerland for the summer, and in Italy or France for the winter" (Pilgrim 4:537–38). Dickens's wording ("Italy *or* France") was telling, for this was the sticking point in his discussions with Catherine. Writing to Madame de la Rue on 17 April, he explained that while *he* wished to live in Genoa, Mrs. Dickens did not, although he had "beset her in all kinds of ways," but making it clear that he and his correspondent were not to be deterred from meeting: "I think I should take a middle course ... and, coming as near you as I could, pitch my tent somewhere on the Lake of Geneva—say at Lausanne, when I should run over to Genoa immediately" (Pilgrim 4:534).

In May, Catherine's description of their trip was more definitive, particularly in regard to its southern boundary, a line that she herself drew. "We are on the move again," she wrote Margaret Holskamp, who knew the de la Rues and had discouraged the advances of Augusta's brother William. "Mr. Dickens" hoped to write his "new monthly book ... in perfect quiet," Catherine explained, and was "very anxious to know more of Switzerland, so we are going to spend the summer there at Lausanne. ... The winter we shall very likely spend in Paris, but we shall not go any further south."[36] Using the plural pronoun in her letter rather than the singular which her husband used in *his,* and the imperative tense instead of his conditional one, Catherine spoke for Dickens as well as herself on this matter, even while expressing deference to him and his wish "to know more of Switzerland." He might "beset" her, but her mind was set, impervious to his influence in this regard.

Having seen to the baby's christening in April and hosted a wedding breakfast for Dickens's brother Alfred, who married Helen Dobson in May, Catherine devoted one of her last days in England to Kitty Macready, dining with her and Georgina on the twenty-first. She took Fanny Burnett to see Dr. Elliotson, amid the

35. Ibid.

36. ALS Catherine Dickens to Miss Holskamp, 28 May 1846, Fales Library & Special Collections, New York University.

"immense number of things" she had to do before her departure.[37] The women were overjoyed when Elliotson told them, erroneously, that Fanny was not suffering from consumption. With Georgina, Anne, Louis Roche, two nurses, and the six children, the Dickenses left London for Switzerland on 31 May, having rented out Devonshire Terrace for one year to Sir James Duke. Traveling on the Rhine, they arrived at Lausanne on 11 June and four days later moved into Rosemont, their home for the next five months. Situated on a hill overlooking the lake and mountains, Rosemont was large enough to provide a study for Dickens and a spare room for visitors. They paid £10 monthly in rent, with an extra ten francs for a leased piano, and hired a local cook and coachman. From their house the Dickenses could walk to town and make use of the English church and the English library.

Within a fortnight of their arrival Charley was enrolled as a boarder at a nearby school in the hope of his learning French, living apart from the family six days of the week, while Mamie and Katey were taught at Rosemont by a French-speaking governess. With outdoor festivals, boating expeditions, and a "juvenile party" for Katey's seventh birthday,[38] the children were well entertained. Although there were now half a dozen of them, three under six years old, eight adults provided varying degrees of supervision: their parents and their aunt, a governess and two nurses, as well as Anne and Roche, who sometimes took one or more of the older children on special outings.

By the end of June, Dickens had started *Dombey and Son,* and he and Catherine had joined a new circle: its members included William Haldiman, a philanthropist and former M.P. for Ipswich; Richard and Lavinia Watson and their three young children, the husband a retired cavalry officer and former M.P. for Canterbury, his wife the daughter of a peer; and William and Mary de Cerjat and their daughter. With Catherine and Georgina, these friends formed an appreciative audience for Dickens's works in progress. In September, Dickens read the first monthly number of *Dombey* to them at Rosemont and the second in October. At a third gathering in November he read his latest Christmas story, *The Battle of Life.*

With their new friends, Catherine, her husband, and her sister explored their surroundings, taking short excursions to Vevay. The three embarked on their own four-day expedition to Chamonix at the end of July, crossing mountain passes on mules, which they rode for several hours at a time, and gaining spectacular views of Mont Blanc. In early September they joined eight others on an expedition to St. Bernard, ascending on mules to a mountaintop convent to sleep. The dangers of the region were evident. On 21 July an Englishwoman whose husband insisted on

37. Ibid.
38. Christiana Weller Thompson, 1846 diary, MS Meynell Family Papers, Greatham.

carriage rather than mule travel was killed near Lausanne when their vehicle fell into a ravine; and on their way back from Chamonix the Dickenses came upon a German woman who had fallen from her mule and broken her leg and to whom Catherine and Georgina tended as she was carried to Lausanne.

In midsummer Catherine conceived her seventh child, Sydney; at the time, Alfred was nine months old. She was soon joined in Lausanne by a pregnant friend—Christiana Thompson, who arrived with her husband on 10 August, renting a house there until April. Dickens felt very differently about Mrs. Thompson, "large in the family way," than he had about the "etherial" Miss Weller (Pilgrim 4:615, 70). The beautiful young woman in whose face he had once seen "an angel's message" proved "to have a devil of a whimpering, pouting temper," he complained (Pilgrim 4:70, 615). "Mrs. Thompson disappoints me very much," he told Émile de la Rue in August. "She is a mere spoiled child, I think, and doesn't turn out half as well as I expected. Matrimony has improved him, and certainly has not improved her.... I wish her well through [her confinement],—but upon my Soul, I feel as if her husband would have the worst, even of that" (Pilgrim 4:604).[39]

Catherine felt differently than Dickens did about Christiana, however. While he worked on *Dombey and Son* and *The Battle of Life*, took long walks with T. J. Thompson, and went off by himself to Vevay for a brief visit with the de la Rues, Catherine called on Christiana, taking drives with her or walking together into Lausanne, where they read in the English library and shopped for watercolor frames. When Catherine called on Christiana, Georgina sometimes came along, playing the piano that the Thompsons had rented with their house.

In Switzerland as elsewhere, Catherine heard her husband pass judgment on women he deemed unwomanly, unladylike, and in need of correction. Shortly before they left London for Switzerland, he began making plans for Urania Cottage, a home dedicated to the discipline and reformation of fallen women from the working classes, to be established in London the following year with funds provided by Angela Burdett Coutts. When he was in Geneva with Catherine and Georgina, however, it was the lapses of *aristocratic* women that caught his eye. At the end of September the three dined with Lady Walpole and Lady Pellew, who were "both very clever," Dickens felt, but who shocked him by smoking cigars "in the most gentlemanly manner" and using language generally reserved for men. "Kate and Georgy...were decidedly in the way, as we agreed afterwards," he told Forster. "Such a Braver of

39. For an insightful discussion of Dickens's changing feelings about Christiana and her similarity to Mary Hogarth, see Slater, *Dickens and Women*, 88–91. Bodenheimer sees him connecting Christiana to young Fanny Dickens as well (*Knowing Dickens*, 102).

all conventionalities never wore petticoats," he wrote Macready of Lady Walpole. "It is not her fault, if Scandal ever leaves her alone" (Pilgrim 4:634, 647).

Although she neither smoked nor cursed and remained free from scandal, Christiana was more willing to brave convention than were other women in Catherine's circle. Dickens criticized Christiana accordingly, yet also tolerated her for the sake of her husband and Fred, who was engaged to her sister Anna in the summer of 1846. In Christiana, Catherine found a married woman who was neither submissive nor restrained in her speech ("the Ladies talked as much as Mrs. T.," Richard Watson remarked of some acquaintances),[40] and whose activity as a new mother called into question the conventions of childbearing. Her daughter Elizabeth was born on 3 November, and Christiana joined the Dickenses for a farewell dinner at her home little more than a week later, when many first-time mothers would still be in their rooms.

As she had in Genoa when Dickens dreamed of her dead sister, Catherine attended to and supported her husband in Lausanne, where he was struggling to write his Christmas book in "an uncommon depression of spirits" at the end of September (Pilgrim 5:19) and feared he might need to cancel it altogether. Traveling with him to Geneva, where they were later joined by Georgina, Catherine kept him company and saw to his needs while he worked on *The Battle of Life,* a story celebrating self-sacrifice on the part of each of a pair of sisters.[41] By seeking self-fulfillment rather than embracing self-sacrifice, Christiana provided Catherine with a significant counterexample. Whether in her marriage, her music, her drawing, or her eager responsiveness to what she found beautiful, Christiana valued emotional and artistic self-expression and implicitly questioned, through her own behavior, the "home-adorning, self-denying qualities"[42] that Dickens celebrated among his female characters and encouraged in his wife. As she did with her sister Mary and their Scremerston cousin, Catherine expressed herself differently to Christiana than she did to those with whom she made "a point of being on [her] Ps and Qs," as Mary had put it ten years earlier.[43] After leaving Lausanne, Catherine wrote to

40. Richard Watson, diary, 15 July 1846, quoted in Pilgrim 4:605 n. 4.

41. This story is often taken as a key to Dickens's triangulated love for the Hogarth women, since the hero, engaged to one sister, eventually marries the other. Such readings treat Catherine and Georgina as interchangeable—in Dickens's thinking and in his life—and pay no heed to *their* perceptions. I return to the Hogarth sisterhood in Interlude 2.

42. Charles Dickens, *The Battle of Life,* in *Christmas Books,* 2 vols. (Boston: Houghton Mifflin, 1894), 1:243.

43. ALS Mary Hogarth to Mary Scott Hogarth, 26 January 1837, D. Jacques Benoliel Collection of the Letters of Charles Dickens, 83-1842, Rare Book Department, Free Library of Philadelphia.

Christiana in early December, and Christiana responded on New Year's Day. Regrettably, only the record of their correspondence survives—in Christiana's diary—not the letters themselves.

"SO CRUELLY HUSTLED AGAINST THE PORTALS OF LIFE"

On 16 November the Dickenses left Lausanne for Paris, their party crossing the Jura in two carriages with a third carrying their luggage. Within three days of their arrival they had rented 48 Rue de Courcelles, in Faubourg Saint-Honoré, a house with a small courtyard and garden. Among its oddities was a dining room painted to resemble a wooded grove, with mirror fragments placed on the walls and ceiling among fictive tree branches. Poorly insulated, the house was expensive to heat; in December and January water froze in the rooms overnight. In Paris, unlike London, Sunday was a workday for many laborers and shopkeepers, and even the busiest streets seemed unsafe at night; out with her brother-in-law to see the palace illuminated, Georgina witnessed an assault and robbery on the main boulevard.

Despite the differences between the cities, Catherine, her husband, and her sister found many of the same pleasures in Paris that they did at home, frequenting the theaters and socializing with writers and actors. Accompanied by Dickens, Catherine called on some well-known Parisians, among them François Régnier, whom they saw perform in a revival of Molière's *Don Juan*. But it was Forster, not Catherine, who joined Dickens on his visit to Victor Hugo and family. Hugo was notorious for his infidelities, and Dickens thought that Adèle, Hugo's wife, looked "as if she might poison his breakfast any morning" (Pilgrim 5:15). Having given birth five times, however, Mme. Hugo condoned her husband's adultery because it put an end to her own childbearing.

Before the Dickenses arrived in Paris, their stay had been cut from seven to four months because of Catherine's pregnancy. They planned to return to England in March and rent temporary London lodgings, since Sir James Duke would remain at Devonshire Terrace until July. But their residence in Paris was shortened further when Charley fell ill in London, where he had started King's College School in February, staying with the Hogarths until he could move into a residence with headmaster John Major when classes began. At the end of January, Charley traveled from Paris to London with Forster, a fortnight's guest of the Dickenses. The trip began inauspiciously for the ten-year-old, who was forced to leave his luggage behind. "To our great consternation," Catherine told Angela Burdett Coutts, "his trunk, by a great mistake of our Courier's, exceeded the limits allowed for the Malle Poste, and they refused to take it." Although Charley was scheduled to meet with Miss Coutts on 3 February, Catherine feared he might not make the meeting. Unless his trunk arrived, and with it his proper attire, "his grandmother [might] withhold him . . . until the next day."[44]

Catherine's concern for social proprieties soon gave way to alarm over Charley's health. In London for purposes connected with *Dombey and Son,* Dickens spent a February weekend with the boy, and Catherine received word on the twentieth that Charley "look[ed] very well and very happy—sen[t] all sorts of loves—and talk[ed] incessantly" (Pilgrim 5:30). But the day after Dickens returned to Paris, he and Catherine learned that Charley had contracted scarlet fever and had been removed from school to the Hogarths' by Forster and Elliotson. Three months earlier, an Edinburgh physician had diagnosed Fanny Burnett as consumptive, to the grief of the Dickenses. Now "dear Charley" lay in bed, wrapped in blankets, with "the Fever . . . crimson on him" (Pilgrim 5:41).

Rushing to London with Roche, the couple found lodgings on Chester Place, near the Hogarths on Albany Street. Although they were close by Charley, neither parent was permitted to see him; the doctors feared that Catherine, in her third trimester, would contract the illness from either her son or her husband. Nonetheless, Charley was the focus of attention at his grandparents' and had the company of his aunt Helen and his uncle Edward, only four years his senior. Charley was soon out of danger, and Catherine and her husband could write reassuringly to Georgina, who had been left in Paris to care for the five younger children with Anne's help and a fund of £80.[45] Withdrawn from King's College School, Charley returned to his old schoolmaster, Joseph King, as a weekly boarder as soon as he was fully recovered.

Toward the end of March, Roche accompanied Georgina, Anne, and the children back from Paris. With the exception of Charley, who joined them in April, the family members were reunited at their temporary lodgings on 27 March. As usual, the Dickenses, with Georgina, Forster, and Maclise, celebrated their anniversary in Richmond on 2 April. At her eleventh anniversary celebration Catherine was near the end of her seventh full-term pregnancy. With the exception of 1842, she had been carrying a child for part of every year of her married life. Although she had suffered from postpartum depression after the births of Charley and Mamie and been apprehensive toward the end of her fifth pregnancy, her deliveries had been painful but uncomplicated and had required little medical attention. That changed in 1847 with the birth of Sydney at Chester Place.

44. ALS Catherine Dickens to Angela Burdett Coutts, 1 February 1847, MA 1352, the Morgan Library & Museum, New York.

45. Charles Dickens, Esq., Account Ledger, Coutts & Co., London.

Catherine went into labor on 17 or 18 April, but the delivery did not progress normally as the others had. It was not simply a case of false labor—the "numerous 'false starts'" that preceded Walter's delivery in 1841.[46] The available evidence suggests instead that Sydney was a breech baby and that his presentation was an unusual one—not the frank breech, in which the baby assumes a pike position and the bottom is delivered first, but either a complete breech (with the baby in a cannonball position) or a footling. While any breech presentation was a cause for concern, substantially increasing perinatal mortality, a footling breech was especially worrisome and called for medical intervention. After the baby emerged as far as the umbilical cord, maneuvering was necessary to prevent serious damage or death, and unless the mother's cervix was fully dilated, it would not allow for passage of the upright head.

Realizing the danger to Catherine and the baby, Dickens rushed out in search of medical aid and brought back two doctors: Henry Davis and Charles Locock, Queen Victoria's obstetrician. Dickens was "wild" with anxiety, and Davis, far from reassuring the father, told him that "he had seen but one such case" in his years of experience. "Of course my dear Kate suffered terribly," Dickens told Macready the next day, "but thank God she is as well today as ever she has been at such a time" (Pilgrim 5:58). A week later he told Kitty Macready, "My young 'ooman continues, thank God, to thrive brilliantly," nevertheless confessing that he had been "horribly alarmed" (Pilgrim 5:61). Having heard about the difficult birth and empathizing with the baby as much as with Catherine, Francis Jeffrey inquired after them before Sydney was three months old. "How is the poor child who was so cruelly hustled against the portals of life at his entry?" Jeffrey asked. "And his dear mother?"[47]

Although Catherine recovered from Sydney's birth without any particular trouble, she was not yet through for the year with the dangers and anxieties of pregnancy; 1847 would end—and 1848 begin—with a second childbearing crisis. As before, Catherine remained out of social circulation for three or four weeks following Sydney's delivery. The day after his birth, Georgina brought Mamie and Katey to a children's party at the Macreadys', and she rather than Catherine accompanied Dickens to a dinner party at Forster's on 9 May, the older children joining them in the evening. On the thirteenth Georgina was in their box at the St. James Theatre

46. ALS John Dickens to George Franklin, 14 February 1841, D. Jacques Benoliel Collection of the Letters of Charles Dickens, 87-1942, Rare Book Department, Free Library of Philadelphia; "John Dickens and George Franklin: Five Letters, 1839–1841," transcribed by David Parker, *Dickensian* 99, no. 3 (Winter 2003): 227.

47. Francis Jeffrey to Charles Dickens, 5 July 1847, in *Life of Lord Jeffrey*, 2:427.

with Maclise, Jerrold, and others to see an amateur performance of *Hernani* while her sister stayed home.

Catherine marked the end of her confinement by going with Dickens and Georgina to Brighton for the last two weeks of May; Charley, Mamie, and Katey followed them to the coast after a time. Back in London she met the opera star Jenny Lind at the Macreadys' and saw her perform in Donizetti's *Figlia del Reggimento*. The Dickenses hosted a dinner party in June, with Thackeray and Catherine's Edinburgh friends the Allans among their guests. Joining the Macreadys for their anniversary celebration and the christening of baby Cecilia, Catherine heard Joseph Staudigl, the acclaimed bass, perform. At a breakfast for the educator Samuel Wilderspin, she listened to her husband and others describe the achievements of the Infant School Society, dedicated to helping children from the working classes.

The Dickenses left London for Broadstairs at the end of June, the children, Sydney included, having contracted whooping cough and been advised to go there for their health. While the children recuperated, their parents entertained; among their visitors that summer were Miss Coutts, staying in nearby Sandgate, and Hans Christian Andersen, on his first visit to England. Back from Switzerland, the Thompsons visited as well, bringing along Anna, toward whom Dickens felt undiminished antipathy. Christiana was in the third trimester of her second pregnancy and gave birth to her daughter Alice in September.

In Broadstairs six years earlier, Catherine's husband had joked with Maclise about visiting prostitutes nearby, but the Dickenses maintained their monogamous relationship, and with it their ability to conceive. Dickens might know where prostitutes lived in Margate, but when he went there in September 1847, Catherine accompanied him, and the two saw *As You Like It* at the local theater. Despite the alarm generated by Sydney's delivery, Catherine was once again pregnant in the fall. The unfortunate end of that pregnancy, her ninth, was anticipated that summer by the happier result of another, the first for Annie Leech, wife of John Leech, the *Punch* illustrator.

To benefit fellow writers Leigh Hunt and John Poole, Dickens and the amateur players he directed arranged to perform *Every Man in His Humour* in Manchester on 26 July and in Liverpool two days later. Organized by Dickens and journalist Mark Lemon, a large party of friends traveled from London by rail. The Lemons and the Leeches joined Catherine, Georgina, and Dickens, as did Fanny and William Ayrton, T. J. and Christiana Thompson, and Fred. While most of the men performed, their wives did not, professional actresses having been hired instead. As Dickens confessed to Forster in 1846, referring to a portrait of an actress and kinswoman of the Lemons on display in their home, "if Kate had been a Columbine her portrait would not be hanging, 'in character,' in Devonshire-Terrace" (Pilgrim 4:582).

Dickens was anxious to shield middle-class women from undue publicity, yet Annie Leech gained the spotlight on their trip home. Returning from Liverpool on 30 July in the same train compartment as Catherine and Dickens, she went into labor, was wheeled out of London Station in a bath chair, and gave birth in a room at the Victoria Hotel. Her experience lent force to the belief that train travel could induce labor, a stock joke among Victorians and one that Dickens himself used in his fiction. Although Mrs. Leech's emergency created "confusion and distress" (Pilgrim 5:134), both she and the baby were "'going on' famously," her husband reported in mid-August.[48] In September, six-year-old Walter started school with Mr. King, accompanying Charley from Broadstairs to London to meet their headmaster. One month later the family moved back to Devonshire Terrace, which had been renovated with gas lighting, its rooms aired and put in order by Josephine Walker, who was regularly hired by the Dickenses for that purpose. Having on hand "a fine haunch of venison,"[49] Catherine invited Thomas Beard, among others, to dine in mid-October, celebrating their return and inaugurating a new series of such entertainments. At the end of November the Dickenses were expected for several days at Rockingham Castle, the Northamptonshire estate of Richard Watson. On the twenty-seventh Catherine left London without her husband, who was detained by troubles at Urania Cottage. The home for "fallen women" had been open for only two weeks, but one of the inmates had already transgressed: "Disappointment Number One," Dickens termed it (Pilgrim 5:204).

"NO GREATER SOURCE OF REGRET TO A MARRIED WOMAN"

An insuperable moral barrier was presumed to separate Catherine Dickens from those living at Urania Cottage. In her husband's fiction she read that fallen women had squandered the "priceless treasures...the Creator bestows but once"—their chastity—and could never regain their lost virtue, though they might gain peace of mind by repenting for the past.[50] Three years after Urania Cottage opened, Catherine herself acknowledged the divide separating her and other respectable

48. John Leech to Charles F. Adams, [16 August 1847], in William Powell Frith, *John Leech: His Life and Work*, 2 vols. (London: Richard Bentley, 1891), 1:236. This letter is misdated by the Pilgrim editors (5:134 n. 3). Sadly, the Leeches' daughter died as a toddler, in March 1849, after declining for nearly a year.

49. ALS Catherine Dickens to Thomas Beard, [7 October 1847], Charles Dickens Museum, London.

50. Charles Dickens, *Oliver Twist*, ed. Peter Fairclough (Harmondsworth: Penguin, 1982), 414. The one "cure" for a woman's stained honor, a traveling salesman in the novel later remarks, is the poison she uses to kill herself (426).

women from the "fallen" when she wrote notes of apology to female guests who had unwittingly crossed that divide at a recent dinner party, the Dickenses having allowed into their midst an unknown acquaintance of Samuel Rogers. Catherine was instructed to write the notes by Dickens, who had learned the truth about Rogers's companion, Pauline Denain, the mother of an illegitimate child born "some indefinite time ago" ("a small faux pas," Dickens facetiously remarked to his wife) and the mistress of Lord Normanby. "Just say 'that her history is not quite correct, you find,'" he told Catherine, providing her with her text, "'and that Rogers was mistaken in presenting her. . . . [Y]ou feel you owe this explanation to them, whom you asked to meet her.' *This you must do at once*" (Pilgrim 6:120).

The perceived and urgent necessity of this measure helps to explain why, in the ten years in which her husband largely managed Urania Cottage and the selection, treatment, and prospects of its residents, Catherine never visited. Nonetheless, in the discipline she received from Dickens and, more generally, the social regulation of her sexuality as a married woman, her own proper history intersected with the "not quite correct" histories of the "fallen," rendering suspect the division between the women and, with it, the alleged privileges of female virtue.[51]

"Tak[ing] some pains to find out the dispositions and natures" of the women living at Urania Cottage, Dickens assured Miss Coutts that he would be able "to exercise some personal influence with them in case of need" (Pilgrim 5:178). Rather than using "*the* influence" to mesmerize them, as he did Catherine, he provided them with incentives for good behavior, adapting the Mark System of Alexander Maconochie, a penal reformer, to reward them for propriety, truthfulness, and industry. Yet in *both* households, Dickens's influence took some of the same forms: "judicious commendation," for example, and "serious and urgent entreaty," combined with praise and encouragement.[52] At Doughty Street and Devonshire Terrace, Dickens commended Catherine's behavior at the expense of Mrs. Hogarth and the Wellers, promoting self-restraint and service to others in his wife; at Urania Cottage, he dismissed self-assertive and insolent inmates, producing what he considered "a very good effect" on those remaining (Pilgrim 6:804). Encouraged, just

51. Margaret Flanders Darby discusses Dickens's interest in and use of the stories of the women who lived at Urania Cottage in "Dickens and Women's Stories: 1845–1848 (Part Two)," *Dickens Quarterly* 17 (September 2000): 127–38. Dickens's relations with the inmates are the subject of Jenny Hartley, *Charles Dickens and the House of Fallen Women* (London: Methuen, 2008).

52. [Charles Dickens], "Home for Homeless Women," *Household Words* (23 April 1853), in Michael Slater, ed., *"Gone Astray" and Other Papers from Household Words*, Dent Uniform Edition of Dickens' Journalism, vol. 3 (Columbus: Ohio State University Press, 1998), 135.

as Catherine was, to value "order, punctuality, and good temper," the advantages of which Dickens outlined and posted on the living room wall of the home (Pilgrim 5:186), the women he disciplined there made the same discovery that Miss Hogarth had when trying to negotiate the terms of her marriage: they had no bargaining power. Told by Dickens that she would "have no Marks for a month" for breaking rules, "Little Willis" tried to "make terms with the establishment," approaching him "diplomatically" for the purpose. When he refused to negotiate, she gathered her few belongings and left (Pilgrim 6:804).

While subject to measures familiar to Catherine as Dickens's wife, those he recruited for Urania Cottage were set apart from her as the mothers of illegitimate children. In his "Appeal to Fallen Women," a pamphlet distributed to female prison inmates, Dickens reminded each prospective recruit that "if she has ever been a mother, [she] has felt shame, instead of pride, in her own unhappy child" (Pilgrim 5:698). His ultimate goal for the women—respectable married life in distant Australia—would free them from shame and make them proud of the births of their children.[53] Indeed childbearing had become for Catherine her primary means of success; by 1847 she was the proud mother of seven. Nonetheless, it also subjected her to a host of constraints, and its legitimacy could not free her from self-recrimination in association with it. Not only was female sexuality itself perceived as a chronic source of instability and disorder;[54] not all pregnancies were successful, and there was "no ... greater source of dread, anxiety, and subsequent regret to a married woman than miscarriage," as one medical guide warned.[55]

Although the vast majority of miscarriages result from genetic defects that render the fetus unviable,[56] women in Catherine's culture were commonly held responsible when they miscarried; the premature end of a pregnancy was blamed on the female constitution, weak *and* strong, and on a lack of prudence on women's part. In Victorian fiction, miscarriages sometimes indict female characters for their

53. As a middle-class reformer, Dickens did not fully recognize the economic basis of the trade in sex or the ability of women to turn from it when their finances allowed, marrying and raising families despite an ideology that deemed them outcasts. He assumed that all "fallen" women felt degraded and ashamed and was annoyed to discover that residents at Urania Cottage could have a healthy sense of self-respect (see, for example, Pilgrim 5:638).

54. See Carol Smart, "Disruptive Bodies and Unruly Sex: The Regulation of Reproduction and Sexuality in the Nineteenth Century," in *Regulating Womanhood: Historical Essays on Marriage, Motherhood and Sexuality*, ed. Carol Smart (London: Routledge, 1992), 7–32.

55. Thomas Bull, *Hints to Mothers, for the Management of Health During the Period of Pregnancy, and in the Lying-in-Room* (1837; New York: Wiley and Putnam, 1842), 101.

56. Gillian C. Lachelin, *Miscarriage: The Facts* (Oxford: Oxford University Press, 1985), 36–43.

willfulness; in George Eliot's *Middlemarch* (1871–72), Dr. Lydgate "wonder[s] over the terrible tenacity" of his seemingly "mild" wife, who goes horseback riding despite his prohibition and suffers "the loss of her baby" as a result.[57] As Thomas Bull put it in *Hints to Mothers,* the causes of a miscarriage could be constitutional or accidental, the first category including "naturally robust and vigorous" physiques as well as "nervous and delicate" ones, and the second involving the injurious behavior of mothers who might not be prone to miscarry but who indulged in "immoderate exercise in dancing, riding, or even walking" and "the fatiguing dissipations of fashionable life." Too *little* exercise imperiled pregnancies as well, for "among those who . . . live luxuriously, and sleep in soft warm beds, there is often a weak condition of the vessels produced, which conveys the blood from the parent for the nourishment of the child . . . and it withers, dies, and is expelled." By attributing miscarriage to a wide range of constitutional "types" and social behaviors, describing it as a "disease" that "grow[s] into a habit," and claiming that it could be avoided with prudence "in the majority of cases," medical men such as Bull traced a largely inevitable physiological event to what they represented as moral causes.[58]

Catherine was following a fatiguing itinerary and thus acting in a way proscribed by Bull when she miscarried on 28 December 1847. Dickens was scheduled to speak at the first annual "Soirée" of the Glasgow Athenaeum, and she traveled with him to Edinburgh on 27 December. Bound for Glasgow the next day, she miscarried in their rail car. Once arrived at the Glasgow station, she was taken to the home of their host, Sir Archibald Alison, undressed, and put to bed, as a doctor was quickly summoned to her side. Having missed the events for which she went to Scotland, she returned with Dickens to Edinburgh on the thirtieth, where they stayed with Francis Jeffrey. Out shopping with her husband on New Year's Day, she was taken ill on the street, put to bed at Jeffrey's, and attended by a second doctor—most likely James Simpson, professor of medicine and midwifery at Edinburgh University. Catherine's relapse forced the couple to cancel their planned visit with Alfred and Helen Dickens and their new baby in Yorkshire on their return, instead traveling directly to London on 3 January.

Once home, Catherine spent a week in bed, suffering from what Georgina vaguely described to friends as an "unfortunate illness" that they all hoped would "not be of long duration."[59] Before leaving for Edinburgh, Catherine had sent out invitations to the annual Twelfth Night party at Devonshire Terrace, which would

57. George Eliot, *Middlemarch,* ed. Gordon S. Haight (Boston: Houghton Mifflin, 1968), 427.
58. Bull, *Hints to Mothers,* 112, 104–7, 101–2.
59. Georgina Hogarth to Thomas Beard, [5 January 1848], in *Dickens to His Oldest Friend,* 274.

center on Charley and other children that year, with some "grown up friends to see them dance."[60] Now it was left to Georgina "to write to everyone" again, explaining that Catherine "was taken so ill on her return from Scotland, that... poor Charley's party must be unavoidably postponed," and promising to reschedule the gathering.[61]

Referring to Catherine's miscarriage three years later, Francis Jeffrey, who had been "frightened" for her at the time, suggested that it could have been avoided; but he blamed Dickens, not Catherine, for the crisis. In Jeffrey's view, Dickens had "imperiled" his wife by bringing her on the trip when she was pregnant.[62] For his part, Dickens blamed neither himself nor Catherine, at least not directly, and treated her feelings of embarrassment ironically. Without specifying the nature of Catherine's illness, Dickens wrote to Georgina from Edinburgh, explaining, in an exaggerated style he deemed feminine, that it had prevented her from attending the "Soirée": "She is frightfully anxious that her not having been to [it] should be kept a secret. But I say that, like murder, it will out, and that to hope to veil such a tremendous disgrace from the general intelligence is out of the question!" (Pilgrim 5:1017).

Dickens's treatment of the miscarriage is itself veiled here; it was not Catherine's absence from the "Soirée" but the reason behind it that distressed her and that she hoped to conceal. But Dickens was not one to grieve over such a loss or to give it more thought than necessary. When his childless sister Letitia had a miscarriage in the spring of 1845, the second one she believed she had suffered, he complained to Thomas Mitton that his mother had wasted "floods" of tears over "failure[s] of that kind" (Pilgrim 4:313), and by 1846 he felt that he and Catherine had enough children to satisfy them. "We want no Babbies here," he joked to Macready before Alfred's christening, quoting his own character Mr. Kenwigs (Pilgrim 4:532). Nonetheless, the phrase he uses to describe the revelation of what Catherine wished to keep secret—"like murder, it will out"—conveys his sense that she bore some blame for the miscarriage, even as he treats facetiously her sense of anxiety and "disgrace."

Ten years earlier Catherine had suffered a miscarriage after Mary's death, but her regret over that loss was overshadowed by the grief of losing her sister. Its cause was beyond her control—a result of the "violent mental emotions" that could suddenly "disturb... the organs of the body," as Bull explained it, especially "in the

60. ALS Catherine Dickens to Thomas Beard, 21 December 1847, Charles Dickens Museum, London.

61. Georgina Hogarth to Thomas Beard, [5 January 1848], in *Dickens to His Oldest Friend*, 274.

62. Francis Jeffrey to Charles Dickens, 6 January 1850, in *Life of Lord Jeffrey*, 2:465.

peculiarly sensitive condition of the pregnant female"[63]—and the experience itself, much more private than her second miscarriage, was less disturbing. While she had one child rather than seven in 1837, less seemed to depend on her identity and success as a mother; married for only one year, she was managing the household with greater autonomy than Dickens would allow her later. Inevitably circumscribed by her recurring pregnancies and deliveries, Catherine found her role further limited by her sister's presence at Devonshire Terrace. Though welcome and helpful in its way, the division of labor it created in the household left Catherine the specialist in childbearing and Georgina the housekeeper and companion to Dickens during her sister's confinements.

Unlike the virginal Georgina, exempt from sexual activity, or the disembodied spirit of Mary described to her by Dickens, Catherine was woman incarnate, her identity as a wife and mother closely tied to her body and its physiological processes. In an unusual show of power ten years into her marriage, Catherine forced her husband to recognize and act on her "state of mind," resisting his influence and setting the terms of their second residence on the continent. But it was her *body* that preoccupied the couple at the close of 1847, her "unfortunate illness" leaving her disappointed in herself rather than with her husband or their marriage. Four months after her miscarriage in Scotland, Catherine was again pregnant— with Henry, her eighth child, born in January 1849, despite a phaeton accident in Broadstairs the previous August that she and her husband feared might result in a third miscarriage. After Henry's delivery, Catherine would give birth twice more, in 1850 and 1852. Yet her renewed success in this regard was double edged; it further identified her as—and with—her body and, combined with Georgina's presence and aid, splintered what could have been a more complex and multifaceted role.

63. Bull, *Hints to Mothers*, 106.

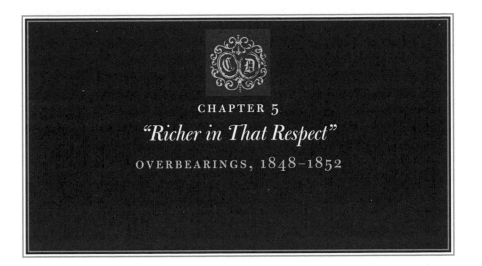

CHAPTER 5

"Richer in That Respect"

OVERBEARINGS, 1848–1852

Come, then, to see us when you can, and bring that true-hearted Kate with
you,—but not as you did last time, to frighten us, and imperil her. Let that
job be well over first, and consider whether it had not better be the last?
There can never be too many Dickenses in the world; but these overbearings
exhaust the parent tree.
—Francis Jeffrey to Charles Dickens, 6 January 1850

"TOO MANY DICKENSES"?

Three weeks before his death, in what was to prove his last exchange with Dickens, Francis Jeffrey replied to a letter he received from Devonshire Terrace toward the close of 1849—a report of "the well-being and promise of [the] children," his six-year-old godson included, and news that Catherine was once again expecting, though she could have been little more than six weeks pregnant at the time. Delighted to receive "such pleasing accounts" of the children, Jeffrey was less pleased by the revelation that a ninth baby was on the way. Rather than offering his congratulations, he wrote of Catherine's pregnancy unsentimentally, as a "job" that must "be well over" before she could safely visit him in Scotland again. Addressing Dickens as he would "a younger brother," he proffered some advice: it would be wise if this child were their last. Harking back to Catherine's miscarriage two years before and the journey he believed had endangered her, Jeffrey used a horticultural image to make his point. Like a fruit tree that "overbears," Catherine was being exhausted by the excessive crop of Dickenses she and her husband were raising. His term "overbearing" signified an injurious overproduction but also conveyed the sense of oppression inseparable from that process: in "overbearing," Catherine herself was oppressed or "overborne."[1] Acknowledging the sexual activity of the Dickenses only implicitly, Jeffrey's horticultural metaphor was both more tactful and more sympathetic than the one Wilkie Collins used to describe a particularly fruitful couple he encountered at Whitby's Royal Hotel in 1861, the wife "a Rabbit with *fourteen* young ones."[2]

In January 1850, when Jeffrey responded to the news of Catherine's pregnancy, English wives were giving birth an average of six times, and one fifth of all families had ten or more children; the queen herself was pregnant with her seventh of nine. Thus the difference between childbearing and *over*bearing could be difficult to determine. In the decades in which Catherine gave birth to her children, Britons were more likely to take pride in their fertility than to feel ashamed of it. Between 1751 and 1831 the British population more than doubled. Although Malthus warned that it would grow geometrically while the resources necessary to support it would not, its increase was heralded on political and military grounds, as Britain went to war, the empire expanded, and its outposts required defense.[3] Not until the second half of the nineteenth century, as contraceptive methods, sexual abstinence, and non-coital sex were practiced more widely by married couples, did family size decrease, with a fall in live births from six to two on average between 1860 and 1940.[4]

Among those in Catherine's circle, family size varied widely. Before their deaths from tuberculosis in 1848 and 1852, respectively, Fanny Burnett had given birth to two children and Kitty Macready to ten, eight of whom survived her. Christiana Thompson was the mother of two, Annie Leech the mother of three, and Nelly Lemon, like Catherine and Kitty, the mother of ten. So too was Rebecca Adcock, the second wife of artist Clarkson Stanfield, with five of each sex. Lavinia Watson had three sons and two daughters, her last born in February 1853, six months after the death of her husband. Mary Ann Cruikshank was childless, as was Catherine's sister-in-law Letitia

1. Francis Jeffrey to Charles Dickens, 6 January 1850, in *Life of Lord Jeffrey,* ed. Lord Cockburn, 2 vols. (Edinburgh: Adam and Charles Black, 1852), 2:465–66.

2. Wilkie Collins to Harriet Collins, 22 August 1861, in *The Public Face of Wilkie Collins: The Collected Letters,* ed. William Baker, Andrew Gasson, Graham Law, and Paul Lewis, 4 vols. (London: Pickering & Chatto, 2005), 1:244.

3. See Linda Colley, *Britons: Forging the Nation, 1707–1837* (New Haven: Yale University Press, 1992), 240.

4. Simon Szreter, *Fertility, Class and Gender in Britain, 1860–1940* (Cambridge: Cambridge University Press, 1996), 393, 1. Szreter rejects the model of Britain's "unitary" population decline, outlining "many distinct histories of fertility change among the different social groups and industrial communities" (5).

until the Austins adopted a son, while Catherine's sister Helen had a boy and a girl in four years of marriage. Between 2 April 1836, when she and Dickens married, and the birth of their tenth child on 13 March 1852, Catherine was pregnant for approximately 2,800 of 5,824 days, slightly less than half the time (fig. 10; table 1).

Dickens first declared himself "quite satisfied" with the number of their children in November 1843, two months before the birth of Frank, their fifth, "importuning the Gods" to spare him in the future (Pilgrim 3:597). In 1845, with Catherine's sixth full-term pregnancy and the birth of Alfred, Dickens began to comment more frequently on the "Anti-Malthusian state" of his household (Pilgrim 6:146), increasingly aware that there could, in fact, be "too many Dickenses in the world." While sensitive to the suffering Catherine endured in labor and delivery, an ordeal that "cast...its shadow" before her in "a very disconcerting manner" (Pilgrim 4:301), Dickens perceived her childbearing as "overbearing" because of the sheer number of dependents to whom she gave birth, not because he thought "the parent tree" was being "exhausted." The worrisome effects of an "Anti-Malthusian state" were primarily financial in his eyes; he would have to provide for and educate his children and prepare seven sons for professions. "Take 'em away to the Fondling," Dickens joked to Macready six months after Catherine delivered Alfred and four months before Kitty delivered Cecilia, her ninth child, recommending that the Macreadys "be examined before the House of Commons Committee on Population" (Pilgrim 4:532). Suggesting that labor pains might be a deterrent to childbearing during Catherine's seventh full-term pregnancy and following Kitty's ninth, Dickens comically refused to try using mesmerism to ease them, fearing that the Macreadys might then only stop at eighteen (Pilgrim 4:647). Despite the joke, Dickens arranged for Catherine to be anesthetized during her eighth delivery. Her labor pains would be eliminated through the use of chloroform, its effects compared to those of mesmerism by contemporaries.

As both Catherine and her husband knew, there were more effective ways to limit family size than the pains of labor, though neither acknowledged them in writing. Catherine was probably reticent about discussing with her friends a subject deemed "unnatural" and unladylike,[5] and Dickens skirted the issue while bemoaning their fertility. "So you want a godchild," he replied to the novelist Catherine Gore in September 1852, when Plorn was five months old:

May I never have the opportunity of giving you one! But *if* I have—if my cup (I mean my quiver) be not yet full—then shall you hear again from

5. Kathryn Gleadle, *British Women in the Nineteenth Century* (New York: Palgrave, 2001), 81.

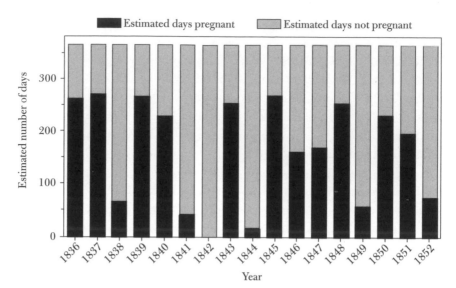

FIGURE 10. *Estimated days pregnant and not per year, 1836–1852.*
Data for figures 10 and 11 and tables 1 and 2 based on Catherine's dates of delivery
and miscarriage. Estimated dates of conception based on an average gestation period of 268 days
for full-term pregnancies and 60 days for miscarriages.

TABLE 1. *Catherine's dates of delivery and miscarriage, with estimated*
dates of conception

Births and miscarriages in chronological order	Estimated dates of conception	Dates of delivery or miscarriage
Charley (Charles Jr.)	13 April 1836	6 January 1837
miscarriage	15 March 1837	14 May 1837 (est.)
Mamie (Mary)	11 June 1837	6 March 1838
Katey (Catherine)	3 February 1839	29 October 1839
Walter	16 May 1840	8 February 1841
Frank (Francis)	22 April 1843	15 January 1844
Alfred	2 February 1845	28 October 1845
Sydney	24 July 1846	18 April 1847
miscarriage	29 October 1847	28 December 1847
Henry	22 April 1848	16 January 1849
Dora	21 November 1849	16 August 1850
Plorn (Edward)	19 June 1851	13 March 1852

the undersigned Camel that his back is broken by the addition of the last overbalancing straw.

What strange Kings those were in the Fairy times, who, with three thousand wives and four thousand seven hundred and fifty Concubines, found it necessary to put up prayers in all the Temples for a prince as beautiful as the day! I have some idea—with only one wife and nothing particular in any other direction—of interceding with the Bishop of London to have a little service in Saint Pauls beseeching that I may be considered to have done enough towards my country's population. (Pilgrim 6:756)

Implying that prayer and divine intervention are the only means available to him to halt Catherine's childbearing, Dickens humorously disavows his part in producing his own children, or recognizes it only obliquely, as he struggles—"my cup (I mean my quiver)"—to find the right image for his reproductive role before representing himself as a mere beast of burden with no choice in the matter. Yet the fact that Plorn *was* the Dickenses' last child suggests that the pair may have exercised more control over conception than Dickens's metaphors suggest.

Two months after delivering Plorn, Catherine turned thirty-seven, an age at which she was probably still capable of conceiving another child. In the mid-nineteenth century the mean age at last childbirth among Englishwomen was forty-one;[6] Catherine's own mother had given birth to twins at forty. Unless Catherine suddenly became infertile, she and her husband must have acted to prevent a thirteenth pregnancy—whether by having intercourse infrequently, abstaining from it altogether, and/or engaging in sexual activity that was noncoital. That they did not simply leave the possibility of conceiving another child to God, nature, or chance seems all the more likely when we consider the range in intervals between each pair of Catherine's successive pregnancies (her "conception waits," eleven in all) and recognize that these intervals correspond to a range in frequency of sexual intercourse, such frequency being the most important factor in the timing of conception among fertile women without the use of contraception. Studies indicate that, for such women, brief conception wait intervals of three to four months generally result from fifteen to twenty acts of intercourse per month, intervals of eleven to twelve months from four acts of intercourse per month, and intervals of twenty-two to forty-four months from fortnightly or monthly acts (fig. 11; table 2).[7]

6. John Bongaarts, "The Proximate Determinants of Natural Marital Fertility," in *Determinants of Fertility in Developing Countries,* vol. 1, ed. Rodolfo A. Bulatao and Ronald D. Lee (New York: Academic Press, 1983), 127.

7. These findings are based on clinical studies as well as mathematical models. See ibid., 116; and Szreter, *Fertility, Class and Gender in Britain,* 395.

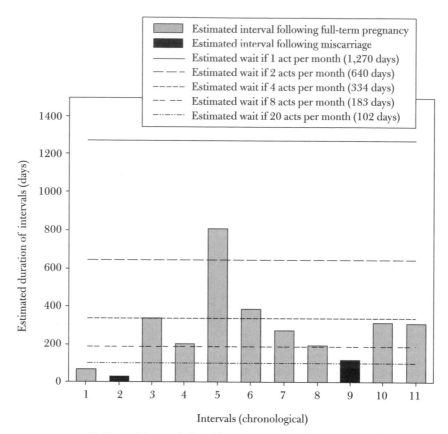

FIGURE 11. *Estimated intervals (1–11) between pregnancies, 1837–1851. (Correlations of estimated intervals to frequency of intercourse are provided in John Bongaarts, "The Proximate Determinants of Natural Marital Fertility," pp. 116–17.)*

TABLE 2. *Intervals between Catherine's dates of delivery and miscarriage and her estimated dates of next conception*

Interval number	Date of delivery or miscarriage to next estimated conception date	Interval length in days
1	6 January 1837–15 March 1837	68
2	14 May 1837 (est.)–11 June 1837	29
3	6 March 1838–3 February 1839	335
4	29 October 1839–16 May 1840	201
5	8 February 1841–22 April 1843	804
6	15 January 1844–2 February 1845	384
7	28 October 1845–24 July 1846	270
8	18 April 1847–29 October 1847	194
9	28 December 1847–22 April 1848	117
10	16 January 1849–21 November 1849	310
11	16 August 1850–19 June 1851	307

It may seem strange to characterize Catherine's twelve pregnancies and ten children as the result of planning or restraint of *any* kind, the assumption being that the Dickenses' sexual activity was limited primarily by circumstance: his work schedule, her confinements, and their travels and time apart. Nonetheless, under what demographers consider "a fertility-maximizing regime,"[8] Catherine could have given birth to more children than her ten, particularly since she did not experience the prolonged periods of postpartum amenorrhea that are triggered by nursing and often prevent breast-feeding mothers from conceiving for months after childbirth. In a century in which "coital spacing" was the principal method of birth control among married couples,[9] the Dickenses may have employed that method at least some of the time, and not only after the birth of Plorn. The longest interval between Catherine's twelve pregnancies—the nearly twenty-nine months separating the birth of Walter from the conception of Frank (interval 5 in fig. 11)—seems the most likely instance, since that gap coincides with their anticipation of, and travels during, their six-month tour of North America, when it would have been particularly inconvenient for Catherine to be pregnant or confined.

The remainder of Catherine's conception wait intervals are considerably shorter, though there are some notable variations. While the time separating Walter's birth from Frank's conception would be most likely to result when intercourse takes place less than twice a month, five of Catherine's eleven intervals would be expected from weekly intercourse, two of her intervals from biweekly intercourse, and three from intercourse at least as often as every other day. Of the three shortest intervals, two follow Catherine's miscarriages in 1837 and 1847. These reflect the rapid return to ovulation in women whose pregnancy ends in miscarriage rather than full-term delivery;[10] but they also suggest that Catherine may have been particularly anxious to become pregnant again after experiencing what she considered the loss of a child.

As the mother of ten, Catherine suffered some of the damaging physical effects of what obstetricians now term "great grand multiparity"[11]—effects that include

8. Szreter, *Fertility, Class and Gender in Britain*, 395.

9. Ibid., 394.

10. See, for example, M. L. Donnet et al., "Return of Ovarian Function Following Spontaneous Abortion," *Clinical Endocrinology* 33, no. 1 (1990): 13–20.

11. Use of the term "multiparity" among British physicians and the medical consideration of its effects date from the 1860s. In the 1880s, expert James Matthews Duncan, in *On Fertility in Woman* (London: J. & A. Churchill, 1884), classified "families above ten" as "excessive" and "dangerous to the lives and injurious to the health of both mothers and children" (33, 74), and by the 1930s, "the dangerous multipara" was a familiar phrase; see, for example,

pelvic floor dysfunction (incontinence and genital prolapse), diabetes, recurrent breech presentations, macrosomic (high birth weight) deliveries, and an elevated risk of cervical cancer, to which Catherine succumbed in 1879.[12] Nonetheless, she wanted to have children, enjoyed motherhood, and never voiced regret at giving birth ten times. If she ever felt, with Francis Jeffrey, that certain of her pregnancies were "overbearings," she kept those feelings to herself. Insofar as Catherine might be seen to express regret over her childbearing, she did so indirectly, in relation to her first five deliveries, not her last—that is, in her tearful confinements of 1837 and 1838 and her apprehensions before Frank's birth in 1844. When, in 1859, she recalled the birth of "little Dora," her "9th child," she represented it as a welcome sign of the affection she and Dickens had felt for each other in 1850,[13] not as the burdensome task Jeffrey refers to in his letter.

It may seem ironic that Catherine was more accepting of her multiparity than Dickens was, since she was the one who suffered most directly and palpably from its effects. But she also benefited from repeated childbearing in ways that her husband could not, since her sense of worth, purpose, and community was largely dependent on it. Not only did the births of her children and her children's children testify to a marriage that was long-loving, but also they provided her with some of her most important and enduring ties and constituted the "wealth" she produced and accrued as a married woman without earning power or property rights. "I congratulate you now most heartily on the birth of your first granddaughter," Catherine characteristically wrote to her friend Mary Chester, married to painter George Chester, in 1869. "Bessie [Charley's wife] had her *fifth* daughter about six weeks

---

B. Solomons, "The Dangerous Multipara," *Lancet* 2, no. 8 (1934): 8–11. While "grand multiparity" describes women who deliver at least five times, "great grand multiparity" describes those who have ten or more children.

12. See B. M. Audu et al., "The Influence of Reproductive and Marital Factors on Cervical Dyskaryosis," *Journal of Obstetrics and Gynaecology* 21, no. 6 (2001): 622–25; E. Maymon et al., "Peripartum Complications in Grand Multiparous Women," *European Journal of Obstetrics, Gynecology, and Reproductive Biology* 81, no. 1 (1998): 21–25; K. Fuchs et al., "The 'Grand Multipara'—Is It a Problem?" *International Journal of Gynaecology and Obstetrics* 23, no. 4 (1985): 321–26; E. Fornell et al., "Factors Associated with Pelvic Floor Dysfunction," *Acta Obstetrica et Gynecologica Scandinavica* 83 (2004): 383–89; and A. T. Abu-Heija and H. El Chalabi, "Great Grand Multiparity: Is It a Risk?" *Institute of Obstetrics and Gynaecology* 18, no. 2 (1998): 136–38.

13. Catherine Dickens to Angela Burdett Coutts, 18 July 1859 (copy in the hand of Katey Perugini), Charles Dickens Museum, London.

ago, so you see I am richer than you in that respect, but I have only one grandson, *Charles the 3rd.*"[14]

Rather than referring to Thomas Malthus or to committees on population in her letters, as Dickens does, Catherine responds to news of births among relatives, friends, and acquaintances "safely confined" with congratulations and delight.[15] She is interested in the details of labor, concerned with the well-being of mother and child, and pleased when a delivery goes quickly, particularly in the case of "a first." "Dear Bessie was safely delivered at ½ past two o'clock this morning of a fine little girl," Catherine announces to Nelly Lemon in 1862. "She had an excellent time for a first child, as she was only really ill from ½ past eleven and it was all well over within three hours."[16] Catherine made a point of reading the births columns in the daily papers, eager to catch the news that shaped the lives of the women around her. "We see, in the Times of yesterday, which we received here this morning, that dear Helen's confinement has taken place, and that she has a son," Catherine wrote to Helen Tagart, the new grandmother, from Boulogne in July 1854. "I lose no time in writing to offer you our warmest congratulations on the event, and to say that we are very anxious indeed to hear how Helen and her baby are going on and I shall think it very kind if you or [daughter] Emily will write me a line here to let me know. Perhaps you are with Helen?"[17]

As her letters reveal, childbearing gave Catherine and her friends a strong sense of community. From a first delivery to a last, it was a subject of common interest and experience and a means of bringing together female relations, often reuniting grown daughters with their mothers—hence Catherine's question to Mrs. Tagart. Both Catherine's mother and her mother-in-law were present at Charley's birth, and once they returned to their own homes, Mary Hogarth took their place, seeing to her sister's needs. Catherine's last deliveries, like her first, brought Hogarth women together. When Dora was born at Devonshire Terrace, Mrs. Hogarth stayed with Catherine during her confinement, with supplemental help from Helen, while Georgina supervised the older children in Broadstairs.

14. ALS Catherine Dickens to Mrs. Chester, 16 September 1869, D. Jacques Benoliel Collection of the Letters of Charles Dickens, 86-2745, Rare Book Department, Free Library of Philadelphia.

15. ALS Catherine Dickens to George Cattermole, 9 October [1843], Dunedin Public Libraries, Dunedin, New Zealand.

16. ALS Catherine Dickens to Mrs. Lemon, 31 October 1862, Charles Dickens Museum, London.

17. ALS Catherine Dickens to Mrs. Tagart, 6 July 1854, Charles Dickens Museum, London.

But while childbearing placed Catherine in a supportive network of women, her deliveries after 1847 positioned her in a very different community as well: as a female patient and challenging obstetrical case to be discussed, diagnosed, and treated by a cohort of male physicians, in consultation with her husband. Following her seventh delivery, Catherine became a proving ground for therapeutic innovation, most notably the controversial use of chloroform during labor and delivery. First anesthetized for Henry's birth in 1849, she was not "present" for the delivery, entering a temporary state of unconsciousness in which the dissociation of her mind from her body liberated her from pain but was itself symptomatic of troubling new ways in which she was being perceived.

"WOMEN WILL BETIMES REBEL AGAINST ENDURING THE USUAL TORTURES"

Considered in its immediate context—in terms of the debate in the late 1840s over obstetric anesthesia—Catherine's willingness to try chloroform for her eighth delivery recalls her joking skepticism about Eve's transgression in the Garden. While her favorite joke questioned the biblical account of Eve's temptation, her attempt to allay the pains of labor was understood by chloroform's opponents as subverting Eve's punishment after the Fall. "It has been ordered, that 'in sorrow shall she bring forth,'" a writer in the *Edinburgh Medical and Surgical Journal* noted in July 1847, six months after James Young Simpson first administered anesthesia to an obstetric patient in the city of Catherine's birth, reprimanding the doctor for "forgetting" chapter 3 of Genesis.[18]

As Simpson recalled, patients, doctors, and members of the clergy sometimes voiced this concern when he began using anesthesia for deliveries, and while a minister of his acquaintance absolved a woman who felt she had sinned by mitigating her labor pains, not all clergymen were willing to follow suit. "A few of the more narrow minded...joined in the cry against the new practice," Simpson noted, one declaring chloroform to be a "decoy of Satan, apparently offering itself to bless

18. "Injurious Effects of the Inhalation of Ether," *Edinburgh Medical and Surgical Journal* (July 1847), quoted in James Young Simpson, *Anaesthesia, or the Employment of Chloroform and Ether in Surgery, Midwifery, etc.* (Philadelphia: Lindsay & Blakiston, 1849), 110. As Donald Caton explains, Simpson and his colleagues preferred chloroform to ether because it was "much easier to administer...and less irritating to the lungs and throat." Its damage to the liver went unrecognized for over fifty years. See Donald Caton, *What a Blessing She Had Chloroform: The Medical and Social Response to the Pain of Childbirth from 1800 to the Present* (New Haven: Yale University Press, 1999), 10.

woman, but, in the end . . . rob[bing] God of the deep earnest cries which arise in time of trouble for help."[19]

Simpson responded to his critics in an "Answer to the Religious Objections Advanced Against the Employment of Anaesthetic Agents in Midwifery and Surgery," published in December 1847. Here Simpson refuted scriptural objections to his use of anesthesia by noting that God promised to lift the "primeval curse" against Eve; by outlining ways in which people already used technology to ease suffering; and by disputing the interpretation of the Hebrew word for "sorrow" *(etzebh)* in Genesis as "pain," arguing instead that God punished Eve with "labor" or "toil," inflicted on women in childbirth regardless of their level of suffering. "Anaesthesia does not withdraw or abolish that muscular effort, toil, or labour," he assured his readers, "for if so, it would then stop, and arrest entirely the act of parturition itself. But it removes the physical pain and agony otherwise attendant on these muscular contractions and efforts."[20]

While Simpson's "Answer" was seen to meet the religious objections of his critics,[21] the debate over chloroform continued, the grounds shifting among various anxieties provoked by its use. Most obviously, patients and physicians were concerned about the physical safety of anesthesia, numerous deaths and complications having been attributed to it. As medical writers explained, chloroform put obstetrical patients at risk, since physicians relied on the reactions of the women in the course of delivering them, particularly during difficult births. When obstetrical instruments were used, "to render . . . patients insensible, is greatly to increase their danger," a reviewer noted in the *London Journal of Medicine,* citing John Banner of the Liverpool Royal Institution: "Men are not all equally clever and expert in the application of the forceps; and much injury has been avoided by the patient's expressions of pain when there has been a wrong application of them."[22] G. T. Gream, a medical officer at Queen Charlotte's Lying-in Hospital, agreed: "By depriving the patient of sensation, we take away a great guide to the

19. James Young Simpson to Dr. Protheroe Smith, in *Anaesthesia,* 123.

20. James Young Simpson, "Answer to the Religious Objections Advanced Against the Employment of Anaesthetic Agents in Midwifery and Surgery," in *Anaesthesia,* 111, 113–15.

21. Review of S. William J. Merriman, *Arguments Against the Indiscriminate Use of Chloroform in Midwifery* (1848); G. T. Gream, *Misapplication of Anaesthesia in Childbirth* (1849); and W. F. Montgomery, *Objections to the Indiscriminate Administration of Anaesthetic Agents in Midwifery* (1849), *London Journal of Medicine* 7 (July 1849): 636.

22. Ibid., 638.

correct application of the forceps."[23] The insensibility of female patients was seen as dangerous for another reason: because medical attendants were suspected of violating women unable to object or defend themselves. In the 1850s the *Lancet* warned British physicians about the "temptations the anesthetized patient might present" after a Philadelphia practitioner was found guilty of sexual assault in such a case.[24]

While chloroform left women's bodies vulnerable, the "destruction of [their] consciousness" was troubling in and of itself. At least one "eminent London divine" termed it "unnatural," Simpson recounted, while some of his colleagues objected that they were "not entitled to put the activity and consciousness of the mind of any patient in abeyance."[25] Even more troubling to some practitioners was the growing perception that the mind was not, in fact, *put* in abeyance by chloroform—or so the alleged "intoxication" of women by the anesthetic suggested.[26] Unless a heavy dose was administered, and administered *quickly,* patients were "deprived" of one type of sensation only to be provided with another. As Gream put it, chloroform gave rise to "obscene expression and actions" and to "lascivious dreams" among those to whom it was administered, a result of the drug's "irritation of the cerebellum" in combination with "the excitement incidental to manipulation of the sexual organs...or to the presence of the foetal head within the pelvis."[27] Gream's observations were supported by those of W. Tyler Smith, who claimed that when anesthesia was given to women in childbirth, "sexual orgasm...substituted for their natural pains—an exchange which women of modesty would more shrink from, than the liveliest agony."[28] Although "the very ice of chastity" is found in "the women of England," the *London Journal of Medicine* observed, numerous accounts of "lascivious ravings" in "parturient women...under the influence" had

23. G. T. Gream, *Misapplication of Anaesthesia in Childbirth, Exemplified by Facts* (London, 1849), quoted in *London Journal of Medicine* review, 638.

24. Mary Poovey, *Uneven Developments: The Ideological Work of Gender in Mid-Victorian England* (Chicago: University of Chicago Press, 1988), 39. Poovey cites "Care in the Use of Chloroform," *Lancet* 2 (1854): 495.

25. Simpson, *Anaesthesia,* 120, 183–84.

26. *London Journal of Medicine* review, 635.

27. Gream, *Misapplication of Anaesthesia,* quoted in *London Journal of Medicine* review, 638.

28. W. Tyler Smith, *Lancet* 1 (1848): 376, quoted in Poovey, *Uneven Developments,* 38.

been reported, and thus it was recommended that medical attendants use a higher dose of chloroform to prevent "these unpleasant manifestations."[29]

As Mary Poovey argues in discussing the chloroform debate, the lasciviousness the drug was believed to evoke in respectably de-eroticized women threatened to undermine ideas of sexual difference that childbirth presumably reinforced.[30] This threat was compounded by reports that patients were demanding chloroform for their deliveries, forgetting their social position and urging pregnant friends to do the same.[31] Obstetricians were being "dragooned" by "conceited or ignorant women" who made "a pastime of . . . quackeries," a *Lancet* writer warned.[32] Simpson criticized his wary colleagues, asserting that "women themselves will betimes rebel against enduring the usual tortures and miseries of childbirth" rather than defer to doctors too apathetic or prejudiced to alleviate their pain.[33] Yet Gream found such arguments "pernicious" and believed that they left medical men with "no voice in the matter" while giving women a false idea of their "rights."[34]

Catherine did not demand chloroform as her "right" but evidently wished to use it, and Dickens "promised her that she should have it" (Pilgrim 5:487), Sydney's delivery having been difficult and frightening. The two were aware of the controversy surrounding obstetrical anesthesia; Dickens had five of Simpson's pamphlets in his library when it was catalogued in 1870, and he echoed their claims in recounting Henry's birth. The couple had most likely met Simpson in Edinburgh after Catherine's second miscarriage. Francis Jeffrey, their host at the time, knew Simpson, having confidentially consulted with the famous doctor about the medical treatment of his own wife.[35]

29. *London Journal of Medicine* review, 638. Simpson acknowledged that "small doses" of anesthesia "are accompanied with excitement and talking," but he disputed their allegedly lascivious character, charging that those who have "averred" such things were only revealing "the sensuality of their own thoughts" (*Anaesthesia,* 145, 148).

30. Poovey, *Uneven Developments,* 50.

31. G. T. Gream, *Remarks on the Employment of Anaesthetic Agents in Midwifery* (London: Churchill, 1848), 34–35.

32. *Lancet* 2 (1847): 677, quoted in Poovey, *Uneven Developments,* 47.

33. James Young Simpson, "Superinduction of Anaesthesia in Natural and Morbid Parturition," paper read to the Medico-Chirurgical Society of Edinburgh, 1 December 1847, in *Anaesthesia,* 101–2.

34. Gream, *Remarks on the Employment of Anaesthetic Agents,* 5–7.

35. Francis Jeffrey to James Young Simpson, two letters, n.d., J.Y.S. 667 and 668, James Young Simpson Papers, Royal College of Surgeons of Edinburgh.

There is only one detailed description of Catherine's 1849 anesthetization, provided by her husband to Macready two weeks after she gave birth. Dickens's account shows that he and Catherine had considered the dangers of anesthesia and felt confident that they could avert them. Dickens arranged for Samuel John Tracy, an expert on the use of chloroform, to administer it while others focused on the delivery itself. In 1847 Tracy had given ether to the first woman to have a cesarean section under general anesthesia at St. Bartholomew Hospital, and he had invented an apparatus for the inhalation of ether before chloroform became the anesthetic of choice. Positioned at Catherine's side, Tracy applied chloroform in controlled doses, with a handkerchief, monitoring her pulse and respiration. The delivery was left to Henry Davis and Charles Morgan, both of whom objected in vain to the use of chloroform on their patient.[36] "Chloroform did wonders" for Catherine, Dickens told William Empson, Jeffrey's son-in-law, on 21 January 1849, five days after the birth; although Henry's delivery "was almost as bad a one as its predecessor[,] . . . she knew nothing of it" (Pilgrim 5:478).

The use of chloroform on Catherine reveals Dickens's concern with her comfort and well-being during the delivery, which he described as if it were a shared experience; a number of plural pronouns recur in his detailed account. Yet even more clearly than her other deliveries, Catherine's anesthetized childbirth reveals what *wasn't* shared between them: the conscious experience of the event and the control and authority associated with consciousness. Despite anxieties about the liberating effects of chloroform for women—freed from labor pains and, allegedly, from propriety and restraint—the drug's effects were also confining. As medical historians point out, Victorian advocates of obstetric anesthesia numbered among its advantages its ability to "subdue [women's] resistance to medical authority"; chloroform was even caricatured in the nineteenth-century press as a "prescription for scolding wives" and a "taming of the shrew."[37]

At first glance, Dickens's account of Catherine's eighth delivery gives no indication of any such "taming." "Kate is wonderfully well—eating mutton chops in

36. See John L. Thornton, "Samuel John Tracy (1813–1901): The Early Use of Anaesthetics at St. Bartholomew's Hospital, London," *Anaesthesia* 7 (April 1952): 72–76. Although Tracy, Morgan, and Davis go unnamed by Dickens, his bank records reveal their involvement in Catherine's delivery.

37. Ornella Moscucci, *The Science of Woman: Gynaecology and Gender in England, 1800–1929* (Cambridge: Cambridge University Press, 1990), 126; Martin S. Pernick, *A Calculus of Suffering: Pain, Professionalism, and Anesthesia in Nineteenth-Century America* (New York: Columbia University Press, 1985), 86, 174.

the drawing room," and "sends you her dear love," he reported to Macready on 2 February 1849, two weeks after Henry's birth.

> The boy is what the Persian Princes might have called a "moon-faced" monster. He did not, however, come into the world as he ought to have done (I don't know in what we have offended Nature, but she seems to have taken something in us amiss) and we had to call in extra counsel and assistance. Foreseeing the possibility of such a repetition of last time, I had made myself thoroughly acquainted in Edinburgh with the *facts* of chloroform—in contradistinction to the talk about it—and had insisted on the attendance of a gentleman from Bartholomew's Hospital, who administers it in the operations there, and has given it four or five thousand times.... The doctors were dead against it, but I stood my ground, and (thank God) triumphantly. It spared her all pain (she had no sensation, but of a great display of sky-rockets) and saved the child all mutilation. (Pilgrim 5:486–87)

Catherine's anesthetization ensured her safety and the baby's, Dickens explains, though as it is, Henry resembles a "'moon-faced' monster"—as opposed to the "moon-faced" beauties who figure in the *Arabian Nights*.

Rather than suffering through what was likely another breech delivery, Catherine was spared its pain. More importantly, she escaped the nervous "shock" produced by a long and agonizing labor. So Dickens contends, echoing Simpson's defense of chloroform and attributing Catherine's rapid recovery to the drug.

> It enabled the doctors to do, as they afterwards very readily said, in ten minutes, what might otherwise have taken them an hour and a half; the shock to her nervous system was reduced to nothing; and she was, to all intents and purposes, *well*, next day. Administered by some one who has nothing else to do, who knows its symptoms thoroughly, who keeps his hand upon the pulse, and his eyes upon the face, and uses nothing but a hand kerchief, and that lightly, I am convinced that it is as safe in its administration, as it is miraculous and merciful in its effects. This the Edinburgh Professors assured me, and certainly our experience thoroughly confirms them. (Pilgrim 5:487)

Ostensibly, Catherine's experience with chloroform represents a victory over her wary and conservative doctors, which is achieved by her husband for her sake: "I stood my ground...(thank God) triumphantly." Possessing "the *facts*" about obstetrical anesthesia, Dickens overcomes the objections of Davis and Morgan, enlightening *them*. They ultimately concede that, with anesthesia, they accomplished the maneuvers necessary for the delivery in ten minutes rather than ninety.

Yet Henry's birth represents, more significantly, a triumph over Mother Nature, who had perversely set obstacles in its way. Henry "did not...come into the world as he ought to have done," Dickens jokes, he and Catherine somehow having "offended Nature." Instead of being natural—or unnatural—the birth is technological and scientific, an instance of medical specialization and its advantages, and constitutes a victory of male medical expertise over natural forces—the "miracle" of chloroform instead of the miracle of birth. But as a triumph over Mother Nature, Catherine's delivery also represents a triumph over Catherine herself. Safely and painlessly delivered of a breech baby, happily eating mutton chops in the drawing room two weeks later, Catherine enjoys her success in childbearing. Yet her victory is compromised by the method through which it is achieved: the dissociation of her mind from her body through the "destruction of consciousness" and her consequent objectification—incapable of guiding her doctors, cooperating with them, or questioning their decisions, and seemingly absent from the difficult delivery. "She knew nothing of it," Dickens contends.

By the time Dickens is through recounting the event to Macready, Catherine is not only an unconscious and unfeeling body ("she had no sensation") but a depersonalized and disassembled one as well—"the pulse" on which the anesthesiologist keeps his hand and "the face" on which he keeps his eyes. Deprived of integrity and agency in Dickens's description, she recalls the "unresisting" and "apathetic" mother who is prevented by her anesthetization from "those sudden shrinkings and changes of position [from] which the boldest and firmest woman cannot sometimes abstain," as Simpson writes.[38] Whether a woman demonstrates boldness and firmness or the failure of such traits in refusing to hold still during her delivery, she exhibits the volition that chloroform checks, transmuting her into a "relax[ed]...maternal passage" readily accessible to her medical attendants and their instruments.[39] As Dickens conceives of it, Catherine's delivery testifies not to her own strength or endurance but rather to the foresight and courage of her husband and the knowledge of "the Edinburgh Professors," confirmed in their assurances about chloroform, its powers, and their own.

<hr/>

38. James Young Simpson, "Results of the Practice of Anaesthesia in Midwifery," *Edinburgh Monthly Journal of Medical Science* (October 1848), reprinted in *Anaesthesia,* 144.

39. Ibid. As Poovey notes, "representing woman as an 'unresisting body' removed the grounds for any objections actual women might pose to the doctor's interpretation." The letters from practitioners that Simpson reprinted "exult in the power with which chloroform could 'lay the most restless or ungovernable patient quiet on her pillow'" (*Uneven Developments,* 29).

In using anesthesia for Henry's birth, the Dickenses aligned themselves with medical innovators and reformers, Catherine's eighth delivery reenacting in miniature a larger medical debate, with her consulting physicians defending their conventional mode of practice and Dickens, with Tracy, following "the Edinburgh Professors" and emerging triumphant. Catherine seems aligned with the latter party, yet her *own* success and interests are less than clear. Delivered without her knowledge or conscious participation, she becomes a female "system" that others manage and control. While her anesthetized delivery relieved her from pain and anxiety, it also encouraged Dickens to think of her at a remove, despite their continued intimacy and affection—to talk *about* her as much as *with* her in matters pertaining to her well-being, consulting with medical men and close male friends on the "subject" of his wife, and, unwittingly or not, devaluing her own perceptions.

Catherine's state of unconsciousness in labor while she is surrounded by "thinking men" is connected to another notable absence: the narrative gap central to the event. Her experience of the delivery, like her experience of mesmerism earlier in the decade, is related by Dickens, not herself. This may seem inevitable. Yet women who experienced the effects of chloroform had tales to tell, though these were usually made public in a way that suited their doctors, the experts authorized to write on the subject. As Poovey notes, women's firsthand accounts are scarce not because of "a person's inability to narrate unconsciousness" but because "the right to write about the body belonged to men" at midcentury; women were quoted only "when their words supported a medical man's position, and even then these passages emphasized primarily the difference between women's unsophisticated attitude . . . and the doctor's scientific understanding."[40]

In fact, Catherine described her experience of Henry's birth to her husband—and probably to several others—although she did not give her description written form. Out of necessity, then, we must rely on her husband's account of the delivery to reconstruct her experience of it. We need not accept Dickens's account as definitive, however. Just as we resisted his magnetic powers when reconstructing Catherine's experience of submission to him, acknowledging the agency she exercised in her mesmerized state, so we can counter her objectification in his narrative of her unconscious delivery—by reading between the lines, placing *our* emphasis differently from *his,* and recognizing Catherine's presence in her seeming absence.

In the 1840s, Dickens joked about using mesmerism to ease childbirth pains while Simpson faced criticism for failing to see that it might "entirely supercede"

---

40. Poovey, *Uneven Developments,* 218 n. 71, 43–44.

chloroform in labor and delivery.[41] The tie between chloroform and mesmerism is significant for Catherine's story, for under the influence of both, she suspended her agency and her consciousness, submitting to male authority and control. Catherine became a mesmerized subject willingly and proved able to break her trance. But having submitted to anesthetization, she could not will herself back to consciousness. Even so, her powers of mind continued to function during her mental "absence," although their workings were subconscious and acknowledged by Dickens only in a parenthetical aside ("she had no sensation, but of a great display of sky-rockets"). While Catherine's vision of a fireworks display is not necessarily a sexual one and was not interpreted by Dickens as such, it connects her to the women whose allegedly unruly thoughts and behavior under the influence of chloroform marked a presence that could not be altogether suppressed or ignored. Despite the efforts of medical attendants to enforce "the strictest quietude" around anesthetized women so as to keep them from talking,[42] they nonetheless continued to think and to interpret their experiences, whether in a dream state or a waking one, and whether silent or vocal. Catherine's "great display of sky-rockets" reminds us of the importance of what, to Dickens, seems merely parenthetical, material largely unspoken, displaced, or encoded in her story—thoughts and feelings suppressed or articulated only indirectly, subconsciously, or subtextually: the telling silence and gesture, the dream, the mistake.

"It is not cool at all, oh no," Charley wrote to his mother from Eton in 1851 after Catherine mistakenly sent the fourteen-year-old an angry letter written to his father by Rosina Bulwer Lytton, estranged from Sir Edward.[43] In her letter, Rosina complained that the two men, engaged to perform for Queen Victoria in *Not So Bad As We Seem* to benefit the Guild of Literature and Art, were "even *worse* than [they] seem," and she threatened "to attend" and disrupt "the Fooleries."[44] We cannot

41. "Religious Objections to Chloroform Anticipated," *India Register of Medical Science*, February 1848, J.Y.S. 226, James Young Simpson Papers, Royal College of Surgeons of Edinburgh, transcribed by J. R. Maltby, 2001. Simpson was criticized privately and in medical journals for failing to recognize the importance of "mesmeric births." In February 1848 an old medical acquaintance complained to him that he "never mentioned" mesmerism and referred him to a London *Times* notice of a delivery accomplished during "mesmeric sleep." J.Y.S. 228, James Young Simpson Papers, Royal College of Surgeons of Edinburgh, transcribed by J. R. Maltby, 2001.

42. Simpson, *Anaesthesia*, 148.

43. ALS Charley Dickens to Catherine Dickens, 11 May 1851, Lytton Papers, quoted in Pilgrim 6:388–89 n. 2.

44. Rosina Bulwer Lytton to Charles Dickens [May 1851], Lytton Papers, quoted in Pilgrim 6:388 n. 2.

tell if Catherine "meant" for Charley to read this letter, although she was no doubt struck by Rosina's threats and claims, and by Dickens's efforts to silence them. Bulwer Lytton would later have Rosina confined to a lunatic asylum after she took her marital protests to the streets in the summer of 1858 but in May 1851 it was Dickens who arranged for a police detective to attend rehearsals and performances of the play in case Rosina should appear.[45]

Unlike Rosina, Catherine wrote politely to Bulwer Lytton over the years, though she, too, may have been upset by all the time and energy that Dickens, with Rosina's husband, was devoting to amateur theatricals and the causes they helped support. A proper lady, Catherine did not express anger any more openly than she did sexual desire. Yet she silently set off fireworks on occasion and let others besides her husband speak for her when she chose to remain silent, including women much more clearly dissatisfied than herself.

NOT SO BAD AS SHE SEEMS

For all their differences, Rosina Bulwer Lytton and Catherine Dickens shared common ground: both were unfairly charged with mental illness by their estranged husbands, charges echoed by critics and biographers well into the twentieth century. The case against Rosina depends in part on allegations that she was a woman "on whom maternity sat very lightly"—an unfeeling mother who wrote novels rather than caring for her children and heartlessly sent her babies out to nurse.[46] The case against Catherine traces the "mental disorder" with which Dickens would charge her in 1858 to her supposed maternal difficulties in 1850 and 1851—her reputed bout with a disabling postpartum depression following the birth of her ninth child, Dora, culminating in a "nervous breakdown" the following year. While Edgar Johnson, Peter Ackroyd, and most other Dickens biographers seem interested in the state of Catherine's mind during her late childbearing period, when Dickens and the medical experts were increasingly focused on her body, they assume that a woman's thoughts and behavior are governed by her allegedly unstable reproductive system and that, if Catherine was ailing or unhappy in the early 1850s, postpartum depression was necessarily the cause. To the extent that Catherine was "depressed" in 1851, her feelings resulted from the *death* of baby Dora, not from Dora's *birth*. To understand Catherine's difficulties properly, we need to consider her care for Dora during the baby's illness and apparent recovery in February, followed by the baby's

45. See Virginia Blain, "Rosina Bulwer Lytton and the Rage of the Unheard," *Huntington Library Quarterly* 53, no. 3 (Summer 1990): 211–36.

46. Ibid., 221. Here Blain quotes from Alice Acland, *Caroline Norton* (London: Constable, 1948), 82, to challenge claims that Rosina was a negligent mother.

sudden death in mid-April, and recognize her "breakdown" for what it was: a normal reaction of grief to the loss of her child, the first of three to predecease her.

Catherine must have conceived Dora toward the end of November 1849, ten months after the birth of Henry. In the interval, she and Dickens hosted large dinner and evening parties at Devonshire Terrace and spent the summer at Bonchurch on the Isle of Wight. Catherine's circle of women acquaintances had broadened as she met Jane Carlyle, novelist Elizabeth Gaskell, and naturalist Phebe Lankester, and her friendships with Nelly Lemon and Annie Leech became more intimate.[47]

Although Dickens described her as "rather unwieldy for going out" within a month of her confinement (Pilgrim 6:132), Catherine remained active during her ninth full-term pregnancy. She went to the opera with the Hogarths, dined at the Macreadys', and celebrated her fourteenth anniversary with Dickens and Forster in Richmond. The banking records reflect her household activity for 1849 and 1850 and show that the amount of money specifically allotted to her by her husband exceeded that allotted to himself for the first time since 1837: her £139.18 to his £135.16 in 1849, and her £193.13.6 to his £169.5 in 1850.[48] Busy with the eight children, Catherine invited guests to Charley's thirteenth birthday party in January 1850 and prepared him to leave for Eton a few days later. Writing to Edward Chapman, she explained that she wanted "a nice Bible and Prayer Book for him," asking the publisher to send several with a price list so that she could choose the one she thought best. "For [her] little girls," Catherine requested three other books from Chapman, *Elizabeth; or the Exiles of Siberia* among them.[49] With Georgina, she visited Charley at Eton. Mindful of the children's health, particularly during the 1849 cholera outbreak, she discouraged Dickens from socializing with friends whose children were ill, worried that he might "bring...home infection" (Pilgrim 5:530).

Catherine gave birth to Dora on 16 August 1850, but her ninth delivery is less fully documented than her eighth. Although she referred to Dora's birth in writing to Angela Burdett Coutts after her separation from Dickens, Catherine did not disclose any of the details surrounding the delivery, and Dickens evidently did not write about it to Macready, his usual confidant on such matters. In August 1850 the actor was in London; on the brink of retirement, he was preparing to move from

47. Planning to attend the annual dinner of the General Theatrical Fund in May 1849 with Georgina, Mrs. Hogarth, and Helen, Catherine wrote to "dearest Annie," who would be joining them, advising her friend on what to wear. ALS Catherine Dickens to Annie Leech, 16 May 1849, D. Jacques Benoliel Collection of the Letters of Charles Dickens, 62-0537, Rare Book Department, Free Library of Philadelphia.

48. Charles Dickens, Esq., Account Ledger, Coutts & Co., London.

49. ALS Catherine Dickens to Mr. Chapman, [4 January 1850], British Library.

Clarence Terrace to Sherborne in Dorset. He may have heard about the event from Dickens in person, or perhaps he seemed too busy for such confidences—or too mournful, having lost his eldest daughter, Nina, less than six months earlier.

From Dickens's banking records, we know that Charles Morgan attended the birth and that Samuel Tracy was once again present to administer chloroform. A monthly nurse may also have been hired, since John Dickens sent a £20 check to an unknown recipient on his son's behalf for services provided during Catherine's ninth confinement. As they did for her eighth delivery, Morgan received £5 and Tracy £3.3.[50] The news that Dickens relays in August 1850 is glowing but vague. Catherine is "happily confined," he informs journalist W. H. Wills on the sixteenth, and "in a noble condition," he tells Miss Coutts one week later. "Kate, brilliant! Ditto, little Dora!" he writes artist Frank Stone (Pilgrim 6:149, 155). By mid-August, Georgina had gone to Broadstairs with the children and servants, and Dickens joined them on the evening of Dora's birth, leaving Catherine in the care of Mrs. Hogarth and Helen. Within hours of his departure from Devonshire Terrace, Mrs. Hogarth sent "good tidings" of Catherine, followed by "excellent accounts" on the eighteenth and nineteenth (Pilgrim 6:151). By then Catherine had decided to join her husband and children on 6 September, and Dickens was pleased to learn of her plans. "We all want you very much," he assured her; "without you we shall be quite incomplete and a great blank everywhere" (Pilgrim 6:152, 150). Traveling between London and Broadstairs as he worked on *David Copperfield,* Dickens told Georgina in early September that Catherine was looking well; before leaving Devonshire Terrace, she had already started to plan family dinners (Pilgrim 6:164, 162). With Dora and Mary Gartland, the baby's wet nurse, Catherine left London for the coast on the day she had named, escorted by her husband.

Despite Catherine's steady recovery in the weeks following Dora's birth, most of the standard biographies represent her as afflicted with postpartum depression at the time. "All the evidence suggests that she suffered from a peculiarly intense form of post-natal depression and illness... culminating in bad attacks of migraine as well as a general 'giddiness' or 'sickness,'" Ackroyd writes, dismissing firsthand accounts that point to a different conclusion.[51] Summarizing the events of 1850–51 in the lives of the Dickenses, the editors of the Pilgrim *Letters* also refer to Catherine's

50. Charles Dickens, Esq., Account Ledger, Coutts & Co., London.

51. Peter Ackroyd, *Dickens* (New York: HarperCollins, 1990), 620. Catherine's *real* state was "not... always visible" to those around her, Ackroyd claims, dismissing credible witnesses. Ackroyd's scholarship is particularly unreliable at this point. Among his errors, he misidentifies James Wilson as "Dr. Watson" and Knotsford Lodge as "Knutsworth" (621). In *Charles Dickens* (New Haven: Yale University Press, 2009), Michael Slater makes no mention

"post-natal" illness, though they are somewhat more conjectural in their claim, noting that in March 1851, eight months after Dora's birth, "Catherine was sufficiently unwell from a nervous illness (probably abnormally long-lasting attacks of migraine combined with post-natal depression) for Dickens to take her for treatment under Dr. James Wilson at Malvern" (Pilgrim 6:viii–ix).

While Ackroyd fails to provide a source for his claims about Catherine's "post-natal" crisis, the Pilgrim editors cite Dr. W. H. Bowen's *Charles Dickens and His Family* (1956) on the subject. Annotating Dickens's first letter to Dr. Wilson, written on 8 March 1851, they attribute to Bowen the idea that "Kate was probably suffering . . . from post-natal depression, following the birth of Dora the previous August" (Pilgrim 6:309 n. 4). However, Bowen's analysis is riddled with misjudgments and contradictions. His diagnosis of Catherine is avowedly a matter of "guess work,"[52] and it is based on a misconstruction of events leading to her treatment by Wilson. Despite Dickens's accounts of Catherine's quick recovery in August and September 1850, Bowen asserts that "for a time" after the birth, "both mother and child were ill," and that only when Catherine was convalescing did she go to Malvern. Returning to London after Dora's death, Catherine suffered a "nervous breakdown," Bowen contends, having had already suffered periodically from a "neurasthenic state"—a psychiatric condition he believes was first manifested in 1845, when Catherine objected to Dickens's mesmeric treatment of Madame de la Rue.[53]

We might protest that Catherine's reaction to her husband's intimacy with another woman not only adhered to Victorian social convention but also seems reasonable enough today. But Bowen himself casts doubt on his argument about Catherine's pathology as he struggles to accommodate evidence running counter to it. Having described Catherine's "neurasthenia" and her "nervous breakdown," he goes on to argue that "there is nothing pointing to a lack of competence" on her part and "no reason to believe that Mrs. Dickens was inefficient as wife or mother."[54] Given the speculative nature of Bowen's argument as well as its striking contradictions, it seems remarkable that Dickens scholars have been willing to rely on it uncritically.

In 1837 and 1838 Catherine did suffer from postpartum depression, but when her confinements became less restrictive after Mamie's birth, her nearly month-long periods of depression ceased. Although Catherine suffered from migraines in

---

of postpartum depression in his brief reference to Catherine's treatment in Malvern, noting instead that she was "seriously ill with some kind of nervous trouble" (325).

52. W. H. Bowen, *Charles Dickens and His Family* (Cambridge: W. Heffer, 1956), 95.

53. Ibid., 94–95, 91–92.

54. Ibid., 94, 92.

the winter of 1850–51, and the lightheadedness and vision problems that often accompany them, she had apparently suffered in this way for several years, and there is no indication that her headaches were tied to or symptomatic of postpartum depression. For three weeks following Charley's birth, Catherine had to be persuaded to eat and was often found crying. After the birth of Dora, by contrast, she was "excellent" and "brilliant," "rosier" and "better" than before (Pilgrim 6:164)—eager to join the family in Broadstairs and setting her own time for doing so. Within a week of the delivery she was up and writing letters, and three weeks after giving birth, she was reunited with her children as planned. By early October she was entertaining visitors and guests. With her return to Devonshire Terrace toward the end of October, she resumed her usual London activities, receiving a check from Dickens for £35.4 for unspecified expenses in mid-November.[55] December was especially busy, with dinner and evening parties on the third, eighth, and fifteenth, a visit from Lavinia Watson on the fifth, an extended family gathering on Christmas Day, and a New Year's Eve party with music and dancing well into the early morning hours. It is difficult to see "a peculiarly intense form of post-natal depression" in all this.

A few days before Catherine left Devonshire Terrace for Broadstairs with her newborn in September 1850, Dickens began to plan for another round of amateur theatricals, to be performed at Bulwer Lytton's Knebworth House later that year. He gave Catherine the roles of Mrs. Humphries in *Turning the Tables* and Tib in *Every Man in His Humour,* with Georgina playing Bridget in Jonson's comedy and Constance, the young ward, in *Animal Magnetism.* At the end of October, ten weeks after Dora's birth, Catherine began rehearsals at Fanny Kelly's Royalty Theatre. She proved unable to perform in the Knebworth theatricals, but this was only because of an accident during the second rehearsal, when she bruised her foot in a trapdoor someone had left open onstage. Even then, she was determined to participate, if only as an audience member, arranging to travel to Knebworth when the others did, resting her swollen foot on a support. Up and walking by the end of November, she acted in the theatricals Dickens managed at Rockingham Castle in mid-January 1851, performing the part of Lady Maria Clutterbuck in *Used Up,* a farce adapted from the French by Dion Boucicault.

While Dickens thrived on managing and performing in these amateur productions, Catherine seems to have been less enthusiastic about them. Her role as Lady Maria was comic but unflattering—a supposed widow engaged, by mere chance, to the play's dissipated and insulting protagonist—and she may have felt annoyed by the playful flirtation that Dickens carried on with Mary Boyle, Lavinia Watson's distant cousin, who starred as Mary Wurzel opposite his Sir Charles Coldstream.

---

55. Charles Dickens, Esq., Account Ledger, Coutts & Co., London.

After a week at Knebworth in November and more than a week at Rockingham in January, Catherine was eager to be back at Devonshire Terrace with her children. Yet none of these feelings point to an underlying illness, and when Dickens wrote to Lavinia Watson in March, telling her that he was "uneasy about Kate, who has an alarming disposition of blood to the head" (Pilgrim 6:311), he thought the news would come as a surprise.

Within two weeks of her return from Rockingham, Catherine was consoling Nelly Lemon on the loss of her eighteen-month-old daughter and facing a similar crisis herself. "Dickens's baby was ill, and I was fearful for it; but all was well when we came away."[56] So Macready wrote in his diary for 2 February 1851, having dined at Devonshire Terrace with Kitty and half a dozen others that evening. James White, a minister, was among the guests, and Dora seemed so very sick that the Dickenses asked him to baptize her then and there. As Catherine had written to her cousin nearly fifteen years earlier when Charley was about Dora's age, "the consequences of a child's dying without being baptized are very dreadful as they cannot be buried on consecrated ground."[57] Dickens told Annie Leech on 3 February, "Our poor little Dora is very ill—with something like congestion of the Brain," and "though better this morning, is not out of danger" (Pilgrim 6:280). While he attended Macready's farewell performance at the Haymarket with the Leeches that evening, Catherine stayed home to nurse the baby.

Dora's diagnosis—brain "congestion"—was familiar to Victorians and signified a seizure disorder, thought to result from an impeded return of venous blood to the heart and hence its dangerous accumulation "in the encephalon."[58] But within a few days Dora was much better. "My sister's little baby . . . is recovering nicely though still very weak," Georgina told Mary Ellen Greville, Fanny Kelly's daughter, on 8 February;[59] "getting on bravely," Dickens wrote Forster (Pilgrim 6:284). Catherine herself felt much less worried about the baby by mid-February, when she sent "good accounts of all at home" to her husband, who had left for a five-day trip to Paris with John Leech (Pilgrim 6:289). On the eleventh the Macreadys joined

56. William Macready, *Diaries of William Charles Macready,* ed. William Toynbee, 2 vols. (London: Chapman and Hall, 1912), 2:491.

57. ALS Catherine Dickens to Mary Scott Hogarth, 30 May [1837], D. Jacques Benoliel Collection of the Letters of Charles Dickens, 86-2740, Rare Book Department, Free Library of Philadelphia.

58. Edward Liveing, *On Megrim, Sick-Headache and Some Allied Disorders: A Contribution to the Pathology of Nerve-Storms* (London: J. and A. Churchill, 1873), 286.

59. Georgina Hogarth to Mary Ellen Greville, 8 February 1851, Sotheby's catalog, 27 April 1971, quoted in Pilgrim 6:284 n. 3.

Catherine for dinner in Dickens's absence. Noting the event in his diary, the actor made no mention of Dora, which suggests that his fears for the baby had passed.

With the relief of Dora's recovery, Catherine sought treatment for the headaches that both she and Dickens attributed to a vascular cause. "I have been suffering for some time [past] from a fulness in the head, which has lately increased so much, & caused me such violent headaches & c, that I have been ordered to go at once to Malvern and try what change of air and cold water will do for me," she told Fanny Kelly on 11 March, an account she provided to Effie Ruskin as well, adding "I cannot say how long we may be absent but I hope not long."[60] Three days earlier Dickens had written to James Wilson, who treated Bulwer Lytton in the mid-1840s and inspired his laudatory *Confessions of a Water-Patient* in 1845. Wilson's water cure, imported from Gräfenberg, Austria to Malvern in 1842, was gaining in popularity; Darwin and Tennyson, among other notables, sought treatment there.

To Wilson, Dickens identified Catherine's ailment as "a nervous one." Dora's brain congestion fell into the same category. Catherine's disorder was "of a peculiar kind," Dickens explained, and Dr. Southwood Smith had already formed an opinion of it and considered "great caution necessary." Smith wanted his views relayed to Wilson, but Dickens said he would wait to do so until he and the doctor met. In the meantime, Dickens told him, Anne Brown would travel to Malvern to find lodgings for her mistress. Dickens would join his wife, as would his wife's sister, and they would likely "remain at Malvern some time," with several of the children "probably following" (Pilgrim 6:309).

Dickens's use of the term "peculiar" to describe Catherine's ailment might seem to support the contention that she was suffering from postpartum depression, by conveying an idea of the abnormality of her case. In 1858 he referred to "the peculiarity of her character" when attempting to discredit her in what has come to be known as the "violated" letter (Pilgrim 8:740). But throughout his correspondence, Dickens uses "peculiar" to mean "particular," not "aberrant" or "odd,"[61] and in describing Catherine's illness to Dr. Wilson, he has a particular diagnosis in mind: a "tendency" or "disposition of blood to the head" rather than postpartum

60. Catherine Dickens to Fanny Kelly, 11 March 1851, Sotheby's catalogue, 27 April 1971, quoted in Pilgrim 6:309 n. 4; ALS Catherine Dickens to Effie Ruskin [Millais], 9 March 1851, MA 1338 M.14, the Morgan Library & Museum, New York. Effie's marriage to John Ruskin was annulled in 1854 and she married John Everett Millais the following year.

61. Dickens speaks of "sweet smells . . . quite peculiar to the country" (Pilgrim 4:580), and of God's "peculiar love and care" (Pilgrim 1:516); and he tells an aspiring author in the United States that the "impediments and difficulties" facing him are "not peculiar to America" (Pilgrim 1:535). There are dozens of such examples.

depression. This "tendency" was "not at all a new disorder with her," he told correspondents, but had afflicted her "at intervals these 3 or 4 years," and was "attended with giddiness and dimness of sight" (Pilgrim 6:311, 314). For this reason he had "resolved to carry her down to Malvern, and put her under rigorous discipline of exercise, air, and cold water" (Pilgrim 6:311).

According to the "determination theory" of nineteenth-century medical experts, a "determination" or "tendency" of blood to flow to the head might be caused by "too violent or too quick an action of the heart" or, in childbearing women, by the "state of plethora" (excess) associated with pregnancy, "the balance of such plethora . . . determined towards the head," with symptoms including headache, vertigo, confusion, and temporary vision loss.[62] In a case such as Catherine's, "great caution" was necessary not because she was badly depressed or on the brink of a nervous breakdown but because the unequal circulation and overfull vessels that were causing her headaches could lead to a stroke, it was thought. As Wilson himself put it, "very great care and discrimination" were required "where there is a determination of blood to the head."[63] In terms of the vascular theory of nervous disorders accepted by the Dickenses and their doctors, the application of cold water to Catherine's extremities would draw blood away from her head and thereby equalize her circulation, reducing if not altogether eliminating her headaches and the "fulness" that caused them.

Unlike postpartum depression, a "tendency of blood to the head" was understood to afflict both men and women, and the treatment a patient of either sex would receive for it from Wilson was standardized. To equalize the circulation and create a "determination of blood . . . to the lower extremities" and the body's surface,[64] cold water was applied by means of compresses, showers, and baths, and by "packing" or wrapping the body in wet sheets. At various hours, the patient might take a shallow bath, a sitz bath, a head bath, and/or a douche bath (or shower), administered in a column of water up to four inches wide from a height of ten to twenty feet, and appropriate for those with "fulness of the head" only if that condition was not "apoplectic."[65] Walks in the Malvern hills supplemented these treatments, as did a healthy diet and early hours. As Wilson and others recognized, the removal of

62. C. H. Parry, "Memoirs of the Medical Society of London," quoted in Liveing, *On Megrim,* 280; David D. Davis, M.D., *Elements of Obstetric Medicine,* 2nd ed. (London: Taylor and Walton, 1841), 702–3.

63. James Wilson, *The Practice of the Water Cure, with Authenticated Evidence of Its Efficacy and Safety* (London: H. Bailliere, 1844), 67.

64. Ibid., 75.

65. Ibid., 74.

patients from their homes and their accustomed tasks and routines was central to the cure.

On 13 March, Catherine arrived in Malvern with Dickens and Georgina, joining Anne at Knotsford Lodge. Dickens traveled back and forth to London, where the children remained with the servants, while Catherine underwent her regimen of baths and walks. Within a week Dickens reported that she had "derived great advantage" from Wilson's treatment and was "much better" (Pilgrim 6:320, 322). Within ten days she was "getting on famously" (Pilgrim 6:326). On 20 March, Catherine herself reported that she was "a great deal better," corroborating her husband's accounts.[66]

Catherine's rapid improvement in Malvern suggests that the ailment long dubbed "post-natal" by Dickens critics may have been due to a different kind of confinement—that imposed on her by her gendered domesticity. Because "water doctors" conceived of the human body as a system to be "roused" to "self-restorative efforts" regardless of gender,[67] encouraged women as well as men to exercise, and privileged health over fashion, prohibiting tight lacing,[68] their cure challenged Victorian ideas of sexual difference and was embraced as equitable by social reformers, particularly in the United States.[69] Certainly the treatment Catherine received from Wilson differed radically from that she received from Samuel Tracy, who literally immobilized her in the delivery room. As the medical historian Susan Cayleff argues, Victorian hydropaths typically refused to see women as "chronically infirm" and instead gave their female patients a chance to participate actively in their care.[70]

Unlike his fellow hydropaths, however, James Wilson was originally trained as an accoucheur, or male midwife. "Present at the confinements of nearly a thousand ladies,"[71] he had a special interest in what he understood to be the problems caused by "menstruation, pregnancy, parturition, 'change of life,' &c." and promised to establish or restore regular monthly menstrual cycles among his amenorrheic patients and to relieve the "local congestions" he attributed to the onset of

66. Catherine Dickens to Joseph Howe, 20 March 1851, Sotheby's catalog, 23 July 1982, quoted in Pilgrim 6:309 n. 4.

67. James Wilson, *Prospectus of the Water Cure Establishment at Malvern* (London: Cunningham, 1843), 27–28.

68. See Harriet Martineau, "Malvern Water," *Household Words*, 11 October 1851, 70.

69. See Susan E. Cayleff, *Wash and Be Healed: The Water-Cure Movement and Women's Health* (Philadelphia: Temple University Press, 1987), especially chap. 2.

70. Ibid., 16.

71. Wilson, *The Practice of the Water Cure*, 26.

menopause.[72] In his view, the balanced "economy" of a healthy body was disrupted not just by dissipated living or infectious disease but by the very condition of being female: as a result of menstruation *or* its absence and by childbearing *or* infertility.

The exercise Wilson prescribed for Catherine might challenge conventional ideas of female weakness, yet his general handling of her case did not, since he consulted with her husband and her husband's male proxy about her treatment and progress rather than with the patient herself. Although Catherine may have corresponded with Wilson about her condition, the tone in which Forster reported to him about her on Dickens's behalf makes such an exchange seem unlikely. "I really think that Mrs. Dickens is somewhat better since her return," Forster told Wilson on 17 April, after she left Malvern for Devonshire Terrace following the death of Dora. "She grieves bitterly, of course—but I fancy the grief & suffering less morbid than it was for the first twelve hours.... Mr. Dickens will be well pleased to hear from you," Forster added. "I know the reliance he places on your judgment" (Pilgrim 6:353 n. 4, 383 n. 5). In this circuit of male knowledge, interchange, and mutual reliance, Catherine was the subject of discussion among the men, not a participant in her own right.

"OUR LITTLE DORA'S DEATH"

Within two weeks of Catherine's stay in Malvern, her illness was eclipsed by that of her father-in-law, suffering from acute bladder disease. In London on 25 March to begin rehearsals for the May production of *Not So Bad As We Seem,* Dickens learned of his father's need for emergency surgery. Writing to Catherine that day, he told her how shocked he had been by the news and described John Dickens's room as "a slaughter house of blood," though he was still hopeful that his father would pull through. The children were "well and happy," he assured her. He dined with them on the twenty-sixth before his return to Malvern, and spent part of his morning with Dora, who was "charmed" to see her father (Pilgrim 6:333–34).

Catherine was with Georgina and Anne at Knotsford Lodge when her father-in-law died on the thirty-first, Dickens having returned to London in time to be at the bedside with his mother and other members of the family. While Catherine remained with Anne in Malvern to continue her treatment, Georgina returned to London to see to the children's mourning. Because the funeral took place on 5 April, Catherine spent her fifteenth anniversary apart from her husband, who marked the occasion with Forster, the two toasting her health. "The children are all well and happy as possible," he wrote her from home, imagining the "dull time" she must be having in Malvern "with no amusement but baths—and little to look at but bad

72. James Wilson, *The Principles and Practice of the Water Cure; and Household Medical Science,* 3rd ed. (London: John Churchill, 1854), 335.

weather" (Pilgrim 6:347–48). With Forster and Georgina, he joined Catherine late on the day of his father's funeral, parting with her again on the eighth and again on the fourteenth, when he was scheduled to speak at the annual General Theatrical Fund dinner.

As Catherine later claimed, the letters she received in Malvern from her husband capture the intimacy between them at the time. Writing to her from London, he describes his father's surgery in "a shaking hand," sketches the dreary breakdown of a moving van outside his window, and details his suffering before and after his father's death, confiding that he "sometimes felt" as if he "could have given up, and let the whole battle ride on over [him]" (Pilgrim 6:333–34, 348). Despite such confidences, Dickens continued to believe that Catherine was set apart from him by nature and, as his wife, required his guidance and correction. The way in which he broke the news of Dora's death to her—more precisely, the way in which he *withheld* the news—suggests as much.

On 14 April, Dickens had been holding Dora before he left Devonshire Terrace for the General Theatrical Fund dinner. The baby seemed fine, but she died suddenly while he was giving his speech. Forster told him of his loss when he had finished. Dora's death certificate cites "teething" as the cause; Victorians associated that painful process with "nervous excitability" and "convulsive attacks,"[73] and the finding of the doctor in attendance as well as Mamie's recollections indicate that the baby succumbed to a seizure disorder or to the disease or defect that produced it.[74] With Lemon and Forster, Dickens sat up through the night. Wary of leaving Devonshire Terrace, he sent Forster to Catherine with a letter explaining that Dora had been "suddenly stricken ill" and, though resting quietly, was unlikely to recover. Forster would escort Catherine home from Malvern, since she would "not like to be away" under the circumstances. "If—*if*—when you come, I should even have to say to you 'our little baby is dead,'" Catherine read toward the close, "you are to do your duty to the rest, and to shew yourself worthy of the great trust you hold in them" (Pilgrim 6:353–54).

"Written on the day after our little Dora's death. Catherine Dickens." So Catherine inscribed the envelope that contained the letter from her husband, recording the fact that he suppressed in the letter itself. Despite its restrained and factual tone—or

73. John Epps, *Domestic Homoeopathy: or Rules for the Domestic Treatment of the Maladies of Infants, Children, and Adults* (Boston: Otis Clapp, 1848), 219. Mrs. Beeton includes "coma and fits" among the consequences of teething in her *Book of Household Management*, facsimile ed. (1861; reprint, East Sussex: Southover Press, 1998), 1046.

74. As Mamie recalls, "the baby was seized with convulsions, and was dead in a few minutes." Mamie Dickens, *Charles Dickens by His Eldest Daughter* (London: Cassell, 1885), 90.

rather by means of it—Catherine's simple sentence conveys the mixed feelings her husband's communication evoked. Catherine's note underscores the discrepancy between what she was told by her husband and the truth about Dora, which Dickens claimed to reveal: "I will not deceive you. I think her *very* ill" (Pilgrim 6:353). In his deception, Catherine undoubtedly recognized his desire to shield her, as she herself tried to shield those she loved—by setting aside her black-edged mourning paper when sending her son Alfred news of her father's death, for example, so as to soften the shock.[75] Catherine's recognition that Dickens wished to protect her seems implicit in her annotation—and all the more poignant if she wrote it after their separation. But her note also registers the knowledge that Dickens withheld, in a tone that conveys her self-possession and strength, and suggests that she might as well have received the news from the outset, as Dickens himself seemed to recognize at the time. "So good and amiable," Catherine was "resigned to what has happened," he told Bulwer Lytton a few days after Dora's death, "and can speak of [her loss] tranquilly" (Pilgrim 6:356). Critics often comment on Dickens's letter to Catherine, foregrounding what they see as its kind and necessary untruths. On the one hand, it reveals Dickens's goodness; on the other, it captures Catherine's fragility. With his wife already in a "nervous" state, the argument goes, Dickens feared that the news "might...lead to some kind of breakdown."[76] "Dickens wrote this most affectionate letter out of regard for his wife's delicate state of health," one critic notes, and as a means of "gently prepar[ing] his sick wife" for the revelation, writes another.[77] "A touching example" of Dickens's "native delicacy" and "solicitous for [Catherine's] peace of mind," it is "just the sort of letter Dickens would write when his heart-felt sympathy went out to some stricken soul."[78]

"Affectionate," "gentle," "touching"—with such terms critics commend Dickens's thoughtful deception of Catherine and gauge her "nervous," "delicate," and "stricken" state. Yet a different set of terms might apply equally well to Dickens's letter, those that convey the instruction and control that underlie his solicitude. Although critics see Dickens's characteristic delicacy here—"just the sort" he would extend to "some stricken soul"—his letter is expressed with a telling specificity. In its language and tone, it could only have been written to a woman, and to one

75. ALS Catherine Dickens to Alfred Dickens, 16 February 1870, MS 2563, by permission of the National Library of Australia, Canberra.

76. Ackroyd, *Dickens,* 627.

77. Walter Dexter, *Mr. & Mrs. Dickens: His Letters to Her* (London: Constable, 1935), 155 n; Michael Slater, *Dickens and Women* (London: J. M. Dent, 1983), 130.

78. G. M. Young, "Mr. and Mrs. Dickens," in *Victorian Essays,* ed. W. D. Hancock (London: Oxford University Press, 1962), 83; Bowen, *Charles Dickens and His Family,* 95.

woman in particular: the wife who owed her obedience to him. Dickens's letter is kindly meant, but with the sort of kindness he so often expressed to Miss Hogarth during their courtship in his loving letters of command, correction, and approval. Indeed Dickens's letter about Dora consists of a lengthy series of imperatives: "observe," "Mind!" "You must," "you would," "you will," "Do your duty," "come home with perfect composure," "shew yourself worthy." She is to "remember what [he has] often told her" and strive to meet his expectations, inspired by his "perfect confidence in [her] doing what is right" (Pilgrim 6:253-54). As he had in 1835, Dickens invokes the "perfect" Catherine—her "real" self, as he wishfully imagines her—who will avoid the example of Mrs. Hogarth, all too expressive in her maternal grief.

As these echoes from Dickens's courtship suggest, his "management" of Catherine and her grief reveals at least as much about their marital dynamic and his desire for control as it does about her need for support, and renders suspect the diagnostic use to which critics put his letter. The gentle way in which Catherine was treated by her husband after her return from Malvern has been similarly misinterpreted as evidence of a nervous breakdown. In fact, Dickens's effort to provide her with "kind friends," "change of scene," and "mental diversion" was a standard and common-sense response to a mother's bereavement, typically recommended by Victorian physicians for "ordinary and healthy grief."[79]

That Catherine rather than her husband would be the grieving figure in the family is not surprising. Dickens mourned for Dora, breaking down "completely" a day or two after the baby's death, Mamie recalled.[80] But Dora's death occurred in the midst of preparations for the May production of *Not So Bad As We Seem*, and those involved in the amateur theatricals depended on his activity as their manager and fellow actor. In the hiatus between writing *David Copperfield* and *Bleak House*, Dickens was also busy editing his weekly periodical *Household Words*, just beginning its second year of publication, and under considerable pressure to read and return material to W. H. Wills, his sub-editor. By contrast, Catherine was focused on the home and the children, and was in a position to miss Dora more keenly than he was. Not having seen the baby for the month she was in Malvern, Catherine likely regretted what she had termed her "truancy" a decade before, even though this time she had been away for medical treatment. "I was obliged to be so long away from the children when I was at Malvern that I fear I cannot leave them again for

79. John Charles Bucknill and Daniel Hack Tuke, *A Manual of Psychological Medicine* (London: J. and A. Churchill, 1879), 447.

80. Mamie Dickens, "Charles Dickens at Home, by His Eldest Daughter," *Cornhill*, n.s. (January 1885): 58.

more than a few days at a time," Catherine wrote Bulwer Lytton in June, declining an invitation to Knebworth.[81]

For the grieving mothers in her circle, Catherine prayed for God's "support and comfort,"[82] and she relied on her faith to overcome her own grief. More immediately, she took comfort in her husband's efforts to cheer her and direct her thoughts to practical matters—most obviously their need to find a new home, since their lease on Devonshire Terrace would expire later that year. "I am anxious to direct Kate's attention to our removal, and to keep it engaged," Dickens told Frank Stone on 18 April (Pilgrim 6:357), arranging to call within a week at Tavistock House, Tavistock Square. The Stones were moving down the row, from Tavistock to Russell House. From mid-May through October the Dickenses would stay at Fort House in Broadstairs, avoiding the crowds and callers in town for the Great Exhibition. But they would need a London residence by November. "I am taking Mrs. Dickens out, under a variety of pretences," Dickens wrote Wills on 20 April, arranging to show Catherine the back rooms at 16 Wellington Street, the *Household Words* office, which he proposed using as makeshift London quarters during the summer months.

Catherine was busy with friends and obligations as she mourned for Dora, thanks in part to her husband's efforts. Within two weeks of her return from Malvern, she received £12.12.6 from him, most likely to pay the servants their quarterly wages.[83] She toured Tavistock House on 21 April and in May called with Dickens on the naturalist Richard Owen. After attending the dress rehearsal of *Not So Bad As We Seem* on 12 May with other wives of cast members, she traveled back and forth from Broadstairs for performances on the sixteenth and twenty-seventh. After three weeks at Fort House, she, Georgina, and Dickens spent several days with the Macreadys at Sherborne. The £46 that Catherine received before the trip suggests that the sisters traveled there first while Dickens worked at *Household Words*.[84] By the end of June, Catherine was once again pregnant, giving birth for the tenth and final time in March 1852. Thus Dickens's occasional remarks on Catherine's delicate state that summer likely reflected her pregnancy as much as her grief, recalling comments he sometimes made when she was expecting in years past.

81. Catherine Dickens to Edward Bulwer Lytton, 11 June 1851, Lytton Papers, quoted in Pilgrim 6:410 n. 4.

82. ALS Catherine Dickens to Matilda Butler, 5 December [1877], Charles Dickens Museum, London.

83. Charles Dickens, Esq., Account Ledger, Coutts & Co., London.

84. Ibid.

The Dickenses entertained dozens of visitors and houseguests that summer and fall, including Douglas Jerrold, Frank Stone, Augustus Egg, and Forster as well as the Lemons, the Willses, and R. H. Horne and his wife, Kate. In September and October they turned their attention to renovations at Tavistock House, which Dickens had decided to lease. Their new home was larger than Devonshire Terrace by half a dozen rooms, though badly in need of cleaning and repair. Dickens paid £1,542 for a term of forty-five years, agreeing to cover taxes and remodeling costs. Although he rather than Catherine sent detailed suggestions and instructions to those working on repairs, he had done exactly the same in 1839 before their move to Devonshire Terrace. Married to a micromanager, Catherine was left to select wallpaper, decide which of the bedrooms would be theirs, and reconfigure the pantry. She made cleaning arrangements with Josephine Walker and helped see to the security of belongings temporarily left behind by the previous occupants. With Dickens she traveled to London while the children remained with Georgina in Broadstairs, and met with William Cubitt, their contractor. Catherine is "all over paint," Dickens wrote comically to Richard Watson and Henry Austin, and he and she both were "patched with oil and lime and haggard with white lead" (Pilgrim 6:526, 533).

Overseeing "the Progress of things" at Tavistock House in mid-November, as the family prepared to move and Dickens was away with the amateur players in Bath and Bristol, Catherine reported that all was going well and won his praise for her "methodical, business-like, and energetic state" (Pilgrim 6:536–37). "I am continually thinking of the House in the midst of all the bustle, but I trust it with such confidence to you that I am quite at my ease about it," he assured her (Pilgrim 6:539). As early as September, Dickens had trusted to Catherine, vouching for her help with the move. "Kate will come to town with me, and will be happy to do anything...to accommodate and please us all," Dickens told Stone on 30 August (Pilgrim 6:474). By then Catherine was back to "herself," with service to others her norm.[85] "Talfourd comes down [to Broadstairs] with me," she heard from Dickens in mid-September. "See that Georgina's room is made as comfortable as possible.... You will bring the little carriage to meet the cheap Express. Dinner at ½ past 5" (Pilgrim 6:482).

85. Writing to Georgina from Genoa in October 1853, Dickens asks "how Kate is," telling her he "fanc[ies] from [Kate's] letter, though [he] scarcely know[s] why, that she is not quite as well as she was at Boulogne" weeks earlier (Pilgrim 7:181). Without Catherine's letter, it is impossible to consider what gave him cause for concern; but if Catherine was dispirited that fall, her being so might be due to Dickens's decision to vacation in Europe for two months with Wilkie Collins and Augustus Egg rather than his wife and family.

Among other details from the time, Dickens's reliance on Catherine and her willingness "to accommodate and please" discredit the tale of an 1851 breakdown, her alleged postpartum depression said to usher in years of wifely incompetence. Yet such allegations are best answered by Catherine herself—less by her heeding Dickens's instructions than by her ability to issue her own. In the volume she authored in 1851 on how to prepare and assemble meals, her language becomes as imperative as Dickens's can be when he writes to her. "Set on the fire four ounces of pearl barley, with three Scotch pints (or six quarts) of salt water," she begins her recipe for Scotch broth.

> When it boils skim it, and add what quantity of salt beef or fresh brisket you choose, and a marrow bone or a fowl, with a couple of pounds of either lean beef or mutton, and a good quantity of leeks, cabbages or savoys, or you may use turnips, onions, and grated carrots; keep it boiling for at least four or five hours; but if a fowl be used, let it not be put in till just time enough to bring it to table when well done, for it must be served up separately.[86]

Catherine's collection of "useful recipes" and "bills of fare" was published as *What Shall We Have For Dinner?* by Bradbury and Evans, under the pen name "Lady Maria Clutterbuck." The date of the book's initial publication is uncertain, since no copies of a first edition seem to survive, but a second edition appeared in October 1851 and a "new edition" in February 1852.

Like so much else associated with Catherine in 1851, *What Shall We Have For Dinner?* has been used against her—taken as a sign of her reputed incompetence, her uncontrolled appetite, and the harm these did her husband. Until recently the book was described as at best an antidote thoughtfully prescribed for her "nervous disorder" by Dickens, who may have given her the idea for the book.[87] At worst it has been characterized as "muddled, inept and unhelpful," a work that reveals Catherine's unhealthy "obsession" with food and explains the failure of her marriage.[88] "The

86. Lady Maria Clutterbuck [Catherine Dickens], *What Shall We Have For Dinner? Satisfactorily Answered by Numerous Bills of Fare for from Two to Eighteen Persons,* 2nd ed. (London: Bradbury and Evans, 1851), 43.

87. Michael Slater, *Dickens' Journalism: "The Uncommercial Traveller" and Other Papers, 1859–70,* Dent Uniform Edition, vol. 4, ed. Michael Slater and John Drew (Columbus: Ohio State University Press, 2000), 420. Slater conjectures that Dickens may have suggested Catherine "compile for publication a collection of her menus and recipes" in "his attempts to distract her and help her to recover some equilibrium" (420).

88. Margaret Lane, *Purely for Pleasure* (New York: Alfred A. Knopf, 1967), 234–35.

emphasis on rich and starchy dishes... makes one wonder whether Dickens's growing distaste for his marriage... may not have been—at least partly—due to the fact that while still young she became mountainously fat," Margaret Lane writes.[89] Dame Una Pope-Hennessy concurs, arguing that "quicksilvery" Dickens, a "sufferer... who early became hard-arteried and generally gouty," was victimized by his "plump" and "placid" wife and her cooking, neither one meeting his "exacting" standards.[90]

In using Catherine's book to "explain" and disparage her body, these writers objectify its author and miss her point. They distort her physical appearance and describe as "monstrous" what was seen quite differently by at least some of her contemporaries—Henry Morley, for example, who first met Catherine, six months pregnant, in December 1851. "Mrs. Dickens is stout, with a round, very round, rather pretty, very pleasant face, and ringlets on each side of it," he told his fiancée. "You will be just according to her own heart, and will like each other in five minutes."[91] Misinterpreting her bills of fare as well as their consequences, her critics also mistake the aims of the genre in which Catherine writes. With "gender and class role behavior... laid out as precisely as a puff pastry recipe," one historian of the period writes, Victorian cookbooks were meant to feed social ambitions, not physical hunger.[92]

Instead of representing *What Shall We Have For Dinner?* as a source or symptom of illness, obesity, and mismanagement, Susan Rossi-Wilcox in *Dinner for Dickens* sees it as proof of Catherine's culinary knowledge. Placed in the context of Victorian food culture and culinary history by Rossi-Wilcox, Catherine's book reveals what critics overlook: her pragmatic ability to design menus that balance dishes prepared on the stove, baked in the oven, and roasted; to use foods available throughout the year; and to incorporate inexpensive cuts of meat and leftovers into her family meals.[93] For Lane, Catherine's recipe for Italian cream helps to account for the "monstrous alteration in her appearance" by 1851; for Rossi-Wilcox,

89. Ibid.

90. Dame Una Pope-Hennessy, "Dinner with Mr. and Mrs. Charles Dickens, *Wine and Food* 44 (Winter 1944): 215.

91. Henry Shaen Solly, *The Life of Henry Morley, LL.D.* (London: Edward Arnold, 1898), 201.

92. Colleen Cotter, "Claiming a Piece of the Pie: How the Language of Recipes Defines Community," in *Recipes for Reading: Community Cookbooks, Stories, Histories*, ed. Anne L. Bower (Amherst: University of Massachusetts Press, 1997), 71; Michael Mason, "A Little Pickle for the Husband," *London Review of Books*, 1 April 1999, 35.

93. Susan M. Rossi-Wilcox, *Dinner for Dickens: The Culinary History of Mrs. Charles Dickens's Menu Books* (Totnes: Prospect Books, 2005), 84, 98, 104.

it marks an innovative approach to "a well-known Victorian dessert," using lemon juice rather than gelatine as a thickener.[94]

Rossi-Wilcox's reassessment of Catherine's book helps us to read it as its original audience did, to recognize the skill and invention it exhibits, and to understand its popularity in the 1850s, as it appeared in several subsequent editions.[95] But Catherine's book not only suggests her competence as a hostess and domestic manager; it also allows us to hear her voice in an assertive and self-confident timbre, as she explains the dos and don'ts of kitchen practice. "Mind it does not break," Catherine warns those turning out their molded Italian cream; "garnish it with fruit, jelly, or with flowers." Neck of mutton "should be stewed gently for a long time . . . but not boiled to rags as it usually is," and "if given as a remedy for a severe cold, it is much better not to remove the fat, as it is very healing to the chest." Asparagus should be simmered and "rubbed through a tammy" to make soup—"not an easy matter if they be not very young."[96] So Catherine advises her readers, drawing on her expertise as cook, nurse, and grocery shopper.

In her study of kitchen writings, Janet Theophano describes recipe collections as autobiographies and important sources of women's history, "a written legacy of [women's] art and their lives."[97] Whether we trace its origins to a suggestion from Dickens, to the cooking Catherine and her husband reportedly did with the Lemons occasionally,[98] or to the domestic know-how conveyed to her by her mother, never wealthy enough to hire a cook, Catherine's volume helps us understand the experiences she valued and the ways in which she defined herself. Including menus for gatherings of twenty and dishes that were expensive to prepare and labor intensive—"nearly an hour" required to whip an Italian cream—Catherine signals her class status.[99] She draws on her time abroad when she explains how puddings are prepared "in many parts of the continent, as well as throughout Switzerland,"[100] while her recipes for Scotch broth, Scotch minced collop, and Kalecannon, like her

94. Ibid., 114.

95. Rossi-Wilcox lists editions of 1854, 1856, and 1860, noting changes among them.

96. [Dickens], *What Shall We Have For Dinner?*, 42–45.

97. Janet Theophano, "A Life's Work: Women Writing from the Kitchen," in *Fields of Folklore: Essays in Honor of Kenneth S. Goldstein*, ed. Roger D. Abrahams, Michael Robert Evans, Charles Greg Kelley, and John McGuigan (Bloomington, Ind.: Trickster, 1995), 296.

98. According to the Lemons' descendants, their daughter Betty left a record of visits paid by the Dickenses, during which they "often helped to cook supper," to the annoyance of the Lemons' cook. Later "the couple would retire to the study to jot down the recipes." See Laura Peek, "Cookbook Reveals Dickens Nakedly as Chef," *Times* (London), 22 December 2001.

99. [Dickens], *What Shall We Have For Dinner?*, 42.

100. Ibid., 45.

measures in Scotch pints as well as English quarts, identify her country of birth and make use of its standards and culture.

Yet even as Catherine provides us with a self-portrait in her recipes and bills of fare, Dickens infringes on her identity as a published author by assuming "her" voice. In the comic introduction he contributed to Catherine's volume, he explains, *as* Lady Maria, the importance she places on her culinary skills as a means of satisfying her husband and keeping him at home. "My attention to the requirements of his appetite secured me the possession of his esteem until the last," Dickens writes, but "my experience in the confidences of many of my female friends tells me, alas! that others are not so happy in their domestic relations." Lady Maria has thus written her book "to rescue many fair friends" from the "domestic suffering" caused by their own incompetence, which drives their husbands away, helping the women to make their homes "attractive."[101] In this act of ventriloquism Dickens provides Catherine with a conventionally feminine reason for writing, despite the strong sense of self her book conveys, the gratification she likely received from becoming a published writer, and the motive for authorship implied by her recipe for "Eve's Pudding," with its allusion to women's desire for knowledge as a source of independence and power.[102]

Collaborating with her husband on *What Shall We Have For Dinner?* Catherine got a taste of what it was like to contribute to *Household Words*—to have her work revised by Dickens or framed by his writing in a way that redefined her aims. But Catherine's status as an author is even more tenuous than that of writers whose work appeared anonymously in Dickens's periodical, because the records that usually surround authorship are wholly absent in her case. There are no references to her book in any of her extant letters or her husband's; no contract has been found, nor is there any mention of *What Shall We Have For Dinner?* in the financial accounts of Bradbury and Evans. Although there are joking references to her publication in the pages of *Punch*, edited by Mark Lemon, none specifically refers to Catherine herself.[103] We know of her authorship solely from family histories and word of mouth.

101. [Charles Dickens], introduction to *What Shall We Have for Dinner?* v–vi.

102. Catherine's recipe for "Eve's Pudding" simply calls for "half-a-pound of finely chopped apples" (48), but some versions make the tie to Genesis explicit, rhyming "half a dozen" with "fruit which Eve did once cozen." See "Mother Eve's Pudding—A Recipe," in *The Mirror of Literature, Amusement, and Instruction,* vol. 4 (London: J. Limbird, 1824), 440.

103. In October 1851, a boa constrictor in the Zoological Gardens swallowed the blanket in its cage, and *Punch* acknowledged the publication of Catherine's book in that context, under the heading "What Shall We Have for Dinner?": "Lady Maria Clutterbuck writes to us

More aptly than the birth and death of Dora or Catherine's treatment in Malvern, her venture into authorship served as a threshold to the 1850s, the decade in which her childbearing ended and she could assume less specialized, body-centered functions within her family. With the birth of Plorn on 13 March 1852, she was attended by Davis and Morgan for the last time and may have received one final dose of chloroform, from Dr. Henry Lee.[104] In 1852 Catherine prepared Charley for six months of study in Germany to ready him for a business career. She advised Charles Knight on the subject of governesses, introducing him to Mademoiselle St. Amand, who instructed Katey and Mamie on weekday mornings. With Georgina, Nelly Lemon, and Mrs. Wills, she traveled to Birmingham in May to see the amateur players perform and spent her thirty-seventh birthday with her husband and the Lemons. At Dover with her family for the summer, she entertained the usual round of visitors and guests, among them one of her Thomson cousins, who brought news of the Duke of Wellington's death. With Georgina and the amateurs, she went to Newcastle and Sunderland for performances in late August and attended the opening of Manchester's Free Library in early September. She mourned for Kitty Macready and corresponded with Lavinia Watson, widowed while pregnant with her fifth child.

Putting her own confinements behind her, Catherine was ready to expand her role and assume more autonomy than sixteen years of childbearing had allowed her. For two months in 1853 she became the surrogate head of household when Dickens left England for an extended continental tour with Wilkie Collins and Augustus Egg. But as her venture into authorship suggests, autonomy could prove elusive for Catherine. In the double bind in which she was placed, she was encouraged to act on her own authority by her husband yet often told what to think, do, or say— endowed with powers that were only nominally hers. The reliance Dickens placed on Georgina, and Georgina's relative privilege as a single woman in the household, made matters worse.

----

to say that 'the problem of the Boa Constrictor swallowing the Blanket is easily accounted for. The poor creature was tired of having nothing but *volaille* for dinner, so he thought he would just try a *Blanquette*'" (*Punch* 20 [1851]: 237).

104. In mid-March, Dickens's account at Coutts shows £5 paid to Morgan, £5.5 to Davis, and £3.3 to Lee.

INTERLUDE II

"Catherine Georgina"; or, What's in a Name?

*Of course I cannot be "cross" with you, or angry at your letter—as I
know your trouble is not your fault—but you may imagine I am not
much delighted at receiving it—I will lend you the money—on the strict
understanding that it is a loan—and a loan to you—not to your Husband.
The money is to be entirely in your hands—paid by you and repaid to me
by you—and I must have it back my dear Katie as soon as you can possibly
let me have it for I have great money anxieties of my own this year—and I
require literally every shilling I possess.*
—ALS Georgina Hogarth to Katie Cornelius Romer, 14 November 1877,
HM 28211, Huntington Library

TRIOS AND TRIANGLES

In January 1868, nearly a decade after Catherine separated from her husband and,
as a consequence, from Georgina, a new pupil was admitted to the North London Collegiate School for girls. "Student #1402" in the school's admission book
was the twelve-year-old daughter of a pianoforte dealer who lived on Harrington
Street in Camden, one Edward Cornelius.[1] Yet it is the daughter's name—and the
identity of her mother—that have bearing on Catherine's story. What the admission book didn't note was that Catherine Georgina Ann Cornelius was the child
of Anne Brown, long the lady's maid of Catherine Dickens and, since September
1855, known as Mrs. Edward Cornelius.

1. "Admission Book, with Index, for Names of children on Entering School, with Age & c.
London," f. 33, North London Collegiate School Archives.

One of the five servants employed at Devonshire Terrace in 1841, Anne was hired in 1838, when she was seventeen years old. In addition to performing the usual tasks of a lady's maid, and some of those more commonly assigned to nursemaids and housemaids, she traveled to North America with her mistress in 1842 and accompanied the Dickenses on their European tours, living with them in Italy, Switzerland, and France. She found Malvern lodgings for Catherine in March 1851 and remained with her at Knotsford Lodge when Georgina returned to London after John Dickens's death. If Anne was not with Catherine, she was likely to be found with Georgina. When Charley had scarlet fever in 1847 and his parents rushed from Paris to be near him, Anne remained behind with Catherine's sister to help with the five younger children, and she and Georgina traveled to Boulogne together to secure summer lodgings for the family in 1854.

A domestic servant, Anne traveled second class; she slept in the women's cabin on American steamers, rode in the second of the three carriages that carried the family from Switzerland to France, and sat in different rail cars than her mistress did when touring with the amateurs in England. On the 1851 census return for Knotsford Lodge, she appears on a separate sheet from Catherine and Georgina, divided by seven places from those "lodgers" as a servant. Nonetheless, she was one of "the whole trio," as Dickens referred to Catherine, Georgina, and Anne (Pilgrim 6:737). Having worked for, and with, both Hogarth sisters for more than a dozen years by the time she left Tavistock House to marry, Anne knew Catherine and Georgina well. It seems apt that she would commemorate "the trio" in 1856, grouping their names together in christening her daughter—and all the more significant because Catherine and Georgina are so often defined against each other in Dickens scholarship, as critics and biographers read backward from 1858. Relying largely on Dickens's statements about the separation and citing the stipulations of his will, they depict the sisters as antagonists or rivals, the alleged inadequacies and placidity of the one played off against the reputed competence and energy of the other. Anne's act of naming reminds us of what is all too frequently forgotten: that Catherine and Georgina were sisters before the first became Mrs. Charles Dickens and the second the novelist's "pet...sister in law" (Pilgrim 4:255). It also shows that two decades into the Dickenses' marriage, and within two years of their separation, the sisters' names could be linked without irony by someone who knew them intimately, Anne's act pointing to what was long a mutually supportive and affectionate relationship.

Catherine Georgina Ann: the name bears repeating because Dickens so often speaks for these women, misrepresenting their relationships and exaggerating their differences to justify his own behavior. The maid as well as the mistress and her sister played a part in this ventriloquist's act, as Dickens used Anne to testify against his marriage in 1858, in the "violated" letter, providing her with the necessary script:

> Mrs. Dickens and I . . . are, in all respects of character and temperament, wonderfully unsuited to each other. . . . An attached woman servant (more friend to both of us than a servant), who lived with us sixteen years, and is now married, and who was, and still is, in Mrs. Dickens's confidence and in mine, who had the closest familiar experience of this unhappiness, in London, in the country, in France, in Italy, wherever we have been, year after year, month after month, week after week, day after day, will bear testimony to this. (Pilgrim 8:740)

Lest Anne forget her lines or need prompting, Dickens gave her a copy of this opening paragraph of the letter, which he wrote out for her in his own hand.

Dickens did not mesmerize Anne Brown as he did Catherine, at least not in a literal sense, though he put words in her mouth. But he exerted his magnetic powers over Georgina—quite literally—in what served as an initiation rite of sorts. In the summer of 1842, at the very time when his sister-in-law was becoming a member of his household, Dickens displayed for Forster and Maclise, among other guests assembled at Devonshire Terrace, his ability to control her consciousness as well as Catherine's, sending "Miss Hogarth . . . in[to] violent hysterics" in the usual prelude to the magnetized state, as Macready recorded, though his host's power "could not affect" *him*.[2]

Dickens's ability to "affect" both Catherine and Georgina and place them under his spell was one of several ways in which he laid claim to them: "my pair of petticoats," as he put it, "my Venuses," "my womankind," "my two ladies" (Pilgrim 3:440, 387, 580, and 6:779); or, as Thackeray referred to the sisters after catching a glimpse of them with "the great Dickens" in 1849, "his wife" and "his Miss Hogarth," all "abominably coarse vulgar and happy."[3] Like Macready and Thackeray, we need to resist Dickens's magnetism, breaking the spell under which he has long held Catherine and Georgina—and those who rely solely on his voice to write about the Hogarths. Insofar as possible, we need to let the sisters speak for themselves about their own tie, making the most of their surviving accounts, disentangling

2. William Macready, *Diaries of William Charles Macready, 1833–1851*, ed. William Toynbee, 2 vols. (London: Chapman and Hall, 1912), 2:179–80.

3. W. M. Thackeray to Mrs. Brookfield, 24 July 1849, in *Letters and Private Papers of William Makepeace Thackeray*, ed. Gordon N. Ray, vol. 2 (Cambridge: Harvard University Press, 1946), 569, quoted in Pilgrim 5:573 n. 3.

their voices and perspectives from those of Dickens, and supplementing their narratives with source material of various kinds provided in a range of hands.

Doing this does not discount Dickens's importance to their life stories or deny his part in the trio they formed. If Catherine's relationship with Georgina was triangulated with Anne Brown, it was much more famously so with Anne Brown's master, in the "threesome" or "ménage-à-trois" so often discussed by critics interested in Dickens's fantasies and needs.[4] Yet there are three sides to *all* triangles and vastly different ways to give them shape. In the standard geometry of Dickens studies, the novelist appears at the apex of a love triangle and the Hogarth sisters below, their own connection notably foreshortened. To understand that sisterhood, we need to think equilaterally, to use as our model a triangle in which *any* of three equivalent points serves equally well as apex and none of its sides gets short shrift.

ONCE A HOGARTH, ALWAYS . . .?

Georgina is known to posterity as the sister-in-law of Charles Dickens rather than as the sister of Catherine Hogarth, and much more profoundly than in Mary Hogarth's case, her sense of self was shaped by her dealings with her eldest sister's husband. Mary's camaraderie with Catherine developed through their teenage years, the pair first making their way around London in 1832. But Georgina was only eight years old when Catherine married. Joining her sister's family at fifteen, she was thirty-one when Catherine left Tavistock House for Gloucester Crescent, and thus lived with Mrs. Charles Dickens twice as long as she did with Catherine Hogarth. Unlike Mary, who stayed with her married sister on and off for only one of her seventeen years, Georgina was a full-fledged member of the Dickens household for nearly three decades and was supported solely by her brother-in-law for much of her life. Inevitably, then, her relationship with Catherine was triangulated with Dickens in a way that Mary's was not.

Nonetheless, Georgina *was* a Hogarth and grew up in a family in which sibling relations were affectionate and playful. Twelve years younger than Catherine and eight years younger than Mary, she was usually left behind when her teenage sisters went on their London adventures, and grouped by them with the babies of the family—the "little pets," Mary called them[5]—forming a trio with twins Helen and Edward rather than with Catherine and Mary. "Georgie and the dear twins" were

---

4. Albert J. Guerard, *The Triumph of the Novel: Dickens, Dostoevsky, Faulkner* (New York: Oxford University Press, 1976), 72.

5. ALS Mary Hogarth to Mary Scott Hogarth, 26 January 1837, D. Jacques Benoliel Collection of the Letters of Charles Dickens, 83-1842, Rare Book Department, Free Library of Philadelphia.

an item in the reports Catherine sent to their cousin in Scotland, the three children having come down with the measles all at once.[6] Like the twins, Georgina was taught her first letters by her older sisters and had her playtime with them. If Georgina is celebrated, in part, as the "Auntie" willing to play with young Dickenses on the floor at Devonshire Terrace, that is largely due to what she learned from Catherine and Mary through their care for her at their own home.

There were brothers in the family, too—five in all—and the sisters were close to them as well, although the boys' schooling and careers often took them away from home. In 1837, when Georgina was ten, "dear little Jamie and William" were studying in Hamburg and "getting quite little Germans by their own account," Mary reported. Robert would be leaving England to take a position in Mexico, and parting with him would "be a great trial." But George Jr. would remain in London, where he was earning the praise of his master and "had his Salary raised in consequence of his good conduct." However good his conduct, George still enjoyed teasing his sisters; looking over Mary's shoulder, he told her he pitied whoever received her letters, filled as they were with family gossip and crosshatching.[7] When George died unexpectedly in 1841, four years after Mary, Georgina joined Catherine for her first extended stay with her married sister; they mourned for their brother together, shortly before the Dickenses, with Anne, left England for North America.

Absent for six months, Catherine wrote to Georgina, sending her a "long letter" from Baltimore in March, probably one of a series.[8] Although there appears to be only one surviving letter of the many they exchanged over the years—a note from Georgina to "Dearest Kate" that dates from 1877[9]—their 1842 correspondence likely focused not only on the American tour but also on the welfare of the Dickens children, whom Georgina, with Mrs. Hogarth, was visiting while their parents were away. In 1842 the Hogarth twins were nearly ten, but the four Dickens children were five and under. When Catherine returned home, it seemed sensible for

6. ALS Catherine Hogarth to Mary Scott Hogarth, [4 July 1835], D. Jacques Benoliel Collection of the Letters of Charles Dickens, Rare Book Department, Free Library of Philadelphia.

7. ALS Mary Hogarth to Mary Scott Hogarth, 26 January 1837, D. Jacques Benoliel Collection of the Letters of Charles Dickens, 83-1842, Rare Book Department, Free Library of Philadelphia.

8. ALS Catherine Dickens to Frederick Dickens, 22 March 1842, The Henry W. and Albert A. Berg Collection of English and American Literature, New York Public Library.

9. ALS Georgina Hogarth to Catherine Dickens, n.d. [1877], D. Jacques Benoliel Collection of the Letters of Charles Dickens, 87-1968, Rare Book Department, Free Library of Philadelphia. Though undated, Georgina's letter concerns Catherine's friend Linda Scates (Mrs. Dutton Cook), who gave birth at 69 Gloucester Crescent in 1877.

Georgina to join her as a mother's helper, all the more so because the Hogarths were often hard-pressed for funds.

Georgina was young but astute and well read, as were all the Hogarths. Like Mary and Catherine as teenagers, she had a satiric eye. For Catherine, the companionship she provided was an antidote of sorts to Dickens's close friendships with Forster and Maclise, neither of whom was married and with whom he was often engaged, and the two sisters started to make the social rounds together. "Mrs. Dickens and Miss Hogarth called; wished us to dine," Macready noted in his 1842 diary, in what became a common refrain. "Mrs. Dickens and Georgina called"; "Mrs. Dickens and Georgina Hogarth came to dine with Catherine"; "Mrs. Dickens, Miss Hogarth": in variations such as these, the two sisters appear and reappear in Macready's diary over the years.[10]

The adventures on which Catherine and Georgina embarked with *Dickens* are well known to us because of the prominence he often gives them in his letters. We hear in great detail about their ascent of Mount Vesuvius in 1845, for example, and the difficulties encountered when their party made their way, with danger, down the icy slope. But because virtually all their letters to each other have disappeared, we know much less about the activities of the two sisters alone. Nonetheless, pictures of their daily lives, the pleasure they took in each other's company, and their sense of solidarity emerge in letters to and by others, and in the diaries of acquaintances and friends: when "Mrs. D and Miss H" go calling in Lausanne and Georgina plays the piano for her sister and Christie Thompson during a "very merry" evening;[11] or when Catherine introduces guests to "her sister Miss Hogarth" in their early Tavistock House days and watches the good impression made by the "pretty" girl, a "lively young damsel...rather good looking."[12] The two sisters keep watch at Dora's crib after the baby falls ill, taking solace in her apparent recovery. "Mrs. D & [Miss] H" stand "stiffly" together in the Brighton lodgings of Fred and Anna Dickens while a "very cordial" Charles mesmerizes his *other* sister-in-law to ease her chronic pain;[13] and in Genoa they complain to each other about Susan Atkins, their irritating houseguest, earning them Dickens's reproof.

10. Macready, *Diaries,* 2:179, 185, 338, 401.

11. Christiana Weller Thompson, 1846 diary, MS Meynell Family Papers, Greatham.

12. ALS Caroline Norton to Catherine Dickens, n.d. [August 1842], MA 104, the Morgan Library & Museum, New York; Henry Shaen Solly, *The Life of Henry Morley, LL.D.* (London: Edward Arnold, 1898), 200.

13. Christiana Thompson, 1850 diary, MS Meynell Family Papers, Greatham, quoted in Pilgrim 6:73 n. 1.

Georgina was typically commended by the Dickenses, not criticized, and she felt affection and pride rather than irritation as a member of their household—pride in her sister and her brother-in-law, and pleasure in her importance to both, her feelings evident in letters she writes on their behalf. She frequently explains what "[her] sister...desires [her] to say" or what Dickens "desired [her]...to write."[14] "Charles (who has gone to Bath today to dine with Mr. Landor on his birthday) desired me...to...ask if you would dine with us, on his own birthday," Georgina tells Thomas Beard after the birth of Frank. "By that time dear Kate will be down again and will dine with us."[15]

As these letters remind us, Georgina was living with the Dickenses in part to serve them, and her relationship with Catherine combined affection and fellow feeling with a degree of subordination, as sibling relations often do. Dickens might use mesmerism to gain and display authority over his sister-in-law when she joined their household, but Catherine had helped to raise Georgina and exercised *her* authority over her sister by virtue of the twelve years separating them.

In the mid-1840s Catherine was clearly the senior partner in their relationship and held the upper hand; she was "the lady...par excellence," as Dickens put it "in compliment to Kate" (Pilgrim 4:594), and her questions or requests to Georgina were sometimes indistinguishable from instructions and commands. "Kate says will you bring her a box of tooth powder. Anne knows where it is." So Dickens conveyed his wife's message to his sister-in-law in 1845. When Dickens wrote this letter, his very first to Georgina, she was soon to meet them in Naples but had been left behind in Genoa with the children and servants for a month while the couple traveled to Rome. "Also," Kate wished him to say, "will you take counsel with Charlotte about colour...and have the darlings['] bonnets made at once.... Kate would have written," Dickens added, "but is gone...to a day-Performance of the opera, to see Cerito dance" (Pilgrim 4:261–62).

14. Georgina Hogarth to Christiana Weller, [16 October 1845], MS Meynell Family Papers, Greatham, reprinted in David H. Paroissien, "Charles Dickens and the Weller Family," *Dickens Studies Annual* 2 (1972): 38; Georgina Hogarth to Thomas Beard, 30 January [1844], in *Dickens to His Oldest Friend: The Letters of a Lifetime,* ed. Walter Dexter (London: Putnam, 1932), 272. When Dickens is ill and Catherine "occupied in attending on him," Georgina tells Cornelius Felton, "they beg me to send both their loves...and to say how sorry they are that we are not likely to see you again before you go abroad." ALS Georgina Hogarth to Cornelius Felton, 2 June 1853, H715L 1853 June 2, William Andrews Clark Memorial Library, UCLA.

15. Georgina Hogarth to Thomas Beard, 30 January [1844], in Dexter, *Dickens to His Oldest Friend,* 272.

Combining her efforts with those of nursemaid Charlotte and lady's maid Anne, Georgina might free Catherine for such pleasures. But more often than not, Georgina's work enabled Catherine to perform labors of her own—to meet with or write to those Dickens could not and to serve as his consort, accompanying him to Scotland in 1847 and to Manchester and Birmingham in 1848. In the division of labor that developed between the sisters, Georgina was a part-time nursemaid and Catherine the domestic manager, and both were secretaries and hostesses for Dickens. Georgina taught the children to write and, in the summer and fall, could be found on the beach with them and Charlotte, while Catherine planned meals with the cook, brought the pony carriage, with Topping the manservant, to meet Dickens at the station, and paid the servants their quarterly wages if her husband did not. For a time, Katey was troubled with nightmares. When she woke in the night, Georgina was more likely to put her back to bed than either of Katey's parents; if Dickens fell ill, his wife was the one to nurse him.

In discussing the division of labor in the Dickens household, critics and biographers often claim that by the early 1850s, Georgina had replaced her older sister as domestic manager. W. H. Bowen identifies 1851 as the year of Dickens's domestic "reorganization," while Arthur Adrian asserts that Georgina was "already largely in charge of the household" by that time. According to Peter Ackroyd, the younger Hogarth had "supplanted much of her sister's role" by 1856.[16] The banking records tell a different story, however. They show that, from 1846 through 1857, Georgina, like Anne and the other servants, generally received a quarterly payment from her brother-in-law, an allowance roughly equivalent to the wages paid to a governess, housekeeper, or head nurse at the time, while Catherine received, usually more frequently, the larger sums necessary to run the household.

Dickens wrote his first check to Georgina in February 1844, when Catherine was confined after the birth of Frank; the £5 may have been intended to cover some household expenses during that three-week period. Georgina did not receive another check from Dickens for nearly two years, when her quarterly allowance began: £5 at the end of January 1846 and again at the beginning of May, before the family left for Switzerland and France. In roughly the same period, from February through May 1846, Catherine received five checks totaling £70.10.6. Left by the Dickenses in Paris in March 1847 with Anne and five of the children, Georgina had £80 at her disposal, but once she had returned home, her allowance resumed: £7 in

16. W. H. Bowen, *Charles Dickens and His Family* (Cambridge: W. Heffer & Sons, 1956), 95; Arthur A. Adrian, *Georgina Hogarth and the Dickens Circle* (London: Oxford University Press, 1957), 33; Peter Ackroyd, *Dickens* (New York: HarperCollins, 1990), 766.

April 1847, raised to £7.10 in December, the added forty shillings per year making for a total annual payment of £30.

On occasion Georgina received an extra £5 with a quarterly payment; in 1848 her four checks totaled £35 rather than £30, as they did in 1851. In 1852 she received four payments of £7.10; in 1853 Dickens supplemented these with an additional £15. In 1854 and 1855 her payments were slightly under £30 (£27.3 and £24.2.6, respectively), then as much as £50.18 in 1856, but back down to £32.10 in 1857. Until 1858 Georgina's allotment in the Coutts account was always significantly smaller than her sister's in any given year. Between 1848 and 1857, the year preceding the separation, the amount of money that was spent or handled specifically by Catherine in the account ranged from £49.12.6 (in 1852) to £956.7.6 (in 1853), with a yearly average of £352 over the ten-year period.[17] From the financial records and what they reveal about the workings of the household, it is difficult to see Georgina becoming its manager until the year in which Catherine separated from her husband.

The problem with claims that Georgina assumed this position earlier than she actually did goes beyond questions of timing to the very terms in which her relationship with Catherine is usually formulated. "To supplant," "to supersede": using such language, critics imagine the Hogarth sisters as natural antagonists and competitors vying for primacy at Dickens's side. They pit an "efficient, intelligent," if ambitious Georgina against her rather pathetic and "clumsy" sister, whom they depict as fearful of being usurped but too "slow" and "lethargic" to prevent it.[18] It is true that Georgina stepped in for Catherine when the latter was confined and remained with Dickens when her sister was pressured to leave him. But it is *also* true that Georgina had hoped to avert the separation and that Catherine *wanted* Georgina to remain when she herself could not. "I have heard Miss Hogarth bitterly assailed for remaining with Mr. Dickens's household after her sister left," Jane Panton recalled, "but I have also often heard Mrs. Dickens say that her presence among 'the children' was her one comfort and consolation, and that she wished people who did not know all would not talk."[19] These details complicate and challenge the way in which the relationship has been represented and suggest that the sisters were cooperating with each other even as their tie was being compromised.

17. Charles Dickens, Esq., Account Ledger, Coutts & Co., London.

18. Ackroyd, *Dickens,* 763–66.

19. Jane Ellen Panton, *Leaves from a Life* (New York: Brentanos, 1908), 144–45. A fiction writer and author of books on domestic management and interior decoration, Panton was the daughter of the artist William Powell Frith and his wife, Isabella.

Catherine and Georgina were not fixed in their positions and feelings, nor did the power dynamic between them remain unchanged. Although Catherine continued as the household's manager, her authority over her younger sister diminished as Georgina became an adult and as Georgina's presence and contributions to the family became increasingly important to Dickens. To understand this changing dynamic, however, we need to look beyond the contrasting "natures" of the two sisters as they have often been represented and instead consider their differing positions and obligations in the household. Although Georgina was subordinate to Catherine as the younger, unmarried sister, she possessed crucial advantages as a single and celibate woman. Free from the physical demands and perils of childbearing as well as the legal confines of coverture, Georgina could achieve an equivalence with Dickens that his wife could not. Although Dickens and those who echo him depict Georgina as a woman "sacrificed" to her sister's family (Pilgrim 8:740), Georgina herself seems to have perceived *Catherine's* sacrifice in becoming a wife and mother, having witnessed its physical and social consequences at first hand. Valuing what she termed her "free will,"[20] Georgina chose to remain single, declining at least one marriage proposal, and probably two.[21] As critics so often argue, the difference between the sisters can help us account for Georgina's "rise," but only if we recognize those differences for what they were: a product of social circumstances and expectations. The two sisters were set apart not by their "natural" possession (or lack) of grace, energy, and efficiency but by their marital status, a dozen pregnancies, two miscarriages, and the births of ten children.

Catherine gave birth six times in the first decade in which she and Georgina lived together with Dickens, and her late-term pregnancies, deliveries, and confinements broadened Georgina's range of responsibilities for weeks at a time just as they narrowed Catherine's during those intervals. Between January 1844 and March 1852, Catherine was confined for at least twenty weeks (including the recovery that followed her second miscarriage), and she was in the last trimester of pregnancy for a full year and a half. Georgina's celebrated activity as Dickens's "little right hand" (Pilgrim 7:724) had its origins in the restrictions imposed on her sister by virtue of repeated childbearing.

Georgina first managed the family's social arrangements after Frank's birth in 1844, organizing Dickens's birthday party. When Catherine miscarried three years

---

20. Georgina Hogarth to Percy Fitzgerald, 17 January [1868], in Arthur Adrian, "Georgina Hogarth to Percy Fitzgerald: Some Unpublished Letters," *Dickensian* 88, no. 1 (1992): 11.

21. According to Gladys Storey, who had the information from Katey Perugini, Forster had proposed to Georgina (Pilgrim 7:172 n. 1), as had Augustus Egg.

later and was forced to stay in bed, her sister wrote the necessary letters postponing their Twelfth Night party. Two weeks before Alfred was born in 1845, Georgina, with Dickens, attended Christiana Weller's wedding while Catherine rested at home, and soon after the delivery she took her nieces and nephews on their outing to the Lord Mayor's Show. Three weeks after Sydney's birth in 1847, it was Georgina rather than Catherine who accompanied Dickens to a dinner party at Forster's; the next evening she joined her brother-in-law in a theater box "crowded" with friends, but from which her sister was missing.[22] In 1849, a few days after Catherine delivered Henry, Georgina went with Dickens to a dinner party at the Tagarts'. In Broadstairs the next year, when Catherine was confined with Dora, Georgina served as Dickens's "little housekeeper," to whom Wills would write if accepting an invitation to visit (Pilgrim 6:158). There, Georgina heard Dickens read the seventeenth number of *David Copperfield*, while Catherine remained at Devonshire Terrace with two-week-old Dora. Having passed a restless night a few days later, Dickens woke Georgina at 5 am for company, his sister-in-law performing what had been his wife's exclusive role.

To Catherine, Georgina's temporary assumption of duties and pleasures in her stead meant something different than it did to her husband. "Going out very little" when she was "shortly expecting [her] confinement[s],"[23] Catherine understood Georgina to be filling in for her while her own social activities were suspended. "I am not going out very much at present as I am not very well," Catherine told Jane Loudon, responding to a party invitation one month before Henry's birth, "but my sister will have great pleasure in accompanying the children."[24] To Dickens, however, Georgina was not simply filling in for Catherine; she was willingly assuming the duties that, under other circumstances, Catherine was obligated to perform. This distinction in Dickens's thinking was clear from his earliest days with Catherine—when, training his fiancée for marriage, he contrasted *her* obligation to serve him with the kind compliance of Mary, what was "entirely expect[ed]" of a wife being seen as a virtue in her sister (Pilgrim 1:65).

Like Catherine, Georgina was financially dependent on Dickens. Yet she enjoyed certain liberties that her married sister did not—liberties in expression, in outlook, and in physical activity. Six weeks postpartum in 1845, Catherine "walked . . . impossibly slowly," Dickens complained after strolling with her to Covent Garden Market

22. Macready, *Diaries*, 2:366.

23. ALS Catherine Dickens to Miss Holskamp, n.d. ["Monday morning"], Fales Library & Special Collections, New York University.

24. ALS Catherine Dickens to Jane Loudon, 19 December [1848], Fales Library & Special Collections, New York University.

(Pilgrim 4:64). But Georgina always made an excellent walking companion, going with Dickens on brisk and extended jaunts. "Georgy is very well, and takes long country walks with me," Dickens told Lavinia Watson later in 1845 (Pilgrim 4:390). "I wish you were here to take some of the old walks," he wrote his sister-in-law from Genoa in 1853. "It is quite strange to walk about alone" (Pilgrim 7:181).

Dickens encouraged Georgina's verbal license as well as her physical activity, contrasting Catherine's propriety of expression with her sister's more blunt and mocking commentaries. "Mrs. Dickens sends you her best regards," he told an ailing William Bradbury in 1849, "and Miss Hogarth says she thinks you are shamming" (Pilgrim 5:633). "Kate and Georgy send their best regards," Dickens wrote Douglas Jerrold in 1846. "The latter small person was making me weak with laughter only last night, by imitating Mrs. Bradbury, in a manner quite inconceivable" (Pilgrim 4:645). When Charles Knight visited the Dickenses in Dover in 1852 and Catherine talked with him politely about his daughter's "governess plans,"[25] Georgina comically disparaged him behind his back, calling him an "old Donkey" and suggesting that his interest in governesses was inappropriate—"that he 'philanders.'" Dickens remarked to Wills, "I don't know what that involves, or where it ends," conveying Georgina's snide remarks to his sub-editor and clearly enjoying them (Pilgrim 6:739). Although Dickens sometimes criticized Georgina for going too far in mocking their friends and guests—such as when he reprimanded her for being "foolish" in disparaging Susan Atkins to Forster (Pilgrim 4:215)—he often encouraged this propensity, facetiously referring to "dear Susan" in his own letter to his sister-in-law (Pilgrim 4:262) and making Georgina's fondness for "disparaging people" the subject of comic sketches. Writing to John Leech from Broadstairs in 1849, Dickens "imitates" Georgina in an impromptu stage dialogue and imagines himself "fiercely" reproving her for being unable to "hold [her] tongue," even though her point about a local woman's drinking problem was common knowledge (Pilgrim 5:624).

To Cornelius Felton in 1854, Georgina characterizes herself as a woman who knows her place. "I am no politician or I should have no difficulty in filling my letters with public affairs," she writes, "but I think it safer to keep within my depth."[26] Relegating herself to the private sphere and what she suggests are its shallows, Georgina embraced her womanly position and the limitations associated with it. She deferred to Dickens as "the Head" of the household in the years following the separation and concluded that "his own decision will be the best" when her wishes

25. Charles Knight to "Dear Mary," 10 August 1852, quoted in Alice A. Clowes, *Charles Knight: A Sketch* (London: Richard Bentley, 1892), 124.

26. ALS Georgina Hogarth to Cornelius Felton, 23 January 1854, Harvard University Archives, Pusey Library.

diverged from his.[27] While Georgina's celibacy gave her control over her own body and exempted her from the physical burdens of her sister's repeated childbearing, it too had its drawbacks. Referred to as "the Virgin" by Dickens (Pilgrim 4:339, 5:41), Georgina allegedly felt compelled to obtain medical certification of her virginity to quell allegations of sexual intimacy with her brother-in-law in the aftermath of the separation.[28]

Yet Georgina's ability to push the limits of propriety with her outspokenness, and to choose the difficult position of housekeeper to the brother-in-law who lived apart from her sister, marked her relative privilege as a *feme sole* entitled to the autonomy denied to married women under common law. Even as she deferred to his authority, Georgina could identify with Dickens and participate in a number of his masculine activities. As Maclise's 1843 sketch of Catherine, Georgina, and Dickens suggests, this privilege was apparent to some of those in the Dickens circle from nearly the start of Georgina's residence in the household (fig. 12). In his sketch, Maclise places Catherine in the middle position. Representing the threesome in 1843, without the "advantage" of hindsight, the artist identifies Catherine, sister to one and wife to the other, as the figure linking the trio together and emphasizes Georgina's physical resemblance to her. With slight modifications, the outline of Georgina's face and the shape of her eye, nose, mouth, and chin mirror those of her elder sister. The fall of hair on Georgina's forehead ends where that on Catherine's begins, the uninterrupted line conveying Maclise's sense of the continuity between the women. Yet the sketch also captures Georgina's similarity to Dickens, despite the distance between them in the composition. As the *feme covert,* Catherine bows her head submissively, peering up to see what the others do. By contrast, Georgina looks forward, her head upright and her line of vision identical to that of Dickens.

Shortly before Maclise produced his sketch, in the same year in which Georgina joined the Dickenses, Victorians began their parliamentary debate over a bill legalizing marriage to a deceased wife's sister. Opponents of the bill argued that such a marriage would harm rather than help Englishmen by destroying a bond untainted by sexual feeling. As one member of Parliament put it, should a union with a sister-in-law be allowed, "we shall be deprived of that pure love and affection,

27. Georgina Hogarth to Percy Fitzgerald, 27 October and 16 December [1867], in Adrian, "Georgina Hogarth to Percy Fitzgerald," 9–10.

28. According to Michael Slater, "a doctor's certificate of virginity may have been obtained for Georgina" in the fall of 1858, after Dickens received a letter alleging that a Glasgow newspaper editor was circulating the story that Georgina had three children by her brother-in-law. In the 1930s Henry Dickens told Gladys Storey that the family still possessed the certificate. Michael Slater, *Dickens and Women* (London: J. M. Dent, 1983), 172, 415 n. 34.

FIGURE 12. *Daniel Maclise, drawing of Georgina Hogarth, Catherine Dickens, and Charles Dickens (1843), V & A Drawing Collections, Victoria and Albert Museum.*

unconnected with any thought of marriage, which adds so much to the charm of life."[29] A husband's relationship with his sister-in-law was both frank and affectionate, it was argued, and combined "playful confidence" with respect: "In no situation, perhaps, is a female seen to greater advantage.... [S]he is never so much at her ease, never so agreeable or attractive, never apparently less selfish, or more amiable."[30] In a debate over marriage, surprisingly enough, marital relations were consistently devalued by those on *each* side of the question and "pure" relations valorized. Those supporting the bill argued not that the sister-in-law would make a loving wife to a widower but that she would make a good mother to her dead sister's children, a devoted aunt rather than a callous stepmother.[31]

Both Maclise's sketch and the parliamentary debate over the Deceased Wife's Sister Bill help explain how Dickens could privilege Georgina at Catherine's expense. They also shed light on the value Georgina placed on her tie to her sister's husband. What Georgina gained from Dickens was not so much a "pure" bond with a "brother" as a more equitable and frank relation with a non-kinsman than any marriage would likely allow her. The nature of the partnership Georgina gained through her sister's union thus illuminates what Dickens found "unaccountable" in her and what critics usually attribute, too readily and simply, to her devotion to the novelist: her decision to remain single. "We have had no marriages or givings in marriage, here," Dickens told William de Cerjat in 1849. "We might have had, but a certain young lady . . . is hard to please" (Pilgrim 5:683). "Not married yet—nor going to be," Dickens wrote Lord Robertson of Georgina in 1851 (Pilgrim 6:444). "Georgina is not yet married . . . and not in the least likely to be," he repeated to de Cerjat in 1852. "She seems unaccountably hard to please" (Pilgrim 6:671). "A general sentiment expressed this morning, that Georgina ought to be married," Dickens wrote Catherine from Lausanne in 1853. "Perhaps you'll mention it to her!" (Pilgrim 7:167). But Georgina had already "said No" to Augustus Egg, as Dickens confided

29. *Hansard*, 3rd ser., civ, 1237 (Thursday, 3 May 1849), quoted in Cynthia Fraser Behrman, "The Annual Blister: A Sidelight on Victorian Social and Parliamentary History," *Victorian Studies* 11, no. 4 (June 1968): 492.

30. Marriage Law Defence Association (A Sister and a Widow), no. 5, *An Englishwoman's Letter to the Right Honourable Sir Robert Harry Inglis, bart. M.P. on the proposed Alteration of the Marriage Law* (1849), quoted in Sybil Wolfram, *In-Laws and Outlaws: Kinship and Marriage in England* (New York: St. Martin's Press, 1987), 34.

31. As Elizabeth Gruner notes, the Deceased Wife's Sister Bill became "a 'children's relief bill,'" with the image of the motherly aunt obscuring the more troubling vision of a sexual union between sister and brother-in-law. Elizabeth Gruner, "Born and Made: Sisters, Brothers, and the Deceased Wife's Sister Bill," *Signs* 24, no. 2 (Winter 1999): 434.

to Angela Burdett Coutts. Remaining with the Dickenses instead of "brightening up [that] good little man's house" (Pilgrim 7:172), she refused to take the hint. Holding her head upright, unbowed by marriage even as she saw to others' needs, she declined to follow Catherine's lead.

"ANNE CORNELIUS, MOTHER-IN-LAW"

By the time Catherine separated from Dickens and Georgina, Anne Cornelius had returned to work at Tavistock House, at least temporarily, staying there when the family was away at Gad's Hill, the Dickenses' country home in Kent. As Catherine's lady's maid—and "more friend to both of us than a servant," according to Dickens—she had been privy to their deteriorating relations in the fall of 1857, when Dickens wrote to her from Gad's Hill, telling her of carpentry work to be done at Tavistock House, where he would no longer be sharing a bedroom with Catherine. "I want some little changes made in the arrangement of my dressing-room and the Bathroom," he began his letter. "And as I would rather not have them talked about by comparative strangers, I shall be much obliged to you, my old friend, if you will see them completed before you leave Tavistock House." Directing the carpenter, Anne was to see to it that Dickens's dressing room became his bedroom, with a "small iron bedstead" he had ordered for it soon to arrive; and she was to have the doorway connecting his new bedroom to Catherine's blocked off—fitted with shelving and sealed with a door. "The sooner it is done, the better," he told her (Pilgrim 8:465).

What Dickens's "old friend" thought of this arrangement—and of Catherine's departure from Tavistock House seven months later—is unknown to us. Evidently Anne did not record her perspective on the household and its events. Like Georgina, she remained with Dickens rather than going with Catherine to Gloucester Crescent as Charley did, but such behavior in a servant paid by, and answering to, her master is hardly surprising. Although he refers to Anne's testimony in his support in the "violated" letter, we don't know if she was at all convinced by Dickens's revisionist history of his marriage or by his claims that it had been unhappy from the start. After all, Anne had been a witness to many happy years between Catherine and Dickens, and had heard him praise his wife—as they traveled under trying circumstances in North America, for example. In writing to Miss Coutts in May 1858 to defend his behavior, Dickens grouped Anne with those who found Catherine difficult if not impossible to live with ("the companionship would wear her to death" [Pilgrim 8:560]), but that group included the people closest to his wife—her staunchest supporters, in fact—who *sought* Catherine's companionship after the separation: her mother and her sister Helen.

Whatever Anne's view of Dickens's claims, an arrangement in which she would leave Tavistock House with her mistress was clearly untenable. While Catherine employed a cook and a housemaid at Gloucester Crescent, she could not afford to pay a lady's maid on her streamlined budget even had Anne been willing to anger Dickens by casting in her lot with his wife. With her own husband often unemployed as a result of pulmonary troubles, Anne kept up her association with Dickens, receiving his occasional wages and, at times, additional financial support. Payments to her in the Coutts account follow Catherine's departure: £3 on 21 April 1859, for instance, and £7.10 three weeks later.[32] In 1868 Dickens came to her assistance when Edward Cornelius was unemployed; he asked Mamie and Georgina to assess her situation and see to her needs. Kate Cornelius became a pupil at North London Collegiate at this time, and Dickens paid for her schooling, as he did the tuition of two other pupils enrolled there since 1862—Florence and Maria Dickens, daughters of his late brother Alfred. They were joined at the school by a third sister, Katherine, in 1869.[33]

Catherine may have seen Kate Cornelius at North London Collegiate. She paid at least one visit to its boardinghouse, in March 1867, spending an evening with some of the girls.[34] In the years that followed her separation, Catherine assisted some of her former servants, providing recommendations and advice. If she saw Anne and Kate Cornelius, however, their meetings went unrecorded, and by the late 1870s they had almost certainly lost touch. Although Anne survived her former mistress by more than a decade, neither she nor her daughter is mentioned by Catherine in her will, while Catherine's "late faithful servant Sarah, now the wife of Benjamin Slade," receives a cameo brooch set in gold.[35] Yet Georgina made a point of writing to "dear old Nanny," as she called Anne, the day after Catherine's death, in one final acknowledgment of what had once been "the whole trio." "My poor sister died yesterday morning ... quite peacefully at the end, Thank God!" Georgina assured Anne, sending her "best love" to the trio's namesake.[36]

32. Charles Dickens, Esq., Account Ledger, Coutts & Co., London.

33. "Admission Book," ff. 23 and 35, North London Collegiate School Archives.

34. Catherine's visit of 26 March is recorded in the journal of Septimus Buss for 1867, North London Collegiate School Archives. I am grateful to Leon Litvak for alerting me to this fact.

35. Catherine Dickens, Last Will and Testament, 1878.

36. ALS Georgina Hogarth to Anne Cornelius, 23 November 1879, HM 28198, Huntington Library.

Georgina communicated with Anne into the 1890s; their last correspondence dates from 1893. In the months following Charles Dickens's death, she and Mamie raised a subscription for Anne, once again in financial difficulties. At Forster's suggestion they solicited contributions from friends who once knew her, collecting £150. At the time, Anne was subletting unfurnished apartments in a house she and her husband rented, but they were in debt to their landlord, and Georgina and Mamie hoped she would use the money to let "*furnished* apartments" more profitably. "We gave her £50 the other night for the paying of her landlord and the buying of furniture," Mamie told Alfred Dickens in October 1870. "She was most grateful, & very much affected, poor dear!"[37] Having helped establish Kate Cornelius at North London Collegiate on Dickens's behalf, Georgina and Mamie continued to pay her tuition and kept track of her progress as a teacher in training, praising her industry and cleverness, taking note when she passed her initial government exam, and hoping that she would "be able to earn her own living as a pupil teacher."[38] Yet Georgina was angered by Anne and Kate when, in 1873, they ignored her advice and, against her protests, Kate married, still in her teens. Anne had been thirty-four when she married; Kate was half that age. "We knew she was engaged, but she is not 18 yet and we understood that there was to be no question of marriage for two years, and we strongly advised that there should *not* be," Georgina complained to solicitor Frederic Ouvry, speaking for herself and Mamie. "However it seems our advice is not to be taken; and we can do no more than protest. The young man she is going to marry is steady and industrious, so I hope it will turn out well."[39]

While Catherine's experience suggests that a marriage can last for decades, produce many children, yet still turn out badly, it seems that Kate Cornelius had better luck in her union with the French-born John Romer, with whom she was still living in 1901, the year of Queen Victoria's death. Despite Georgina's fears that marriage would waste the girl's training and diminish her earning power, anxieties reinforced by Kate's struggle against debt in her early years with John Romer, she worked successfully as a music instructor and schoolteacher from her twenties well into middle age while also bearing six children over the course of nearly two decades. Anne made her home with her daughter and son-in-law after her own husband's death,

37. Mamie Dickens to Alfred Dickens, [October 1870], typescript, Charles Dickens Museum, London.

38. Georgina Hogarth to Annie Fields, 5 August 1872, FI 2701, Huntington Library, quoted in Adrian, *Georgina Hogarth and the Dickens Circle*, 202–3; Mamie Dickens to Alfred Dickens, [October 1870], typescript, Charles Dickens Museum, London.

39. Georgina Hogarth to Frederic Ouvry, n.d., Ouvry Papers, Charles Dickens Museum, quoted in Adrian, *Georgina Hogarth and the Dickens Circle*, 203.

living with the couple in her last years. Having been one of a trio with Catherine and Georgina in her twenties and thirties, Anne spent her sixties and seventies in a triangle of a different sort, identified on the 1881 census return as "Anne Cornelius, mother-in-law."

Catherine formed part of a similar trio in the last two decades of *her* life, spending time with Charley and his wife, Bessie Evans, although she shared their home only during her holidays. Sometimes perceived as meddling and burdensome, the mother-in-law figure is vulnerable to hostility and ridicule, and this certainly proved to be the case with Dickens and Mrs. Hogarth. But Catherine's relationship with Charley's wife proved much warmer and more mutually supportive than Mrs. Hogarth's with her eldest daughter's husband, with Bessie feeling for the "poor dear" and serving as Catherine's confidante.[40] While the trios Catherine had formed with Georgina and Anne and with Dickens and Georgina had dissolved by the late 1850s, there were others to be formed after the separation, substantially different in their grounding and ultimately more rewarding in their dynamics: not only the trio of Mrs. Dickens, "Mrs. Charles,"[41] and Charley, but also that of Catherine, Helen, and Helen's daughter May, named for their dead sister Mary.

40. Alfred Dickens quotes from Bessie Dickens's letter to him, in ALS to G. W. Rusden, 11 August 1870, Rusden Manuscripts, Trinity College Archives, University of Melbourne.

41. So Catherine refers to her daughter-in-law in writing to Matilda Butler (from "my bedroom" at Gad's Hill) in August 1877, ALS Charles Dickens Museum, London.

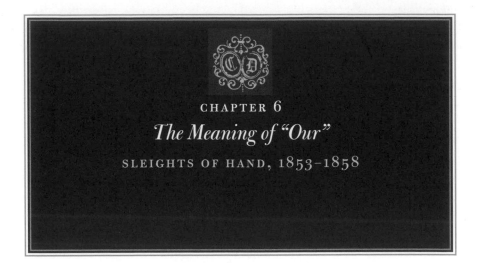

What do our keenest powers of observation avail . . . when they attempt to
unravel the sorceries of such a conjuror as the Chevalier de Caston—the
man who could name the cards which distant persons had silently taken
from an unbroken pack, with his back turned and blindfolded, and at the
distance of a drawing-room and a half? . . . This Chevalier de Caston, by
the way, was the only professor of his art who succeeded in puzzling Charles
Dickens, himself a consummate and experienced conjuror.
—H. F. Chorley, *Autobiography, Memoir, and Letters* (1873)

MIND READING

Gathered with friends and family members in Bonchurch on the Isle of Wight in
the summer of 1849, Catherine watched as "the Unparalleled Necromancer Rhia
Rhama Rhoos"—her husband, dressed as an Eastern conjuror—performed a series
of magic tricks. She saw coins vanish and reappear, cards leap from a pack and re-
materialize after being burned, a friend's watch cut from a loaf of bread, and a plum
pudding cooked in a hat that remained somehow undamaged in the process. In
Dickens's nimble hands, a wooden figure dubbed "the travelling doll" miraculously
disappeared, leaving only its dress behind. As Dickens announced in his playbill,
the doll "passes from visibility to invisibility with an expedition so astonishing that
no eye can follow its transformations" (Pilgrim 5:707).

Married to an amateur conjuror as well as a mesmerist, Catherine invited friends
to several such performances over the years and had seen Dickens work his sleights
of hand since the early 1840s, when he and Forster bought "the entire stock in trade
of a conjurer" (Pilgrim 3:416). Dickens used the supplies at New Year's Eve and

birthday parties. "Only think of that excellent Dickens playing the *conjuror* for one whole hour—the *best* conjuror I ever saw," Jane Carlyle told Jeannie Welsh in December 1843, after a party for Nina Macready, recounting feats that she thought "would enable him to make a handsome subsistence let the bookseller trade go as it please."[1] Thus when the celebrated French conjuror Alfred de Caston appeared at a soldiers' camp near their Boulogne lodgings in October 1854, the Dickenses made a point of seeing him perform. Sitting next to her husband in the front row, Catherine became a participant in de Caston's act, selected by the conjuror to help demonstrate his mind-reading powers.

One of the staples of mid-Victorian conjuring, "mind reading" depended on a performer's legerdemain skills. Asking several audience members to write words of their choice on slips of paper, which they folded and placed in a container, the conjuror would remove one of the slips unobserved, read it offstage as an audience volunteer selected a second slip of paper (presumed to be the first), and then secretly switch the two slips, "demonstrating" the knowledge he had surreptitiously gained of the original.[2] But in Catherine's exchange with de Caston, no such switch seemed possible. Without leaving the stage, the "Chevalier" himself wrote two undisclosed words on a blank piece of paper, which he folded and gave to Catherine to hold. "Madame," he then asked her, "will you think of any class of objects?"

"I have done so."
"Of what class, Madame?"
"Animals."
"Will you think of a particular animal, Madame?"
"I have done so."
"Of what animal?"
"The lion."
"Will you think of another class of objects, Madame?"
"I have done so."
"Of what class?"
"Flowers."
"The particular flower?"
"The rose."

1. Jane Carlyle to Jeannie Welsh, 23 December 1843, in *Jane Welsh Carlyle: Letters to Her Family, 1839–1863*, ed. Leonard Huxley (London: J. Murray, 1924), 170.

2. See Henri Garenne, *The Art of Modern Conjuring* (London: Ward, Lock & Co., 1886), 198–200.

Instructed by de Caston to open the slip of paper she was holding, Catherine discovered what he had written there: "*The Lion, the Rose.*" "Nothing whatever had led up to these words," Dickens marveled to Forster, "and they were the most distant conceivable from Catherine's thoughts when she entered the room. . . . I never saw anything in the least like this; or at all approaching to the absolute certainty, the familiarity, quickness, absence of all machinery, and actual face-to-face, hand-to-hand fairness between the conjuror and the audience, with which it was done" (Pilgrim 7:434).

Unlike the mediums who held séances in London in the mid-1850s, de Caston made no claims to clairvoyance. In fact he identified himself as an "opponent of all marvel-mongers, ancient and modern."[3] Nonetheless, his ability to anticipate and prerecord Catherine's thoughts, at least in appearance, may have struck her as uncanny—if only because it seemed strangely familiar. Despite Dickens's assertion that he had never seen "anything in the least" like de Caston's feat, he himself had worked similar "magic" on Catherine, using mesmerism to control her mind but also writing down the thoughts he had determined she would have, ideas that had value, he claimed, because they were Catherine's and not his.

Dickens's "read" Catherine's mind and recorded her thoughts not on slips of paper he handed her from a stage but in letters he posted to her while he was away. In one she received from Italy in December 1853, after Dickens visited members of their old Genoa circle, Catherine learned that she possessed the "power" to become reconciled with Augusta de la Rue while also learning what she would think, feel, and say in properly exercising it:

> I see that you have it in your power to set it right at once by writing [Madame de la Rue] a note to say that you have heard from me, with interest, of her sufferings and her cheerfulness—that you couldn't receive her messages of remembrance without a desire to respond to them—and that if you should ever be thrown together again by any circumstances, you hope it will be for a friendly association without any sort of shadow upon it. Understand above all things, that I do not ask you to do this, or want you to do this. I shall never ask whether you have done it or not, and shall never approach the subject from this hour. . . . But I am confident that if you could do this without any secret reservation in your own mind, you would do an unquestionably upright thing, and would place yourself on a far better station in your own eyes. . . . But I most earnestly repeat, for all that, that it would be utterly valueless and contemptible if it were done through a grain of any other influence than that of your own heart, reflecting on what I have written here. (Pilgrim 7:225)

3. L. W., "Sorcery, Ancient and Modern," *Eclectic Magazine,* n.s., 1 (March 1865): 393.

When de Caston "read" Catherine's mind, he may have employed a ruse or exchange that neither she nor Dickens observed, or he may have guided her word
choice subliminally; an image of English monarchy might bring to mind the lion
and the rose, commonly linked in representations of kingship. Dickens's method of
"conjuring" Catherine differed from these but was similarly deceptive. Inviting—
indeed encouraging—her to think (and write) for herself, he had already determined
how she was to do so. Although he tells her to follow her own heart and mind, he
dictates to her the terms of her proposed note, word for word, even as he denies
making any such proposal or having an interest in the matter. While he seems to
devalue his influence over her and to acknowledge her power rather than his, he
issues a series of directives ("set it right," "say that," "respond to them") couched
in the conditional tense ("you could," "you would"). In a psychological sleight of
hand, he thus represents his ideas and desires as Catherine's, creating the illusion
of her autonomy.

Dickens worked a second trick in his letter, transforming his own suspect position with Madame de la Rue into Catherine's unworthy position, and making his
obsession with another woman appear a matter of artistic temperament rather than
marital disloyalty. "Nine years have gone away" since they were in Genoa, Dickens
reminds Catherine; implying that she had magnified what she found improper in
1845, he supposes that "whatever looked large in that little place" had "shrunk to
its reasonable and natural proportions" by now.

> You know my life too, and my character, and what has had its part in mak-
> ing them successful; and the more you see of me, the better perhaps you may
> understand that the intense pursuit of any idea that takes complete posses-
> sion of me, is one of the qualities that makes me different—sometimes for
> good, sometimes I dare say for evil—from other men. Whatever made you
> unhappy in the Genoa time had no other root, beginning, middle, or end,
> than whatever has made you proud and honored in your married life, and
> given you station better than rank, and surrounded you with many enviable
> things. (Pilgrim 7:224)

Dickens represents his preoccupation with another woman as "the intense pursuit of
[an] idea"—mesmerism, presumably. Inverting its dynamics, he depicts himself as
the one possessed. While conceding that the "complete possession" such ideas take
of him might lead to evil as well as good, he acknowledges only the benefits Catherine reaps from his difference from others, not the harm it might do her. Rather than
righting himself with Catherine in revisiting the past, then, he justifies himself to
her and emphasizes *her* obligation to do right by those he alleges she wronged, her
"position beside these people" neither "good" nor "amiable" nor "generous"—"not

worthy of [her] at all." But if she does the "upright thing," she must do so for the right reason—on the basis of her own thought and feeling, not his—otherwise her actions will be "utterly valueless and contemptible" (Pilgrim 7:225). Turning the tables on Catherine, he places her in the wrong, recounting what he represents as her mistakes in the past and emphasizing her moral vulnerability in the present.

Over the next few years a "restless" Dickens, struggling against middle age, would become intensely preoccupied with two other women, the first much more fleetingly than the second. His handling of his relations with Madame de la Rue in 1853 anticipated sleights of hand Catherine was yet to observe, when Dickens became reacquainted with the former Maria Beadnell in 1855, only to let Ellen Ternan "take . . . complete possession" of him in 1857.

Subject to Dickens's conjuring in the mid-1850s, Catherine sought to distinguish illusion from reality in their relationship and in her husband's relations with other women, invited to think and act for herself yet discouraged from or criticized for doing so (fig. 13). From her perspective, the years immediately preceding her separation were marked, in part, by deceptive appearances and distressing transformations, leading to what has been represented by Dickens scholars as her own disappearing act. Finished with childbearing by 1853 and serving as surrogate head of the household during Dickens's repeated absences, Catherine "ventured" to act on her own judgment and authority, as she put it to Miss Coutts.[4] But when she did so, Dickens was sometimes irritated—and ultimately irate. By 1858 his affection for her had vanished, and she became as invisible in his eyes as the "traveling doll" he made disappear during his "cabalistic" performances (Pilgrim 5:707).

Conjured out of existence as far as Dickens was concerned, Catherine remains subject to scholarly "sleights of hand," as critics and biographers mistake the illusion of her disappearance for the reality, overlook her significance to the plotlines their work unfolds, and on occasion transform letters she authored into writings "by" Dickens. While correcting such misattributions and considering their implications, we might also revisit the scene in which de Caston "succeeded in puzzling Charles Dickens" and entertain yet another possible explanation for his ability to read Catherine's mind, one that grants her more agency than do other explanations—applying what H. F. Chorley, recounting his own experience with the "Chevalier," terms "the theory of complicity."[5] Although Dickens confidently reported to Forster that the words "lion" and "rose" were "the most distant conceivable from Catherine's

4. ALS Catherine Dickens to Angela Burdett Coutts, "Monday" [1 February 1858], MA 1352, the Morgan Library & Museum, New York.

5. Henry Fothergill Chorley, *Autobiography, Memoir, and Letters*, comp. Henry G. Hewlett, 2 vols. (London: Richard Bentley, 1873), 2:222–23.

FIGURE 13. *Catherine Dickens (ca. 1852–1855), daguerreotype by John J. E. Mayall, reproduced by kind permission of Colin Axon. Photo by Jim Styles.*

thoughts when she entered the room" (Pilgrim 7:434), he may have known less about her mind than he assumed. Indeed, Catherine may have been performing her own sleight of hand during de Caston's performance, entering in league with him to out-conjure the conjuror beside her. This explanation seems more plausible than it otherwise might when we consider Catherine's response to an 1853 wager between her husband and Clarkson Stanfield which she congratulated Stanfield "on having won."[6] Whether or not Catherine out-conjured Dickens in 1854, she would expose his sleights of hand several years later, in speaking of his improper attachment to Ellen Ternan and reminding friends and acquaintances of her presence at Gloucester Crescent, despite her disappearance from Tavistock House.

"UNPROTECTED FEMALES"

In November 1853 Catherine wrote to Miss Lawrence of Balsall Heath, responding to an invitation to stay at her family's home the following month, when Dickens would be reading in Birmingham. Miss Lawrence's note had been forwarded to Catherine in Bonchurch, where she was "paying a visit just now," and she apologized for her delayed reply. "Mr. Dickens is in Italy, taking a little vacation after his hard work," Catherine told her, but she could speak "in his name and [her] own" in thanking her correspondent yet declining the "most kind and hospitable" offer. "We shall not be able to have the pleasure of availing ourselves of it," Catherine went on, since "several friends . . . are going to accompany us to Birmingham, and Mr. Dickens will feel himself obliged to remain at the Hotel on their account."[7] "You were 'quite right' in your reply to the Lawrences," Dickens told Catherine two weeks later, writing from Venice and using one of Forster's pet expressions to commend her (Pilgrim 7:216). But in the same letter, Dickens proved less pleased with another decision Catherine had made in his absence: to pay the visit to their friends the Whites which she mentioned to Miss Lawrence.

> From what Georgina says, and from what Forster indicates that he supposes you to have told me, I infer that your stay at Bonchurch was sufficiently disagreeable. But you know my old principle; that there are very few people indeed, in whose house it will ever do to stay. Such social confidence requires in the hosts, ease, tact, good humour, liveliness, and above all hospitality and generosity.—I am afraid the last is hardly as general a quality as I once

6. ALS Catherine Dickens to Clarkson Stanfield, 13 May 1853, STN/5/23, National Maritime Museum, Greenwich.

7. ALS Catherine Dickens to Miss Lawrence, 10 November [1853], Special Collections and Digital Programs, Margaret I. King Library, University of Kentucky.

hoped. . . . I am quite certain it is not to be found under White's waistcoat, and I wonder you ever went there. (Pilgrim 7:216)

What her husband "always . . . ma[d]e a rule" was a refrain in Catherine's letters, as she explained to correspondents why it was "impossible . . . to comply" with their requests or accept their offers,[8] and she knew his "old principle," as he reminded her from Venice. Nonetheless, she failed to follow it in staying with the Whites, Dickens made clear.

He implied that Catherine made matters worse by remaining silent on the subject of Bonchurch and forcing him to "infer" that her visit was unpleasant, although he knew that she had told him of it in a "missing letter" he had "give[n] . . . up for lost" (Pilgrim 7:215). But Dickens generally felt that his subordinates were telling him too little during his trip to Italy, and he was easily irritated on that score. Not only was one of Catherine's letters missing. In those he received, she left him wondering about some of her purchases, while Wills failed to describe "one single paper that has been put into Household Words," though Dickens had "now been two months away," "Imagine this," Catherine read; "I have not . . . the least idea of anything that was developed at the Audit Meeting—of the state of the accounts—of the reported condition of H.W.—of the sum placed to my credit—or anything else. . . . I don't even know what the nights are on which I am to read! I have been turning over in my mind for some time, an improvement in the Study, which I wish you would have completed *at once*," he went on, his abrupt shift in focus making sense, psychologically, after his litany of complaints:

> A covering for the mantelpiece—covered shelf you know, like that in the drawing room, and a trifle broader than the mantelpiece now is—of green velvet, about the color of the green leather to the bookcase, or a trifle darker if necessary—with a green fringe intermingled with red. The form of the fringe to be, in little, something of the shape of the cornice-fringe of the curtains—so as to carry that idea, through. The green should be of a tint that will carry through both the bookcase green and the carpet green—generally—so that the greens will all tone in. Get an estimate from Shoolbreds, and then have it made and put up. The glass will have to be raised, you know, and put upon the shelf—as in the drawing room. (Pilgrim 7:215–17)

Kept in the dark by Wills and "impatient" to hear more from Catherine (Pilgrim 7:185), Dickens sought to reestablish control by directing his wife in a new project,

8. ALS Catherine Dickens to Mr. Smith, [9 August 1852], Charles Dickens Museum, London.

his desires ("I wish") becoming underlined commands ("completed *at once*"). Telling her what she knows ("you know . . . you know"), he limits her discretionary power. His detailed instructions leave little to her judgment or taste. Yet as long as Dickens remained away from her, he was unsure if she was compliant. "I wonder whether you will have done the study mantelpiece by Sunday morning!—I hope so," he wrote her one week later (Pilgrim 7:225).[9]

As Wills filled in for Dickens at *Household Words,* Catherine filled in for her husband at home from mid-October through mid-December, despite the time she spent away from Tavistock House herself, visiting Macready at Sherborne with Georgina and Forster before going to Bonchurch and the Whites. While Dickens toured the continent with Collins and Egg, Catherine acted as his proxy, attending to correspondence and invitations, paying necessary social calls, conveying messages to Wills and Forster, and managing household and traveling expenses. Her name appears in a flurry of entries in the Coutts bank ledger during Dickens's 1853 absence, with a total of £173.16 going to her for bills and drafts in the month of October.[10]

Like Wills, left to manage *Household Words,* its payroll, and its accounts, Catherine took on extra responsibilities while Dickens was away. But unlike the subeditor, she was a wife and a dependent—in Dickens's absence an "unprotected female," as was Georgina—and thus more closely instructed and supervised. From Rome, Dickens told Wills to "keep 'Household Words' imaginative" without telling him precisely how he was to do so (Pilgrim 7:200); from Venice, Dickens told Catherine that the new shelf in his study was to be "a trifle broader" than before, its green at most "a trifle darker" than the bookcase, specifying tints and shapes and leaving little to her imagination (Pilgrim 7:216–17). Joking to Wills before his departure, Dickens defined the nature of Catherine's "power" for his sub-editor, who had offered to assist the Hogarth sisters while their guardian was away. "Many thanks for your kind letter, both on my own behalf, and on that of the unprotected females," he wrote Wills on 9 October. "They are sincerely sensible of your offer, and Mrs. Dickens begs me to say that she will not hesitate to give you all the trouble in her power!" (Pilgrim 7:161).

Granting Catherine the power to give trouble, Dickens implicitly distinguished *her* surrogate authority from Wills's. Like their neighbor Miss Cardale, whose 1854 wedding left "all the women and girls" at Tavistock House "stark mad" with

9. Catherine may have obtained an estimate as instructed, but she did not hire Shoolbreds for the job; instead Dickens paid £7.15.6 to his carpenter for work done within two weeks of his return. Charles Dickens, Esq., Account Ledger, Coutts & Co., London.

10. Ibid.

excitement, Catherine was "uterine" in her behavior and might require "despotic conjugal influence" or "stern . . . command" (Pilgrim 7:320). So Dickens joked with Wills after his return. As Catherine well knew, her ability to act in the name and place of her husband was highly circumscribed, and whether he was abroad or at home, her authority differed markedly not just from his but from that of his male proxies.

This was due, in part, to her ignorance of the manly concerns Dickens and his friends discussed "in bearded confidence" (Pilgrim 7:376)—business matters, most obviously. When she and her family were living in Paris in 1855 and Dickens had to leave abruptly for London, Catherine learned only then how to bank in France, instructed in a letter from her husband, who arranged to have her drafts as well as his honored at Ferrère Laffitte's (Pilgrim 7:731).

But Catherine's authority as Dickens's proxy was limited more generally by her "natural" subordination as a woman, an idea that structured household power dynamics. Animated by her knowledge of her husband, his expectations, and feelings, Catherine might carefully apply his principles to reach decisions in his absence, only to have her decisions overturned. Dickens, not Catherine, had the authority to exercise discretion and bend the rules, as he sometimes demonstrated in her presence, undermining her exercise of power. When Kate Horne was invited to Sunday dinner at Tavistock House in July 1852, she called on Catherine to explain that she would have a friend visiting whom she couldn't leave behind. As Mrs. Horne relayed the incident to her husband, R. H. Horne, "Mrs. Dickens said she was very sorry but I knew how strange & shy 'Charles' was and that he could not endure any stranger when they dined quietly alone, as they intended to do on Sunday. Presently, however, he came in and Mrs. Dickens told him I could not dine there, and why. He said 'I shall be most happy to see any friend of Mrs. Horne's; she sanctifies the stranger & c.[']"[11] Subject to such reversals, Catherine was wary when Dickens urged her to judge for herself—to consider matters "in [her] own eyes" and follow the "influence . . . of [her] own heart" (Pilgrim 7:225)—knowing her word was not the last in most matters.

Kate Horne found Catherine "very kind" and underscored the consideration shown her by Mrs. Dickens in letters to her husband, who had gone to Australia to write about gold prospecting for *Household Words*.[12] But the lesson of Catherine's subservience was not lost on Mrs. Horne, even as she played along with Dickens's flirtations—amused when he suggested that "he and [she] must someday go to Italy

11. ALS Catherine Horne to R. H. Horne, 11 July [1852], HM 37767, Huntington Library.

12. ALS Catherine Horne to R. H. Horne, 24 June [1852], HM 37767, Huntington Library.

together" or told her that she looked "provokingly well."[13] Describing herself as "very independent" to Catherine,[14] whose wifely submission she observed at close hand, and increasingly disenchanted with her own husband, his inadequacies as a provider, and the inequities of coverture generally, Mrs. Horne developed a clear if cutting sense of what male "protection" was worth—in her case, less than nothing. Left with debts she couldn't pay by Horne, whose Australian plan proved a failure, and "want[ing] some money badly to pay off . . . bills,"[15] she accepted a post in London at the Ladies' Guild, a female cooperative run by Caroline Hill, where she learned to paint glass to resemble marble. By August 1853 she was "'in receipt' of a sovereign a week & . . . getting on splendidly,"[16] determined "to keep [her] situation" when her husband returned. "Then we will both go to our work every day," she told him.[17]

By January 1854 Kitty Horne had reenvisioned their relationship again and decided to end their marriage, whether or not she could do so legally. Warning her husband to "prepare [his] mind for what 'might' be a most painful surprise," she announced that she was his "wife no longer" and could "never again be to [him] anything but a friend." She had worked her way through coverture, acquiring "strength and . . . independence" in her successful "struggle [to] maintain [her]self body and soul." She reclaimed her body as her own, and although she could remain his wife "outwardly," she thought it best not to do so, since she understood from his comments about the Brownings and their reputedly sexless marriage that he "would seek elsewhere what [she] did not give [him]," and that was something she "would not endure."[18] From his old friend Mary Gillies, Horne heard in greater detail what Kitty felt she had gained in his absence, and what she was rejecting in ending their marriage: "work which seemed successful—the sense of independence—a growing interest in the movements of the time[,] . . . a love of freedom—of time at her own disposal—of absence of all little cares & minor details of cookery &c.—a power to

13. ALS Catherine Horne to R. H. Horne, 12 July [1852] and 1 May [1853], HM 37767 and 37777, Huntington Library.

14. ALS Catherine Horne to R. H. Horne, 24 June [1852], HM 37767, Huntington Library. Here Mrs. Horne quotes a letter she had recently written to Catherine Dickens.

15. ALS Catherine Horne to R. H. Horne, 22 October [1852], HM 3777, Huntington Library.

16. ALS Catherine Horne to R. H. Horne, 3 August [1853], HM 37780, Huntington Library.

17. Ibid.

18. ALS Catherine Horne to R. H. Horne, 6 January 1854, HM 37784, Huntington Library.

read what she likes, to go where she likes—a hatred to the idea of being trammelled ever again and having to submit to the will of another"[19]—and so Gillies's catalog of Kate Horne's newfound freedoms went on.

After she declared herself a "wife no longer," the Dickenses continued to see her, inviting her to stay with them in Boulogne in the summer of 1854, as they had invited her to their seaside lodgings in the past. Before she took her post at the Ladies' Guild, her husband had suggested to her that she might work for the Dickenses, though she apparently scoffed at the idea: "As you would not have minded my being a governess at the Dickens[es'] (!)," she told him in August 1853, "I conclude you would not mind my post at the Guild being known, so I keep it secret no longer."[20] Happy with their French governess, the Dickenses were unlikely to have hired their friend, but they were sensitive to her financial struggles. In 1852, Catherine arranged for "the brougham . . . to take [Mrs. Horne] home" after a dinner party to save her any expense.[21]

While Kitty emphasized her independence to Catherine and disclosed to Mary Gillies her "hatred to . . . having to submit to the will of another" in marriage, she struck a different, archly feminine key in her banter with Dickens. She secured his sympathy and help not as an articulate critic of coverture who sought to regain her autonomy but as an attractive middle-class woman striving to support herself because she had married a failed provider.

Having achieved *within* marriage many of the freedoms that Kate Horne regained outside it, Christiana Thompson earned no such sympathy from Dickens. Catherine had not seen Christiana since 1850, when she and Georgina stood by while Dickens mesmerized her sister Anna. But she heard of her three years later, when Dickens called on the Thompsons in Nervi, near Genoa, and took offense at what he saw. Not only were the two daughters "untidy," their hair oddly "cropped"; their mother was "greatly flushed and agitated. . . . We had disturbed her at her painting in Oils; and I rather received an impression that what with that, and what with Music, the household affairs went a little to the wall" (Pilgrim 7:178). Writing to Georgina, Dickens was more severe, identifying Christiana's "excitability and restlessness" as "a positive disease" and parodying her defense of her painting against those who thought she should focus exclusively on music: "She said—so fast, that she seemed to leave out all small words—'Assure you Mr. Dickens—shall

19. ALS Mary Gillies to R. H. Horne, 2 January 1854, HM 37756, Huntington Library.

20. ALS Catherine Horne to R. H. Horne, 3 August 1853, HM 37780, Huntington Library.

21. ALS Catherine Dickens to Catherine Horne, "Sunday Evening" [June 1852], HM 37741, Huntington Library.

see my pictures yet—in Exhibition in London Royal Academy.—Play great deal better since painted than ever did....Painting's poetry and Music's poetry, and poetry breaking out of a person in one, breaks out in the other—naturally—must be so'" (Pilgrim 7:212).

Dickens claimed to "have thought a good deal about Christiana" while in Italy (Pilgrim 7:212), but in describing her "agitation" and "excitability" to the Hogarth sisters, and her spirited defense of her work "in Oils," he completely misunderstood her behavior. Christiana was agitated and defensive in Dickens's presence not because she was "diseased" but because her sister Anna was badly mistreated by Dickens's brother Fred, who bullied his wife, in part, by opposing her artistic pursuits. Since the Weller sisters last saw Catherine and Dickens in 1850, Anna had "burden[ed]" Christiana with "unhappy confidences," disclosing some of the painful details of her married life, particularly Fred's "*spite* against" her art. "I have been longing to write . . . but I can hardly regret my silence," Anna told her sister in January 1852, since she could not send "a welcome & cheerful epistle . . . unless [she] could have drawn it from some other source than home." Anna was suffering from Fred's "violent & disgusting treatment—[as] unreasonable as cruel"; he not only called her an unfit companion but also threatened to get medical "advice" that would justify his "put[ting] a stop to [her] Painting."[22] In June 1854, six months after Kate Horne declared herself a "wife no longer," Anna left Fred, moving back to her parents' home "in consequence of ill-treatment" and her husband's "neglect to supply her with food and other necessaries."[23] Although Anna returned to him the following January, she obtained a judicial separation on the grounds of adultery in 1858, only a few months after Catherine separated from Fred's older brother through other means.

As Kate Horne understood it, a husband's "protection" required submission, constraint, and dependence; for Anna Dickens, it brought "violent & disgusting treatment," "daily bitterness," and "aggravations [that] pass all bounds."[24] To Catherine, it was less illusory, though Dickens's guidance was sometimes indistinguishable from control, and the "many enviable things" he supplied were laden with wifely obligations. Catherine never declared herself a "wife no longer," but her response to the protection her husband offered could be as equivocal as that

22. Anna Dickens to Christiana Thompson, [?10] January 1852, typescript, Meynell Family Papers, Greatham.

23. Anna Dickens, Petition for Judicial Separation, 30 October 1858, MS Principal Probate Register, quoted in Pilgrim 7:361 n. 3.

24. Anna Dickens to Christiana Thompson, [?10] January 1852, typescript, Meynell Family Papers, Greatham.

protection itself. Having been urged by Dickens to correspond with Madame de la Rue to set herself right, Catherine complied, yet in a way that subverted her husband's aims and instructions. Rather than expressing interest in her correspondent's "sufferings and . . . cheerfulness" and hoping for a "friendly association," as Dickens advised, Catherine wrote her about some "Italian dishes," most likely requesting or enclosing the pertinent recipes. And while Dickens insisted that his part in the matter was now over and that he would "never ask" whether Catherine had written or "approach the subject from [that] hour," she made a point of telling him of her action by asking him to inquire after her letter when he next wrote to Émile in March 1854. "Mrs. Dickens and Georgy send their loves," Dickens noted, "and the former wants to know whether Madame De la Rue ever received her letter about the Italian dishes'?" (Pilgrim 7:289).

INVISIBLE INK

Like so many of the letters we know Catherine wrote solely from the correspondence of others, the one she composed to Madame de la Rue near the start of 1854 has vanished. Dickens's reference to it suggests the difficulties of learning about Catherine's writings and expressions from his own—for as the editors of the Pilgrim *Letters of Charles Dickens* observe in their annotation, Dickens omits the opening quotation marks when he cites Catherine to Émile ("Mrs. Dickens . . . wants to know whether Madame De la Rue ever received her letter about the Italian dishes'?"). He thus fails to indicate where his language ends and Catherine's begins. Despite our uncertainty over which words "belong" to Catherine, we understand that her letter concerned "Italian dishes." But the missing quotation mark in Dickens's letter points to a larger and more significant set of practices—or illusions—that compromise Catherine's meaning and make her authorship disappear: the misattribution to Dickens of some of the letters she wrote, the transformation of her writing into "his" by virtue of his postscripts, and the characterization of Catherine as a mere copyist or amanuensis. Each of these "tricks" unduly limits her powers of expression and her significance as a person in her own right.

At the Lord Mayor's dinner on 2 May 1853, Catherine met Harriet Beecher Stowe, touring Europe with her husband after the success of *Uncle Tom's Cabin* (1852). "We ladies . . . went into the drawing-room," Stowe recalled, and she and Catherine spoke. Catherine had read Stowe's best-seller and six months earlier had been among the first to sign an antislavery address from the "Women of Great Britain and Ireland to Their Sisters, the Women of the United States," sent to Mrs. Stowe with over half a million signatures. Dickens had mixed feelings about the American and her novel, but Stowe enjoyed meeting the Dickenses, and Catherine's "air of frankness, cheerfulness, and reliability" impressed her, leaving her "desiring to know more."[25] Soon after meeting the Stowes, the Dickenses called on them in Walworth, and the day after the Lord Mayor's dinner, Catherine wrote to "Professor & Mrs. Beecher Stowe," inviting them to Tavistock House on the fourteenth.[26] Catherine was brief but filled most of the page with her script, using the third-person voice on behalf of herself and her husband. She had written for herself and Dickens in the third person before and would do so for five more years. The last such letter she composed was dated 8 June 1858, shortly after the separation, and addressed to the treasurer of the Foundling Hospital and his wife: "Mr. and Mrs. Charles Dickens regret extremely that, as they will be out of town on Sunday the 13th next, they cannot have the pleasure of accepting Mr. and Mrs. Gregory's kind invitation to Luncheon on that morning" (Pilgrim 8:581). Without noting when the invitation was received, the editors remark that "the reply was Catherine's responsibility and should have been sent earlier" (Pilgrim 8:581 and n. 2).

If such replies and invitations were "Catherine's responsibility," however, and were written in her hand, then they are the letters of Catherine Dickens, not those of her husband, and ought not to be included in the Pilgrim edition as such. Yet Catherine's letter to the Stowes appears as *Dickens's* letter. Only in the small print of the text's bottom margin do we learn that the manuscript is "in Catherine's hand," and without any recognition of her as its author (Pilgrim 7:77 n. 2). Similarly, Catherine's letter to the Gregorys appears in the Pilgrim edition as Dickens's letter; here, too, her handwriting rather than her authorship is acknowledged, and in a reduced font further diminished by parentheses: "MS (in Mrs CD's hand)" (Pilgrim 8:581). At one and the same time, the editors chastise Catherine for writing a tardy response and elide her authorship, denying her the very agency on which their blame must rest.

The twelve-volume Pilgrim edition of Dickens's letters is the work of four decades of meticulous scholarship to which those in Dickens studies are heavily indebted. Because of the editors' attention to Catherine's letters, dozens of which they cite in footnotes, and their recognition of Dickens's distorted representations of his wife in 1858, their volumes are invaluable to those interested in Catherine's story. Nonetheless, their attribution to Dickens of the third-person letters Catherine wrote on the couple's behalf is regrettable because it obscures the experience and person behind them. Catherine's invitations and replies to invitations illuminate her responsibilities as hostess and domestic manager. But the letter she wrote

25. Harriet Beecher Stowe, *Sunny Memories of Foreign Lands* (London: G. Routledge & Co., 1854), 127.

26. AL Catherine Dickens to Professor & Mrs. Beecher Stowe, 3 May 1853, G341, Gimbel Collection, Beinecke Rare Book and Manuscript Library, Yale University.

to the Stowes also reflects her presence at the Lord Mayor's dinner and her meeting with the Americans, just as her letter to the Gregorys suggests the strain placed on her at the time of the separation. It does so in its timing—in what may have been her delayed response to an invitation that arrived at Tavistock House as she was in the throes of leaving it permanently—but in its language as well. Her phrase "regret extremely" is unusual among such replies. Rather than simply expressing her disappointment at missing a luncheon, it likely conveys her unhappy estrangement from Dickens, whom she would no longer accompany to such gatherings.

Equating the joint marital identity of the Dickenses with that of the husband, these misattributions reinforce the logic of coverture while promoting Dickens's claims, as literary genius, to texts authored by subordinates. When Dickens himself writes a letter on behalf of "Mr. and Mrs. Charles Dickens," as he did to the duke of Devonshire in 1848 (Pilgrim 5:272–73), he is acknowledged as its author, but Catherine cannot write for herself and her husband in this way without being considered his amanuensis and her letter becoming "his."[27]

An editorial practice that too readily credits Catherine's letters to Dickens reenacts the novelist's own appropriations of Catherine's correspondence and correspondents—his tendency to intervene in her communications and make her writing his own, in part by means of his postscripts. In September 1853 Catherine wrote to Macready of her upcoming visit to Sherborne, naming 24 October as the date for her arrival with Georgina and Forster. Dickens carried her letter from Boulogne to London, but before mailing it added a postscript inside the flap of her envelope, altering her arrangements after meeting with her male escort. "As I forewarned you," he wrote her from the office, "Forster's day for Macready *must be* a Saturday. I have therefore added a postscript to your letter (so written and in such ink that it is no great matter what you say therein, as I defy Macready to read it), importing that on F's account the day is changed to Saturday the 22nd. of October" (Pilgrim 7:138). In his postscript Dickens tells Macready that Forster "suggests as an improvement on Catherine's suggested day, Saturday the 22nd," which their host should "now understand . . . to be the day appointed," Dickens having "full power to change the day according to [Forster's] necessities" (Pilgrim 7:139).

27. The only time a third-person communication written on behalf of the couple appears in the marginal notes of a Pilgrim volume, where Catherine's letters generally appear, that communication is understood to be purely mechanical—a matter of filling in blanks on a printed card: "'Mr. and Mrs. Charles Dickens. Return thanks for the Honor of Mr. William Ainsworth's obliging enquiries' (the names apparently in Catherine's hand; the rest printed)" (Pilgrim 1:260 n. 2).

This "improvement" on Catherine's plans seems practical. Understanding business matters—in this case the *Examiner*'s publishing schedule—Dickens presumably knew what Catherine did not: that Forster, as editor, would have to leave town earlier than she wished because the *Examiner* appeared on Saturdays. But as the "forewarning" Catherine received makes clear, she already knew about Forster's schedule and was really questioning the force of male "necessities" when she proceeded with her plans. Like Forster, she may have been faced with obligations—social or family duties that would keep her in town through Sunday. In altering her arrangements, Dickens reminds his wife that *male* needs are imperative (they "*must be*"). He further discounts her view by disparaging her letter as so illegible that its contents are irrelevant. Because the document has not survived, we cannot judge how easy or difficult it was to read, although the address Catherine inscribed on the envelope is legible enough. But the illegibility of women's letters generally—in their subject and style as well as their script and crosshatching—was a standing joke in the nineteenth century and a way of putting aspiring female authors in their place. As Henry Tilney tells Catherine Morland in *Northanger Abbey* (1818), "the usual style of letter-writing among women is faultless, except in three particulars... a general deficiency of subject, a total inattention to stops, and a very frequent ignorance of grammar."[28]

Dickens's critique of Catherine's letter—"so written and in such ink"—draws on this stereotype at the same time that it subordinates female desires to male "necessities." Judged to produce "illegible" letters that "defy" reading, the ink in which Catherine writes might as well be invisible—as is Catherine's correspondence with Macready. Just as Dickens overrides the plans Catherine makes in her letter, so his postscript replaces her letter in the library housing what remains of the correspondence, the page on which she wrote to Macready having vanished and the envelope that once contained it, and on which Dickens added his note, appearing in its stead (fig. 14). In a sleight of hand repeatedly staged in libraries and archives, the postscript becomes the letter in the couple's exchange with a friend, the text of Dickens's addendum included in the Pilgrim edition as any other letter would be. In small print, and within parentheses, the editors refer to Catherine's original letter to the actor in the headnote to what appears as Charles Dickens "*To* W. C. Macready, 7 [September 1853]": "MS Yale University Library (written inside flap of envelope of Mrs. CD *to* Macready)" (Pilgrim 7:138). But the archivist of Yale's Gimbel Collection catalogues the two sentences Dickens added to Catherine's letter as "A.L.s.

28. Jane Austen, *Northanger Abbey*, ed. James Kinsley and John Davie (1818; Oxford: Oxford University Press, 2003), 16.

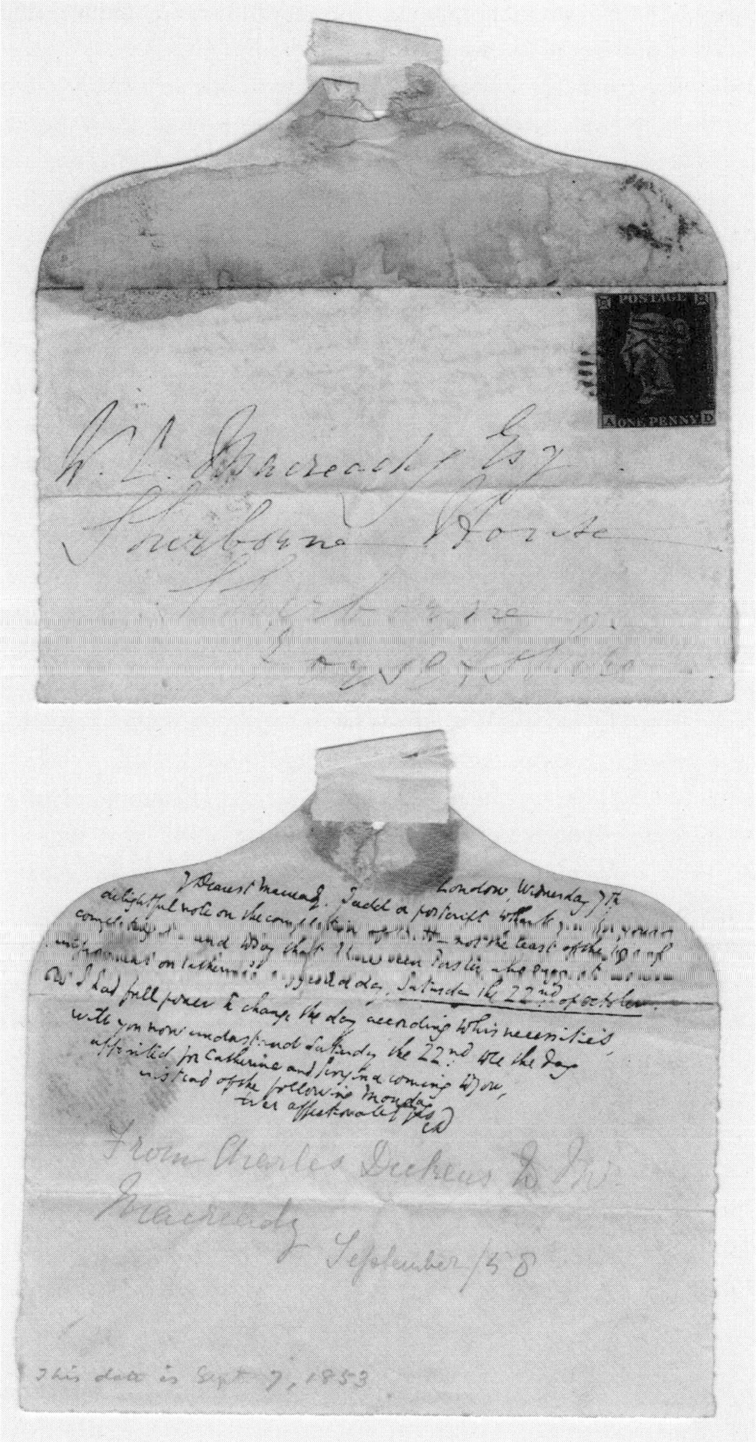

FIGURE 14.
Envelope addressed to W. C. Macready by Catherine Dickens, with postscript by Charles Dickens inside flap, September 1853, G257, Gimbel Collection, Beineke Rare Book and Manuscript Library, Yale University.

[autograph letter signed] of 7 September 1853," a "'postscript' written on the inside of an envelope," saying nothing of Catherine's missing "script."[29]

While Catherine's letter to Macready has vanished, others are invisible because they were never written, as Dickens intervened in Catherine's exchanges, responding in her stead. "I take it upon myself to answer your letter to Catherine as I am referred to in it," he told Lavinia Watson in November 1854, after she mistook another author's journalism for his. "The Walk is not my writing. It is very well done by a close Imitator. Why I found myself so 'used up', after Hard Times, I scarcely know" (Pilgrim 7:453). So Dickens answers for Catherine, forestalling her authorship in defining his own. In 1854 Catherine's cookbook appeared in a revised and expanded "New Edition" by "Lady Clutterbuck," with twice the original number of recipes and with Dickens's 1851 introduction.[30] His phrase "used up" would have recalled for his correspondent the play that he, Catherine, and others performed at the Watsons' and from which Catherine took her pen name. The only reference to "cooking" in his letter, however, pertains to Sir John Franklin and his men, who allegedly resorted to cannibalism while lost in the Arctic (Pilgrim 7:456).

Dickens speaks for and as Lady Maria in his introduction to Catherine's cookbook, yet he repeatedly prevented Catherine from making him and his writings her own subject. Just as he answered for her in November 1854, when he was referred to in the letter she received from Mrs. Watson, so he did again in September 1855, when Mrs. Watson asked her about the novel that became *Little Dorrit*. "Catherine tells me that you want to know the name of my new book. I cannot bear that you should know it from anyone but me. It will not be made public until the end of October; the title is NOBODY'S FAULT. . . . I am getting on pretty well—have done the first two numbers—and am just now beginning the third; which egotistical announcements I make to you, because I know you will be interested in them" (Pilgrim 7:703–4).

What is obscured by these "egotistical" communications and interventions is Mrs. Watson's connection to Catherine, her primary correspondent in the household. The disappearance of the women's correspondence and the substitution of Dickens's replies for his wife's unduly diminish Catherine's role in the story once conveyed by these writings and give the false impression that she and Mrs. Watson had no real tie. On 21 May 1855 Dickens described to Lavinia his vexation at

29. John B. Podeschi, *Dickens and Dickensiana: A Catalogue of the Richard Gimbel Collection in the Yale University Library* (New Haven: Yale University Library, 1980), 343.

30. Susan Rossi-Wilcox discusses the 1854 edition and reprints its recipes in *Dinner for Dickens: The Culinary History of Mrs. Charles Dickens's Menu Books* (Totnes: Prospect Books, 2005), 77, 69–74.

having missed her when she called two days before. "The fault was not mine," he claims. "On my infallible slate of engagements, was this inscription: Mrs. Watson here at 3. . . . Consequently, when I came home (having only run down to the office) at ten minutes before three, conscious rectitude sustained me under your having come and gone. In which proceeding you have no kind of justification" (Pilgrim 7:626). Dickens's remarks and the story told by the Pilgrim *Letters* suggest that Mrs. Watson mistimed her visit, missing the very person she hoped to see. What goes unrecognized in a plot based solely on Dickens's letter is the actual reason for her call. The day in question was 19 May 1855—Catherine's fortieth birthday— unacknowledged in the Pilgrim *Letters* but commemorated with visits, cards, and gifts by those in the Dickens circle, some of whom always celebrated the event with Catherine and her husband.

Thus in May 1857 Dickens declined an invitation from the Earl Stanhope, explaining that "the Nineteenth being Mrs. Dickens's birthday, I gave a promise that she should make her first appearance [at Gad's Hill Place] on that occasion, and asked some of her friends to come down for two or three days" (Pilgrim 8:325). One year earlier, anticipating his marriage to Eliza Colburn, Forster had sent Catherine a moving and grateful letter with his birthday gift, wishing "many, many most happy returns to you & to us all on this day which for so many years we have passed together," adding: "I do not know how it is that I associate you so much with the change that is about to befall me—& that I have never felt so strongly as within the last few months how much of the happiness of past years I owe to you.—But at least I know that you will kindly wear now & then for my sake the little thing that now accompanies this note," and closing "with increasing wishes & prayers for your continued happiness."[31] Clearly, then, on the day of which Dickens writes in 1855, Mrs. Watson didn't wait for his return because she was at Tavistock House to see Catherine. Having visited with Mrs. Dickens and congratulated her on turning forty, Lavinia went her way.

As she did with Mrs. Watson, Catherine developed her own friendship with Angela Burdett Coutts, although Dickens intervened in their correspondence as well, laying claim to letters addressed to Catherine by Miss Coutts and, shortly before the separation, harshly berating his wife for writing to their friend on her own initiative. Miss Coutts's decision to drop Dickens after the separation and to visit and assist Catherine at Gloucester Crescent suggests that he overestimated his importance to the heiress while underestimating her regard for his wife. More than a dozen surviving letters exchanged between the two women from 1843 to 1871 attest to their

31. John Forster to Catherine Dickens, 19 May 1856 (copy in unknown hand), Charles Dickens Museum, London.

connection, as Catherine gives her friend news of "dear little Charley,"[32] thanks her for visits, gifts, and newspaper clippings, borrows her box at Drury Lane, confides to her about her marriage and separation, and expresses her affectionate regard. "So glad to have this opportunity of saying dear Miss Coutts what however I hope you already know, how much and affectionately I think of you," Catherine wrote in 1856.[33]

In his dwindling exchanges with Miss Coutts after June 1858, Dickens describes Catherine as both an illusion and an illusionist, a "blank" where a figure once was and a performer whose affectionate "act" with the children should not be believed (Pilgrim 10:356, 8:632). But because some of Catherine's correspondence with Miss Coutts survives, Dickens cannot work his usual "magic," though *his* letters, if read in isolation, make Catherine's significance to Miss Coutts fade. "I am inexpressibly vexed to find that Mrs. Dickens, in my absence and without my knowledge, wrote to you yesterday about her brother. I had not told her of the contents of your last kind note to me, concerning him. That is her only excuse; and I hope you will forgive her more freely and more readily than *I* do" (Pilgrim 8:512). So Dickens tells Miss Coutts in February 1858.

Yet Catherine needed no excuse or forgiveness for writing to Miss Coutts about Edward—not only because Dickens neglected to tell her that their friend had already responded to him on the subject, but also because the women had their own relationship in which Catherine understood she could discuss such matters. "I know that with your usual friendship and kindness you will pardon my thus troubling you on my brother's behalf," Catherine confided in the letter that angered Dickens.

> You may remember that Charles wrote to you now some weeks ago about my youngest Brother Edward who owing to one of the great failures in Sheffield lost an excellent position there, and had the world to begin again.
>
> Soon after Charles wrote to you about him, he was offered and accepted a situation in the City as Cashier in a large Wholesale Furniture Silk Warehouse, but for reasons with which I need not trouble you, he finds it impossible to continue in it. I ought however to add that it is from no fault of his that he leaves. I venture therefore dear Miss Coutts to ask you if you should hear of any situation likely to suit him, if you would do me the great kindness to

32. ALS Catherine Dickens to Angela Burdett Coutts, 1 February 1847, MA 1352, the Morgan Library & Museum, New York.

33. ALS Catherine Dickens to Angela Burdett Coutts, 9 January 1856, MA 1352, the Morgan Library & Museum, New York.

bear him in mind, as I need not tell you I am deeply interested in his procuring employment more particularly as my Father is not able to do much for him, and it is a serious and anxious thing for him, that my Brother should be unemployed.[34]

Catherine exercised her own agency in contacting Miss Coutts "in [Dickens's] absence and without [his] knowledge," writing not simply as his wife but as the friend of kind Miss Coutts and as a Hogarth: a daughter whose anxious father could do little for his son; a sister whose youngest brother "had the world to begin again." Within three months, Catherine herself would make a new beginning. Unwilling to forgive what required no forgiveness, Dickens identified Catherine as a Hogarth in May, transforming his wife into a single woman through an act of legal conjuring.

TURNING TABLES

Of all the "sleight-of-hand tricks" performed for London audiences in the 1850s,[35] table turning received the closest scrutiny. Scientists, ministers, and journalists investigated the claims of mediums to communicate with spirits who allegedly tilted, turned, and rapped messages on séance tables; many attempted to recreate these feats or expose the fraud. Observers were struck by the phenomena, if skeptical about what produced them. "Albeit I have never yet had any reason to believe in the supernatural, I cannot possibly deny that the table began, very soon after we had formed the prescribed chain, to play the wildest pranks," Mrs. W. Pitt Byrne recalled, describing a London séance conducted by an American, Mrs. Haydon, at the home of a friend.[36] For £25, the "lady-professor" would conduct private séances,[37] but families often chose to "spin tables" without professional aid—the Dickenses among them. In the spring of 1853 Catherine repeatedly participated in table-turning experiments at Tavistock House, first with her husband, their daughters, Georgina, and the governess, along with the Regniers; and then with Cornelius Felton. "We tried it at Dickens's," Felton recalled, "with a fixed

34. ALS Catherine Dickens to Angela Burdett Coutts, "Monday" [1 February 1858], MA 1352, the Morgan Library & Museum, New York.

35. Mrs. W. Pitt Byrne, *Gossip of the Century: Personal and Traditional Memories,* new ed., 4 vols. (London: Downey & Co., 1899), 1:169.

36. Ibid., 1:172.

37. Ibid., 1:170.

determination to give the experiment a perfectly fair chance" and "neither table, nor hat, nor anything else, moved a hair's breadth."[38]

Writers in *Punch* attributed "the circulation of the table" to "the circulation of the bottle," with alcohol the only "spirit" involved in the "farce."[39] But cultural historians attribute the Victorian fascination with table turning to its transgressive potential and its emotional appeal. The séance enabled female mediums to speak for and as departed male spirits while also helping participants overcome their sense of loss. As Alex Owen explains, "many nineteenth-century believers came to spiritualism" through the deaths of family members, with "spirit communication" and "'the sound of a voice that was stilled'" offering "'unspeakable consolations'" and meeting "emotional needs."[40]

Dickens was skeptical of spiritualism from the start, parodying it in *Household Words* articles and in his account of a Pembroke table that "gamboled" around his study (Pilgrim 7:92). But while the table-turning experiments in which Catherine and he engaged proved a failure, the Dickenses made contact with "departed spirits" in another sense, as figures from their past returned to them in middle age, marking as well as meeting emotional needs: not only Maria Beadnell (Mrs. William Winter), as Dickens critics often note, but also Scrope Ayrton, the brother of Fanny and Matilda, Mary and Catherine Hogarth's closest teenage friends. With these figures came two others from the past: Charles Dickens and Catherine Hogarth before their introduction. In 1855 Catherine was the forty-year-old matron of Tavistock House; having borne ten children, she made no claims to youth and was resigned to becoming "old Mrs. Dickens" in time.[41] But her husband was troubled by his sense of aging and what he now felt, when in "low spirits," to be the "one happiness" he had "missed in life," he told Forster (Pilgrim 7:523). In the first stages of a midlife crisis, he proved as receptive to long-stilled voices as the most celebrated medium could hope to be.

38. Cornelius Conway Felton, *Familiar Letters from Europe* (Boston: Ticknor and Fields, 1865), 32.

39. "Turning the Tables," *Punch* 24 (1853): 189. See also Dickens's "Well-Authenticated Rappings," *Household Words,* 20 February 1858, one of several articles he wrote or published on the subject.

40. Alex Owen, *The Darkened Room: Women, Power, and Spiritualism in Late Victorian England* (Philadelphia: University of Pennsylvania Press, 1990), 82, 105–6. Owen quotes from Morell Theobald, *Spirit Workers in the Home Circle* (London: T. Fisher Unwin, 1887), 80–81.

41. ALS Catherine Dickens to Georgina Weiss, 20 October 1867, Cambridge University Library, Add. 9180 (no. 66).

Catherine was home in December 1854 when George Beadnell, Maria's father, called at Tavistock House, and she received him in Dickens's absence. The two men had not corresponded since 1852, when Dickens, declining an invitation, imagined himself "exactly 19" in sending his love to Maria through her father (Pilgrim 6:660). Two months after Catherine saw Beadnell, Maria herself wrote to Dickens, for whom "three or four and twenty years vanished like a dream" (Pilgrim 7:532). He and Maria went on to exchange a series of nostalgic and confessional letters which he assured her were "between [them]selves alone" (Pilgrim 7:544) and which Catherine never read, although they would return to haunt an elderly Georgina when Maria's daughter put them up for sale in 1905. "No one but myself has the slightest knowledge of my correspondence," Dickens wrote Maria, and he "could be nowhere addressed with stricter privacy or in more absolute confidence than at [his] own home" (Pilgrim 7:543).

For our purposes, what is most striking about these letters is what they reveal not about Mrs. Winter or Dickens's feelings for her (she was "once . . . the Angel of [his] soul" [Pilgrim 7:534]) but rather about his state of mind three years before his separation from Catherine. Though addressed to Maria, Dickens's letters are primarily about himself—his "earnest," "boyish heart"—who he once was and what he has become (Pilgrim 7:534, 538), and they capture his difficult discovery that he has grown middle-aged. Dickens's letters also reveal his willingness to carry on a "tender" correspondence behind Catherine's back and to feel justified in doing so. He imagines "dangerous" and secret meetings with Maria, accepts and "reciprocate[s]" her emotional proposals "with [his] whole soul," and suggests that she call at Tavistock House when "it is almost a positive certainty" that Catherine will be out, all the while claiming to be acting "in perfect innocence and good faith" (Pilgrim 7:544–45).[42]

Even before Dickens realized that Maria was not the attractive woman he remembered, he did not "for a moment sincerely believ[e] that it would have been better if [they] had never got separated," he confided to Forster (Pilgrim 7:557). In

42. These letters are widely discussed by critics and biographers. In *Dickens and Women* (London: J. M. Dent, 1983), Michael Slater notes that their tenderness "is primarily directed towards [Dickens's] younger self" (65), while Rosemarie Bodenheimer, in *Knowing Dickens* (Ithaca: Cornell University Press, 2007), finds them "shocking to behold," with Dickens "fully immersed in a David Copperfield vision of himself, minus the comic irony" (81). Peter Ackroyd, in *Dickens* (New York: HarperCollins, 1990), claims that "none of these letters would have been written . . . if it were not for the deep unhappiness of Dickens's present life" (728), implying that Catherine was to blame for Dickens's midlife crisis, although Katey argued that her father would have treated *any* wife of twenty years the way he treated Catherine. See Gladys Storey, *Dickens and Daughter* (London: Frederick Muller, 1939), 134.

1855 Dickens might dwell on other routes his life could have taken, but he did not wish he had married Maria instead of Catherine, who figured in his letters to Mrs. Winter and gave their reunion its proper social footing. "Mrs. Dickens will come to you, to arrange a day for our seeing you and Mr. Winter . . . quietly to dinner," he told Maria in his opening letter (Pilgrim 7:533). And so Catherine did, calling at Artillery Place on 27 February and arranging for a dinner on 7 March. By the end of that month Maria was as much Catherine's acquaintance as Dickens's—even *more* so, in fact, since the novelist, quickly disillusioned with the forty-four-year-old "Angel" of his youth, was now avoiding her and leaving his wife and Georgina to politely maintain the connection he had so eagerly reestablished. On 30 March, Catherine and Georgina shared with Maria a box at the Adelphi, but Dickens did not appear. When Maria complained to him of his absence, he told her that his work and its demands "mastered" his "whole life," though he did not expect her to understand "an author's mind" (Pilgrim 7:583–84).

In 1855 an aging Dickens saw something of himself in Charley, then eighteen, despite his belief that his eldest son resembled Catherine and lacked the determination that had defined him at that age. Accounting for the strength of his feelings when Maria emerged from the past, Dickens reminded Forster, "This began when I was Charley's age . . . at a time of life when four years are equal to four times four" (Pilgrim 7:557). Like her husband, Catherine could see her younger self in the child named for her. Mamie's idolization of her father and Katey's temperamental resemblance to him have obscured their ties to their mother in their teens, as have Dickens's claims, in 1858, that they "harden into stone" near Catherine (Pilgrim 8:559). But to those in the Dickens circle, "darling" Katey's winning traits were "something else [they] ha[d] to thank [Catherine] for,"[43] and their letters from the 1850s describe "dear Mrs. Dickens" accompanying her "young ladies" to dances,[44] hosting their birthday parties, and teaching domestic skills to the girls and their friends. In Katey's own letters and reminiscences of her "dear mother," we see the strength of their mutual feeling. Known as "Lucifer Box," Katey was as different from her mother as Charley was from his father. Nonetheless, Catherine and Katey saw themselves mirrored in each other—all the more clearly as the Dickenses' marriage deteriorated and Katey felt and responded to what both mother and daughter perceived as Catherine's wrongs. When, shortly before the separation, Dickens insisted that his wife

43. ALS Annie Thackeray to Catherine Dickens, [n.d.], MA 104, the Morgan Library & Museum, New York.

44. ALS Albert Smith to Catherine Dickens, "Monday" [1853], II.a.49, Congregational Library, London.

call on Ellen Ternan, Katey insisted that her mother "not go!"[45] Although Catherine tearfully submitted to Dickens where Katey would have angrily refused, each felt the insult and indignity, and Catherine's departure from the Dickens household precipitated Katey's two years later.

We don't know if Catherine, at forty, imagined the alternate routes her life might have taken had she married a different person or if she thought herself quite as lucky in marrying Charles Dickens as he considered her to be. Whatever use she made of her memories as Miss Hogarth, Catherine was brought back to her teenage years at the close of 1854, shortly before Dickens replied to Maria and "became" nineteen again—when she received a letter from her husband, in Bradford to read *A Christmas Carol* for a benefit and likely to see Scrope Ayrton there. Catherine had last seen the family in 1847, when Fanny and William Ayrton joined the amateurs on their trip to Manchester for a performance of *Every Man in His Humour*. The reappearance of Scrope, a barrister and commissioner of bankruptcy, and a bachelor into his forties, likely revived Catherine's memories of his company and escort in 1832–1834, when she, Mary, Fanny, and Matilda were the best of friends and Scrope the eligible older brother.

Whether or not she imagined, in the mid-1850s, alternative plotlines for her life, Catherine did so for some of the women in her circle; the situations of Kate Horne and Anna Dickens, their marriages dissolving, required as much, as did the rumored engagements of young Helen Tagart.[46] As the daughters of her friends married, as Helen Hogarth reached a marriageable age and Georgina received and declined at least one proposal, Catherine focused on the choices women faced in shaping their lives as well as the possibilities that went unrealized because of the decisions they reached.

Like other wives of her acquaintance, Catherine was not confined to a single plotline or character, despite the restrictions of coverture. Dickens might invoke what he considered Catherine's "real" self, but she negotiated among and helped to construct a range of identities that reflected her network of relationships and called into question the primacy often ascribed to the "naturally"

45. Storey, *Dickens and Daughter*, 96. In *Katey: The Life and Loves of Dickens's Artist Daughter* (London: Doubleday, 2006), Lucinda Hawksley discusses Katey's response to Dickens's treatment of Catherine in 1857–58, noting her sympathy with her mother: "Katey's determination not to abandon her mother drove, for the very first time, a wedge between her and her father" (128).

46. Mrs. Tagart feared that Catherine was on the "wrong scent" about Helen, who was engaged to Mr. Harvey but paired by some with Mr. Paget. ALS Catherine Dickens to Mrs. Tagart, 4 March 1853, Charles Dickens Museum, London.

selfless wife and mother. Yet while Catherine's identity as Mrs. Charles Dickens did not constitute her authentic or essential self, her experiences as Dickens's wife were recorded on her body in a way that Dickens's as a husband were not recorded on his—because of their sexual difference and Catherine's sixteen years of childbearing. So their paired photographic portraits in middle age suggest, the counterpoint between the figures more striking than in Samuel Laurence's paired portraits of 1837–38 (fig. 15).

To prepare Dickens for their reunion in 1855, Maria Winter described herself to him as "toothless, fat, old, and ugly" (Pilgrim 7:544). At forty, Catherine was neither toothless nor ugly, and well into her fifties, her friends did not find her old; "although a grandmother," Catherine was "still not an 'old' person," William Hardman noted in the 1860s.[47] Having borne ten children, however, Catherine was variously described as "stout," "large," and "fat"[48]—considerably heavier in the mid-1850s than she had been before her marriage in 1836.

Catherine's body in middle age has been a focus of attention in Dickens scholarship, usually in brief but cutting remarks on the separation and the role Catherine's alleged failings played in it—"the fat-emblazoned scandal" of 1858, as two critics term it.[49] What is represented as her corpulent, aging body often serves as an embodied explanation of what went wrong in the marriage. It provides a convenient means to define her middle-aged lassitude against Dickens's energetic youthfulness, her appetite against his abstemiousness, her self-indulgence against his drive and self-control, a counterpoint implicit in Dickens's infrequent but cutting references to what he perceives as Catherine's corporeality. Toward the end of 1854, for example, Dickens promises to place at Leigh Hunt's disposal their brougham, the "little pill-box on wheels which staggers about town with Mrs. Dickens" (Pilgrim

47. William Hardman, *The Letters and Memoirs of Sir William Hardman, 2nd ser., 1863–1865,* ed. S. M. Ellis (New York: George H. Doran, 1925), 8.

48. To Henry Morley in 1851, Catherine appeared "stout," her face "very round" and "pleasant"; see Henry Shaen Solly, *The Life of Henry Morley, LL.D.* (London: Edward Arnold, 1898), 201. To Charles Kingsley in 1855, Catherine was a "fat vulgar vacancy"; quoted in Susan Chitty, *The Beast and the Monk: A Life of Charles Kingsley* (New York: Mason/Charter, 1975), 174. To Harriet Beecher Stowe in 1853, Catherine appeared "tall, large, and well developed, with a fine, healthy colour" (*Sunny Memories,* 127). Chitty's biography reveals that Kingsley was often harshly critical of women's bodies—no sooner describing "the most clever, agreeable, well-read woman" than adding, "She weighs 16 stone and has a moustache like a man" (quoted in *The Beast and the Monk,* 175).

49. Michael Moon and Eve Kosofsky Sedgwick, "Divinity: A Dossier, a Performance Piece, a Little-Understood Emotion," in *Bodies Out of Bounds: Fatness and Transgression,* ed. Jana Evans Braziel and Kathleen LeBesco (Berkeley: University of California Press, 2001), 326 n. 19.

7:465). Writing to Wilkie Collins from Paris in April 1856, he describes a dinner to which he took Catherine, their daughters, and Georgina at the Trois Frères: "Mrs. Dickens nearly killed herself, but the others hardly did that justice to the dinner that I had expected" (Pilgrim 8:95).

As these comments suggest, Catherine's corporeality had come to seem burdensome and unbecoming to Dickens, and her appetite self-destructive. He associates her size with her excessive consumption—of labor and goods as well as food. She is the lady of leisure who heedlessly goes visiting "about town" in a carriage that "staggers" under her weight. As critics note, Dickens links economic surplus and luxury with body fat in his metaphors for political economy, the dangers of "economic accumulation and waste" with the "fat female body" specifically. In so doing, he attributes the exploitation of labor to what he represents as the parasitic consumerism of unproductive middle-class women rather than the abuses or greed of capitalists.[50]

50. Ibid., 307–8. See also Joyce L. Huff, "A 'Horror of Corpulence': Interrogating Bantingism and Mid-Nineteenth-Century Fat-Phobia," in Braziel and LeBesco, *Bodies Out of Bounds*, 51–52; and Gail Turley Houston, *Consuming Fictions: Gender, Class, and Hunger in Dickens's Novels* (Carbondale: Southern Illinois University Press, 1994).

Regardless of Catherine's economic status or her role as a middle-class consumer, her corpulence most probably resulted from her "great-grand multiparity," as the births of ten or more children are closely linked to obesity in medical studies. Her weight gain since marriage was likely due to her eating habits as well. A cookbook author and the hostess of frequent and elaborate dinner parties, Catherine was interested in food, its preparation, and presentation, and she enjoyed eating; her own recipes suggest as much. Explanations of "excess" body fat tend to be defensive in our culture, particularly for women. But rather than criticize or justify Catherine for being "stout," "large," or "fat," we ought to note what the very plurality of these adjectives reveals about her body as we know it—as a series of representations conveyed in terms that have varying intonations and serve various ends. Dickens may have perceived Catherine's corpulence as a burden, a sign of excessive leisure or consumption, but a number of other observers did not, Catherine herself among them.

In her own accounts of daily life in the mid-1850s, Catherine is busy and energetic, not leisurely or lethargic. If she uses the brougham, she often does so in the service of her husband and their guests, meeting their needs instead of indulging her own. "I am quite ashamed to write to you, having left town after all, without going to see you," Catherine wrote Mrs. Tagart from Boulogne in July 1854:

> But we left at the last, rather sooner than we intended, as Mr. Dickens was anxious to get away from London to work at "Hard Times," which he is anxious to finish that he may enjoy a complete country holiday afterwards. And we had Mr. Macready staying with us for some days up to the very day we left town and have had a great deal to do, and many places and people to see, so that I really could never manage to take the carriage any distance on my own account, besides having a good deal to do before coming away from town for four months.[51]

Neglecting her friendship, Catherine privileges the needs and desires of her husband, who is eager to leave London and finish *Hard Times*. Her work in relocating their household serves and runs parallel to his. Although Dickens represents Catherine as an unproductive and "staggering" burden that cost him £600 annually in the final version of his will, written in the 1860s, the Coutts bank ledger from the mid-1850s documents her financial restraint as well as her expenditures. When Dickens gave Catherine permission to draw money from their Boulogne bank while

51. ALS Catherine Dickens to Mrs. Tagart, 6 July 1854, Charles Dickens Museum, London.

he was in London in 1854, asking that she not "draw more than [she] really want[s]" (Pilgrim 7:372), she drew none at all.

Recounting their 1856 dinner at the Trois Frères, Dickens contrasts Catherine's self-indulgence with the restraint of Georgina, Mamie, and Katey but tells us nothing about *his* approach to the meal or whether he "did [it] justice." As Dickens's letter to Collins goes on, however, his account of Catherine's appetite gives way to a description of his own, though he fails to acknowledge it as such. Out alone in Paris, he seeks satisfactions that his ladies cannot, in ballrooms that double as high-class brothels and among prostitutes on the streets. The evening after their dinner out, Dickens returned to a place he once visited with Collins:

> On Saturday night, I paid three francs at the door of that place . . . and went in, at 11 o-Clock, to a Ball. . . . Some pretty faces, but all of two classes—wicked and coldly calculating, or haggard and wretched in their worn beauty. Among the latter, was a woman of thirty or so, in an Indian shawl, who never stirred from a seat in a corner all the time I was there. Handsome, regardless, brooding, and yet with some nobler qualities in her forehead. I mean to walk about tonight, and look for her. I didn't speak to here there, but I have a fancy that I should like to know more about her. Never shall, I suppose. (Pilgrim 8:96)

Dickens never elaborates on his interest in the "woman of thirty" or explains its nature, leaving Collins to surmise what type of knowledge he seeks from or about her. It is his "fancy" to seek her on the street, not his "desire." Yet in a letter that represents Catherine "nearly kill[ing] herself" at dinner, the tables suddenly turn, with Dickens himself the consumer.[52] Whatever satisfactions he may seek from the "worn beauty," she is the object of his hunger, an appetite no less pressing than Catherine's because he represents it more poignantly, as incorporeal and unlikely to be fulfilled.

VANISHING ACTS

Dickens's search for the Parisian woman who caught his eye as well as his critical distance from Catherine's body suggest that their sexual intimacy had waned by 1856. From Rome three years earlier Dickens had written to Catherine of his desire "to embrace [her]," signaling their affectionate and still physical bond (Pilgrim 7:198). By October 1857 he had made a point of dividing his bedroom from his

---

52. As Michael Hollington notes, Dickens is not simply the "flâneur" here, the detached city stroller who "feeds" his eye; he is as much the "hunter" as the observer, and "singles out a face he intends to stalk a second night." Michael Hollington, "Dickens, *Household Words,* and the Paris Boulevards (Part Two)," *Dickens Quarterly* 14, no. 4 (December 1997): 201.

wife's, announcing his sexual abstinence as far as she was concerned. Catherine's diminished intimacy with her husband had a greater impact on their marriage than it otherwise might had Georgina not been a member of their household. Catherine's status as Dickens's wife and sexual partner had privileged her in the family, even if her privileges were double-edged. But now that the grounds of her marriage were shifting, the companionship she could offer her husband in middle age was forestalled by his long-standing friendship with Georgina, whom he perceived as more deserving of admiration than Catherine because of her voluntary "sacrifices" yet also more at liberty to join him in his strenuous pursuits. In May 1858 the Hogarths and the Thomsons found Georgina "blinded by the sophistry of her brother-in-law," as her aunt Helen put it, and blinding to Dickens as well. "Eclipsing" Catherine, Georgina rendered her and her "sacred claims" invisible in Dickens's eyes, Helen Thomson alleged.[53] Rather than blaming Georgina for eclipsing her sister, however, or granting Dickens and those who echo him the power to make his wife disappear, we need to make visible Catherine's significance to her family and household, even as her husband's feelings for her changed, by looking at the events of 1856–1858 from her perspective.

Reading backwards from the separation and seeing through Dickens's eyes, some argue that Catherine's bond with her husband had dissolved by the early 1850s or even that the union never *really* existed, since Dickens claimed, in 1858, that his marriage was doomed from the start. While accounts of the atmosphere surrounding the Dickenses in 1857 vary, the tensions between Catherine and her husband were evident from August onward, in the weeks and months following Dickens's introduction to Ellen Ternan.

But in the first half of that year, the Dickenses appeared a harmonious family to numerous friends and acquaintances. As Mary Howitt told "Dear Mrs. Dickens" on 16 January 1857, soon after seeing Catherine's husband, sisters, and children perform in *The Frozen Deep* at Tavistock House, they were a "lovely family group," one "blessed" with "human felicity," Georgina seeming more "like another daughter" to Catherine than a sister.[54] We need to weigh this view of Catherine and her family against that recounted decades later by Lucy Tagart, who remembered that "Mrs. Dickens seemed very unhappy" at a Tavistock House performance of the melodrama but may have been reconstructing matters in light of the subsequent

53. Helen Thomson to Mrs. Stark, [30] August 1858, in K. J. Fielding, "Charles Dickens and His Wife," *Études Anglaises* 8, no. 3 (1955), reprinted in Pilgrim 8:747–48.

54. ALS Mary Howitt to Catherine Dickens, 16 January 1857, MA 104, the Morgan Library & Museum, New York.

separation.[55] In early September 1857 Forster was hoping that Dickens would learn to live with his dissatisfaction, arguing for tolerance and forbearance in marriage and assuring his friend that any differences with Catherine were "bearable." Both men assumed that a separation was "impossible," though Dickens wished otherwise (Pilgrim 8:434). According to Katey, it was in September that her father "set out to accomplish" the separation, a "sad business" that "took eight months to complete."[56]

In the spring and summer of 1857, however, Catherine understood her marriage to be intact. Beginning in June, the family stayed at Gad's Hill Place for the first time, and Dickens anticipated their move by hosting Catherine's birthday party there. When Catherine, still her husband's "deputy," wrote to their acquaintance William Dempster at the end of May, her theme was family unity, conveyed in part through the pronouns that characterize her letter ("we," "us," "our"), "husband, sister, and…daughters unit[ing] with [her]" in its sentiments and expressions. "We were all most happy to hear"; "we shall be always truly interested"; "it has given us…sincere pleasure"; "we hope that it will not be a very distant day"; "we have delivered your kind message"; "we are now leaving London for our little country house in Kent"; "we shall remain until the Autumn." Catherine singles out Dickens's accomplishments and desires in her letter but in a way that suggests her connection to them. "My husband is looking forward with much pleasure to the rest and quiet of the country, after his hard work. He has just completed Little Dorrit, and I hope…that you will like the ending."[57]

In the summer of 1857, the Dickenses hosted Hans Christian Andersen for five long weeks. Andersen's "amiable misperception[s]"[58] of the family have been outlined by critics sensitive to the ironies of his representations—his glimpses of the "happy party round the pianoforte" at Gad's Hill Place, "when Dickens and his wife and the guests sat gossiping."[59] Catherine's own description of family dynamics in late May might be considered equally mistaken—merely wishful thinking on her part. Yet her connection to Dickens and their children as well as her role in the

55. ALS Lucy Tagart to Mr. Nicholson, 29 September 1909, Nicholson Papers, 920 NIC 18/11/3, Liverpool Record Office.

56. Storey, *Dickens and Daughter*, 94–95.

57. ALS Catherine Dickens to William Dempster, 30 May 1857, D. Jacques Benoliel Collection of the Letters of Charles Dickens, 87-1904, Rare Book Department, Free Library of Philadelphia.

58. Slater, *Dickens and Women*, 101.

59. "A Visit to Charles Dickens by Hans Christian Andersen," *Bentley's Miscellany* 48 (1860): 184.

household in the final two years of her residence with them have been badly under-valued by most who write on the subject, guided primarily by Dickens's "restlessness" and dissatisfaction and their knowledge of events to come. It is not simply that Catherine was ignorant of the truth—unaware of her husband's confidences with Maria Winter in 1855 or with Collins and Forster in 1856 and 1857—but that the truth itself was a compound mixture. When Dickens defined the meaning of "our" for William de Cerjat in January 1857—"'our' means, Mrs. Dickens's, Georgina's, and mine" (Pilgrim 8:266)—he was not simply writing from habit or glossing over a reality of marital strife. He was capturing one of the truths of his family life, to which Catherine was then integral.

According to Forster's dating, Dickens discovered "that the skeleton in [his] domestic closet [was] becoming a pretty big one" in mid-April 1856, following his twentieth wedding anniversary (Pilgrim 8:89). That year Catherine may have noticed that her husband's letters to Georgina were sometimes more detailed and engaged than his letters to her, and during one of his absences more frequent—and she was undoubtedly pained when, in the autumn of 1857, he stopped writing to her altogether, using Georgina as his domestic correspondent from that time on. Yet Catherine served as a crucial medium of communication between her husband and their friends in 1856 and 1857, whether he wrote to her or to Georgina: she was the one to whom David Roberts conveyed a "hint" about Stanfield on which Dickens acted (Pilgrim 8:185–86); to whom Ary Scheffer confided his doubts about his portrait of the novelist; through whom Dickens learned that Lord Lyndhurst wished to see *The Frozen Deep* and that Edward Tagart was moved by it; and to whom Miss Coutts made suggestions about improving the play after its final January rehearsal. In moments of crisis, Catherine's primacy with the children was clear, despite Dickens's later assertions that Georgina had long been their "mother." When a diphtheria epidemic broke out in Boulogne in August 1856, Catherine immediately returned home with the younger children, leaving Georgina and Dickens behind. "All the boys were sent to London under their mother's care—those at school here as well as the youngest," Collins reported to his mother on 1 September.[60]

Until the fall of 1857, Catherine remained central to the household's management and economy. Toward the end of 1856, she and Dickens discussed the failings of their new cook, whom they would need to replace, and in January 1857 she went with her husband to Newgate Market to see where he thought she should buy fowl. In 1856, much of which the Dickenses spent in France, Catherine was responsible

60. Wilkie Collins to Harriet Collins, 1 September 1856, in *The Letters of Wilkie Collins,* ed. William Baker and William M. Clarke, 2 vols. (New York: St. Martin's Press, 1999), 1:159.

for nearly £1,000 in expenditures, more than twice the £402.17.6 she spent in 1855, the rise a consequence of their residence abroad. In the same period Georgina received £50.18, up from £24.2.6 in 1855. Catherine managed £139 in 1857 before dropping from the bank account records in November; Georgina received £30 that year, her customary annual allowance.[61] While Catherine waited in Boulogne with the children in October 1855, Georgina helped to find and prepare their Paris lodgings. Once there, Catherine organized the household. "Mr. Dickens me prie de vous dire que" and "voulez-vous nous faire le grand plaisir,"[62] she begins her letters to prospective guests, arranging their dinner parties. At least one of Catherine's shopping lists from their time in Paris survives, since Dickens used the back of the paper to jot down their Champs Elysée address for an acquaintance.[63]

In March 1857 Dickens still spoke of Catherine, like Georgina, as possessing "full powers from the source of all domestic authority": himself (Pilgrim 8:292). His letters sometimes anticipate correspondence to follow from Catherine, who "will not fail, she says, to write" about various matters (Pilgrim 8:210). Among the surviving invitations to the Tavistock House performances of *The Frozen Deep* that Catherine wrote out in a careful hand are those to Sarah Austin, Charles Coote, Mrs. Richard Lane, Daniel Maclise, Annie Thackeray, Mrs. Francis Topham, and Mrs. E. M. Ward. With only minor variations, Catherine offered her correspondents the assurance "that it will give Mr. Dickens great pleasure to have you among the audience at a new play, with which he and all concerned have been taking great pains."[64]

From the amateur theatricals that became so central to Dickens family life in the mid-1850s, Catherine might seem to be excluded, her 1851 performance in *Used Up* her last. When *The Lighthouse* was staged at Tavistock House in June 1855, Georgina played Lady Grace opposite Dickens's Aaron Gurnock, and Mamie, Charley, and Edward Hogarth all had roles, as did Katey and Georgina in *Mr. Nightingale's Diary*, the farce that followed. When *The Frozen Deep* was performed at Tavistock House in January 1857 and at the Gallery of Illustration in July and August, Georgina (Lucy Crayford), Helen Hogarth (Mrs. Steventon), Katey (Rose Ebsworth), and Mamie (Clara Burnham) appeared alongside Dickens (Richard Wardour), Charley

61. Charles Dickens, Esq., Account Ledger, Coutts & Co., London.

62. Catherine Dickens to Gabriel Legouvé, 29 March [1856], in E. W. F. Tomlin, "Newly Discovered Dickens Letters," *TLS*, 22 February 1974, 184; Catherine Dickens to Madame Scribe, [1856], quoted in Neil C. Arvin, "Some Unpublished Letters to Eugène Scribe," *Sewanee Review* 33 (July 1925): 260.

63. Sotheby & Co., Catalogue of Sale (1964), 11.

64. ALS Catherine Dickens to Mrs. E. M. Ward, 1 December 1856, British Library, Add. 54316, f. 228.

(Lieutenant Steventon), and Edward Hogarth (Bateson). As rehearsals got under way in November 1856, Catherine left on a visit to the Macreadys at Sherborne, her absence from Tavistock House and from the cast mirrored in the play itself, which foregrounds the danger posed to the heroine by her old Scottish nurse and celebrates the bond between fathers and daughters. "I must have my father near me, or I can never enjoy myself as I ought," Rose proclaims in the opening scene.[65]

Offstage, however, Catherine was an important figure in the Tavistock House performances. "Everybody who comes, is to be shown up into the Drawing Room to Mrs. Dickens," her husband instructed their servant John Thompson (Pilgrim 8:254 n. 3). In the role of hostess, Catherine treated audience members as private guests and gave the theatricals their domestic character. Appearing as "herself" on performance nights, she had the "natural" air for which Katey and Mamie were praised onstage.[66]

In the acting of the Dickenses, what was perhaps least natural was their devaluing of the maternal in *The Frozen Deep*, with Katey, as Rose, claiming to live solely for her father and Mamie, as Clara, deserted by her mother and endangered by the superstitious visions of her nurse. After her parents separated, Katey wrote—and destroyed—a biographical account "clearing her mother of false accusations"; and she told her friend Gladys Storey that in 1858 she had taken "her mother's part in-so-far as it was possible for her to do so," with Dickens "sternly impress[ing] upon [the children] that 'their father's name was their best possession.'"[67] Although Henry and Mamie defined themselves as their father's children, some of the siblings favored their bond with Catherine, and most openly acknowledged what Collins termed "their mother's care," knowing that, as Catherine put it, she was "very happy to have all . . . [her] dear children at home."[68]

In the summer of 1857, the separation Catherine dreaded was not one from her husband but from her "beloved Walter,"[69] then sixteen. He sailed for India on

65. Charles Dickens and Wilkie Collins, *The Frozen Deep*, in *Under the Management of Mr. Charles Dickens: His Production of "The Frozen Deep,"* ed. Robert Louis Brannan (Ithaca: Cornell University Press, 1966), 103. For details on the play, its authorship, and its treatment of gender relations and family dynamics, see Lillian Nayder, *Unequal Partners: Charles Dickens, Wilkie Collins, and Victorian Authorship* (Ithaca: Cornell University Press, 2002), chap. 3.

66. *Morning Herald,* 8 January 1857, quoted in Pilgrim 8:247 n. 5.

67. Storey, *Dickens and Daughter,* 91, 95.

68. ALS Catherine Dickens to Mrs. Brown, 16 July 1856, MA 1352, the Morgan Library & Museum, New York.

69. ALS Catherine Dickens to Angela Burdett Coutts, 8 March 1864, MA 1352, the Morgan Library & Museum, New York.

20 July, having passed his exam as an East India Company cadet in April, and was likely to see military action almost immediately, since the Sepoy Rebellion had begun in May (fig. 16). On the morning of 19 July, Catherine and Walter said their good-byes; they would never see each other again. For Catherine there would be several such partings. Charley had finished his schooling in Leipzig in 1854 and, after a brief stint at a London broker's, had obtained a position at a banking house, Baring Brothers, in September 1855, at an annual starting salary of £50. But he was the only one of the seven boys whom Dickens intended for a career in England. Although the departures of the younger boys were temporary in the mid-1850s, they had been gradually disappearing from Tavistock House for long intervals since 1853, with four of Catherine's sons leaving for Boulogne before the separation, sent to the Reverend Matthew Gibson's school when they were eight or nine years old: Frank and Alfred in 1853, Sydney in 1855, and Henry in 1858 (fig. 17). "The boys went back to school yesterday, with their elder brother for escort," Collins wrote from Folkestone in September 1855. "We saw them off and little Sydney (going to school for the first time) accepted his fate like a hero. His pluck was undiminished when I last saw him, very small and flushed[,] . . . a threatening sea before him, and the horrid perspective of the schoolmaster awaiting him on the opposite shore."[70] Like Sydney, Walter put on a brave face when he left in 1857, "cut up for a minute" but "recover[ing] directly, and conduct[ing] himself like a Man," Dickens thought (Pilgrim 8:381). Catherine was spared the sight of Walter's sailing, since he was escorted to Southampton by his father and eldest brother, who saw him aboard the *Indus*.

Walter's departure and his "manly" behavior did nothing to calm the midlife stirrings of his father, who discovered incarnations of his younger self in his eldest sons. "Seeing Charley and [Walter] going aboard the Ship before me just now, I suddenly came into possession of a photograph of my own back at 16 and 20, and also into a suspicion that I had doubled the last age," Dickens wrote Edmund Yates on 19 July. "Before you know that Time has flapped his wings over your head," Dickens warned the father of three, "you will find those babies grow to be young men" (Pilgrim 8:379). By the end of the summer Dickens had seized on a way to reverse this process and halve his age, fixing his romantic attentions on Ellen Ternan, the aspiring young actress born in the same year as his daughter Katey.[71]

70. Wilkie Collins to Edward Pigott, 2 September 1855, in *The Public Face of Wilkie Collins: The Collected Letters,* ed. William Baker, Andrew Gasson, Graham Law, and Paul Lewis, 4 vols. (London: Pickering and Chatto, 2005), 1:129–30.

71. For an excellent account of Ellen Ternan, her relationship with Dickens, and her life after the novelist's death, see Claire Tomalin, *The Invisible Woman: The Story of Nelly Ternan and Charles Dickens* (New York: Knopf, 1991).

FIGURE 16. *Walter Dickens in Uniform (1857), photograph,*
Charles Dickens Museum, London.

Dickens met Ellen, her widowed mother, and her sisters in August 1857 as a
result of efforts he and his colleagues were making to benefit the family of Douglas
Jerrold, who had died in June. Dickens organized events in London for the Jerrold
Fund, giving three readings of *A Christmas Carol* at St. Martin's Hall as well as four
performances of *The Frozen Deep* with the amateurs at the Gallery of Illustration.

FIGURE 17. *Henry and Frank Dickens in the later 1850s, photograph,*
Charles Dickens Museum, London.

He also agreed to three final performances of the melodrama at Manchester's Free Trade Hall during the third week of August, substituting professional actresses for his female relations, with Maria Ternan performing as Clara, Ellen as Lucy Crayford, and their mother as Nurse Esther. Shortly before Dickens began London rehearsals with the Ternans, Catherine had been examined by a doctor at Gad's Hill; she may have been suffering from sciatica, which plagued her in the summer of 1858. But she was well enough to travel to Manchester on the twentieth with Dickens, their daughters, Georgina, and the amateurs, the family group returning to London on the twenty-fifth. Within ten days of their return, Dickens had left with Collins for a two-week tour of Cumberland, Lancaster, and Doncaster—to work on a collaborative story for *Household Words* but also to see the Ternans, who were performing in Doncaster. Dickens may have been attracted to Maria initially, but by mid-September he had fixed his attentions on Ellen, referring to her in letters to

Wills as "the little—riddle" and to himself as "the riddler" (Pilgrim 8:451), taking her and her relations on carriage rides in the countryside and, by mid-October, arranging with J. B. Buckstone for her to perform at the Haymarket Theatre in London and paying him £50.

To Catherine over the next few months, her husband's attraction to the young actress was painfully clear. Besides the new bedroom arrangements at Tavistock House, there were Dickens's extended absences from home, his refusal to write to her when he was away, his efforts on behalf of Ellen and the Ternans, and the arrival of some jewelry for the young woman, a gift from Dickens mistakenly delivered to his home. Catherine was unconvinced by her husband's insistence that he had often given such gifts to fellow performers, and she objected to his behavior as she had to his intimacy with Madame de la Rue in the mid-1840s. But Catherine's position with her husband had changed. Now an object of his antipathy, she had lost the leverage she possessed in 1845. There were tearful arguments to which Katey, and perhaps others, were privy and which ended with Catherine's doing as her husband willed—calling on the Ternans, as if to sanction and make proper his relations with them.

At odds with Dickens, who sought a separation while insisting he had done no wrong—who was making Catherine's home unendurable, Helen Thomson reported, and acting "like a madman," Katey recalled[72]—Catherine was also pressured to leave her husband by her mother and her sister Helen, who deeply resented Dickens's behavior and keenly felt what they perceived as Catherine's injury. Early in May 1858, Dickens took up temporary quarters at the *Household Words* office while the Hogarths helped Catherine prepare to leave Tavistock House—first for a two-week stay in Brighton with her mother and then for a permanent residence elsewhere in London, the location yet to be determined. Wherever she made her home, Charley would join her; having come of age, Catherine's eldest could choose to do what he felt was right by his mother.

With the exception of Walter, all the children had been home for vacation in December 1857, but only Plorn, Mamie, and Katey were at Tavistock House in May when Catherine departed.[73] Within the next decade the family would disperse: Katey would marry Charles Collins, Sydney would join the navy, Frank would sail

72. Helen Thomson to Mrs. Stark, [30] August 1858, reprinted in Pilgrim 8:746; Storey, *Dickens and Daughter*, 94.

73. Katey gave 29 April as the date of her mother's departure, though Dickens told Miss Coutts on 9 May that he had "come for a time to the office, to leave [Catherine's] Mother free to do what she can at home, toward the getting her away to some happier mode of existence" (Pilgrim 8:560), and Catherine was still using Tavistock House as her address on 19 May.

for India and Alfred and Plorn for Australia. With Dickens "only too anxious to send his sons away to the ends of the earth," as one of those he consulted about them saw it,[74] most of the boys disappeared to colonial outposts. Whatever their feelings about the separation, they were aligned with their mother as exiled subjects of their father's will.

74. John Lehmann, *Ancestors and Friends* (London: Eyre Spottiswoode, 1962), 165–66. The author is the grandson of Frederick Lehmann, whom Dickens consulted about Alfred.

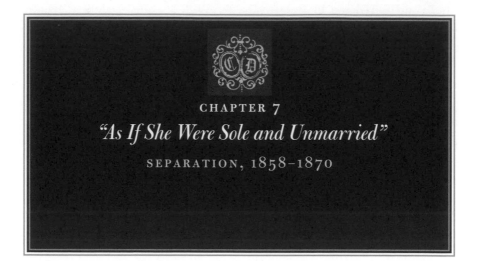

CHAPTER 7

"As If She Were Sole and Unmarried"

SEPARATION, 1858–1870

*As to the platonic attachment he has the bad taste and boldness to profess
to a young actress, and which he wrote to his elder children their mother
had not character to appreciate, and which he has intruded upon the notice
of the public in his foolish and egotistical statement, I can only compare
it to "the wicked fleeing where no man pursueth." What has the public to
do with what ought to be his private affairs? Conscience makes cowards of
men. But I must check my pen. His poor, dear wife is silent and forbearing,
and I must try to imitate her.*
—Helen Thomson to Mrs. Stark, [30] August 1858

"NOTWITHSTANDING HER COVERTURE"

On 4 June 1858 Catherine signed the deed of separation that her solicitor, George
Smith, brought to her in Brighton. A densely written three-page legal document,
the deed had been drawn up by Smith and edited by Frederic Ouvry, Dickens's
solicitor, as well as by Dickens himself. The itemized bill Smith submitted to "C.
Dickens Esq." the following month included charges for drawing up the deed and
producing a fair draft but also for "attending at several places enquiring for the
address of Mrs. Dickens" on 3 June (fig. 18).[1] Catherine's solicitor had found it difficult to locate his client, whose whereabouts were generally unknown—one sign of
the uncertainties that surrounded her as a married yet separated woman positioned
between her familiar life at Tavistock House and what would soon become her new
existence at 70 Gloucester Crescent, Regent's Park.

---

1. George Smith, itemized bill, Ouvry Papers, 25.15, Charles Dickens Museum, London.

Arranging the terms of their separation by means of a deed—in effect, a financial contract—the Dickenses signed a document that was not recognized under common law and violated the principle of coverture. But since the 1600s the Court of Chancery had recognized and enforced separation deeds, which allowed a husband to provide his wife with a separate settlement of property, vested in male trustees, and released him from liability for her debts.[2] Accordingly, the phrase "notwithstanding her coverture" recurs throughout the Dickenses' separation deed.

Whatever the pressures placed on her to do so, Catherine "voluntarily" separated from her husband by means of a contract: her signature marked her consent. Mutually agreeing to their new arrangements, the pair avoided the publicity and legal difficulties that would have attended any attempt on Catherine's part to obtain a judicial separation, a decree that could be granted by the newly established Divorce Court, that defined husbands and wives as antagonists, and that would have required proof of spousal wrongdoing that Catherine did not possess.

Before 1858, the right to divorce or separate was granted only by the ecclesiastical courts. Until the year of the Dickenses' marital breakdown, the type of divorce that allowed for remarriage (divorce *a vinculo matrimonii*) was almost exclusively the prerogative of wealthy husbands and required not only an ecclesiastical decree but also an action for "criminal conversation" against a spouse's lover as well as an act of Parliament. Although the ecclesiastical courts had allowed married women to separate on the grounds of adultery, cruelty, or desertion (divorce *a mensa et thoro*), they could not remarry and did not regain their property rights under common law. In passing the Matrimonial Causes Act of 1857, however, Parliament reformed marriage law and established a civil court for judicial separation and divorce in London. The new law continued to reflect the sexual double standard, treating a wife's adultery as a more serious offense than a husband's. But it was now possible, under certain circumstances, for a married woman to divorce or separate from her husband through secular rather than ecclesiastical channels, and in either case to regain her property rights, as Anna Dickens did when she left Fred.

Initially, Mrs. Hogarth and Helen had encouraged Catherine to bring an action for judicial separation against Dickens. As Helen Thomson told her friend Mrs. Stark in August 1858, they felt that the case belonged in "a public court," and she regretted that her relatives did not seek that "proper issue," instead "over-ruled by the casuistry of the lawyer" and "the entreaties" of Mark Lemon and Charley, who was eager to release "his poor mother ... from all the anxious agitation of further delay"—and knowing, too, Dickens's "stubborn and unyielding temper."

2. Lee Holcombe, *Wives and Property: Reform of the Married Women's Property Law in Nineteenth-Century England* (Toronto: University of Toronto Press, 1983), 31–32, 42–43.

FIGURE 18.
George Smith, itemized bill for legal costs, July 1858, Ouvry Papers, Charles Dickens Museum, London.

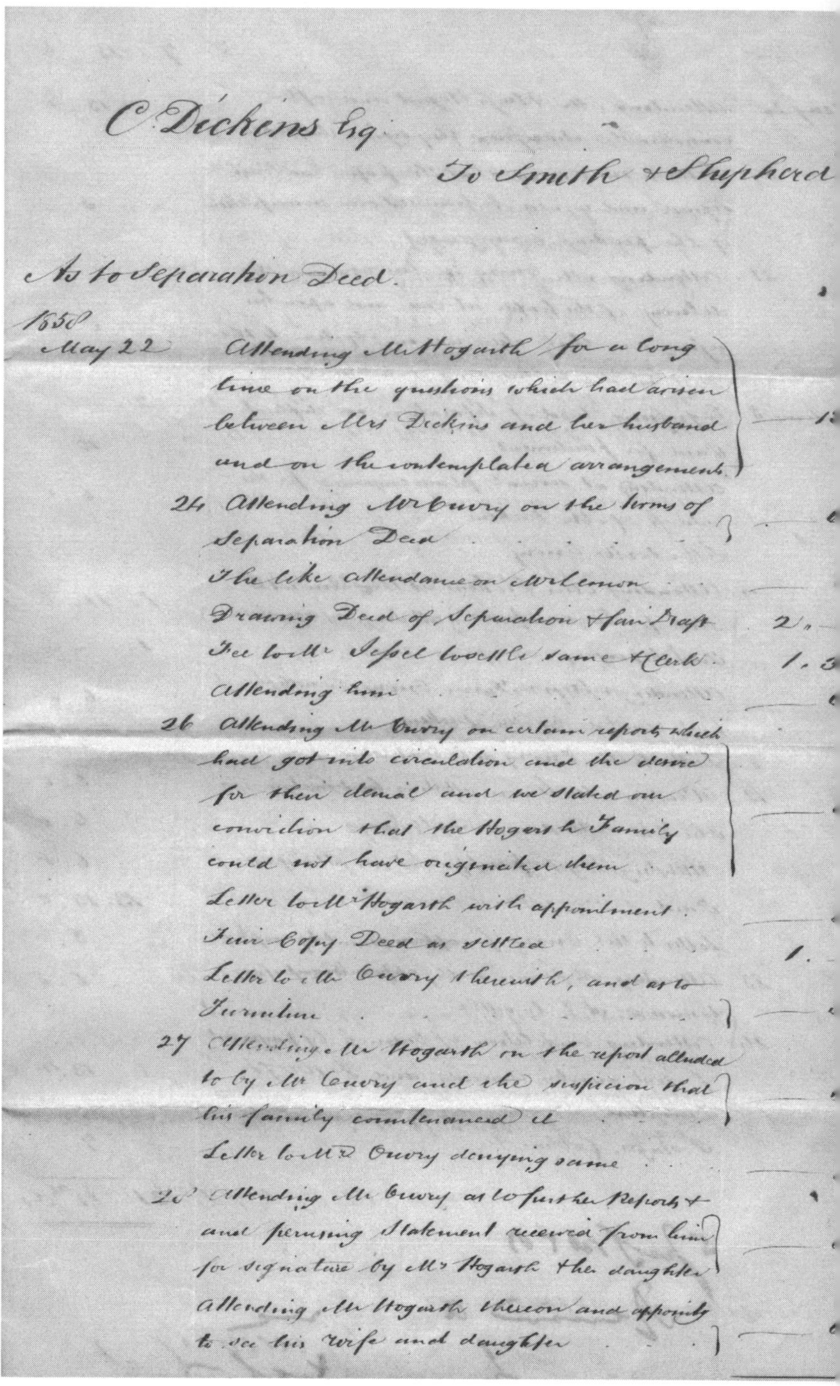

C Dickens Esq

To Smith & Shepherd

As to Separation Deed.

1858

May 22 Attending Mr Hogarth for a long time on the questions which had arisen between Mrs Dickens and her husband and on the contemplated arrangements

24 Attending Mr Ouvry on the terms of Separation Deed

The like attendance on Mr Lemon

Drawing Deed of Separation & fair Draft 2..

Fee to Mr Jessel to settle same & Clerk 1.3

Attending him

26 Attending Mr Ouvry on certain reports which had got into circulation and the desire for their denial and we stated our conviction that the Hogarth Family could not have originated them

Letter to Mr Hogarth with appointment

Fair Copy Deed as settled 1.

Letter to Mr Ouvry therewith, and as to Furniture

27 Attending Mr Hogarth on the report alluded to by Mr Ouvry and the suspicion that his family countenanced it

Letter to Mr Ouvry denying same

28 Attending Mr Ouvry as to further Reports & and perusing Statement received from him for signature by Mrs Hogarth & her daughter

Attending Mr Hogarth thereon and appointing to see his wife and daughter

1848   £ 7 . 15 . 6

May 26   Attending Mr & Mrs Urgent and after   13 . 4
    considerable discussion they signed the paper

29   Letter to Mr Owry that the paper had been
    signed and would be handed over on completion   5
    of the pending arrangement

31   Attending Mr Owry on his requiring the
    delivery of the paper at once, and upon his
    assurance that there was no objection to the   6 . 8
    Deed as drawn handing it to him signed

June 3   Engrossing Deed of Separation in duplicate   2 . —
    Paid for parchment   10 . —
    Attending at several places enquiring for the
    address of Mr Dickens   6 . 8
    Letter to Mr Owry

4   Attending Mr Dickens at Brighton with
    Deed for his execution, & obtaining the execution   1 . 11 . 6
    Paid Expenses   1 . —
    Attending Messrs Farrer Owry & Co with the
    part executed by Mr Dickens   6 . 8

8   Letter to Mr Owry as to completion of Deed   3 . 6
12   Attending Mr Lemon attesting his signature   6 . 8
    The like Attendance on Mr Evans   6 . 8
    Attending to get principal Deed Stamped   6 . 8
    Paid   £2 . 15 . 0
    Letter to Mr Owry for appointment to complete   3 . 6

23   Attending Mr Lemon with appointment for
    tomorrow at 1 to settle   6 . 8

24   Attending completion of business by payment
    of first quarter's Annuity, and £100 for   13 . 4
    Furniture
    Postages, Cab hire &c   7 . —

             £ 31 . 4 . 4

5 July 1858

Received the above

Catherine's aunt wrote, "I deeply regret that they did not abide by their own convictions," for "one cannot consent to do evil and expect good to come of it."[3] To pursue a judicial separation, however, Catherine would have had to charge her husband with adultery, incest, sodomy, desertion, or physical cruelty: such were the required grounds. To pursue a divorce, she would have had to charge him with adultery as well as bigamy, incest, sodomy, or cruelty. Although her mother, her youngest sister, and her aunt believed that Dickens and Ellen Ternan had committed adultery by the spring of 1858, Catherine seems to have had her doubts, and with good reason. As Claire Tomalin notes, Dickens was infatuated with Ellen and had begun to support her, but they may not have become sexually intimate until the early 1860s, when, both Tomalin and Robert Garnett conjecture, Ellen gave birth to a son who died in infancy, as Henry Dickens claimed.[4] Catherine's husband did not simply wish to seduce Ellen, Tomalin argues. "Trapped in his own morality," he wanted "to start life again as a romantic bachelor, in romantic purity."[5]

With nine children and a wife of twenty-two years, Dickens could not return to bachelorhood. But the separation deed seemed to grant him the next best thing; at a price, it effectively liberated him from his responsibilities and obligations as a husband. "She the said C[atherine] T[homson] Dickens shall not nor will at any time or times hereafter molest or disturb the said C[harles] Dickens," the deed stipulated, "nor shall commence or prosecute any suit or suits in any court or courts or take any other proceedings at law or in equity for compelling or obliging him the said C[harles] Dickens to cohabit or live with her the said C[atherine] T[homson] Dickens or to allow her any support maintenance or alimony whatsoever other than and beyond the annuity herein before covenanted to be paid." In their early negotiations Dickens had offered Catherine "£400 a year and a brougham."[6] The final version of the deed omitted the brougham and gave Catherine the "clear yearly sum of £600 by 4 equal quarterly portions." Entitling her to inherit property and make her own will, and granting her "free access to all or any of her children at all places…[and] at all times," the deed exempted Catherine from some of the

3. Helen Thomson to Mrs. Stark, [30] August 1858, in K. J. Fielding, "Charles Dickens and His Wife," *Études Anglaises* 8, no. 3 (1955): 215, reprinted in Pilgrim 8:747.

4. See Claire Tomalin, *The Invisible Woman: The Story of Nelly Ternan and Charles Dickens* (New York: Knopf, 1991), 140–44; Robert R. Garnett, "The Crisis of 1863," *Dickens Quarterly* 23, no. 3 (September 2006): 181–91.

5. Tomalin, *Invisible Woman,* 107.

6. ALS John Forster to Frederic Ouvry, 22 May 1858, Ouvry Papers, 25.2, Charles Dickens Museum, London.

restrictions placed on married women and freed her from her responsibilities toward her husband just as it liberated Dickens from his duties toward her.

> Notwithstanding the marr[iag]e that has been had between them...it shall and may be lawful for the said C[atherine] T[homson] Dickens...to live separate and apart from him the said C[harles] Dickens in such sort and manner as if she were sole and unmarried. And that he the said C[harles] Dickens shall not nor will compel or attempt to compel the said C[atherine] T[homson] Dickens to cohabit and live with him by any legal proceedings...or in any manner assume claim or exercise any rule constraint authority or control over or upon the said C[atherine] T[homson] Dickens or directly or indirectly...molest interrupt or disturb her...in her way of living or in her liberty or freedom of going to and staying in such place or places as she shall think fit or for any cause or under any pretense whatsoever sue or prosecute any person or persons for receiving harbouring protecting or assisting the said C[atherine] T[homson] Dickens.[7]

Ironically, Catherine had neither sought nor desired this "freedom," which still left her dependent on men. Her coverture might be suspended, yet her legal agency was vested in and mediated by the male trustees the deed named: Mark Lemon and Frederick Evans. Once Catherine signed the document on 4 June and her husband on the tenth, Smith brought it to Lemon and Evans, whose signatures were also required, and who were understood to provide Catherine with the guardianship that her husband had withdrawn. Although Dickens wrote some of his first checks for his wife's support to Catherine herself—£100 on 5 July 1858, £100 on 7 September, and £150 on 15 September[8]—his initial £200 payment was made to Ouvry and then transferred to Lemon as one of Catherine's trustees, as were all Dickens's quarterly payments from December 1858 onward. "Received the 24th June 1858 of Charles Dickens Esq. the sum of two hundred pounds—one hundred pounds part thereof being balance of quarter's annuity due 12 June instant—the residue thereof being an agreed payment on account of furniture."[9] So Lemon acknowledged the funds he received on Catherine's behalf (fig. 19).

By the standards of the day, the separation deed was liberal in its treatment of Catherine, and Dickens claimed that its "pecuniary" terms were "as generous as if Mrs. Dickens were a lady of distinction, and [he] a man of fortune" (Pilgrim 8:741).

7. Deed of Separation (draft), Ouvry Papers, 35, Charles Dickens Museum, London.

8. Charles Dickens, Esq., Account Ledger, Coutts & Co., London.

9. Mark Lemon, autograph, stamped receipt, 21 June 1858, Ouvry Papers, 25.16, Charles Dickens Museum, London.

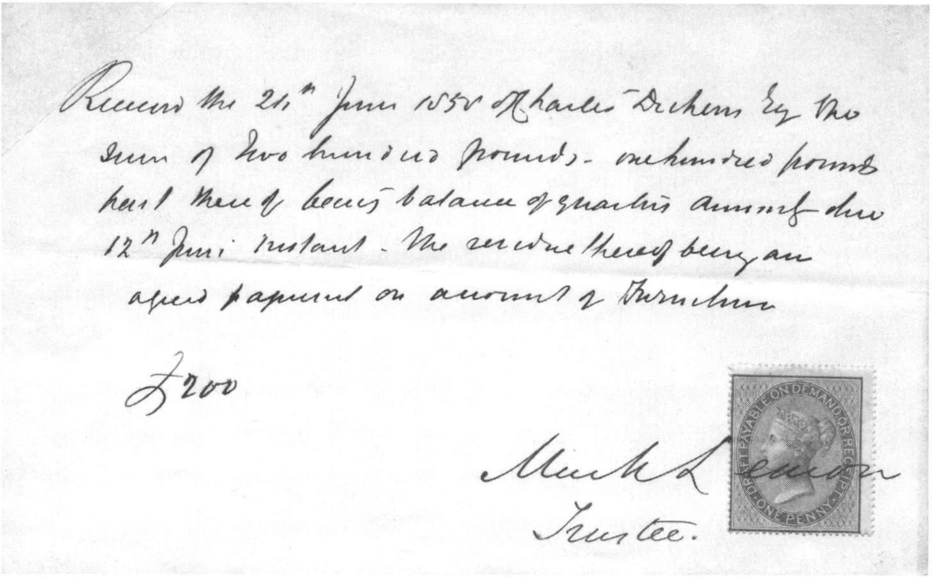

FIGURE 19. *Receipt for £200 signed by Mark Lemon, Trustee, 24 June 1858,*
Ouvry Papers, Charles Dickens Museum, London.

It gave her £200 more annually than Rosina Bulwer Lytton received from the settlement she and her estranged husband had signed in April 1836. Catherine rather than her husband was the one to leave their home, but her new residence was located in an attractive middle-class neighborhood slightly northeast of Regent's Park, and her yearly £600 was equivalent to the annual salary of a middle-class professional man. W. H. Wills earned £416 a year as sub-editor of *Household Words* in the 1850s, in addition to his profits as a part owner, while the starting salaries of junior clerks in the civil service ranged from £125 to £300 in the mid-1850s, and for those employed in banks and law offices from £50 to £100.[10] In the 1860s the London *Times* suggested that a salary of £300 was necessary to allow a middle-class man to marry, live in a semidetached house, and employ one general servant.[11] As Shirley Brooks remarked to William Hardman when the wife of a well-known art dealer separated from her husband in the 1860s, "she wipes her eyes on a settlement of £500 a year: there are worse pocket-handkerchiefs."[12]

10. Geoffrey Best, *Mid-Victorian Britain, 1851–1875* (New York: Schocken Books, 1972), 89–90.

11. Sally Mitchell, *Daily Life in Victorian England* (Westport, Conn.: Greenwood Press, 1996), 36.

12. Shirley Brooks to William Hardman, [November 1867], in *The Hardman Papers: A Further Selection (1865–1868)*, ed. S. M. Ellis (London: Constable, 1930), 293.

On her settlement, Catherine could afford to employ two servants and would not need to cook or clean. Although the 1861 census returns for Catherine's household were destroyed in World War II, the 1871 returns list two women in her service: Sarah Hatfield, her forty-year-old cook, and Matilda Wright, her twenty-seven-year-old housemaid. Catherine's new home was much more modest than either Devonshire Terrace or Tavistock House, but for a middle-class household of four—Catherine, Charley, and two live-in servants—it was spacious enough. Their three-story dwelling, on a pleasant curved street, had been built within the decade. The last in a row of connected terraces, and facing southeast, it overlooked a yard with trees and garden. A kitchen and servants' quarters were in the basement, a dining room and hall on the ground floor; there were front and back parlors on the first story and small bedrooms on the first and second floors.

Catherine appears to have left Tavistock House around her forty-third birthday. Her letter to Miss Coutts of 19 May suggests that she had hoped to avert the separation to the last. "Many, many thanks for your true kindness in doing what I asked," Catherine wrote. "I have now, God help me only *one* course to pursue."[13] Miss Coutts invited Catherine to live with her and her widowed companion Hannah Brown on Stratton Street in Piccadilly. Declining the kind invitation, Catherine spent the second half of June with the Lemons at their home in Crawley after her two weeks at Brighton with her mother. By mid-July she was living with Charley at Gloucester Crescent and distributing new calling cards to friends and acquaintances. "I enclose you a few of my cards as you kindly wished me to do," she told Miss Coutts on the twelfth, her friend determined to spread word of her new location and help her adjust to her changed circumstances.[14]

Because of the cost of new furnishings, Catherine immediately found herself short of funds, despite having received her quarterly allowance. Writing to Ouvry on 1 July with an estimate for Catherine's furniture, Lemon identified objects that, on her current budget, she would have to do without—items that helped define upper-middle-class life among Victorians, such as a piano and a brougham.

> You will see that £300 will barely cover what is necessary omitting altogether those articles against which I have placed a * & not including a piano. Of course I do not presume even to suggest any alteration or addition to what has been done, but if nothing more is given it is proposed to order only

13. ALS Catherine Dickens to Angela Burdett Coutts, 19 May 1858, MA 1352, the Morgan Library & Museum, New York.

14. ALS Catherine Dickens to Angela Burdett Coutts, "Monday morning" [12 July 1858], MA 1352, the Morgan Library & Museum, New York.

those articles carried out in the margin until Mrs. Dickens can spare from her income (doing away with the little carriage) enough to purchase what is required for the drawing room.[15]

In response, Dickens agreed to give Catherine £100 more for furnishings; hence his check to her for that amount, cashed on 5 July, which may have helped her purchase the seven-octave cottage piano she owned at the time of her death. "I will take care that Mrs. Dickens has the cheque," Lemon told Ouvry on 2 July, "& explain to her the kindness which has caused it to be sent."[16]

In agreeing to provide Catherine with "free access to all or any of her children," Dickens could lay claim to further kindness, curtailing his absolute custody rights as a father. Although the Custody of Infants Act of 1839 permitted mothers innocent of adultery to petition the Court of Chancery for custody of children seven years of age and younger and for regular access to older siblings as well, the children of any marriage belonged to their father under common law. "If a father was not guilty of utterly gross or dangerous misconduct towards his children," Mary Lyndon Shanley explains, "his right to their custody and guardianship was practically absolute."[17] Rather than ending with death, that right extended beyond the father's lifetime, since he could name the guardian or guardians of his choice for his underage children in his will. Given Dickens's rights under the law, the deed Catherine signed was enlightened in acknowledging her maternal claims, a point her husband underscored when writing to Charley in mid-July: "I myself took out of our Deed of separation the usual formal clause inserted by her own solicitors; that she should have access to the children except at Tavistock House. That exception seemed to me to convey an unnecessary slight upon her, and I said that she should see them there or anywhere" (Pilgrim 8:602).

Yet what was allowed to Catherine in theory was not granted to her in practice as far as her contact with the children was concerned, and her access to them was subject to restrictions imposed by Dickens and outlined in his letter to Charley, who relayed them to his mother. "'I positively forbid the children ever to utter one word to their grandmother or to Helen Hogarth. If they are ever brought into the presence of either of these two, I charge them immediately to leave your mother's house and come back to me. . . . I positively forbid the children ever to see or to

15. ALS Mark Lemon to Frederic Ouvry, 1 July 1858, Ouvry Papers, 25.13, Charles Dickens Museum, London.

16. ALS Mark Lemon to Frederick Ouvry, 2 July 1858, Ouvry Papers, 25.14, Charles Dickens Museum, London.

17. Mary Lyndon Shanley, *Feminism, Marriage, and the Law in Victorian England* (Princeton: Princeton University Press, 1989), 132.

speak to [Mark Lemon], and for the same reason I absolutely prohibit their ever being taken to Mr. Evans's house.'" Although "you have a distinct right to see the children when where or how you please," Charley assured his mother after echoing his father, "he places these restrictions on their visits, which . . . he has the most perfect right and power to do. . . . [H]e has, as their father, an absolute right to prevent their going into any society which may be distasteful to him, as long as they remain under age. I think it necessary to point this out to you *strongly,* in order that there may be no unnecessary and useless talk on this matter."[18]

In suggesting that the society of Helen and Mrs. Hogarth was now "distasteful" to his father, Charley was putting it mildly. Dickens's hostility toward his in-laws was nothing new. In July 1854 he wrote to Georgina of her mother's "imbecility," a label he applied to both her parents in April 1856 (Pilgrim 7:376, 8:99). At that time they were staying at Tavistock House with Helen, Edward, and Charley while the rest of the Dickenses were in France. Anticipating his return to London, Dickens complained to Wills that his "constitution [was] already undermined by the sight of Hogarth at breakfast" (Pilgrim 8:99), a remark he repeated to Lemon the same day.

Until the separation Dickens had not been critical of Helen, whom he included, with her twin brother, in the cast of *The Frozen Deep.* But as Dickens negotiated the terms of the separation with the Hogarths, he accused Helen and her "wicked mother" of spreading rumors about his alleged sexual impropriety (Pilgrim 8:565), rumors that linked him to Georgina as well as Ellen Ternan. Dickens was wrong in believing that the Hogarths suspected their middle daughter of such behavior. To Helen Thomson, Georgina appeared "an enthusiast" who blindly "worship[ed] [Dickens] as a man of genius"; to her parents, she misconceived her duties in her fidelity to him.[19] But Dickens's connection to Ellen Ternan was an entirely different matter.

Dickens himself had been discussing his domestic affairs for several months, but in a way that put Catherine in the wrong. While a "serio-comic" Dickens told Émile de la Rue, in October 1857, that Catherine was incapable of happiness and "excruciatingly jealous" without cause, he told Miss Coutts on 9 May 1858 that his wife "has always felt herself at the disadvantage of groping blindly about [him] and never touching [him], and so has fallen into the most miserable weaknesses and

18. ALS Charley Dickens to Catherine Dickens, 13 July 1858, HM 18483, Huntington Library, quoted in Pilgrim 8:602 n. 5.

19. Helen Thomson to Mrs. Stark, [30] August 1858, reprinted in Pilgrim 8:748; ALS George Smith, statement drafted for George Hogarth, 27 May 1858, Ouvry Papers, 25.4, Charles Dickens Museum, London.

jealousies. Her mind has, at times, been certainly confused besides" (Pilgrim 8:472, 560). Mrs. Hogarth and Helen, however, were telling a very different story, one in which Catherine's jealousy was painfully well founded and the only confusion was Dickens's in forgetting his marriage vows. From what can be gathered from Helen Thomson's narrative, from the account Katey provided to Gladys Storey, from the reports of several contemporaries, and from Dickens's own indignant letters, the Hogarths did not hesitate to voice their belief that Ellen had become Dickens's mistress. Whether or not they knew that Charley had "caught" his father walking with Ellen on Hampstead Heath, as Annie Thackeray told a friend,[20] they were aware of Dickens's unusual interest in and support of the attractive young actress. On 26 May, Dickens learned that Mrs. Hogarth had recently conveyed "amazing slanders" to a mutual acquaintance, who promptly informed him of that fact (Pilgrim 8:568).

What Dickens learned of the Hogarths' talk fueled his sense of self-righteousness and his determination to exonerate himself and the women whose "purity" he felt his in-laws had questioned. In the midst of working up the separation deed, he broke off negotiations, refusing to settle any property on Catherine until Mrs. Hogarth and Helen signed a document asserting that rumors about him were false and expressing their belief that he and those disparaged with him were innocent. As long as allegations of immorality were "hanging over" his client, Ouvry told Smith—allegations "supposed to be sanctioned by some members of his wife's family"—"Mr. Dickens will not sign any deed."[21] Although the women capitulated to Dickens's demands, signing a retraction at the end of May, they did so out of expediency, not from any feeling of respect for Catherine's husband or conviction that justice was being done.

"A MATTER OF GRIEF TO US"

Smith's bill indicates that he met with George Hogarth "for a long time" on 22 May to discuss "the contemplated arrangements" for Catherine. Two days later he met with Ouvry and then with Lemon to review "the terms of [the] Separation Deed." By 26 May the focus of discussion had shifted. Smith now met with Ouvry to discuss "certain reports which had got into circulation and the desire for their denial." Smith "stated [his] conviction that the Hogarth Family could not have originated them," but neither Ouvry nor Dickens was persuaded. During the next two days,

---

20. "Charley met his Father & Miss whatever the actress' name out walking on Hampstead Heath," she reported in an undated letter to Amy Crowe; quoted in Tomalin, *Invisible Woman*, 111.

21. ALS Frederic Ouvry to George Smith, 28 May 1858, Ouvry Papers, 25.7, Charles Dickens Museum, London.

Smith discussed with the Hogarths "the report alluded to by Mr. Ouvry and the suspicion that [the Hogarth] family countenanced it," and he corresponded with Dickens's solicitor in an attempt to resolve the conflict.[22] On 27 May, Smith drafted a letter in the voice of Mr. Hogarth, which the latter agreed to sign:

> I can have no difficulty or hesitation in assuring you that the report that I or my wife or daughter have at any time stated or insinuated that any impropriety of conduct had taken place between my Daughter Georgiana [sic] and her Brother in Law Mr. Charles Dickens is totally and entirely unfounded.
>
> It is of course a matter of grief to us that after the unfortunate differences which have arisen between my daughter Mrs. Chas. Dickens and her husband, my daughter Georgiana [sic] should remain with his family[,] but while we regret what we regard as a mistaken sense of duty[,] we have never for one instant imputed to her any improper motive for so doing.[23]

"Mr. Hogarth . . . is willing to sign the enclosed letter," Smith told Ouvry, "and I will be glad to know whether it will be satisfactory."[24]

As Smith soon learned, Ouvry and Dickens found the letter wholly inadequate. Not only was it written in the wrong voice—that of George Hogarth rather than his wife and daughter Helen—but also the charge that it repudiated was stated too baldly and too narrowly defined. "The slanders in circulation go beyond the specific charge which Mr. Hogarth repudiates," Ouvry told Smith, "and with reference to the disgusting and horrible nature of that charge I cannot think it desirable that it should be distinctly written down even for the purpose of denial."[25]

In turn, Ouvry composed a statement "for signature by Mrs. Hogarth and her daughter," which Dickens then edited, and which was handed to Smith on 28 May. Ouvry's draft read:

> It having been stated to us that in reference to the differences which have resulted in the separation of Mr. and Mrs. Charles Dickens, certain statements have been circulated that such differences were occasioned by circumstances deeply affecting the moral character of Mr. Dickens. We solemnly declare that such statements did not originate with, and have not been circulated by

22. George Smith, itemized bill, Ouvry Papers, 25.15, Charles Dickens Museum, London.

23. ALS George Smith, statement drafted for George Hogarth, 27 May 1858, Ouvry Papers, 25.4, Charles Dickens Museum, London.

24. ALS George Smith to Frederick Ouvry, 27 May 1858, Ouvry Papers, 25.5, Charles Dickens Museum, London.

25. ALS Frederic Ouvry to George Smith, 28 May 1858, Ouvry Papers, 25.7, Charles Dickens Museum, London.

us or either of us. We know that the statements are wholly repudiated by Mrs. Dickens and we believe them to be entirely destitute of foundation. We pledge ourselves on all occasions to contradict them.

Rather than giving his in-laws the chance to vindicate themselves and deny responsibility for the rumors in circulation, Dickens revised Ouvry's draft to make their guilt implicit. "We solemnly declare that we now disbelieve such statements," Dickens's version read. "We know that these are not believed by Mrs. Dickens and we pledge ourselves on all occasions to contradict them as entirely destitute of foundation."[26] Neither Helen nor Mrs. Hogarth "disbelieved" the rumors about Ellen or wanted to sign the document. But after what Smith described as a "considerable discussion," he noted that "they signed the paper," which they saw as a necessary evil: the means of ensuring Catherine's settlement.[27]

When Smith then offered "to hand to [Ouvry] the paper . . . signed by Mrs. Hogarth and her daughter, in exchange for the deed when completed," Dickens's solicitor balked, insisting that Smith deliver the statement without receiving the deed in return and forcing Catherine's representative to rely on "the word of [Ouvry] and of [his] client and trust that no further impediment . . . will arise."[28] Although Smith received the deed by 3 June, Dickens was clearly determined to wield the upper hand and demonstrate that the Hogarths had no bargaining power. "The proposed arrangement will be carried out, though without any legal obligation," Ouvry told Smith,[29] reminding him, his client, and her relatives of Catherine's dependence on her husband's generosity and goodwill.

Dickens's negotiations with the Hogarths in May 1858 illuminate the power dynamics among them, with Dickens proving to be the strongest party. But their conflict also represented a struggle over the authorship of a narrative of origins—the story of a marital breakdown and its causes.[30] Not surprisingly, Dickens wished to be its sole author. He told it privately at first, in letters to various friends, but then made it public, in a statement for the press. If his in-laws were determined to make

26. Ouvry Papers, 25.6, Charles Dickens Museum, London. Ouvry's portions are written in blue ink and Dickens's emendations in pencil.

27. George Smith, itemized bill, Ouvry Papers, 25.15, Charles Dickens Museum, London.

28. ALS George Smith to Frederick Ouvry, 31 May 1858, Ouvry Papers, 25.9, Charles Dickens Museum, London.

29. ALS Frederic Ouvry to George Smith, 28 May 1858, Ouvry Papers, 25.7, Charles Dickens Museum, London.

30. As Rosemary Bodenheimer puts it, between *Little Dorrit* and *Great Expectations,* "Dickens had another plot to manage: the destruction of his marriage." Rosemary Bodenheimer, *Knowing Dickens* (Ithaca: Cornell University Press, 2007), 157–58.

his marital breakdown a subject of discussion outside the family, so could he, and with much greater effect: not by means of malicious female gossip but through his authoritative printed word.

In the letters he wrote to Miss Coutts, Macready, and others in May 1858, Dickens described his separation from Catherine as "inevitable," "indispensable and unavoidable" (Pilgrim 8:574, 570)—the result of a marriage that "has been for years and years as miserable a one as ever was made" and in which "Nature" placed "an insurmountable barrier" between husband and wife. "I believe that no two people were ever created, with such an impossibility of interest, sympathy, confidence, sentiment, tender union of any kind between them, as there is between my wife and me," he informed a skeptical Miss Coutts (Pilgrim 8:558). "Our separation is the natural end of a course of years," he told Catherine Gore (Pilgrim 8:574). Representing his marriage as somehow unnatural and doomed from the start, Dickens revised its history to justify his behavior and longings, citing what he alleged were his wife's incapacities, which alienated her from the children as well as himself, he claimed. Catherine was a Medusa figure as Dickens portrayed her to Miss Coutts.

> If the children loved her, or ever had loved her, this severance would have been a far easier thing than it is. But she has never attached one of them to herself, never played with them in their infancy, never attracted their confidence as they have grown older, never presented herself before them in the aspect of a mother. I have seen them fall off from her in a natural—not *un*natural— progress of estrangement, and at this moment I believe that Mary and Katey (whose dispositions are of the gentlest and most affectionate conceivable) harden into stone figures of girls when they can be got to go near her, and have their hearts shut up in her presence as if they closed by some horrid spring. (Pilgrim 8:559)

For Miss Coutts, Dickens underscored Catherine's incompetence and jealousy, but he was inconsistent in his letters, using correspondents to test various accounts of the separation. "There is no anger or ill-will between us," he assured Mrs. Gore after angrily berating Catherine to Miss Coutts, "not the slightest" (Pilgrim 8:574).

After these narrative dress rehearsals, Dickens went public with his story in mid-June, against the advice of Forster and Lemon, seeking to vindicate himself and those linked with him from the "cruel" and "monstrous" charges for which he blamed the Hogarths. Poised to launch what would become a highly lucrative reading tour, Dickens was fiercely determined to safeguard his reputation and attempted to do so through paradoxical means—by publishing a "Personal" statement about "sacredly private" matters, first in the *Times* on 7 June and then in the 12 June *Household Words*. In an "extraordinary...exposure of a family affair"—a narrative that critic Catherine Waters aligns with the emerging genre of "sensationalism"—Dickens undermined the boundary between "private and public," "fiction and truth,"[31] writing:

> Some domestic trouble of mine, of long-standing, on which I will make no further remark than that it claims to be respected, as being of a sacredly private nature, has lately been brought to an arrangement, which involves no anger or ill-will of any kind, and the whole origin, progress, and surrounding circumstances of which have been, throughout, within the knowledge of my children. It is amicably composed, and its details have now but to be forgotten by those concerned in it.
>
> By some means, arising out of wickedness, or out of folly, or out of inconceivable wild chance, or out of all three, this trouble has been made the occasion of misrepresentations, most grossly false, most monstrous, and most cruel—involving, not only me, but innocent persons dear to my heart, and innocent persons of whom I have no knowledge, if, indeed, they have any existence—and so widely spread, that I doubt if one reader in a thousand will peruse these lines, by whom some touch of the breath of these slanders will not have passed, like an unwholesome air.
>
> Those who know me and my nature, need no assurance under my hand that such calumnies are as irreconcilable with me, as they are, in their frantic incoherence, with one another. But, there is a great multitude who know me through my writings, and who do not know me otherwise; and I cannot bear that one of them should be left in doubt, or hazard of doubt, through my poorly shrinking from taking the unusual means to which I now resort, of circulating the Truth.
>
> I most solemnly declare, then—and this I do, both in my own name and in my wife's name—that all the lately whispered rumours touching the trouble at which I have glanced, are abominably false. And that whosoever repeats one of them after this denial, will lie as wilfully and as foully as it is possible for any false witness to lie, before Heaven and earth.[32]

As Dickens should have foreseen, any statement referring to "whispered rumours" about himself and "innocent persons" could only make readers wonder about the accusations and fuel the scandal surrounding the separation. He had made precisely

31. Catherine Waters, *Dickens and the Politics of the Family* (Cambridge: Cambridge University Press, 1997), 3–5.

32. Charles Dickens, "Personal," *Household Words* 17, 12 June 1858, 601, reprinted in Pilgrim 8:744.

this point two months earlier when dissuading William Holman Hunt from publishing a statement in *Household Words* to dissociate the Pre-Raphaelite painter from the figure of an adulterous artist portrayed in Robert Brough's story "Calmuck." "I have not a doubt that it would suggest to the public what they have not the faintest idea of," Dickens told him, "its effect... exactly the reverse of your desire" (Pilgrim 8:548).

Such proved to be the case with Dickens's "Personal" statement. It was left to such papers as *Reynold's Weekly Newspaper* and the *Court Circular* to repeat the "whispered rumours" to which Dickens referred and in the process to support them. "The rumours alluded to by Mr. Dickens have, indeed, been widely circulated, and generally credited in literary and artistic circles," G. W. M. Reynolds editorialized on 13 June. "The names of a female relative and of a professional young lady, have both been, of late, so intimately associated with that of Mr. Dickens, as to excite suspicion and surprise in the minds of those who had hitherto looked upon the popular novelist as a very Joseph in all that regards morality, chastity, and decorum."[33] "The story in circulation is that his wife has left his roof—according to the mildest form of the narrative, 'on account of incompatibility of temper'—according to the worst form, 'on account of that talented gentleman's preference of his wife's sister to herself, a preference which has assumed a very definite and tangible shape.'... Mr. Dickens is in a fair way to figure in the new Matrimonial Court, and in a mode which will add little to his laurels."[34]

"What is this sad story about Dickens and his wife?" Elizabeth Barrett Browning asked in July. "Incompatibility of temper after twenty-three years of married life? What a plea!—Worse than irregularity of the passions it seems to me. Thinking of my own peace & selfish pleasure, too, I would rather be beaten by my husband once a day than lose my child out of the house—yes, indeed. And the Dickens's [*sic*] have children younger than Peninl!—Poor woman! She must suffer bitterly—that is sure."[35]

VOICE LESSONS

As Barrett Browning conjectured, the "poor woman" suffered bitterly, though behind the scenes. In the meetings and negotiations between the Hogarths and George Smith, Catherine took no part. She remained in Brighton, where Smith had brought the deed for her to sign on 4 June. That same day Wills arrived at her lodgings, sent by her husband with a copy of the "Personal" statement. "As you

33. G. W. M. Reynolds, *Reynold's Weekly Newspaper,* 13 June 1858, quoted in K. J. Fielding, "Dickens and the Hogarth Scandal," *Nineteenth-Century Fiction* 10 (June 1955): 72.

34. *Court Circular,* 12 June 1858, quoted ibid., 71–72.

35. Elizabeth Barrett Browning, 11 July 1858, Harry Ransom Humanities Research Center, University of Texas at Austin, quoted in Pilgrim 8:597 n. 1.

are referred to in the article," Catherine read in Dickens's cover letter, "I think you ought to see it. You have only to say to Wills...that you do not object to the allusion" (Pilgrim 8:579). Instead of asking her to consent to the publication of his statement, Dickens tells her, in effect, to refrain from objecting, thus downplaying what he wants of her and compromising her sense of agency. Glossing Dickens's letter, the Pilgrim editors say that Catherine "raised no objection." But we don't know what she said to Wills or if she replied to Dickens in writing, and her reaction later that day suggests that she *did* object, albeit in delayed and mediated fashion. She either gave or sent the statement to her solicitor, who attempted to prevent its publication on her behalf. Nonetheless, it appeared as Dickens planned, and when Lemon as editor of *Punch* and Evans as publisher refused to run the statement there, Dickens broke with them, declaring Catherine's trustees his enemies and assigning them to the proscribed camp of Helen and Mrs. Hogarth.

In his cover letter to Catherine, Dickens held her relatives responsible for his need to publish his "Personal" statement while setting her apart from them. "I will not write a word as to any *causes* that have made it necessary for me to publish the enclosed in Household Words. Whoever there may be among the living, whom I will never forgive alive or dead, I earnestly hope that all unkindness is over between you and me" (Pilgrim 8:578). In May and June, Dickens repeatedly claimed that Catherine believed him innocent of misconduct and that, unlike Helen and her mother, she refrained from what he considered their scandalmongering. "Pray do me the kindness, expressly to detach Mrs. Dickens from these wrongdoings, *now*," he told Ouvry on 26 May. "I do not in the least suspect her of them, and I should wish her to know it. She has a great tenderness for me, and I sincerely believe would be glad to shew it. I would not therefore add to her pain by a hair's breadth" (Pilgrim 8:569). On the twenty-ninth he assured Mary Boyle, "Mrs. Dickens (really, generously indignant at the baseless scandals she hears, whatever her weakness may once have done circuitously, towards originating them) has hastened to declare in writing that there is no other cause for our separation than our having lived unhappily together for some time, and having agreed to live asunder" (Pilgrim 8:573).

If Catherine wrote the declaration to which Dickens refers, it has not survived. Her extant writings about the separation suggest that Dickens was ventriloquizing here—referring to what he "most solemnly declare[d]...in his wife's name" in his "Personal" statement, which Catherine had yet even to see. According to Helen Thomson, Catherine was "silent and forbearing" throughout "her heavy trial," behaving "with dignified and gentle forbearance, and a true Christian patience."[36]

36. Helen Thomson to Mrs. Stark, [30] August 1858, reprinted in Pilgrim 8:748.

Indeed Catherine earned praise in newspaper editorials for her ladylike reticence and was defined against such an outspoken "shrew" as the "virago...Lady Bulwer."[37] But Catherine was not *wholly* silent. On 20 May, Lemon told Forster of a letter, "the second to the same purpose," that she had written and asked him to forward to Dickens on her behalf but that he was reluctant to send.[38] The previous day, Catherine had been outspoken enough to convey to Miss Coutts her deep sense of injury, although she declined to name the person who had inflicted the wound or to discuss in writing the details of her treatment. Thanking her friend for attempting a last-minute reconciliation, Catherine ended her letter by imagining a time when she might freely speak her mind, even as she muted her meaning by using the passive voice: "One day though not now I may be able to tell you how hardly I have been used."[39]

In July 1858 Catherine confided to her aunt Helen that she still loved Dickens and thought of him "too much for her peace of mind."[40] Dickens might still disturb her peace, but such confidences show that his control over her was waning. From the time she left Tavistock House for Brighton, Catherine aligned herself with women who spoke their minds and cultivated their powers of expression, such as Helen Thomson, who adapted Proverbs to her purpose in criticizing Dickens ("the wicked flee when no man pursueth" [28:1]), and Helen Hogarth, who actually supported herself by means of her voice. "Since the beginning of last winter," Helen Thomson proudly told Mrs. Stark, her namesake had been "teaching singing successfully," and had "many pupils in prospect for this season." In the midst of criticizing Dickens, Miss Thomson suggested that she would "try to imitate" Catherine and "check [her] pen." Yet she encouraged her eldest niece to imitate *her* instead—to exchange the passive voice for the active. Like Helen and Mrs. Hogarth, she wanted Catherine to speak out, and she provided a receptive audience for her niece's "bitter recollections and feelings." To Mrs. Stark, Miss Thomson emphasized not only Helen's success in singing but also Catherine's expressive writing, quoting at length from one of "several letters" she had received from her that summer that described her "keen pain." Hoping that God would

37. *New York Tribune,* 16 August 1858, quoted in Pilgrim 8:648 n. 1.

38. Mark Lemon to John Forster, 20 May 1858, in *Mr. & Mrs. Charles Dickens: His Letters to Her,* ed. Walter Dexter (London: Constable, 1935), 278.

39. ALS Catherine Dickens to Angela Burdett Coutts, 19 May 1858, MA 1352, the Morgan Library & Museum, New York.

40. Catherine Dickens to Helen Thomson, quoted in Helen Thomson to Mrs. Stark, [30] August 1858, reprinted in Pilgrim 8:749.

"permit...this page in [Catherine's] life's history to be turned," Miss Thomson urged her niece to author her own story.[41]

Catherine had mixed success in doing so, for she had long been accustomed to subordinating her views to her husband's and was more inclined to use his words than hers to make her case. By the third week in August, she had evidently joined her mother and youngest sister in speaking of Dickens's tie to Ellen Ternan. Hence his resentful remarks to Miss Coutts on the twenty-third: "The weak hand that never could help or serve my name in the least, has struck at it—in conjunction with the wickedest people, whom I have loaded with benefits! I want to communicate with her no more" (Pilgrim 8:632). Dickens ascribes his injury to Catherine's "hand" rather than her voice, yet registers the power of her words. Still, Catherine declined to "strike" with them later that month, when a second published statement by her husband appeared, one considerably more offensive than the first: the "violated" letter.

This document consisted of two parts: a cover letter written by Dickens to Arthur Smith, manager of his public readings, and dated 25 May 1858; and an enclosed statement about the separation which Dickens gave Smith "full permission to show" to others and "beg[ged]" his manager "to show, to any one who wishe[d] to do [him] right, or to any one who may have been misled into doing [him] wrong" (Pilgrim 8:568). Given by Smith to the London correspondent of the *New York Tribune,* according to Forster, the statement was published in that paper on 16 August and then in a number of English papers, including the *Morning Chronicle* and the *Morning Herald,* at the end of the month. Dickens claimed that the statement was "a private document" never intended for publication (Pilgrim 8:650). It "was painfully necessary at the time when it was forced from me, as a private repudiation of monstrous scandals," he assured Ouvry on 5 September, "but that it was never meant to appear in print, I suppose to be quite manifest from its own nature and terms" (Pilgrim 8:648). Yet the nature and terms of Dickens's earlier "Personal" statement also suggest that it was never meant for publication, though it *was;* and Dickens's instructions to Smith in his cover letter cast doubt on his claims to Ouvry, as did the continued friendship between Dickens and his manager.

In the "violated" letter, Dickens focused on Catherine and her alleged failings. Much less circumspect in this account of the separation than he was in *Household Words,* he asserted that he and his wife had "lived unhappily together for many years," invoking Anne Brown as his witness, as we have seen. "I suppose that no two people, not vicious in themselves, ever were joined together, who had a greater difficulty in understanding one another, or who had less in common," he wrote. While such claims misrepresented the history of their marriage, Catherine could

41. Helen Thomson to Mrs. Stark, [30] August 1858, reprinted in Pilgrim 8:748–49, 746.

take some comfort in what Dickens portrayed as the mutual grounds of their unhappiness and misunderstanding. But the contrast he went on to develop between her and Georgina was shocking. "From the age of fifteen," Dickens continued, Georgina Hogarth

> has devoted herself to our home and our children. She has been their playmate, nurse, instructress, friend, protectress, adviser and companion. In the manly consideration toward Mrs. Dickens which I owe to my wife, I will merely remark of her that the peculiarity of her character has thrown all the children on someone else. I do not know—I cannot by any stretch of fancy imagine—what would have become of them but for this aunt, who has grown up with them, to whom they are devoted, and who has sacrificed the best part of her youth and life to them.

Having praised Georgina at Catherine's expense and labeled his wife a neglectful mother, Dickens went on to claim that Catherine had proposed the separation, knowing herself to be psychologically "disordered," and that her proposal was supported by Forster with the children's best interests in mind.

> For some years past Mrs. Dickens has been in the habit of representing to me that it would be better for her to go away and live apart; that her always increasing estrangement made a mental disorder under which she sometimes labours—more, that she felt herself unfit for the life she had to lead as my wife and that she would be better far away. I have uniformly replied that we must bear our misfortune, and fight the fight out to the end; that the children were the first consideration, and that I feared they must bind us together "in appearance."
>
> At length . . . it was suggested to me by Forster that even for their sakes, it would surely be better to reconstruct and rearrange their unhappy home.

Dickens ended by summarizing the terms of the separation, attacking "two wicked persons who . . . coupled with [it] the name of a young lady . . . innocent and pure," and claiming that his wife, "in her better moments," must believe in his "truthfulness" (Pilgrim 8:740–41). To Dickens's statement, the disavowal signed by Helen and Mrs. Hogarth on 29 May was appended. "And thus my poor sister's name and her youngest daughter's is also dragged into public notice," Miss Thomson complained.[42]

"What a dreadful letter that last was!" Barrett Browning told a friend in October. "And what a crime, for a man to use his genius as a cudgel . . . against the woman

42. Ibid., Pilgrim 8:747.

he promised to protect tenderly with life and heart—taking advantage of his hold with the public to turn public opinion against her. I call it dreadful."[43] "Undoubtedly badly treated by her husband," sympathetic strangers thought.[44] Among the couple's friends and acquaintances, Miss Coutts was not alone in allying herself with Catherine. "I knew Charles Dickens well, until after his separation from his wife—*she* I knew after that breach," Phebe Lankester recounted.[45] "My father wrote very strongly to Mr. Dickens," Lucy Tagart noted, and "that was the last intercourse they had."[46] Catherine "was always happy at our house where, after the separation, her husband never came again, so Mama must have taken her part very warmly," recalled Jane Panton.[47] "I put a paragraph into one of my 'Letters' to the American newspaper of which I am a correspondent," Harriet Martineau told Frederick Evans, for "I think it right to tell Mrs. Dickens's old friends in the U.S. that other old friends, who have been intimate in the family during her whole married life, feel towards her an unaltered respect & regard.—This *can* do no harm, & is required...by justice."[48] Helen Thomson was particularly indignant over Dickens's allegations that her niece was "labouring under *mental* disorder" and was an unnatural mother. Catherine was "perfectly sound in mind," her aunt countered to Mrs. Stark, and "all that Georgina did was to teach the little boys to read and write until they went to school," adding, "While...Catherine was having her family fast[,]...was it not natural that she should lean upon the assistance of a sister in the care of her children[?]"[49]

As for Catherine herself, her first known response to the "violated" letter was equivocal: she transcribed her husband's explanation to Ouvry of 5 September, which had been forwarded to her through Dickens's solicitor and her own at Dickens's request. "On coming home here to day from Ireland, for a rest of eight and forty hours, I am exceedingly pained to find that a letter written by me as a private and personal communication, has found its way into some of the London

43. Elizabeth Barrett Browning, 5 October 1858, Maggs Bros. Catalog (Summer 1922), quoted in Pilgrim 8:648–49 n. 4.

44. Henry Spencer Ashbee, diary entry, 3 March 1874, quoted in A. James Hammerton, *Cruelty and Companionship: Conflict in Nineteenth-Century Married Life* (London: Routledge, 1992), 145.

45. ALS Phebe Lankester to Frederick Kitton, 11 January 1889, B271, Charles Dickens Museum, London.

46. ALS Lucy Tagart to Mr. Nicolson, 29 September 1909, 920/NIC 18/11/3, Nicholson Papers, Liverpool Record Office.

47. Jane Panton, *Leaves from a Life* (New York: Brentanos, 1908), 144.

48. ALS Harriet Martineau to Frederick Mullet Evans, 14 November 1860, Bradbury and Evans Papers, Bodleian Library, University of Oxford, MS. Eng. lett. d. 397.

49. Helen Thomson to Mrs. Stark, [30] August 1858, reprinted in Pilgrim 8:747.

papers, extracted from an American paper," she wrote out, copying Dickens's claim that the statement was "painfully necessary" to him but was "never meant" for the press. "I wish you would do me the favor to lose no time in informing Mr. Smith who acted for Mrs. Dickens in our separation, that I am no consenting party to this publication; that it cannot possibly be more offensive to any one in the world than it is to me; and that it has shocked and distressed me very much."[50]

We can only surmise what Catherine's act of transcription meant to her. She may simply have wanted a copy of the document as part of her legal record, but it seems likely that she was trying to come to terms with the affront—struggling to believe that Dickens's distress over the appearance of his letter could somehow match her own, despite his authorship of it. While her relatives dismissed Dickens's claims about the statement and its publication as "artful,"[51] Catherine may have wanted to retain whatever respect for her husband was possible under the circumstances.

Catherine's transcription of Dickens's letter to Ouvry is the text's only surviving version, and thus the Pilgrim editors use it as their source in volume eight. In copying *her* copy, however, they introduce a suggestive error into it. "I am exceedingly pained to find that a letter written *to* me . . . has found its way into some of the London papers,"[52] the Pilgrim text reads, with Dickens *receiving* rather than *writing* the "violated" letter. Catherine made no such mistake. Far from obscuring Dickens's authorship, she remained acutely aware of its power after the separation, using her husband's letters to contest his claims about her and their marriage. After hosting Miss Coutts and Mrs. Brown at Gloucester Crescent in July 1859, Catherine sent them a batch of letters Dickens had written to her in 1850, following Dora's birth, to help her prove that "no unhappiness or estrangement existed" between them "until long after that late date in [their] married life."[53]

But Catherine also corrected Dickens's accounts of their relationship with her own. Although her conversations about her husband, their marriage, and its breakdown are difficult to document, traces of her talk are left in a range of writings—in Dickens's criticism of the "weak hand" that struck him (Pilgrim 8:632); in Catherine's references to subjects she discussed with visitors at Gloucester Crescent; and in letters, reminiscences, and diary entries written by those in her circle after

50. Catherine Dickens, autograph copy of Charles Dickens to Frederic Ouvry, 5 September 1858, British Library, Add. 43689, f. 296.

51. Helen Thomson to Mrs. Stark, [30] August 1858, reprinted in Pilgrim 8:747.

52. Emphasis added. "*For* to me *read* by me," the editors note in volume twelve, restoring Catherine's wording in an appendix (Pilgrim 12:684).

53. ALS Katey Perugini, copy of Catherine Dickens to Angela Burdett Coutts, 18 July [1859], Charles Dickens Museum, London.

the separation which record and respond to her explanations of it. At a party Thackeray hosted in March 1860, for example, the American diplomat John Bigelow dined with Catherine and Mrs. James Caulfield, among others, and learned from Mrs. Caulfield that Catherine identified Ellen Ternan as "the source of the difficulty between [herself] and her husband."[54] Catherine's exchanges with Isabella Frith and her daughter Jane in the 1860s "made...all Charles Dickens' pathos ring untrue" for them, Jane recounted, and his moralizing seem "tongue in...cheek."[55]

While Catherine's voice proved dissonant with her husband's after the separation, Georgina's did not. Once praised by her brother-in-law for her ability to parody and mimic, Georgina became his parrot, echoing uncritically his published remarks about his wife and their marriage, including those in the "violated" letter. "I am now going to tell you something which will, I am sure, surprise you," Georgina wrote Maria Winter on 31 May 1858, explaining "that there was no other way out" than a separation:

> For my sister and Charles have lived unhappily for years—they were totally unsuited to each other in almost every respect—and as the children grew up this unsuitability developed itself more strongly and disagreements and miseries which used to be easily kept out of sight have forced themselves into notice.
>
> Unhappily, also, by some constitutional misfortune and incapacity, my sister always, from their infancy, threw her children upon other people, consequently as they grew up there was not the usual strong tie between them and her—in short, for many years, although we have put a good face upon it, we have been very miserable at home.
>
> My sister has often expressed a desire to go and live away, but Charles never agreed to it on the girls' account; but latterly he thought it must be to their advantage as well as to his own and Catherine's to consent to this and remodel their unhappy home.
>
> So, by *mutual consent* and for the reasons I have told you, *and no other*, they have come to this arrangement.[56]

54. John Bigelow, *Retrospections of An Active Life,* 5 vols. (New York: Baker & Taylor, 1909), 1:264.

55. Panton, *Leaves from a Life,* 145.

56. ALS Georgina Hogarth to Maria Winter, 31 May 1858, HM 18515, Huntington Library, in Dexter, *Mr. & Mrs. Charles Dickens,* 290–91.

Downplaying her importance to Dickens and what friends came to perceive as her "anomalous and unnatural position in the household,"[57] Georgina emphasized Mamie's status as the new mistress of Tavistock House, as Dickens did. The eldest daughter, Mamie was "naturally taking her mother's place as mistress of the house," Georgina explained. "She and Katy and I *work* amongst us, but all the dignity will be [hers]."[58] Paired with Mamie rather than Catherine from this time on (fig. 20), Georgina spoke as Dickens's agent over the next twelve years and, after his death, served as his medium, co-editing with Mamie the first edition of his letters, a project that revealed her reverence for his words as well as her willingness to rework them to protect his image.

"OUR DEAR MOTHER HAS SUFFERED VERY MUCH"

Of all the allegations Dickens leveled against Catherine in 1858 and Georgina dutifully echoed, the most hurtful and unjust was the charge that she was an incompetent mother who foisted her children onto "someone else." It was all the more bitter to Catherine because the children, belonging by law to their father, were not allowed to live with her if they so desired. Only Charley, at twenty one, could elect to join her at Gloucester Crescent, although at least one of his brothers, eleven-year-old Sydney, also expressed a wish to do so. In late July or early August 1858, during their school vacation, the boys stayed for a few days with their mother, who recounted details of their visit to Helen Thomson.

> I need hardly tell you, dearest Aunt, how very happy I have been with my dear boys, although they were not allowed to remain with me so long as I wished, yet I think we all thoroughly enjoyed being together. . . . I cannot tell you how good and affectionate they were to me. One of them, little Sydney, was full of solicitude and anxiety about me, always asking what I should do when they were gone, and if I would not be very dull and lonely without them; he should so like to stay. Upon the whole their visit has done me much good, and dear Charl[ey] is so kind and gentle, and tried to cheer me. I trust by God's assistance to be able to resign myself to His will, and to lead a contented if not a happy life, but my position is a sad one, and time only may be

57. Annie Fields, diary entry, 25 February 1870, quoted in Arthur A. Adrian, *Georgina Hogarth and the Dickens Circle* (London: Oxford University Press, 1957), 131.

58. ALS Georgina Hogarth to Maria Winter, 31 May 1858, HM 18515, Huntington Library, in Dexter, *Mr. & Mrs. Charles Dickens*, 291.

FIGURE 20. *Georgina Hogarth and Mamie Dickens (ca. 1860), photograph,*
Charles Dickens Museum, London.

able to blunt the keen pain that will throb at my heart, but I will indeed try to struggle hard against it.[59]

Anxious to establish social normalcy for her children and show them that, notwithstanding her changed circumstances, her ties to old friends remained intact, Catherine took the boys to call on Miss Coutts, eager to share her enjoyment of their reunion with her friend and supporter.

To her aunt, Catherine noted that she and the boys were "not allowed" to stay together beyond a few days. Despite the deeded assurance of her "free access to all or any of her children at all places," Dickens did not honor that clause, pressuring the children to keep their distance from their mother. Thus, instead of creating two family centers, the separation placed Catherine on the margins. In his memoirs Henry claimed that he visited Catherine at Gloucester Crescent with his father's "full knowledge and acquiescence."[60] Yet Katey provided a very different account of the situation. For nearly two years after the separation, her father "would scarcely speak to [her] because she visited her mother."[61] If the children were to call at Gloucester Crescent, they would appear to "reproach" their father, Katey explained, and most found it difficult to do so. Dickens did not "forbid" their visits, but he made them "fully aware that he did not like them going."[62]

In his public statements, Dickens wrote of the understanding that existed among his family members about the separation. Its origins, circumstances, and arrangements were "throughout, within the knowledge of [his] children,"[63] he claimed, without "a shadow of doubt or concealment" between his children and him: "All is open and plain among us, as though we were brothers and sisters" (Pilgrim 8:741). To the children, however, Dickens appeared far from "brotherly," requiring their allegiance and communicating about the separation only to the three eldest, when trying to persuade them that their mother misconstrued his tie to Ellen. According to Katey, she, Mamie, and Charley were aware of their parents' difficulties, but "the other six children . . . were kept in ignorance."[64] As Alfred observed in 1870, "not one word on the subject *ever* passed from the lips of either father or mother. Of the

---

59. Catherine Dickens to Helen Thomson, quoted in Helen Thomson to Mrs. Stark, [30] August 1858, reprinted in Pilgrim 8:749.

60. Henry Dickens, *The Recollections of Sir Henry Dickens, K.C.* (London: Heinemann, 1934), 19.

61. David Parker and Michael Slater, "The Gladys Storey Papers," *Dickensian* 76 (Spring 1980): 4.

62. Gladys Storey, *Dickens and Daughter* (London: Frederick Muller, 1939), 219.

63. Charles Dickens, "Personal," 601.

64. Storey, *Dickens and Daughter*, 95.

causes which led to the unfortunate event," he continued, "we know no more than the rest of the world," adding, "Our dear mother has suffered very much."[65]

During their twelve years apart, Catherine and her husband each had allies among the children. Of the eldest three, Charley sided with his mother and Mamie with her father, while Katey was painfully divided in her allegiances. Henry identified with Dickens and Sydney with Catherine, while Alfred claimed to "love them both equally."[66] These divisions do not fall into a neat pattern or correspond to birth order or gender, though they show that Catherine was not the negligent, unloving and unloved mother that Dickens made her out to be.

Of the nine children, the one who openly advocated for Catherine was Charley. Always close to his mother, he was by 1858 an adult capable of acting on his own feelings and judgment, and he took up his "quarters" with Catherine on 14 July.[67] Dickens repeatedly claimed to have encouraged his eldest son to live with Catherine on Gloucester Crescent. "Charley's living with his mother to take care of her, is *my* idea—not his," Dickens wrote John Leech, whom he reprimanded for telling a mutual acquaintance "that Charley sides with his mother" (Pilgrim 8:575).[68] Yet Charley's own letters show that the decision to live with Catherine was his own, inspired by his sense of justice, duty, and affection. Although Charley did not break with his father, sometimes visited Gad's Hill Place, and denied "any feeling of preference" for his mother,[69] his sympathies lay with Catherine. To her he was always "dear Charley"—"such a real blessing and consolation"—the "kind and gentle" son who cheered her through bitter days, provided her with companionship, and guided her around the pitfalls of her new life.[70] While regretting his role as "the medium" of communications from Dickens about the "absolute right[s]" of fathers, he

65. ALS Alfred Dickens to Mr. Rusden, 11 August 1870, Rusden Manuscripts, Trinity College Archives, University of Melbourne.

66. Ibid.

67. ALS Charley Dickens to Catherine Dickens, 13 July 1858, HM 18483, Huntington Library, quoted in Pilgrim 8:602 n. 5.

68. "Charley takes care of his mother at my express request," Dickens told Mrs. Gore, "as an act of duty, and on the express stipulation that there is to be nothing in the nature of a parting between him and us" (Pilgrim 8:524).

69. Charley Dickens to Charles Dickens, 10 May 1858, copy in Charles Dickens's hand, D. Jacques Benoliel Collection of the Letters of Charles Dickens, Rare Book Department, Free Library of Philadelphia, Pilgrim 8:575 n. 1.

70. ALS Catherine Dickens to Angela Burdett Coutts, 17 March 1860, MA 1352, the Morgan Library & Museum, New York; Catherine Dickens to Helen Thomson, quoted in Helen Thomson to Mrs. Stark, [30] August 1858, reprinted in Pilgrim 8:749.

explained those rights to his mother, detailing the prohibitions placed on her visits with the children in the hope of preventing further conflict.

Indirectly though effectively, Charley expressed his disapproval of his father's treatment of Catherine—in part by allying himself with the *Punch* circle: the Lemons and the Evanses as well as Thackeray. Like others associated with *Punch*, Thackeray voiced his sympathy for Catherine, "the poor matron" forced to leave her home "after 22 years of marriage," calling Dickens's behavior "a fatal story for our trade."[71] As Dickens requested of him in May 1858, Thackeray "corrected" those who linked his fellow novelist to Georgina Hogarth but did so in terms that offended. "Last week going into the Garrick I heard that Dickens is separated from his wife on account of an intrigue with his sister in law," Thackeray told his mother. "No says I no such thing—its [*sic*] with an actress—and the other story has not got to Dickens's ears but this has—and he fancies that I am going about abusing him."[72] That summer their connection was further strained after Dickens's protégé Edmund Yates slandered Thackeray in *Town Talk*. In what came to be called the "Garrick Club affair," Thackeray brought his complaint to club members, and Yates was expelled over Dickens's protests. In December 1858 Charley joined the fray, criticizing Yates in *Punch*, whereupon Dickens had Charley's name removed from the club's list of proposed members. As Thackeray told William Webb Synge, Dickens's "quarrel with his wife has driven him almost frantic. He is now quarrelling with his son; and has just made himself friends of the whole Garrick Club, by withdrawing his lad's name, just as it was coming up for ballot . . . and the poor boy is very much cast down at his father's proceedings."[73]

By strengthening his ties to the Evanses, Charley more pointedly defied his father. Dickens "absolutely prohibit[ed]" his underage children from entering "Mr. Evans's house" after the separation (Pilgrim 8:603) and dissolved his partnership with Bradbury and Evans when they declined to publish his "Personal" statement in *Punch*. But Charley went into the papermaking business with Evans's eldest son, Frederick, becoming his partner in October 1861, and he married Evans's daughter Bessie that November, much to Dickens's chagrin. "Charley . . . will probably marry the daughter of Mr. Evans," Dickens told a correspondent in March 1861, "the very last person on earth whom I could desire so to honor me. . . . It is sure not to answer—if my authority on such a subject can be accepted" (Pilgrim 9:389).

71. W. M. Thackeray [June 1858], in *Letters and Private Papers of W. M. Thackeray*, ed. Gordon N. Ray, 4:86, quoted in Pilgrim 8:580 n. 2.

72. Ibid., quoted in Pilgrim 8:573 n. 5.

73. W. M. Thackeray to William Webb Synge [winter 1858–59], quoted in *Dickens: Interviews and Recollections*, ed. Philip Collins, 2 vols. (London: Macmillan, 1981), 1:69.

Charley rejected his father's authority on this and related subjects, but Dickens downplayed his defiance by blaming his "odious" choice on Catherine. "I wish I could hope that Charley's marriage may not be a disastrous one," he wrote Mrs. Brown two weeks before the wedding. "There is no help for it, and the dear fellow does what is unavoidable—his foolish mother would have effectually committed him if nothing else had; chiefly I suppose because her hatred of the bride and all belonging to her, used to know no bounds, and was quite inappeasable. But I have a strong belief, founded on careful observation of him, that he cares nothing for the girl" (Pilgrim 9:494). When the couple wed at St. Mark's, Regent's Park, on 19 November 1861, Catherine was present, her husband absent. "My son married with my knowledge and consent, because I very well knew that he couldn't help it," Dickens informed Robert Lytton in December. "The name the young lady has changed for mine, is odious to me; and when I have said that, I have said all that need be said" (Pilgrim 9:548).

In making Bessie Evans a second "Mrs. Charles Dickens," Charley dismissed his father's warning that the Dickens children would "waste" and "trifle...with" the family name by associating with those "who have been false to it"—Evans among them, in Dickens's view (Pilgrim 8:608). Charley perceived that those identified as "false" to his father were often true to his mother, and his attachment to Bessie was no doubt strengthened by the support the Evans family provided to Catherine once she left Tavistock House. After her move Catherine sometimes dined with Evans and his children on Sundays,[74] and Margaret Moule Evans, Bessie's eldest sister, became one of Catherine's closest friends, particularly after the death of Margaret's husband, barrister Robert Orridge, in 1866. Catherine warmly approved of Charley's interest in Bessie and encouraged the match. In January 1859 she wrote to Miss Coutts, asking to use her box at Drury Lane, where she and Charley hoped to take Bessie and her younger siblings to the Pantomime.[75] Carrying with her Bessie's *carte-de-visite,* Catherine showed the photograph to Isabella Frith and others, telling them that the young woman in the crinoline would "make Charley a good wife."[76]

74. "She dines at [Evans's] house every Sunday," Harriet Martineau told Fanny Wedgwood in October 1860, "and his second daughter is engaged to young Charles D." According to Martineau, Catherine had "revived" since 1858, "appear[ing] to more advantage than perhaps ever before" and "cheered by the affection of her son-in-law, Mr. Collins, who has brought her daughter [Katey] back to her." *Harriet Martineau's Letters to Fanny Wedgwood,* ed. Elisabeth Sanders Arbuckle (Stanford: Stanford University Press, 1983), 196–97.

75. ALS Catherine Dickens to Angela Burdett-Coutts, 12 January 1859, Fales Library & Special Collections, New York University.

76. Panton, *Leaves from a Life,* 143.

Catherine also sensed that Bessie would make a good daughter. At a time when her own girls were distant, with Katey pressured to stay away from her mother by Dickens and Mamie content to do so, Catherine's tie to Bessie was free from the tensions that existed within her own family. When Bessie gave birth to her first child in October 1862, Catherine was at her side, proud of the way she handled the labor. Catherine's support was warmly returned by her new relation. "She is a dear and affectionate child to me," Catherine wrote Miss Coutts in 1864, after Walter's death. "Both she and dear Charley have been most devoted and kind to me in this time of sorrow."[77]

Charley's marriage followed that of Katey, whose choice of partner, though not proscribed by Dickens, disappointed him. "I do not doubt that the young lady might have done much better," he told William de Cerjat shortly before her wedding to Charles Collins (Pilgrim 9:246). Though less directly than Charley, Katey, too, expressed her unhappiness with her father through marriage, using it to escape what had become an unhappy home.[78] After the separation Katey had more difficulty opposing Dickens than Charley did, wanting to take her mother's part but intimidated by her father's "stern" warnings.[79] If she couldn't confront him or change their household, however, she could leave it, marrying a man eleven years her senior, whom she found "kind" and "sweet-tempered" but with whom she "was not in the least in love."[80] Although Dickens excluded Catherine from their daughter's wedding, which he hosted at Gad's Hill in July 1860, Katey's departure recalled and replayed her mother's. "But for me, Katey would not have left home," Dickens told Mamie when she found him, distraught, in her sister's empty room on the wedding day (fig. 21).[81]

Katey's younger brothers were trained to respect Dickens's authority and abide by his rules. But they, too, indirectly protested their separation from Catherine, sometimes compromising their own well-being, as Katey did, in hurting their father. The "failures" of Dickens's sons, most of whom "disappointed" him, he told Macready in 1866 (Pilgrim 11:150), can be understood in this way. Sydney's

77. ALS Catherine Dickens to Angela Burdett Coutts, 8 March 1864, MA 1352, the Morgan Library & Museum, New York.

78. As Lucinda Hawksley sees it, Katey made an "unsatisfactory" marriage to escape a life "becoming truly intolerable" and possibly to defy her father, who did not consider Charles Collins a good match. Lucinda Hawksley, *Katey: The Life and Loves of Dickens's Artist Daughter* (London: Doubleday, 2006), 142–45.

79. Storey, *Dickens and Daughter*, 95.

80. Ibid., 105.

81. Ibid., 106.

FIGURE 21. *Mrs. Charles Collins (Katey Dickens) in the early 1870s, photograph, Charles Dickens Museum, London.*

behavior provides a case in point. Having decided, at age twelve, to pursue a naval career, he was described by Dickens as "*the* boy of the lot, and the one who will be heard of hereafter" (Pilgrim 9:247). "If he fails to pass [his examination] with credit," Dickens told Wills in 1860, "I will never believe in anybody again" (Pilgrim 9:303). Instead of bringing credit to his father's name, however, Sydney threatened to disgrace it, and in one of the ways most hurtful to his father—by getting into debt. Writing from Vancouver Island in March 1869, as second lieutenant aboard HMS *Zealous,* Sydney warned Dickens that if he declined to pay his son's debts, "the result of your refusal...is not exaggerated—utter ruination."[82] Before Dickens's death in June 1870, Sydney effectually forced his father to renounce him—"to wish that he were honestly dead" (Pilgrim 12:530)—and hence to recognize his fifth son's home as Catherine's, where the boy had "so [wanted] to stay" in 1858.

82. ALS Sydney Dickens to Charles Dickens, 19 March 1869, Ouvry Papers, 27.10, Charles Dickens Museum, London.

Dickens's last letter to Sydney informed him "that he would not be received at Gad's Hill on his return to England."[83] Having pushed his father to this point, Sydney achieved his end. Like Charley, he redefined the margins of his family as its center, becoming "Mr. Sydney Dickens...of 70 Gloucester Crescent, Regent's Park" (fig. 22).[84]

After the separation Dickens aligned his sons with Catherine—not by acknowledging their love for their mother but by blaming their failures on her. In 1854 he had attributed what he saw as Charley's insufficient "purpose and energy" to the "lassitude" his eldest inherited from Catherine along with her "better qualities" (Pilgrim 7:245). By 1867 Dickens had reconceived Charley's "lassitude" as a "curse" Catherine placed on his sons as a group—"my boys with a curse of limpness on them," as he put it. "You don't know what it is to look round the table and see reflected from every seat at it...some horribly well remembered expression of inadaptability to anything," he told Wills that June, writing on Ellen Ternan's monogrammed stationery and complaining of the financial drain placed on him by his "wife's income" (Pilgrim 11:377). If his boys were their mother's sons rather than their father's, they would share Catherine's fate. Arranging to send them to the colonies to establish themselves in life, Dickens saw himself providing a necessary antidote to Catherine's influence. He sought to place them in situations that would force them to overcome their effeminate "limpness" and develop the purpose and energy Catherine allegedly lacked. Becoming financially autonomous, they would no longer be economic burdens like their mother.

The imperial engagements of Dickens's sons might seem to have nothing to do with the breakdown of his marriage or Catherine's departure from Tavistock House. Dickens was hardly unique in sending his sons to the reaches of empire. Anthony Trollope's son Fred went out to New South Wales in 1864, shortly before Alfred did, and Dickens expressed a widely held view when he spoke of the colonies as an opportune place for his sons to "hew out their own paths through the world" (Pilgrim 11:127). His idea of sending Walter to India dated from the early 1850s, years before the separation, and his first thoughts of having Alfred and Frank join their brother preceded it as well. Nonetheless, as Dickens's plans for the boys developed in the late 1850s and the 1860s, his thinking about what India and Australia meant

83. So Georgina told Annie Fields on 18 June 1872, ALS, FI 2707, Huntington Library, quoted in Adrian, *Georgina Hogarth and the Dickens Circle*, 123.

84. "Please describe Mr. Sydney Dickens as of 70 Gloucester Crescent, Regent's Park, Lieutenant in the Royal Navy," Catherine's lawyer told Ouvry when Sydney gained his promotion in 1871. ALS Frank Richardson to Frederic Ouvry, 23 February 1871, Ouvry Papers, 15.33, Charles Dickens Museum, London.

FIGURE 22. *Sydney Dickens in the 1860s, photograph, Charles Dickens Museum, London.*

for them and their manhood intersected with his thinking about Catherine and her alleged weaknesses, with their exile mirroring hers.

The destinies Dickens imagined for his sons might be understood as imperial romances, stories of struggle and triumph that would demonstrate their manly strength and their resemblance to their father—in which each would "conduct...himself like a Man," as Dickens said of Walter (Pilgrim 8:381). "I have always purposed to send [Alfred] abroad," Dickens told W. J. Eastwick of the East India Company; he is "a boy of remarkable character as a combination of self-reliance, steadiness, and adventurous spirit...whom I believe to be particularly qualified for this opportunity" (Pilgrim 8:241–42). Yet as Dickens made arrangements for his "adventurous" boys, his plotlines read another way, as tales of failure and banishment. Dickens compared Walter's departure for India to that of the hero in *The Green Bushes,* an Irish rebel forced to cross "the Big Drink" because of his transgressions (Pilgrim 8:379–80), and though Dickens represented Alfred to Eastwick as self-reliant and steady, he was a boy who had got into debt and whom Dickens hoped "to dispose of...in Australia," as he told Nina Lehmann, Frederick Lehmann's wife, offering "a Patriarchal piece of advice": "Don't have any more children" (Pilgrim 11:25–26).

Picturing the "unfortunate" Alfred "up the country at a lonely station" in the bush, Dickens thought the emigrant would "take...off his coat in earnest to repair his fortunes" (Pilgrim 11:236). Referring to the character "defect" that Dickens believed Plorn shared with Charley—"his want of application and continuity of purpose"—Dickens claimed that his youngest son would "have more pressing need to make a fight against it in Australia than if he were near home" and might "flash up, under such conditions" (Pilgrim 11:363). When Dickens told Plorn, in the fall of 1868, that Australia's "freedom and wildness" were "more suited to [him] than . . . a study or office," he might be seen as complimenting a rough-and-ready character (Pilgrim 12:187). But when Plorn appeared anxious to return to England in 1870, two years after sailing, his father made it clear that he was unfit for the demands of a career back home (fig. 23). Plorn "does not seem to understand that he has qualified for no public examinations in the old country," Dickens complained to G. W. Rusden, "and could not possibly hold his own against competition for anything to which I could get him nominated"; "he seems to have been born without a groove" (Pilgrim 12:530).

If he were to avoid the fate of his brothers, Henry realized, he would have to prove himself worthy of remaining at home—to define himself, as he relentlessly did, as his father's son, not his mother's.[85] Faced with the prospect of a career in the Indian civil service, the destiny Dickens had chosen for his sixth son, Henry asked instead to attend college in England. He was put to the test in 1865, his father requesting his headmaster to determine "whether . . . he really will be worth sending to Cambridge. . . . [I]f you should not be of this opinion, he should decidedly go up for the Indian Civil Service Examination" (Pilgrim 11:93). Despite talk of the strengths necessary for imperial service, Henry understood that it was more a punishment than a reward in his family—at best a therapy for purposeless or incapable sons who, in their father's eyes, took after their mother.

While trying to root out what he identified as Catherine's traits by sending their boys to the colonies, Dickens also freed himself of them at a time when their presence seemed particularly irksome. In the 1860s Dickens devoted himself to Ellen Ternan and led a secret double life as "Charles Tringham," but secrets were difficult to keep with sons at home. Perceiving them as obstacles to his relationship with Ellen, as Catherine was, and as potential observers and critics of his behavior,

85. Henry describes himself as "a son . . . entirely devoted" to his father, "and whose great pride it is to bear [Dickens's] name," recounting Dickens's tearful gratitude at the news that he had won a scholarship at Cambridge. Henry Dickens, *Memories of My Father* (London: Duffield, 1929), 30. "During the latter years of my father's life my whole being was engrossed in his," Henry claims; "since his death I live upon my memory of him, which is a very deep and living thing." *Recollections of Sir Henry Dickens*, 3.

FIGURE 23. *"Plorn" Dickens posed with rifle (ca. 1868), photograph, Charles Dickens Museum, London.*

Dickens became "ruthless" in his treatment of them, Claire Tomalin contends, "obsess[ed] with ridding himself" of them.[86]

As Dickens's eldest son and Miss Coutts's protégé, Charley had been able to fix on a career in England. Hoping to become a London tea merchant, he traveled to Japan, China, and India in 1860, yet did so temporarily and by his own volition. Such was not the case with his younger brothers, who were more easily dispatched

86. Tomalin, *Invisible Woman*, 185. Discussing the fate of Plorn, unwillingly "packed off to Australia" in 1868, Tomalin notes that "Gad's Hill was now entirely free of boys" and that Dickens "displayed the same blend of callousness and sentimentality as when his other boys were banished; the bewildered and tearful 16-year-old was given a letter at parting in which his father told him he loved him and was sorry to part with him, 'but this life is half made up of partings, and these pains must be borne' [26 September 1868].... Even when all the circumstances of Victorian family life and economics are taken into account, it seems a harsh way of treating a not very bright boy" (185).

by their father—some permanently. As Dickens made clear to Frederick Lehmann in 1863, *any* foreign colony would do as a destination for Alfred (fig. 24). "If I could get him abroad...I should prefer it much," Dickens told Lehmann, who had hoped to find work for Alfred in London; "I still hanker after India or some such distant field" (Pilgrim 10:191, 208). Dickens justified his "hankering" by telling Lehmann of his fear that Alfred and Frank, if left together in London, would "spoil...one another" (Pilgrim 10:191). Yet Lehmann, evidently unconvinced, was shocked by Dickens's determination to exile his sons—whether to Ceylon, to China, or to Australia, of which Dickens wrote in turn. Frederick Lehmann's grandson John records in his family memoir: "In 1863 Dickens consulted Frederick, in a series of letters which my father carefully kept from publication during his lifetime, about the possibility of getting...Alfred a business post abroad.... In the end these mysterious negotiations, which must have been decidedly uncomfortable for my grandfather, were cut short by...Dickens's decision to make Alfred learn the silk trade in order to earn a living in China. The wretched boy was, however, eventually sent to Australia."[87]

Catherine had no say in the plans her husband made for their sons. Even before the separation it had been his right to make such decisions, and after 1858 Catherine no longer existed in his eyes. He conveyed his sense of her nonexistence to Miss Coutts, who repeatedly encouraged him to communicate with Catherine in difficult times. "That figure is out of my life for evermore (except to darken it), and my desire is, Never to see it again," he told Miss Coutts in April 1860 (Pilgrim 9:230), as Charley prepared to sail to Hong Kong and Catherine braced herself for the "great trial" of parting with him, though "thankful" for his opportunity.[88] After Catherine learned, in February 1864, of Walter's death in Calcutta on New Year's Eve, Dickens again refused to communicate with her. "A page in my life which once had writing on it, has become absolutely blank," he assured Miss Coutts, and "it is not in my power to pretend that it has a solitary word upon it" (Pilgrim 10:356).

Before she became a widow, Catherine encountered Dickens only once, catching a glimpse of him at the theater one night and breaking down. As Jane Panton recalled the scene, Catherine had gone to the theater with her and her mother, Isabella Frith. When she saw Dickens with friends in the box opposite, she "could not bear it" and was escorted back to Gloucester Crescent by Mrs. Frith, who did what she could to comfort the weeping woman. "I thought I should never be able to leave

87. John Lehmann, *Ancestors and Friends* (London: Eyre & Spottiswoode, 1962), 165–66.

88. ALS Catherine Dickens to Angela Burdett Coutts, 17 March 1860, MA 1352, the Morgan Library & Museum, New York.

FIGURE 24. *Alfred Dickens in the 1860s, photograph, Charles Dickens Museum, London.*

her," Mrs. Frith later told her husband,[89] her sympathy for Catherine no doubt fueled by W. P. Frith's relationship with his mistress Mary Alford, who delivered the first of their seven children in 1856.

Dickens might deny the history of his marriage, imagining its pages "blank," but he could not erase Catherine's importance to their children. She was compelled to part with Frank, Alfred, and Plorn in turn, since Dickens arranged for them to leave England. Yet she spent time with each one before his departure and wrote to them frequently and at length until her death in 1879. Happiest when surrounded by her children and convinced that they did best in their "native air,"[90] Catherine was grieved by their exodus but had no way to prevent it. Frank left for India in December 1863. He and his mother said their good-byes two months before Catherine learned of the loss of her "poor beloved Walter," whom she had been "looking forward with so much joy to the prospect of seeing,"[91] and whose death made her partings with Alfred and Plorn all the more difficult. She hoped they would be happy in the colonies but missed them "most sadly,"[92] telling Plorn she "long[ed] to see [his] face again."[93]

As events proved, her longing went unfulfilled. She was reunited with Frank in March 1871, following his seven years in the Bengal Mounted Police, but after Alfred sailed for Australia in 1864 and Plorn in 1868, neither she nor her husband saw them again. Nonetheless, Catherine provided them with a sense of themselves—and herself—that differed from their father's, one in which they would always have value and an English home regardless of their successes or failures: because they were the children of an "always...loving mother," as she put it.[94] Sent to Australia by Dickens, who saw him as unfit for a career in England, Plorn found a letter from Catherine awaiting him in Melbourne and understood that, to his mother, his experiences were valuable by definition, because they were his. "I...shall expect that long account of [the voyage] you promised me," Catherine wrote in her first

89. Panton, *Leaves from a Life,* 143.

90. ALS Catherine Dickens to Angela Burdett Coutts, 8 March 1864, MA 1352, the Morgan Library & Museum, New York.

91. Ibid.

92. ALS Catherine Dickens to Plorn (Edward Bulwer Lytton) Dickens, 9 October 1868, D. Jacques Benoliel Collection of the Letters of Charles Dickens, 69-3374, Rare Book Department, Free Library of Philadelphia.

93. Catherine Dickens to Plorn Dickens, 6 May 1873, typescript of H1324 (ALS), Gimbel Collection, Beineke Rare Book and Manuscript Library, Yale University.

94. Catherine Dickens to Plorn Dickens, 11 August 1874, typescript, Charles Dickens Museum, London.

letter to Plorn in New South Wales. "The smallest details will of course be deeply interesting to me."[95] Dickens might complain that Plorn "seems to have been born without a groove," but Catherine sounded a very different note. She was "so proud of [her] darling handsome son Plorn," she told him in 1874—not because he had obtained one of those "first positions in the colony" urged on him by his father but simply because, judging from a photograph he sent her, he "seem[ed] to be very tall, and altogether much improved."[96] Catherine hoped he would be "prosperous" as well as "happy" yet would not think less of him if he were not.[97]

"DISCHARGED WITH A GOOD CHARACTER"

Catherine's twelve-year separation from Dickens was punctuated by departures and losses. Her grief over Walter's death was preceded by her mourning for her mother, who died in London on 5 August 1863 after an illness of several months. Mrs. Hogarth's death was closely followed by that of Elizabeth Dickens, who had been cared for in senility by the widow of Dickens's brother Alfred. In February 1870 Catherine wrote to her son Alfred, relating the "sad" end of George Hogarth. Sure of her son's "affectionate sympathy," Catherine described the loss of her "dear father," who, still working in his eighties, fell down a flight of stairs at the *Illustrated London News* office and died of his injuries after "linger[ing] on in great suffering" for "nearly three weeks."[98] Between the deaths of her parents, Catherine also lost a nephew and a brother-in-law, the infant son and husband of her sister Helen.

The 1860s were not simply a decade of losses, however. During her separation, Catherine found joy in the births of her grandchildren and her developing relationships with them. She would read to them on their visits from an oversized picture book she kept in her drawing room—*A Children's Summer* by Eleanor Vere Boyle, a celebration of play. Her griefs were thus counterbalanced with pleasures and consolations. While she "endeavour[ed] with God's help to submit to His will" in her "heavy trial[s],"[99] she was also grateful for her blessings. In the same letter

95. ALS Catherine Dickens to Plorn Dickens, 9 October 1868, D. Jacques Benoliel Collection of the Letters of Charles Dickens, 69-3374, Rare Book Department, Free Library of Philadelphia.

96. Catherine Dickens to Plorn Dickens, 11 August 1874, typescript, Charles Dickens Museum, London.

97. Catherine Dickens to Plorn Dickens, 16 December 1873, typescript, Charles Dickens Museum, London.

98. ALS Catherine Dickens to Alfred Dickens, 16 February 1870, MS 2563, by permission of the National Library of Australia, Canberra.

99. ALS Catherine Dickens to Angela Burdett Coutts, 8 March 1864, MA 1352, the Morgan Library & Museum, New York.

in which Catherine mourned Walter's death, she took comfort in the safe arrival of her second grandchild, "another fine little girl," and was "thankful to say" that Bessie was well.[100] After Plorn left for Melbourne and was "miss[ed]...most sadly" by his mother, Henry made a point of spending time with Catherine, taking her to the dress rehearsal of Mark Lemon's *Falstaff,* which she considered "a most excellent representation." Indeed, "Harry has been with me a good deal during the past week, and he has cheered me up," she told Plorn. So, too, had Charley's success at *All the Year Round,* where he replaced an ailing Wills as sub-editor, "a most capital thing for him," Catherine felt.[101]

At Gloucester Crescent, Catherine strengthened old ties while forming new friendships. Her life was much busier and happier than critics acknowledge. Far from reclusive, she equipped herself to entertain. Among her furnishings was a mahogany dining room set for twelve, and her glassware included a dozen champagne flutes engraved with her initials, for use on special occasions. As before her separation, Catherine hosted and attended dinner parties, received and paid calls, and engaged in a lively correspondence. "You will be glad to hear that I have got safely over my confinement," Catherine read in a letter from a new friend, the novelist Annie Thomas (Mrs. Pender Cudlip), in September 1869. "My son...is such a fine big boy & I am very proud of him already. We purpose having him christened in about a fortnight, as soon in fact as I can go to church with safety. Will you do us the kindness of being his godmother? I shall be so pleased if you will," Thomas urged.[102] "It will give me the greatest pleasure to be one of your guests on the 19th," Wilkie Collins wrote Catherine in November 1867, after she invited him to the anniversary dinner she hosted annually for Charley and Bessie.[103] "Will you favor us with your company to Dinner on Sunday next the 6th," vocalist Louisa Pyne asked in November 1864. "I hope to have the pleasure of your sister Mrs Roney's and your Papa's company also," she added.[104] "Have you an unoccupied evening

100. Ibid.

101. ALS Catherine Dickens to Plorn Dickens, 9 October 1868, D. Jacques Benoliel Collection of the Letters of Charles Dickens, 69-3374, Rare Book Department, Free Library of Philadelphia.

102. ALS Annie [Thomas] Cudlip to Catherine Dickens, 25 September 1869, MA 104, the Morgan Library & Museum, New York.

103. Wilkie Collins to Catherine Dickens, 11 November 1867, in *The Public Face of Wilkie Collins: The Collected Letters,* ed. William Baker, Andrew Gasson, Graham Law, and Paul Lewis, 4 vols. (London: Pickering & Chatto, 2005), 2:91.

104. ALS Louisa Pyne to Catherine Dickens, 2 November 1864, MA 104, the Morgan Library & Museum, New York.

either Thursday, Friday, or Saturday next? And would you like to devote it to seeing my play?" Collins inquired, "very anxious that [Catherine] should see" one of his productions, most likely his 1866 revival of *The Frozen Deep*. "If so, pray send me one line to say which evening you prefer and I will forward the necessary order for a box, immediately, to Gloucester Crescent."[105] "I was much disappointed to be engaged when dear Fanny asked me lately to spend a day with you," Catherine assured Mary Chester, referring to Mary's daughter Fanny Toms, in July 1865. "I write . . . to say how very sorry I am not to have called upon you before leaving town, which I do in a few days. . . . When I return in the middle of September, I shall take an early opportunity of going to see you."[106]

Catherine's friendship with Mary Chester, recorded in over a dozen letters she wrote in the 1860s and 1870s, developed after 1858 thanks to Mark Lemon, a lifelong friend of Mary's husband. Catherine's tie to the wife of Henry Ingram, editor of the *Illustrated London News,* may have formed in the same way. Indeed Catherine owed several new connections to Lemon and others at *Punch,* for whom Dickens's "arrogance" and "unforgivable conduct" toward his wife formed subjects of conversation at their weekly business dinners.[107] Among the magazine's writers and artists, several besides Thackeray invited Catherine to their homes and defended her at Dickens's expense. In November 1859 John Leech included her at a gathering with Shirley Brooks (Lemon's successor at *Punch*), critic E. M. Dallas, his wife, and Billy Russell, a *Times* correspondent. Sitting next to John Everett Millais at dinner, Catherine invited the artist's family to Gloucester Crescent. "Mrs. Dickens . . . desired her best remembrances to you," Millais told Effie, "and hopes you will call and bring the children to see her."[108]

Shirley Brooks dedicated his novel *Aspen Court* to Dickens in 1855, but after the separation Brooks became one of Catherine's strongest advocates. Blaming her husband for the marital breakdown, he described Catherine as a woman "discharged

105. ALS Wilkie Collins to Catherine Dickens, n.d., II.a.49, Congregational Library, London.

106. ALS Catherine Dickens to Mrs. Chester, 26 July 1865, D. Jacques Benoliel Collection of the Letters of Charles Dickens, 86-2743, Rare Book Department, Free Library of Philadelphia.

107. Diary of Henry Silver, quoted in Arthur A. Adrian, *Mark Lemon: First Editor of Punch* (London: Oxford University Press, 1966), 134. Silver "surreptitiously" took notes at *Punch* dinners, writing "under the table" (61).

108. John Everett Millais to Effie Millais, 18 November 1859, in *The Life and Letters of Sir John Everett Millais,* ed. John Guille Millais, 2 vols. (New York: Frederick A. Stokes, 1899), 1:350, 353.

with a good character"[109] and sent her tickets to his plays, comically warning her that he would "sit very near…in order to see that [she] applaud[ed] with all [her] might, and occasionally cr[ied] out that [she] never saw anything half so good."[110] Catherine met Brooks and his wife at dinners hosted by William and Mary Anne Hardman, whose father, James Radley, owned the Adelphi Hotel in Liverpool and considered himself "a very old friend" of Mrs. Dickens.[111] Hardman found Catherine "very agreeable," and he and Mary Anne called on the "much injured wife" at Gloucester Crescent.[112] Hardman's indignation at "the great Charles," who had "so shamefully separated" from his wife,[113] intensified when the novelist refused to communicate with her after Walter's death. "Poor Mrs. Charles Dickens is in great grief at the loss of her second son," he noted. "Her grief is much enhanced by the fact that her husband has not taken any notice of the event to her, either by letter or otherwise. If anything were wanting to sink Charles Dickens to the lowest depth of my esteem, *this* fills up the measure of his iniquity. As a writer, I admire him; as a man, I despise him."[114]

In letters from Gloucester Crescent, Catherine sometimes declined invitations because of her health or her travels. She was unable to visit Eliza Touchet and Anne Buckley, W. Harrison Ainsworth's relations, in December 1858, or "to see the Pictures" George Chester exhibited in the spring of 1869.[115] "Far from well," she could not "venture in the heat as far as Kensington" and the Chesters' before leaving for the coast in August 1865.[116] But more often than not, Catherine ventured out when asked, still a "game" companion. At the end of December 1862 she went to a "wild sort of supper-party" at the Hardmans', with Frederick Evans and the Orridges, among others, where they drank a "concoction of champagne cup and punch" and the gentlemen smoked in the dining room among the ladies; Catherine

109. Shirley Brooks, quoted in William Hardman, *The Letters and Memoirs of Sir William Hardman, 2nd ser., 1863–1865*, ed. S. M. Ellis (New York: George H. Doran, [1925]), 8.

110. ALS Shirley Brooks to Catherine Dickens, "Saturday" [n.d.], MA 104, the Morgan Library & Museum, New York.

111. Hardman, *Letters and Memoirs*, 8.

112. Hardman, *Letters and Memoirs*, 8; Hardman quoted in Ellis, *Hardman Papers*, 288.

113. Hardman, *Letters and Memoirs*, 8.

114. Ibid., 147–48.

115. ALS Catherine Dickens to Mrs. Chester, 3 April 1869, D. Jacques Benoliel Collection of the Letters of Charles Dickens, 86-2744, Rare Book Department, Free Library of Philadelphia.

116. ALS Catherine Dickens to Mrs. Chester, 26 July 1865, D. Jacques Benoliel Collection of the Letters of Charles Dickens, 86-2743, Rare Book Department, Free Library of Philadelphia.

remained until "a quarter past two."[117] At a party there the next May, Catherine met mountaineer Thomas Woodbine Hinchliff and heard her hosts sing from *Tancredi* and Brooks joke irreverently about John William Colenso, the bishop of Natal, at work among the Zulus.

Catherine met Annie Thomas through Brooks. Described by her son-in-law Major William Price Drury as "a close friend of Mrs. Charles Dickens, who held her undivided sympathy in the unhappy dissensions between that lady and her illustrious husband,"[118] Thomas was courted by W. S. Gilbert but married the Reverend Pender Hodge Cudlip in 1867, continuing to write novels as the wife of a country clergyman.[119] She published *Only Herself* with Chapman and Hall in 1869, shortly before the birth of Catherine's godson. Using her birth name for professional purposes, Thomas produced fiction that offended conservative reviewers, who had "hoped marriage might improve her moral tone, but [were] disappointed."[120] While *False Colours* (1865) centers on an unwed mother, her novels generally focus on marriage, the inequities that made wives into childlike dependents, and the transgressions of those who refused to conform. "So you see that my new novel *Only Herself* is just published by Chapman & Hall. I should like to hear your verdict on it,"[121] Thomas told Catherine, who described herself as "*very much* interested" in her friend's fiction.[122]

At Gloucester Crescent, Catherine learned to negotiate new terrain; her household, family structure, and immediate surroundings changed, along with her ways of getting from place to place. In her correspondence she thanked friends and acquaintances for invitations to their homes but also for "information about

117. William Hardman, *A Mid-Victorian Pepys: The Letters and Memoirs of Sir William Hardman,* ed. S. M. Ellis (New York: George H. Doran, [1923]), 229–30.

118. Lieutenant Colonel W. P. Drury, *In Many Parts: Memoirs of a Marine* (London: T. Fisher Unwin, 1926), 105.

119. "Her busy fiction pen was not to be stayed" by her marriage, publisher William Tinsley remarked in *Random Recollections of an Old Publisher,* 2 vols. (London: Simpkin, Marshall, Hamilton, Kent, 1900), 2:249.

120. "Thomas, Annie Hall," in *The Feminist Companion to Literature in England,* Virginia Blain, Patricia Clements, and Isobel Grundy, eds. (New Haven: Yale University Press, 1990), 1073.

121. ALS Annie [Thomas] Cudlip to Catherine Dickens, 25 September 1869, MA 104, the Morgan Library & Museum, New York.

122. ALS Catherine Dickens to Annie [Thomas] Cudlip, 27 July 1872, Fales MSS 40:15, Fales Library & Special Collections, New York University.

the omnibus" that would take her there now that she had no carriage.[123] Yet the continuities between her past and present life were also striking, since Catherine was generally perceived as the same person she had always been. Thus while her husband belittled and renounced her, his own surviving sister did not. Widowed in October 1861, Letitia Austin visited Catherine at Gloucester Crescent. The two women were on familiar terms in the 1860s, and Catherine wrote to Benjamin Webster in 1864 to get a box at the St. James Theatre for her "husband's sister, Mrs. H. Austin," who "had asked [her] to use [her] influence with [him]."[124]

Many old friends made a point of seeing Catherine after 1858, and Catherine, too, stayed in touch with writers, artists, and actors she had known during her years with Dickens. Taking up a popular hobby, she put together an album of *carte-de-visite* photographs in the 1860s, with dozens of the photos and some of the album pages personally inscribed to her. The album reflected her current friendships while giving her a reason to contact those she hadn't seen since leaving Tavistock House. Among the album's contributors were Tennyson, Cruikshank, Bulwer Lytton, Augustus Egg, Caroline Norton, and Harriet Beecher Stowe, as well as Wilkie Collins, Thackeray, and Brooks. "Your most faithful servant," Thackeray wrote on his *carte de visite;* "Your faithful friend," Brooks signed; and "friend forever," Hans Christian Andersen declared.[125] "How time flies!" Ainsworth wrote her, sending his photograph and giving her news of his daughters and the birth of his grandchildren.[126] "According to my promise I send you a photograph of my husband," actress Mary Ann Keeley wrote in March 1862, "and as soon as I have recovered my *beauty* I will go and be *took* by a first rate artist and forward you a specimen."[127]

Catherine also kept in touch with former servants after the separation. By writing repeatedly to Benjamin Webster in 1859 on behalf of Mrs. Gale, "in very poor circumstances," Catherine secured a stall position for her at the Adelphi.[128] After Webster hired the woman, Catherine sent her own thanks, describing a visit just

123. ALS Catherine Dickens to Mrs. Touchet, 23 December 1858, Fales Library & Special Collections, New York University.

124. ALS Catherine Dickens to Benjamin Webster, 29 February 1864, Adam Mills, Rare Books, Cambridge, transcription.

125. Phillips International Auctioneers catalog, 24 March 2000, 217–18.

126. ALS W. Harrison Ainsworth to Catherine Dickens, 8 February 1866, MA 104, the Morgan Library & Museum, New York.

127. ALS Mary Ann Keeley to Catherine Dickens, 9 March 1862, MA 104, the Morgan Library & Museum, New York.

128. ALS Catherine Dickens to Benjamin Webster, 27 February 1859, private collection.

paid to her by Mrs. Gale, "full of gratitude and joy at being engaged. . . . I want to see 'Still Waters,'" Catherine went on to tell him, "and shall be much obliged if you will kindly let me have a Box for Friday evening next."[129]

She remained a steady concert- and theatergoer and an avid reader in the 1860s, with music, drama, and popular literature among her foremost interests, as before. On her shelves at Gloucester Crescent were works by Dante, Scott, De Quincey, Hunt, and Carlyle, a four-volume edition of Poe, and an eight-volume edition of Thackeray. Gaskell, Collins, Jerrold, Ainsworth, Trollope, and Brooks were among the contemporary novelists represented, as were Lemon, Kingsley, and Meredith. Catherine owned a four-volume edition of Barrett Browning's poems as well as volumes of poetry by such writers as Pope, Cowper, Longfellow, Burns, Rogers, and Tennyson.[130]

Catherine read volumes of tragedies and dramatic scenes but preferred to see such works in performance. Requests for boxes "at Drury Lane," "at the Adelphi," and "at the St. James Theatre" run through her correspondence from the period.[131] "I beg to enclose you a box for next Saturday Evening," Dion Boucicault wrote from the Theatre Royal in February 1863, when *The Trial of Effie Deans* was running.[132] "I have much pleasure in placing a box at your disposal for the first performance of David Copperfield on Saturday next," Andrew Halliday told her in October 1869, referring to his adaptation, *Little Em'ly,* at the Olympic.[133]

Attending the stage adaptations of her husband's novels on opening nights, one way of marking her connection to him, Catherine read his fiction and journalism, and the work of his contributors, as they appeared weekly in *All the Year Round.* "It is a great pleasure to me to hear that you like the new story," Collins wrote her in April 1862, when *No Name* was running in serial. "I am trying hard to make it my best—and I hope I shall fasten a strong hold on your interest in the chapters that

129. ALS Catherine Dickens to Benjamin Webster, 7 March 1859, in Hale collection of Dickens and associates autograph letters, Mss. Gr. 155., Special Collections, University of Rhode Island Libraries.

130. Items in Catherine's library, her furniture, music, and works of art are listed in the catalog for the estate sale at 70 Gloucester Crescent on 18 December 1879. British Library, C.194.b.179.

131. ALS Catherine Dickens to Angela Burdett Coutts, 12 January 1859, Fales Library & Special Collections, New York University; ALS Catherine Dickens to Benjamin Webster, 30 July 1859, Charles Dickens Museum, London; ALS Catherine Dickens to Benjamin Webster, 29 February 1864, Adam Mills, Rare Books, Cambridge, transcription.

132. ALS Dion Boucicault to Catherine Dickens, 12 February 1863, MA 104, the Morgan Library & Museum, New York.

133. ALS Andrew Halliday to Catherine Dickens, 5 October 1869, MA 104, the Morgan Library & Museum, New York.

are to come."[134] Catherine also read the monthly *Cornhill,* to which Thackeray, its founding editor, had made her a free subscriber. "Mrs. Charles Dickens . . . has not received the 'Cornhill magazine' this month," she told its publishers in January 1870, "and as it has never missed coming to her she feels quite sure it is owing to a mistake. Mrs. C. Dickens is very glad to have this opportunity of expressing to Messrs. Smith, Elder how much obliged she is to them for their kindness in so regularly sending the Magazine, which she much appreciates."[135] In April 1864 Catherine asked Frederic Chapman, "Will you with your usual kindness to me send me my Husband's new periodical each month," anticipating the monthly publication of *Our Mutual Friend.*[136] Having read, as serials, the novels Dickens wrote after 1858, Catherine made a point of obtaining the volume editions as well. When she received her copy of *Great Expectations* from Chapman and Hall in 1861, she inscribed her name and address on the blank front page in the first volume. By 1879 she owned three complete editions of Dickens's *Works,* in twenty-four, twenty-one, and fifteen volumes, as well as *The Uncommercial Traveller* and *The Mystery of Edwin Drood.*

Despite her husband's refusals to acknowledge her, Catherine continued to identify herself as "Mrs. Charles Dickens" and to refer to Dickens as her husband, taking pride in his latest writings when she could not in the man himself. If she could no longer send Dickens's regards to correspondents, she could send them copies of his works, his novels standing in for their author. "Very many thanks for the Cartes de Visite," she wrote photographer John Watkins in 1862. "I shall be most happy to sit again as you kindly wish, whenever it will be agreeable to you for me to do so. I have much pleasure in sending you one of my husband's works."[137]

After the separation Catherine exchanged letters with Dickens on three occasions: in August 1863, when Mrs. Hogarth died and Catherine sought information from him about the family grave at Kensal Green; in June 1865, when Dickens, Ellen, and Mrs. Ternan were in a railway crash at Staplehurst, Kent, and Catherine wrote to ask about his well-being; and in November 1867, when she wished her

134. ALS Wilkie Collins to Catherine Dickens, 7 April 1862, MA 104, the Morgan Library & Museum, New York.

135. ALS Catherine Dickens to Messrs. Smith, Elder, 7 January 1870, Cornhill Magazine Collection, Harry Ransom Humanities Research Center, University of Texas at Austin.

136. ALS Catherine Dickens to Frederic Chapman, 15 March 1864, MA 104, the Morgan Library & Museum, New York.

137. ALS Catherine Dickens to Mr. Watkins, 12 November 1862, D. Jacques Benoliel Collection of the Letters of Charles Dickens, 87-1902, Rare Book Department, Free Library of Philadelphia.

husband success before his departure for a second American tour. In Dickens's brief replies Catherine may have detected signs of some relenting toward her. Writing to "Dear Catherine" in 1863, Dickens referred to their 1842 American tour as *his* trip ("when I went to America") rather than theirs, offered no word of consolation on her mother's death, and curtly signed his letter "Charles Dickens" (Pilgrim 10:280). Thanking "Dear Catherine" for her next letter two years later, he told her that he had been "shaken" by working "among the dead and dying" at Staplehurst and added "affectionately" before his name (Pilgrim 11:51). Writing to "My Dear Catherine" in 1867, he "accept[ed] and reciprocate[d]" her "good wishes" and signed his letter "Affectionately Yours." Yet the self-righteous tone of his final letter, like its insistent personal pronouns, qualified whatever seemed reciprocal about it. "Severely hard work lies before me," he told her, "but that is not a new thing in my life, and I am content to go my way and do it" (Pilgrim 11:472). If Catherine harbored any illusions that Dickens might want his way to meet hers, they would be dispelled in 1870, when she learned the details of his will.

INTERLUDE III
"Forget Me Not"
CATHERINE AND HELEN

Miss Helen Hogarth (Teacher of Singing) begs to inform her pupils and the
public that she has returned to town for the season and has removed from
Weymouth Street to No. 71 Great Russell Street, Bloomsbury Square.
—*Musical World,* 22 December 1860

"MISS HELEN HOGARTH (TEACHER OF SINGING)"
Writing to "dear Miss Hogarth" in July 1856, on Helen's twenty-third birthday, the contralto Charlotte Dolby wished Catherine's youngest sister "many, very many years of happiness," attaching her letter to a gift from Foster's, the dressmaker's, with "much love." "Will you do me the favor to accept the accompanying head dress?" she asked. "I thought blue 'forget me nots' very suitable for your wear . . . hav[ing] observed that blue is your favorite color."[1] Dolby's gift proved well suited to Helen, less because of its color than its floral motif. Crowned with forget-me-nots, Helen defended the sister whom Dickens slighted and sought to forget from 1858 onward, her thoughtful remembrance of Catherine a foil to his hurtful amnesia.

For Catherine, living at Gloucester Crescent "as if sole and unmarried," Helen became as close a companion as Mary had been when "the girls Hogarth" first adapted to London life in the early 1830s. Through the bequests she specified in her will, Catherine made the tie between Mary and Helen her theme, the connection

1. ALS Charlotte Dolby to Helen Hogarth, 5 July 1856, ENG MS 725/48, Reproduced by courtesy of the University Librarian and Director, The John Rylands University Library, University of Manchester.

she perceived between them less a matter of physical resemblance or shared child-hood experience than one of sisterly solidarity. Born fourteen years after Mary, Helen and her twin brother, Edward, were only three years old when Mary came to Catherine's aid in the first crisis of her married life—the difficult weeks that followed Charley's birth in January 1837, during which Mary "never suffered so much sorrow for any one or any thing before."[2] Helen was too young to comfort Catherine when Mary died that May. But she would devote herself to her eldest sister two decades later in what proved as great a trial: Catherine's loss of Dickens, through estrangement rather than death. In 1858 Catherine took some comfort in Georgina's decision to remain with the children at Tavistock House, although Georgina's misdirected duty to Dickens was a source of regret among their family members, who felt that it "weaken[ed] the defence of her sister."[3] Helen, however, provided the defense that Georgina would not, contesting Dickens's claims about Catherine, voicing her disapproval of his tie to Ellen Ternan, taking part in consultations with Catherine's solicitor, and earning the antipathy of her brother-in-law as the "little serpent" in league with her "wicked" mother (Pilgrim 8:623).

A toddler when Catherine married, Helen played a much more peripheral role among the Dickenses than Georgina did. Although Helen lived at Tavistock House in 1855 and 1856, she did so only briefly, while the Dickenses were abroad and the Hogarths were house-sitting, and she was never a member of her sister's household. When Catherine, pregnant with Sydney, was prohibited from doing so, fourteen-year-old Helen helped her mother care for Charley, who was recuperating from scarlet fever at their home; at fifteen Helen was included in Augustus Dickens's wedding party, signing as one of the witnesses to his marriage with Harriet Lovell. In her teens and early twenties she accompanied Catherine and the other Hogarth women to hear Dickens speak at public events—the 1849 Theatrical Fund dinner, for example—and participated in some of the amateur theatricals he managed. When, in July 1857, she performed as Mrs. Steventon in *The Frozen Deep* alongside Georgina and their nieces at the Gallery of Illustration, she was mistaken by Queen Victoria for Dickens's third daughter. Working with Dickens on other performances to benefit the Jerrold Fund, Helen helped organize the June 1857

2. ALS Mary Hogarth to Mary Scott Hogarth, 26 January 1837, D. Jacques Benoliel Collection of the Letters of Charles Dickens, 83-1842, Rare Book Department, Free Library of Philadelphia.

3. George Hogarth, statement drafted by George Smith, 27 May 1858, Ouvry Papers, 25.4, Charles Dickens Museum, London; Helen Thomson to Mrs. Stark, [30] August 1858, in K. J. Fielding, "Charles Dickens and His Wife," *Études Anglaises* 8, no. 3 (1955): 215, reprinted in Pilgrim 8:747.

concert at St. Martin's Hall, earning his praise ("It is all excellent" [Pilgrim 8:354]) for her efforts.

Yet Helen was the only Hogarth sister "unclaimed" by Dickens, and she felt neither the reverence for nor the debt to him that Georgina did. Though she performed under his theatrical management and read his works as they appeared, she was not the witness to his genius that her sisters were and, unlike Georgina, was never his financial dependent. Trained as a vocalist, she had taken on her own pupils by the winter of 1858 and was a professional musician and wage earner when Catherine separated from her husband. Helen was then twenty-five, an age at which Catherine had already been married for five years and had delivered four children. A single working woman, the youngest Hogarth sister was busy establishing herself as a "professor of music and singing," with advertisements running in *Musical World* from the late 1850s onward. Though still living with her parents and Edward, she was relatively autonomous and not easily intimidated or cowed. When Dickens turned against Catherine, Helen's allegiance was clear: she would say what her more reserved, wronged sister would not. She conceded to Dickens's demand for her signed retraction of remarks allegedly made about him as a pragmatic measure, only "after considerable discussion," fully doubting Dickens's claims in the statement she signed.[4] With her mother, Frederick Evans, and Mark Lemon, Helen became one of the proscribed four to whom Catherine's children were not allowed to speak by their father, and into the 1860s Dickens declined invitations on the grounds that he could "not be a guest at any house where Mrs. Hogarth's youngest daughter [was] received in the same capacity" (Pilgrim 9:214).

As suggested by Dickens's regrets—offered in this case to Albert Smith—Helen's social standing and connections remained largely unaltered by his antagonism toward her. Helen lost contact with Georgina for a dozen years because of the separation, as did Catherine, and until Dickens's death, her affection for Plorn was conveyed to him only indirectly, through his mother. Yet Helen's tie to Catherine grew much stronger as a result of Dickens's animosity, developing into a partnership in which Catherine's intimacy with Mary was recreated, though in subdued and mature form.

As teenagers the two eldest Hogarth girls had given each other an alternative to their sometimes competitive relationships with female friends and their dealings with patronizing male admirers. With their Scottish cousin, they used humor and parody to mock male presumption and set themselves above female rivals, playfully

4. George Smith, itemized bill, Ouvry Papers, 25.15, Charles Dickens Museum, London; Frederic Ouvry and Charles Dickens, statement signed by Mrs. Hogarth and Helen (draft), Ouvry Papers, 25.6, Charles Dickens Museum, London.

assuming powers and privileges they would lose as married women. Returning to "single" life in 1858, Catherine felt "hardly...used" by her husband, but she sought to overcome bitter memories and feelings with Christian resignation—to become "contented if not...happy," as she put it.[5] Her camaraderie with Helen offered her another, more fulfilling way to improve her "sad" position and ease her "keen pain."[6] The keynote of their friendship was not irreverence and humor, as it was for Catherine and Mary, but vocal music; its ability to harmonize and inspire muted Catherine's bitterness, while its performance renewed her sense of community and gave her joy.

"COME, LET US SING"

As a teacher and performer, Helen had a much more modest career than her famous brother-in-law's but one that Catherine could help to manage and promote as she hadn't been able to do for Dickens as his "worser half" (Pilgrim 1:478). While Helen was busy with her students or, after 1864, with her daughter May, Catherine sought audience members and musicians for the concerts her sister organized or in which she sang. "Would you like to go to my sister Mrs. Roney's concert tomorrow?" Catherine asked friends in April 1868, offering to send them tickets and inviting them to a supper to follow at her own home.[7] "I was much grieved to hear from the Howells, only the other day, of your husband's illness," Catherine wrote Angelique Graham, wife of the singer Selwyn Graham, in the early 1870s. "I trust however he is much better, and will be able to sing for my sister Helen...on the 20th next. She begs if he can do so, to let her know at once what he intends to sing, and if he will join in a trio. Please send words of song."[8]

Although Catherine's assistance was informal, Helen's concerts were cooperative ventures. Recalling the "petites concerts" of the Thomsons and Hogarths when Catherine was a girl,[9] the performances on which she and Helen collaborated

5. ALS Catherine Dickens to Angela Burdett Coutts, 19 May 1858, MA 1352, the Morgan Library & Museum, New York; Catherine Dickens to Helen Thomson, quoted in Helen Thomson to Mrs. Stark, [30] August 1858, reprinted in Pilgrim 8:749.

6. Catherine Dickens to Helen Thomson, quoted in Helen Thomson to Mrs. Stark, [30] August 1858, reprinted in Pilgrim 8:749.

7. ALS Catherine Dickens to Mrs. Boyes, 19 April [1868], Charles Dickens Museum, London.

8. ALS Catherine Dickens to Angelique Graham, n.d. [June 1871–September 1873], Cambridge University Library, Add. 9184 (no. 17).

9. George Thomson to Katherine Thomson, 13 August 1819, MS 7198, ff. 29–30, National Library of Scotland.

extended their family tradition. Those with whom Helen sang and Catherine corresponded on her sister's behalf performed a wide range of vocal music, in English, Italian, and German—ballads and serenatas, patriotic pieces and songs from *Faust*. In May 1873, at the last of several annual concerts that Catherine helped Helen organize at the Queen's Concert Rooms, Hanover Square, their friend Selwyn Graham sang Molique's "Soft Blue Eyes," Blangini's duet "Per valli per boschi" with Edith Holman-Andrews, and Balfe's trio "Through the World" with Katherine Poyntz and George Weidge. Catherine's neighbor at 67 Gloucester Crescent, Elizabeth Philp, sang "Restored," Philp's own composition.[10] Combining and recombining their voices in a series of solos, duets, and trios, the group provided Catherine with a more polyphonic model of interaction and performance than had her marriage, dominated as it was by Dickens's authorship and masterful expressions. As George Hogarth noted, vocal music was designed "for one voice or for many" and could be both "heterogenous" and beautiful.[11]

Helen's profession and musical engagements helped Catherine redefine and expand her community at Gloucester Crescent, as she was befriended and drawn out by a host of singers and instrumentalists, many of whom lived nearby: the celebrated vocalists W. H. and Georgina Weiss; their daughter Angelique and son-in-law Selwyn Graham; Elizabeth Philp, a "professor of singing" like Helen; Edward Howell, a violoncellist; and pianist Linda Scates (Mrs. Dutton Cook), Catherine's close friend and neighbor, who lived at 69 Gloucester Crescent with her mother, Mary Ann, and her father, Joseph, a violinist and teacher, and later with her husband, a writer. Both Helen and Linda were elected "Female Associates" of the Philharmonic Society in November 1877, three years after Linda married. With Charley, Bessie, and Helen, Catherine had been among Linda's wedding guests. Catherine spent much of her time in the 1860s and 1870s with her sister, her neighbors, and the members of their musical circle, hosting and attending dinners, participating in impromptu concerts, and discussing vocal and instrumental compositions. Catherine corresponded with Georgina Weiss about marriages and births but also about fine performances—of "Mozart's 'Mass'" and Mendelssohn's "Come, Let Us Sing," for example[12]—her knowledge of the subject reflected in her library, which included two volumes of Beethoven's sonatas, a volume of Chopin's mazurkas, and various collections of operas.

10. The concert was praised in a *Musical World* review, 31 May 1873, 361–62.

11. George Hogarth, *The Philharmonic Society of London* (London: Bradbury and Evans, 1862), 74, 33.

12. ALS Catherine Dickens to Georgina Weiss, n.d. [July 1858–June 1871], Cambridge University Library, Add. 9178 (no. 209).

In 1861 Helen was living at 71 Great Russell Street, Bloomsbury, with her parents, Edward, and their servant Alice Snow. The Hogarths moved to 1 Bloomsbury Square the next year. In her late twenties, Helen found an admirer in the Hungarian-born tenor and composer Alexander Reichardt; eight years her senior, he dedicated his song "Memory" to her. But in 1864, after the period of mourning for her mother ended, Helen married Richard Cusack Roney, the twenty-five-year-old son of barrister James Edward Roney, then deceased, who had lived in Demerara, British Guiana, since the late 1830s. Like his father, Richard Roney began his career in journalism; he was editor of the *China Newsletter* in the mid-1860s. Helen may have met her husband through Dickens. The novelist had shared bachelor lodgings in London with James Roney, a *Morning Chronicle* reporter for a time, and the Dickenses hosted him at Doughty Street in 1838, shortly before he emigrated to the West Indies, and again at Tavistock House in 1856, when he returned for a brief visit after his wife, Matilda, died in London.

On 8 August 1864 Helen and Richard Roney were married at Christ Church, Herne Bay. Catherine knew the seaside town, having spent five weeks there the previous summer, most likely with Helen and their father, following Mrs. Hogarth's death. Catherine and Edward served as the witnesses at Helen's wedding, soon after which the couple settled at 10 Gloucester Crescent, directly across the street from Catherine. Thus instead of dividing Helen from her eldest sister, her marriage brought them into closer proximity. To Catherine's delight, Helen gave birth to a daughter, May Georgina, on 11 April 1865; a second child, a son, died in infancy.

Neither marriage nor motherhood kept Helen from her profession. Two weeks before May's birth, she was making arrangements for a concert in which both violinist Joseph Joachim and tenor John Sims Reeves would perform and editing the program to suit their wishes, the tenor anxious that she move his first piece and the violinist concerned that she place his second properly, since "Spohr will not do to[o] late in the evening, charming as his compositions are." Declaring himself eager to meet Helen's husband, Joachim looked forward to introducing Helen to his wife, the contralto Amalie Schneeweiss, whom he would "fetch" from Paris at the end of April.[13]

Unlike Amalie, who gave up her promising operatic career and put off her concert hall performances to raise her children, Helen had no choice but to remain a working mother. By 1866 Richard Roney had developed Bright's disease, the kidney ailment to which his mother had succumbed ten years earlier. He died from the

13. ALS John Sims Reeves to Helen Roney, 29 March 1865, MA 104, the Morgan Library & Museum, New York; ALS Joseph Joachim to Helen Roney, 21 March [1865], MA 104, the Morgan Library & Museum, New York.

malady in May 1868, less than four years after marrying Helen, leaving her a widow of thirty-five with a young child to support. His death at 10 Gloucester Crescent was followed in February 1870 by that of George Hogarth, attended by Helen and Catherine through his last three weeks. In June of that year Catherine, too, was widowed. "Feel[ing] so much" for each other, the sisters were united by their common losses and "great trial[s]"[14]—the deaths of their parents, of children, and of their husbands. Yet their circumstances differed markedly. Although Catherine's annuity was reduced by more than half with Dickens's death, she was guaranteed enough income to retain her middle-class respectability and remain in her home.[15] Helen had no such guarantee as she made her way in the world, supporting herself and her five-year-old daughter by means of her talents and profession.

MRS. DICKENS, MRS. RONEY, MISS HOGARTH

Within a year of their father's death, Helen moved from Gloucester Crescent to 6 Chalcot Terrace, several blocks west. The change was likely an attempt to economize. Catherine's letters from the period suggest that the move made little difference in the time the sisters spent together. "I saw my sister Helen last night, and she asked me if I would write to you for her this morning," Catherine told Angelique Graham after Helen's relocation. "She asked me to say that she hopes you, and Mr. Graham, will spend this evening with her. I shall be there, and shall have much pleasure in meeting you."[16] Like Catherine at Gloucester Crescent, Helen employed two servants at Chalcot Terrace, Elizabeth and Margaret Phillips, the first May's nurse and the second their cook. But by the summer of 1873 Helen could no longer afford a staff of two. Struggling financially, she secured a teaching position at the Ladies' College in Cheltenham, Gloucestershire, and left London. Though Catherine hoped her sister would flourish, she badly missed her companion. She wrote to Plorn in November of her mixed emotions. "I think I told you in my last letter that I was going to Cheltenham to visit my sister Helen who is settled down there," she reminded him.

14. ALS Helen Roney to Matilda Butler, "Sunday" [9 December 1877], Charles Dickens Museum, London.

15. Some of Catherine's children may have supplemented her annuity after Dickens's death or intended to do so. "I imagine she has not been left much," Shirley Brooks noted in July 1870, "but young C. D. says she shall receive the same as before." Diary of Shirley Brooks, 11 July 1870, the Morgan Library & Museum, New York; transcription kindly provided by Patrick Leary. See also chapter 8.

16. ALS Catherine Dickens to Angelique Graham, n.d. [June 1871–September 1873], Cambridge University Library, Add. 9184 (no. 19).

I remained there for three weeks and was very pleased to be with her again. I miss her so very much here.

However it would be selfish in me to wish her back to the anxious life she had latterly in London, as her position in Cheltenham is an excellent one, both at the Ladies' College, and also she teaches at two large schools and has private pupils as well. She has a pretty, comfortable house in the pleasantest part of the town.

She begged me, when writing to you, to give you her best love. Little May too often speaks of "Cousin Plorn."[17]

Luckily for Catherine, a much less formidable distance divided her from Helen than it did from Plorn. Although they lived in different counties from September 1873 onward, the sisters exchanged two- or three-week visits several times a year. After two weeks with Charley and his family at Gad's Hill at the end of 1873, Catherine expected her sister and niece "to pay [her] a visit of a fortnight,"[18] a pattern that was repeated annually. "I go to Gad's Hill on Xmas Eve as usual, and remain there until the 7th January. When I return I expect Helen and your little cousin May to stay with me," Catherine told Plorn in her December 1874 letter.[19] Catherine always spent October in Cheltenham, and there were spring and summer reunions as well. "I have had a visit from my sister Helen which I enjoyed greatly," Catherine told Alfred's wife, Jessie, in May 1876. "Helen always wishes me to give her love to you and dear Alfred when I write so always take it for granted dear."[20] "I am enjoying my visit to Mrs. Roney," Catherine told her former housemaid Matilda (Mrs. William Butler) in October 1876, a few days after Matilda's wedding, sending "very sincere congratulations, and best good wishes" from Helen's home at 13A Promenade. "She and May are well. They desire to be most kindly remembered to you. I am going to bring their teapot for you."[21] "We shall be in Gloucester Crescent about the 24th," Helen told Matilda on 5 August 1877, anticipating another stay

17. Catherine Dickens to Plorn (Edward Bulwer Lytton) Dickens, 18 November 1873, typescript, Charles Dickens Museum, London.

18. Catherine Dickens to Plorn Dickens, 16 December 1873, typescript, Charles Dickens Museum, London.

19. Catherine Dickens to Plorn Dickens, 11 December 1874, typescript, Charles Dickens Museum, London.

20. ALS Catherine Dickens to Jessie Dickens, 17 May 1876, MS 2563, by permission of the National Library of Australia, Canberra.

21. ALS Catherine Dickens to Matilda Butler, 17 October 1876, Charles Dickens Museum, London.

with Catherine. "We hope to be able to pay you a visit when in London."[22] "I am enjoying my visit to Mrs. Roney, and the weather is now lovely," Catherine wrote Matilda from Cheltenham in October 1877. "Mrs. Roney is out and does not know I am writing, or I am sure she would wish to be kindly remembered to you. May is at home and asks me to give you her love, and a kiss to the dear little baby."[23]

Catherine's continued intimacy with Helen, living in Cheltenham, formed a telling contrast with her more distant relations with Georgina, living in London like herself. After Dickens's death, Catherine and Georgina made a point of seeing each other, and by the time Catherine was dying in 1879, Georgina was a frequent visitor at Gloucester Crescent. Yet their relationship never regained the warmth that had characterized it before the separation.

At intervals in the 1870s, the three surviving Hogarth sisters came together, usually at Catherine's home. When G. W. Rusden, Plorn and Alfred's Australian mentor, visited London in April 1874, for example, Helen traveled from Cheltenham to meet him, dining at Gloucester Crescent with Rusden, Georgina, Mamie, and Henry on the thirteenth. Yet such reunions only underscored what family members already knew: that the Hogarth sisterhood had evolved into two distinct pairs, with Catherine and Helen on the one hand and Georgina and Mamie on the other. Mamie described Georgina as "the aunt *par excellence* . . . the truest, best and dearest friend, companion and counsellor . . . 'The best and truest friend man ever had,'"[24] this last phrase drawn from Dickens's description of Georgina in his will. For their part, Helen claimed primacy with her eldest sister, as Catherine did with her youngest; Helen considered herself "the first" with Catherine, who left her "favourite" objects to her favorite sister in her own last will and testament.[25]

By quoting her father's will in praising Georgina, Mamie suggested that the allegiances and divisions among the Hogarth women and herself were a legacy from Dickens, influencing them from beyond the grave. Yet the dynamics among the foursome had as much to do with their own intrinsic ties, values, and experiences as they did with their histories with Charles Dickens. Although Catherine had become a wife when Helen was a toddler, the two were drawn together as daughters, sisters, and mothers—not simply as women defined in relation to and estranged from the

22. ALS Helen Roney to Matilda Butler, 5 August 1877, Charles Dickens Museum, London.

23. ALS Catherine Dickens to Matilda Butler, 1 October 1877, Charles Dickens Museum, London.

24. Mamie Dickens, *My Father as I Recall Him* (New York: E. P. Dutton, 1898), 10–11.

25. ALS Helen Roney to Plorn Dickens, 13 June 1880, typescript, Charles Dickens Museum, London; Catherine Dickens, Last Will and Testament, 1878.

novelist. Their interest in and warmth toward Matilda Butler make that clear. Not only was Matilda, like Helen, faithful to Catherine, sending "kind remembrance[s]" to Gloucester Crescent after leaving it.[26] She was a mother like Catherine and Helen and, as both had been, a grieving one. "May sends you her love," Helen told Matilda in August 1877, and "is very anxious to see 'Tillie's' baby."[27] "I am knitting some little shoes for the baby," Catherine wrote Matilda a few days later, and she sent some "little warm vests" for the "dear baby" in October, hoping that he was "quite well again" and that his mother had lost her "troublesome cough."[28] When the baby died in December, Catherine quickly responded to the "sad news." "I well know how useless it is to speak of resignation or consolation at such a time," she told her friend, alluding to the deaths among her own children, "but I pray that God will support and comfort you."[29] "I have this morning heard from Mrs. Dickens of your *great trial*," Helen wrote soon afterward, likening Matilda's grief to her own. "I lost my little boy under similar circumstances, as you know—they are both, poor little dears, better off, than to live as *invalids* in this world. That thought, dear Matilda, must console you, but it *is a bitter trial* to lose a child."[30]

"PROPERTY OF MRS. HELEN RONEY, LATE HOGARTH"

To the extent that the Hogarth sisters formed a trio after Dickens's death, they did so by means of "little May," a bridge of sorts among them. When Mrs. Hogarth died in 1863, Georgina did not join her family at the Kensal Green cemetery but was instead at Gad's Hill, preparing to receive the de la Rues. Because George Hogarth died, too, during Dickens's lifetime, Georgina grieved for him apart from her sisters. In February 1870 she noted to Annie Fields that her "poor old Father died on the 12th," but she hadn't seen him at Helen's in his last weeks or met with her fellow mourners.[31] Although Helen moved to Cheltenham only after Dickens's death, Georgina never accompanied Catherine there. But she hosted May in London. In

26. ALS Catherine Dickens to Matilda Butler, 19 May 1877, Charles Dickens Museum, London.

27. ALS Helen Roney to Matilda Butler, 5 August [1877], Charles Dickens Museum, London.

28. ALS Catherine Dickens to Matilda Butler, 10 August and 1 October 1877, Charles Dickens Museum, London.

29. ALS Catherine Dickens to Matilda Butler, 5 December [1877], Charles Dickens Museum, London.

30. ALS Helen Roney to Matilda Butler, "Sunday" [9 December 1877], Charles Dickens Museum, London.

31. ALS Georgina Hogarth to Annie Fields, 25 February 1870, FI 2780, Huntington Library.

December 1874 Helen's daughter, then nine years old, spent Christmas week with Georgina, who found her young niece "a good and considerate child."[32] When Helen lay dying of a "lingering" illness in temporary lodgings in Liverpool, where she had fallen ill while traveling with her daughter in November 1890, Georgina joined May for what proved to be Helen's final three weeks, and was "a good deal tired and shaken by the...attendance."[33] Helen had been dead for two years and Catherine for fourteen when May married W. H. Leon in London on 30 January 1893. But Georgina, with Charley Dickens, served as witnesses to the union, as did two of William Leon's relations.

Georgina's presence at Helen's death and at May's wedding points to the willingness of Dickens's heirs to question and rework his bequests, both emotional and monetary. So, too, does the gift Helen received from her nieces and nephews after Catherine's death. When, in 1880, the income from Catherine's trust reverted to her surviving children under the terms of Dickens's will, they made a point of giving £75 to Helen, although their father had prohibited them from having any contact with their youngest aunt. "Thank you so much for your share of it," Helen wrote Plorn in June 1880. "This money you will be glad to hear, is now a great relief to my mind, and it will also make you very happy to think, could she know it, how repaid your dear mother would be at the kind and generous thought of you all for me. Dear Mamie too, made me a present at Xmas."[34] At May's wedding, Georgina could be seen to offer her own reparations to Helen and Catherine by ensuring that a Hogarth was present at the event. The Hogarth family and its values were important to May, who married a vocal artist and worked as one herself, performing with W. H. Leon, a baritone, in the D'Oyly Carte Opera Company. "She is on the stage," Georgina wrote to Anne Cornelius in 1890, and "very fond of her profession."[35] May appeared as Ruth in *Ruddigore* (1887), as Casilda in *The Gondoliers* (1890 and 1892), as Leila and Fleta in *Iolanthe* (1897), and as Mrs. Partlett in *The Sorcerer* (1897). She probably met her future husband when he joined the company in 1890, singing alongside her in *The Gondoliers.*

32. ALS Georgina Hogarth to Annie Fields, 24 December 1874, FI 2725, Huntington Library, quoted in Arthur A. Adrian, *Georgina Hogarth and the Dickens Circle* (Oxford: Oxford University Press, 1957), 209. Adrian misdates this letter 23 December.

33. ALS Georgina Hogarth to Anne Cornelius, 8 December 1890, HM 28202, Huntington Library.

34. Helen Roney to Plorn Dickens, 13 June 1880, typescript, Charles Dickens Museum, London.

35. ALS Georgina Hogarth to Anne Cornelius, 8 December 1890, HM 28202, Huntington Library.

May drops from sight after 1901, widowed that December, when Leon died of bronchial pneumonia; Powis Pinder replaced him as Lord Mountararat in *Iolanthe*. At the time, the childless couple had been living in Clapham, at 17 Elmhurst Mansion, with a fifteen-year-old maid-of-all-work. Though May's thoughts on her family history are unwritten, we can be guided in speculating about them by our knowledge of her possessions and their fate.

By the terms of Catherine's will, May inherited her aunt Kate's music box and gold brooch "with her grandfather and grandmother's hair in front and her mother's portrait at the back."[36] At her mother's death, May came into possession of a second portrait, with a higher market value—the chalk drawing Samuel Laurence made of Catherine in 1838, for £8.8, the companion piece to Laurence's drawing of Dickens. First displayed at Doughty Street, the portrait was not among the artworks catalogued at Gad's Hill after Dickens's death or mentioned by Catherine in her will. But the label affixed to the drawing's reverse side, which identifies the work as "The property of Mrs. Helen Roney, late Hogarth," reveals that Helen owned it, undoubtedly a gift from Catherine after the separation.[37]

Within a year of Helen's death, May sold the drawing to Horace Pym, a Dickens admirer and friend of Georgina Hogarth. Pym almost certainly approached May to make an offer for it, having purchased Laurence's companion portrait of Dickens several years earlier. While May's decision to sell the drawing might seem to suggest that she placed less value on her tie to Catherine than Catherine placed on her tie to May, it was more likely a sign of her financial difficulties in the 1890s, troubles shared by her mother and her aunt Georgina, who eventually took to marketing her own cherished belongings—selling the manuscript of Dickens's *Cricket on the Hearth* to Walter Spencer, for example, rather than leaving it to Henry Dickens or the British Museum, as she had planned.[38] Helen made similar use of Dickens's autograph writings toward the end of her life, selling to journalist Joseph Hatton at least one of the letters her father had received from the novelist.

May's feelings about Catherine are perhaps most clearly conveyed not by her sale of Laurence's drawing but by a portrait she may have produced herself—a photographic image of Catherine, hand tinted and partly traced over in ink, mounted on cardboard, and cut out like a paper doll. Catalogued as a "family memento" in the Gimbel Collection at Yale, it is inscribed on the back, where "Aunt Kate" is faintly

36. Catherine Dickens, Last Will and Testament, 1878.

37. Andrew Xavier discusses the Laurence portraits and their provenance in "Charles and Catherine Dickens: Two Fine Portraits by Samuel Laurence," *Dickensian* 92 (Summer 1996): 85–90. They are exhibited at the Charles Dickens Museum, London.

38. Adrian, *Georgina Hogarth and the Dickens Circle*, 263.

FIGURE 25. *"Aunt Kate," cutout collotype print, mounted and shaded with brush and ink, H1849, Gimbel Collection, Beineke Rare Book and Manuscript Library, Yale University.*

written in pencil (fig. 25).[39] There were other family members who considered Catherine their "Aunt Kate" and who might have constructed this image—most

39. John B. Podeschi, "H1849 'Aunt Kate,'" in *Dickens and Dickensiana: A Catalogue of the Richard Gimbel Collection in the Yale University Library* (New Haven: Yale University Library, 1980), 527.

plausibly Florence, Maria, and Katherine Dickens, Alfred and Helen's daughters, who lived in London and whom Catherine may have visited at North London Collegiate. But May Roney is the only one of Catherine's nieces and nephews whom she mentions in her will, and their daily contact when May was very young, their extended visits with each other after 1873, and their time spent together when Helen was working make May the most likely artist. If so, she would seem to have been her mother's daughter in her sympathies and vision, since "Aunt Kate" makes a personal and unique image of Catherine out of a mechanically produced one. Its hand coloring and drawing give the figure a sentimental hue and its cut-out shape and dimensions an uncanny reality that representations of Catherine too often lack.

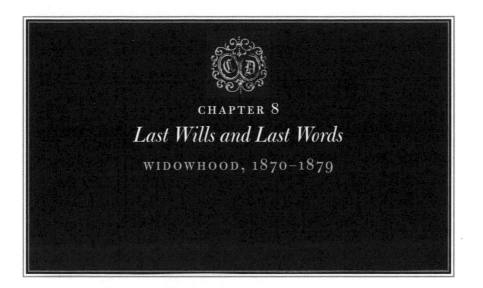

CHAPTER 8

Last Wills and Last Words

WIDOWHOOD, 1870–1879

> *Deepest regret at the sad news of Charles Dickens's death.*
> — Queen Victoria, telegram to Catherine Dickens, June 1870

"THE LAST PROOF OF AFFECTION"

In 1870, the year of Dickens's death, England's most famous widow was Queen Victoria, the ever-grieving "Widow at Windsor." Victoria's beloved Prince Albert had died of typhoid fever in 1861, at the age of forty-two. After Albert's death the queen entered a prolonged mourning period that extended well beyond the conventional limits set for a widow's bereavement in the Victorian age.[1] Not until 1866, after a four-year absence, did Victoria agree to attend the opening of Parliament and exchange her widow's weeds for her robes of state. And even then she remained silent, having arranged for the Lord Chancellor to read her speech. As early as 1863, many of her subjects judged her self-imposed withdrawal from public life to be excessive and resented her willingness to abandon her political duties to indulge in her womanly grief. Public opinion was reflected, for example, in a poster that appeared outside Buckingham Palace in March 1864, announcing that "these commanding premises [were] to be let or sold, in consequence of the late occupant's declining business."[2]

---

1. Victorian conduct manuals advised those newly widowed to wear black for two years and to avoid social engagements for twelve months. See Sally Mitchell, *Daily Life in Victorian England* (Westport, Conn.: Greenwood, 1996), 163.

2. Quoted in Margaret Homans, *Royal Representations: Queen Victoria and British Culture, 1837–1876* (Chicago: University of Chicago Press, 1998), 62.

Historians and critics disagree over the political effects of Victoria's withdrawal into grief in the 1860s. Some argue that the queen's prolonged mourning weakened the authority of the crown by proving that the monarch was expendable. Others characterize her retreat from public life as an effective political strategy, with her invisibility augmenting perceptions of her power or, conversely, her "staged" widowhood disarming anxieties about the political authority of a woman newly freed from her husband's control.[3] But whether Victoria's excessive mourning marked her political savvy or her incompetence, her widowhood underscored the paradoxical position of a female monarch in a patriarchal culture—a woman "expected . . . to mourn deeply" as a dutiful wife but also "to violate mourning practices and appear on display as usual" as England's queen.[4]

As a widow deeply grieved by her husband's death and withdrawn into private life, Victoria could be seen as an "ordinary woman, subject to ordinary feelings."[5] Although she held a uniquely privileged position, the queen actively sought to identify with her widowed subjects, particularly those in the working classes. She commiserated with a cottager near Balmoral whose husband had died soon after Prince Albert, with whom the queen was "thankful to cry," and she responded to the 1862 mining disaster in Hartley by expressing her "tenderest sympathy" for "the poor widows and mothers. . . . Her own misery makes her feel all the more for them," she explained, speaking of herself in the third person.[6]

Despite this emotional link among women high and low, the widowhood of Victoria's subjects differed from hers in one especially striking way. With the single exception of the queen, married Englishwomen were legally empowered by widowhood, regaining the rights they had lost when they became wives, and which the queen alone retained as a married woman. In her famous 1854 critique of marriage law, *English Laws for Women in the Nineteenth Century*, Caroline Norton bitterly contrasts the legal position of Victoria with that of her female subjects, observing that the queen is "the one Englishwoman in England whom injury and injustice cannot reach." Because of the "accident of regal birth," Norton argues, Victoria is invested "with sacred and irrevocable rights, in a country where women have no rights," and "where the signatures of married women are legally worthless; where they cannot lay claim to the simplest article of personal property,—cannot make

3. Ibid., 67; Adrienne Munich, *Queen Victoria's Secrets* (New York: Columbia University Press, 1996), 99.

4. Homans, *Royal Representations*, 59.

5. Ibid., 71.

6. Quoted in Stanley Weintraub, *Victoria: An Intimate Biography* (New York: E. P. Dutton, 1987), 312–13.

a will,—or sign a lease,—and are held to be *non-existent* in law!"[7] Although her tone is less indignant than Norton's, Barbara Leigh Smith Bodichon, writing in the same year, makes the same point: a married queen "is considered by the law as unlike other married women. She can herself purchase land and make leases, receive gifts from her husband, and sue, and be sued alone. She is the only wife in England who has these rights."[8] With widowhood, Englishwomen regained the rights enjoyed solely by a queen regnant or a queen consort during marriage, losing the protection provided by husbands but also freed from their control and entitled to the legal and financial autonomy possessed by single women.[9]

As cultural historians note, the autonomy of the Victorian widow generated "societal unease," as did the challenge she posed to "ideas of respectable femininity" more generally: "In an era when respectable single women were uniformly expected to be chaste and sexually naive, widows were respectable, single, yet sexually experienced. Similarly, despite the ideal of the subjection of a woman to a man[,] . . . many widows were the heads of their own households. Further, although the notion of the fully privatized domestic sphere was widely approved[,] . . . widows frequently turned the home into a source of income."[10] Victorian stereotypes of the widow, often represented as merry or emasculating, register the perceived threat posed by women liberated from the control of a husband, possibly enriched by means of his death, and suddenly entitled to exercise some of the rights enjoyed by men. During the 1860s and the decade's debates over married women's property law, the widow figure assumed added significance—as a woman to whom the rights of the *feme sole* had been restored. Depending on their political sympathies, playwrights, poets, and novelists contrasted the idealized and subservient wife with the domineering widow or questioned the opposition. In *The Merry Widow*, a play he adapted from the French in 1863, Leicester Buckingham does

7. Caroline Norton, *English Laws for Women in the Nineteenth Century*, in *The Disempowered: Women and the Law*, ed. Marie Mulvey Roberts and Tamae Mizuta (London: Routledge/Thoemmes Press, 1993), 159.

8. Barbara Leigh Smith Bodichon, *A Brief Summary, in Plain Language, of the Most Important Laws of England Concerning Women*, ibid., 6.

9. During Victoria's reign, the legal inequities affecting married women under common law were gradually eliminated. The first Married Women's Property Act (1870) gave wives control of their own earnings and certain types of investments and inherited property. The Married Women's Property Act of 1882 granted wives the same property rights enjoyed by unmarried women.

10. Dagni Bredesen, "The 'Widdy's' Empire: Queen Victoria as Widow in Kipling's Soldier Stories and in the *Barrack-Room Ballads*," in *Remaking Queen Victoria*, ed. Margaret Homans and Adrienne Munich (Cambridge: Cambridge University Press, 1997), 222.

the latter, vindicating the seemingly heartless widow in his final act. Although she appears merry after learning of her husband's death abroad, her mirth is a ruse intended to protect her frail mother-in-law from the knowledge that the man they both love is dead. The widow is rewarded for her loyalty and kindness with the unexpected news that her husband is alive—imprisoned rather than buried—and the play ends with her joyful swoon.[11]

In her 1873 novel *The Two Widows,* Annie Thomas treats the stereotype of the merry widow with more complexity than does Buckingham. Instead of simply exonerating the figure, Thomas compares an idealized widow, Mrs. Arthur Waldron, with her vain and callous sister-in-law, the widowed Mrs. George Waldron. After her husband's death, Mrs. Arthur defends her son's property rights rather than her own and sacrifices her happiness to the memory of her dead husband. By contrast, Mrs. George quickly forgets her husband and looks to her own interests, subjecting a host of suitors to "coquettish caprices."[12] Yet Thomas does not simply champion Mrs. Arthur at the expense of Mrs. George. Instead she suggests that the ideal widow is all too eager to "go through a little bit of the suttee business" and justifies the behavior of the scheming widow, at least in part; in Thomas's novel, the widow's will-to-power is best understood as a reaction against the powerlessness of wives. "I really doubt if any woman of five-and-twenty feels anything but sore perplexity and half-repentance when she finds that she has gone into the bondage of a promise to marry," the narrator remarks, before explaining that the "feminine victories" Mrs. George wins over her suitors "are not utterly despicable": for "when one considers how utterly powerless a woman becomes from the day of her marriage, who can marvel at her struggles to develop the attribute [of power] as fully as she can before she [again] goes into bondage? . . . The woman who has been once married knows that though she may shut her eyes to the fact, the fact remains—the man she is going to marry will be her master."[13]

Whether real-life Victorian women felt liberated or constrained by widowhood depended largely on their marital histories and the circumstances in which they were left. For all her newly restored rights as a *feme sole,* a middle-class widow could find herself without any financial support or provided with an annuity too small to maintain her respectability. Much depended on the terms and restrictions of a husband's will. When a married man died intestate in the Victorian period, his

11. See Henry Morley, *Journal of a London Playgoer,* 2nd ed. (1891; reprint, Leicester: Leicester University Press, 1974), 241–42.

12. Annie Thomas, *The Two Widows: A Novel,* new ed. (London: Chapman and Hall, 1875), 238.

13. Ibid., 128, 248, 329.

widow was entitled to one third of his estate if the couple had living children and to one half if they had none. But a husband who made a will could leave his wife as much—or as little—as he desired.

As Isabella Beeton writes in her 1861 *Book of Household Management,* "the last proof of affection which we can give to those left behind is to leave [our] worldly affairs in such a state as to excite neither jealousy, nor anger, nor heartrendings of any kind.... This can only be done by a just, clear, and intelligible disposal of whatever there is to leave."[14] Yet a wife's idea of a "just...disposal" might differ from her husband's. As Leonore Davidoff and Catherine Hall observe in *Family Fortunes,* nineteenth-century testamentary patterns indicate that men increasingly elected to impose restrictions on their bequests: by leaving their widows a life interest in property rather than the property itself, for example; by allowing them the use of property but only until their children came of age; or by stipulating that property was to remain theirs only as long as they remained unmarried.[15]

"MY HUSBAND IN HIS WILL"

Even before her own husband's death brought the point home to her, Catherine Dickens realized that men often placed heavy restrictions on the property they left to their wives. In the year preceding her husband's death, she read Annie Thomas's *Only Herself* (1869), in which these very restrictions provide the central theme. The novel hinges on the status of a widow, Mrs. Bruton, whose husband "left every thing to his wife, subject to...one condition": "If she married a second time, she was to forfeit every shilling of the wealth with which he had endowed her."[16] Although he claims to be protecting his widow from fortune hunters, Mr. Bruton tests and controls her from beyond the grave. In treating this theme, Thomas's novel, typically double-edged, identifies Mrs. Bruton as a transgressive woman who "rejoice[s] much in her recently gained power of doing whatever pleased her" but also criticizes the law that leaves widows feeling this way, having subordinated them to their husbands and made them accountable for their every move. As Thomas puts it, the widow "almost purred to herself in her

14. Isabella Beeton, *The Book of Household Management,* facsimile ed. (1861; reprint, East Sussex: Southover Press, 1998), 1108.

15. Leonore Davidoff and Catherine Hall, *Family Fortunes: Men and Women of the English Middle Class, 1780–1850* (Chicago: University of Chicago Press, 1991), 276. In the 1830s, Davidoff and Hall note, the "customary rights of dower" were legally abolished in England, granting permanent legal control of women's real property (freehold land) to husbands rather than restoring that property to widows by right (276).

16. Annie Thomas, *Only Herself* (New York: Harper & Brothers, [1870]), 25.

intense satisfaction with . . . every thing . . . that left her free. Free to move to the right, without explaining why she didn't move to the left. Free to welcome whom she pleased, and to turn the cold shoulder on whom she pleased. Free, in fact, to live any life she liked."[17]

Unlike Thomas's fictional widow, Catherine Dickens was not discouraged from remarrying by the terms of her husband's will; the possibility of her remarrying after he last revised the document in 1869 did not occur to him. Nonetheless, he imposed substantial limitations on the property he left to his wife, using his will to maintain the restrictions that had been placed on her when they separated. In so doing he provided family members—and the public—with a final representation of Catherine and their marriage, one that reinforced his claims in the "violated" letter but differed markedly from the idea of the union suggested by his first-known will, written three decades earlier.

The few details we possess of that document, which Thomas Mitton helped Dickens draw up in 1838, suggest the happy tenor of the marriage in its early years. "I sat down this evening and put on paper my testamentary *meaning*," Dickens wrote Mitton, hoping his expressions were "sufficiently legal." He continued: "The rough draft of the clauses which I inclose, will be preceded by as much of the fair copy as I send you, and followed by the usual clause about the receipts of the trustees being a sufficient discharge. I also wish to provide that if all our children should die before 21 and Kate married again, half the surplus should go to her, and half to my surviving brothers and sisters, share and share alike" (Pilgrim 1:413–14).

Lacking the "rough draft" and "fair copy" of the 1838 will, we cannot tell how Dickens proposed to divide his estate between his wife and children in the first decade of his marriage. He may have left Catherine a portion of his estate outright and the children another, in trust until they came of age, or he may have left Catherine a restricted life interest in her portion, with that property passing to the children on her death. What we know of the will makes the first possibility more likely, as Dickens seems primarily concerned about leaving Catherine well provided for, not with imposing limits on her use of the property she would inherit. He privileges his tie to her over his ties to his siblings and does so even if she were to remarry after his death. If Catherine survived their children and remarried, she would receive half of Dickens's estate, while his surviving sisters and brothers would share equally in the other half. This division between spouse and siblings differs markedly from the one drawn in the well-known "Will of Charles Dickens" executed in 1870—not because Letitia, his sole surviving sibling, gained precedence over Catherine (in fact Letitia was forgotten) but because Catherine's own sister did.

17. Ibid., 25–26.

Catherine never refers to her husband's 1838 will in her extant letters, though she undoubtedly knew he had made that provision for her and the children. Her sister Mary's death had made the couple keenly aware of how uncertain life could be, and they recognized the plight of middle-class women left in difficult straits by the unexpected death of a husband. Eliza Macrone's dependence on charity concerned the Dickenses in the late 1830s and Elizabeth Smithson's fruitless search for Charles Smithson's will in 1844 was the subject of letters the pair exchanged.

In June 1858 Dickens returned to his will, reworking it with his restructured family in mind. He now sought to ensure, first and foremost, the well-being of Georgina and the children, and to divest Catherine of custody rights should he predecease her. Writing up his memoranda for his solicitor's use, Dickens made Georgina one of his trustees and executors; he set aside a legacy, presumably for Ellen Ternan; and he specified that his estate was to maintain and support Georgina and "any unmarried daughters," and to maintain, support, educate, and establish his underage children: "regard to be always had to the genteel and comfortable support of Georgina Hogarth and any unmarried daughters or daughter of mine," Dickens wrote. "Also," he added, "in trust to pay a certain sum per annum to Mrs. Dickens until the youngest child shall come of age" (Pilgrim 8:750).

While he correlated Catherine's annuity to Plorn's age, Dickens did not leave her custody of him (fig. 26). In his paragraph on custody rights and their permutations, he appointed Georgina and Mamie "joint and sole guardians" of the children; if Mamie married, guardianship would go to Katey and Georgina. Georgina would be sole guardian if both Katey and Mamie married, whether or not Georgina married as well. If she died before all of the children were twenty-one, then Mamie, married or not, would become joint guardian with the surviving trustees. Catherine played no part in any of these variations (Pilgrim 8:750).

When the youngest came of age, whatever remained of the estate would be equally divided among Georgina, Mamie and Katey (if the two were unmarried or widowed), and Catherine, "share and share alike." If Katey and Mamie were married, then Georgina would receive two thirds of the whole balance (amended to one half by Dickens), and Catherine would receive one third (amended to one half by Dickens). If Catherine survived Georgina and the girls were married, she would have one third (amended to one half by Dickens), and the remaining two thirds (amended to "moiety" by Dickens) would be divided among the surviving children, "share and share alike." If Georgina survived Catherine and the girls were married, she would "take the whole absolutely" (Pilgrim 8:750–51 and n. 1).[18]

18. In two undated paragraphs written on the back of the draft of the will drawn up from these notes, Dickens reworked his bequests to Catherine, Georgina, and Mamie; Charley and

FIGURE 26. *"Plorn" Dickens in the 1860s, photograph,*
Charles Dickens Museum, London.

Dickens's memoranda for his 1858 will reflect the unsettled character of his household less than a month after Catherine left it and capture him in the process of redefining his family and the status of its women. The notes and their revisions convey Georgina's rise to prominence in his affections—but also his difficulty

---

Henry Dickens were to invest an unspecified sum of money for each, pay her the income derived from it "during [her] life," and after her death place the sum and/or investments in a trust for their siblings (other than Mamie, who was already provided for) who had come of age (Pilgrim 8:751 n).

in formulating his relative responsibilities to the two Hogarth sisters with whom he had lived. Was Georgina twice as important and deserving as Catherine, Dickens asked himself, or equally so? If Catherine outlived Georgina, she might get as much as one half of what remained in the estate; if Georgina outlived Catherine, she might receive it all. Catherine was never to gain custody of her underage children; Georgina, with or without Mamie or Katey, would have that right. Yet Catherine was acknowledged as "Mrs. Dickens" and due a significant portion of what might remain in the estate once the children were adults. Dickens had pressured her to leave their home, but he could still treat her generously, he suggested, aware of her affection for him even after the separation and exempting her from the "wrong-doings" of Mrs. Hogarth and Helen (Pilgrim 8:569).

By the fall of 1858, however, Dickens had apparently concluded that Catherine, too, was spreading the rumor of his alleged misconduct with Ellen Ternan. When he next revised his will in 1861, he substantially curtailed Catherine's legacy, choosing to leave her a life interest in money placed in a trust, that money to be divided among any surviving children at her death. Under the 1861 will, neither Catherine nor Georgina would inherit principal; but Georgina was named an executor—"for her care and bringing up of all the children," Dickens stated—and once Plorn came of age, the income from whatever remained of the estate would be hers for life, the principal divided among surviving children at her death (Pilgrim 9:464–65).

Since the separation Dickens had used each revision of his will to distinguish between Georgina and Catherine, to Georgina's advantage. In his final version, dating from May 1869, he made his comparison painfully explicit, exempting Georgina from the financial restrictions he placed on Catherine and representing the differences between the two sisters in moral as well as economic terms.

Although a will allowed for "a last proof of affection" that would "excite neither jealousy, nor anger, nor heartrendings," as Mrs. Beeton put it, Victorian life writings as well as Victorian novels are full of instances in which this opportunity is ignored. Dickens's will provided Georgina with a last proof of his affection, but it was heartrending enough for Catherine and left some in their circles "shocked at [its] publication," with its legacies and expressions "fitted to give colour to . . . cruel accusations"[19] against the women Dickens sought to defend and the wife he sought to expose: his very first, unexplained bequest of "£1000 free of legacy duty to Miss

19. Here Annie Fields, in her diary entry for 30 August 1870, describes the reaction of Charles Fechter to Dickens's will; Fields Papers, quoted in Arthur A. Adrian, *Georgina Hogarth and the Dickens Circle* (London: Oxford University Press, 1957), 147. After learning of the will's details and speaking to Wilkie Collins on the subject, American diplomat John Bigelow recorded his impression that Dickens and Georgina "were too intimate" (quoted ibid., 147).

Ellen Lawless Ternan, late of Houghton Place"; his high praise of his "dear sister-in-law Georgina Hogarth"; and his disparaging reference to his burdensome wife, whom he declines to mention by name (Pilgrim 12:730–32).[20]

After leaving Ellen £1,000 and £19.19 each to Anne and Kate Cornelius, and to all those servants who had worked in his household for at least a year, Dickens allotted Mamie £1,000 as well as a £300 annuity contingent on her remaining unmarried. He gave £8,000 to Georgina outright along with his private papers, his jewelry, his "little familiar objects," and "his grateful blessing as the best and truest friend man ever had." Charley received his father's "library of printed books, and [his] engravings and prints," his shirt studs, pins, and sleeve buttons, and two commemorative silver objects; a codicil dated 2 June also gave him his father's share and interest in *All the Year Round.* Dickens left Catherine the income from an £8,000 trust, to be administered by Charley and Henry. Forster, Dickens's "dear and trusty friend," received his gold repeater watch and manuscripts. With Georgina, Forster would manage the estate and/or trust for the children, who (excepting Mamie, provided for separately) would receive equal shares. Appointing Georgina and Forster as guardians for Plorn, still in his teens, and having achieved "the objects" of his will from a legal standpoint, Dickens brought it to an end with a statement that, while legally superfluous, was essential to the legacy he wished to leave his children and his public—a counterpoint between Georgina and Catherine:

> I solemnly enjoin my dear children always to remember how much they owe to the said Georgina Hogarth, and never to be wanting in a grateful and affectionate attachment to her, for they know well that she has been, through all the stages of their growth and progress, their ever useful self-denying and devoted friend. And I desire here simply to record the fact that my wife, since our separation by consent, has been in the receipt from me of an annual

20. Compared by Victorians to Dickens's 1858 statements on the separation, his will evoked public and private disapproval. "[Dickens's] last will betrays the same ungenerous desire to clear himself with the public," one review of Forster's *Life of Dickens* asserted, and "indelicately dragged" his marital quarrel "into the light," his self-defense offered "at the cost of one whose mouth was shut, and who had no door of escape into the excitements of public applause and unbounded popularity." Review, *Every Saturday: A Journal of Choice Reading,* n.s., vol. 1 (Boston: H. O. Houghton, 1874), 284. Michael Slater cites other such responses to Dickens's will and its treatment of Catherine, in *Charles Dickens* (New Haven: Yale University Press, 2009), 618–19, including that of Richard Bentley, who, in July 1870, characterized Catherine as "a quiet inoffensive person" whom Dickens "could not have treated . . . worse" had she been "infamous" (619).

income of £600, while all the great charges of a numerous and expensive family have devolved wholly upon myself. (Pilgrim 12:730–33)

From first to last, Dickens intended his will to be self-justifying, if not just. Having otherwise provided for Ellen Ternan, Claire Tomalin argues, he opened with her legacy, flaunting their relationship in what Tomalin terms "an act of defiance," with "the very smallness of the sum bequeathed to her" designed to "shield her from scandal."[21] He ended with one final, lacerating reference to Catherine, criticizing her for the dependence he had helped to ensure through his training, expectations, and demands. As a middle-class matron and mother of ten, Catherine could not be expected to defray the "great charges of a numerous and expensive family," as Dickens well knew. But he was determined to portray her as the burden he had long borne and as the foil to "ever useful self-denying" Georgina.

Read among family members before Dickens was buried, his will soon made its way into print, appearing in the 1870 edition of *The Mystery of Edwin Drood* published by Fields, Osgood in Boston and in an appendix to Forster's *Life of Dickens* (1872–1874). Ellen Ternan owned a printed copy of the will, which remained "among the few papers... in the household of her family" nearly a century after Dickens's death.[22] By August 1870 Catherine knew portions of the document by heart.

As it did for Catherine and her family members, Dickens's will provides a legacy of sorts for *us*—a last, misleading view of the Hogarth sisters, one unjustly denigrated and the other unduly exalted. It handed down to posterity, as a "simpl[e]... record" of "fact," a distorted and damaging fiction, a legacy we had best choose to reject. Catherine herself declined much of what Dickens hoped to bequeath her: by quoting from her husband's will selectively, in a way that suited her; by easing the divisions he sought to maintain within their family; and by rewriting its history in her own will. With Catherine, we need to revisit and rework Dickens's last will and its representations, making it serve purposes other than those he intended and answering it with narratives of our own.

21. Claire Tomalin, *The Invisible Woman: The Story of Nelly Ternan and Charles Dickens* (New York: Knopf, 1991), 188. As Tomalin writes, Ellen could explain the bequest, the same that Mamie received, "as a little nest-egg for a 'god-daughter' from a family friend—which is indeed exactly how she did explain it" (188). Noting the inadequacy of the £1,000 bequest, Tomalin argues that "the only reasonable assumption is that [Dickens] had made other, proper provision for Nelly through trusts or insurance policies.... There is evidence that this indeed is what he did" (189).

22. Ibid., 188.

Because of the terms of Dickens's will, Catherine's finances did not improve with widowhood, and she remained dependent on male trustees, as she had been during the separation. Whereas Dickens left Georgina £8,000 outright, to spend or invest as she saw fit, he left Catherine a life interest in the same sum, placed in a trust administered by Charley and Henry. At the very moment when she regained her property rights as a *feme sole* under common law, control of the money designated for her maintenance was vested in her sons. Dickens thus perpetuated the financial dependence for which he berated his wife in his will. Because Catherine's £8,000 trust was invested in "the three percents," the widow would have to make do with less than half the income she had received since 1858, with her annuity reduced to £240 from £600. Granted administration of Sydney's estate in June 1872, as his "natural and lawful Mother," Catherine received the payments for his portion of Dickens's copyrights but generally redistributed that income among her surviving children, periodically meeting with her lawyer, Frank Richardson, to sign checks for that purpose.[23] Throughout her widowhood her financial limitations concerned her, and she was careful about expenditures. When she fell and sprained her foot in the early 1870s, the injury worried her, but so too did the expense of hiring cabs to "go everywhere" she used to walk.[24]

After the separation Catherine told her aunt that she still loved her husband, and she was grief-stricken by his death. "Heard that Mrs. Dickens's sorrow was overwhelming," Shirley Brooks recorded on 10 June, the day after Catherine was widowed. "The order was that Mrs. D. is not to be left alone. She wants to see C. D. but I think the permission would be cruel, and the scene shocking."[25] "My sister has been, of course, much afflicted and shocked by her husband's death," Georgina told Mary Howitt that autumn.[26] Catherine allegedly learned that she had been widowed from a poster on the street rather than from a family member,

23. "Administration of the effects of Sydney Smith Dickens deceased," 27 June 1872, Ouvry Papers, 41(d), and "C. Dickens Executors" checkbook, Ouvry Papers, 39(i)41, Charles Dickens Museum, London. At least once, in May 1877, the children insisted that Catherine keep Sydney's share for herself. ALS Georgina Hogarth to Frederic Ouvry, 6 May 1877, Ouvry Papers, 21.18, Charles Dickens Museum, London.

24. ALS Catherine Dickens to Mrs. Chester, n.d. [1871–1873], D. Jacques Benoliel Collection of the Letters of Charles Dickens, Rare Book Department, Free Library of Philadelphia.

25. Shirley Brooks, diary entry for 10 June 1870, the Morgan Library & Museum, New York. Transcription kindly provided by Patrick Leary, 2003.

26. Georgina Hogarth to Mary Howitt, 27 September 1870, quoted in Adrian, *Georgina Hogarth and the Dickens Circle*, 145.

although Katey traveled from Gad's Hill to London to bring her the news.[27] In August, Catherine described to her Boston acquaintance Mrs. Francis Alexander the trauma she suffered with her husband's passing, her need for "a change of scene," and the severe illness from which she was only gradually recovering at Herne Bay.[28] Yet the loss of Dickens proved to be a gain for his widow, though in a social and psychological sense, not an economic one.

Perhaps most obviously, widowhood freed Catherine from the criticism implicit in her husband's ties to Ellen and Georgina, and it allowed her to speak of her painful separation with detachment, as a thing of the past. "I need not tell you," she wrote Mrs. Alexander, "that unhappily for the last twelve years, I was separated from my late husband."[29] Three years later, at the opening of *Heart's Delight,* Andrew Halliday's adaptation of *Dombey and Son,* Catherine spoke to the actor William Farren of her husband's "greatness" with a pride undimmed by feelings of rejection and injury.[30]

Dickens's death left Catherine with considerably less money than had been at her disposal since 1858 and with a new pair of trustees to replace Mark Lemon and Frederick Evans. But it also had the odd effect of improving her social status; it was considerably more prestigious to be Dickens's widow than to be his jilted wife. Although she had not been his companion for more than a decade, Catherine received from Balmoral a telegraphed message of condolence from the queen, as did the widows of other famous men.[31] Four years later, as the representative of her husband, she was asked by committee members of a London workingmen's club to persuade Henry to give a benefit reading from Dickens's works, a task she gladly performed. On 10 December 1874 Henry read *The Cricket on the Hearth* and the trial scene from *Pickwick* to what Catherine described as "a most appreciative audience."[32]

27. Jane Panton, *Leaves from a Life* (New York: Brentanos, 1908), 150; Gladys Storey, *Dickens and Daughter* (London: Frederick Muller, 1939), 137.

28. ALS Catherine Dickens to Mrs. [Francis] Alexander, 22 August 1870, Department of Rare Books and Special Collections, University of Rochester Library.

29. Ibid.

30. William Farren, "A Dickens Memory: To the Editor of 'The Daily Mail,'" *Daily Mail,* 12 September 1928. Catherine's presence at such performances and the tie it reinforced were sometimes remarked in the press. "Mrs. Charles Dickens was...at the Olympic, on Monday night, to witness the revival of 'No Thoroughfare,' and delight again in her husband's humorous creation," the *Penny Illustrated Paper* reported on 18 November 1876.

31. "Mrs. Charles Dickens," *Athenaeum,* 29 November 1879, 694.

32. Catherine Dickens to Plorn (Edward Bulwer Lytton) Dickens, 11 December 1874, typescript, Charles Dickens Museum, London.

Whereas in years past Dickens had used the press to shape the image of his "unfit" wife, Catherine could now oversee and correct those shaping the image of the famous novelist. As Brooks noted on 11 July 1870, Catherine was "resolved not to allow Forster, or any other biographer, to allege that she did not make D. a happy husband, having letters after the birth of her ninth child, in which D. writes like a lover."[33] Rumor had it that Charley would "tell the story [of the separation] himself in *All the Year Round*" if he and his mother were dissatisfied with Forster's account.[34] Corresponding with John Camden Hotten in July 1870, Catherine requested a copy of his newly published *Charles Dickens: The Story of His Life,* agreeing to identify any errors and "communicate them to Mr. Hotten," and prepared to monitor the way in which he represented the novelist's private life.[35] To judge from her letters and the fact of her keeping the book until her death, Catherine was satisfied with Hotten's treatment of her separation, which he declined to discuss, merely mentioning it as "a painful matter, which occasioned a great talk at the time, and led Mr. Dickens's warmest friends to marvel at the course he had thought fit to pursue."[36]

In light of her estrangement from Dickens and his relationship with Ellen Ternan, it is unsurprising that Catherine felt closer to her husband after his death than she had during the twelve years preceding it. She could lay claim to his memory in a way that she had not been able to lay claim to the man himself. Bessie Dickens suggested as much when writing to Alfred of his mother's state of mind in 1870: "Poor dear she is better than I dared to hope she would be, and I am sure that in a little time she will be more settled, and even happier than she has been for years, for she says what is true that she has already lived 12 years of widowhood, and now she feels that there is nobody nearer to him than she is."[37]

Catherine also had the vicarious satisfaction of seeing Charley inherit some of her husband's most prized possessions—his books, engravings, and prints—and enjoyed quoting from the portion of Dickens's will that included this bequest while ignoring the hostile sentence pertaining to her. "My husband in his will has left

33. Shirley Brooks, diary entry for 11 July 1870, the Morgan Library & Museum, New York. Transcription kindly provided by Patrick Leary, 2003.

34. Preface, Pilgrim 1:xvii.

35. ALS Catherine Dickens to J. Camden Hotten, 15 July 1870, Courtesy of Dartmouth College Library.

36. John Camden Hotten, *Charles Dickens: The Story of His Life* (London: John Camden Hotten, [1870]), 243-44.

37. Alfred Dickens quotes Bessie Dickens in a letter (ALS) to Mr. [G. W.] Rusden, 11 August 1870, Rusden Manuscripts, Trinity College Archives, University of Melbourne.

his library of printed books, engravings and prints to my oldest son Charles," she told Mrs. Alexander, who had sent Catherine her condolences but also hoped to retrieve a book of drawings that had been in Dickens's possession since the 1840s. "I have written to him of your little book . . . [and] when the library is unpacked I shall take care that if the book is found it will be restored to you."[38]

Dickens left Catherine none of his personal belongings. His "little familiar objects" went to Georgina, his watch to Forster, and his books, engravings, and prints to Charley—even though some of those books, engravings, and prints belonged to Catherine originally and had been lost to her in 1858: her six-volume edition of Milton from John Macrone, for example. When she left Tavistock House for Brighton, Catherine left behind various objects that had been given to her since her marriage, objects that were not restored to her but became the property of others at Dickens's death: her wedding gift from her husband, the inlaid workbox inscribed "to Kate," went to Georgina, who sold it in her old age; her album of sixteen proofs of George Cruikshank's engravings for *Sketches by Boz,* with "Mrs. Charles Dickens" lettered in gold on the cover, found its way to the bookshelf of Forster, who left it to the Victoria and Albert Museum in 1876; and the drawing of a mother and child that David Wilkie had given her in 1840 was auctioned in July 1870 as part of Dickens's estate, and purchased by Colnaghi and Co. for £136.10. But *as* a mother, Catherine could lay some claim to objects that had been her husband's—because they now belonged to her own beloved Charley. To the limited extent she did, Catherine had reason to quote from her late husband's will and could promise that Mrs. Alexander's book would be returned to her if it was found.

In her letter to Mrs. Alexander, Catherine appropriates for herself Dickens's bequest to Charley, quoting it proudly. Rather than allowing herself to be defined by Dickens's rejection, she reintegrates herself into his life by aligning herself with his heir, but also by placing her separation from Dickens in context: she contrasts "the last twelve years" with the "much happier days" of the 1840s and refers to herself and Dickens as "we." In the cold reply Dickens sent Catherine in 1863 after her mother's death, he referred to their trip to America as if she had never been there, but Catherine writes herself back into the story, using the plural pronoun instead of her husband's singular "I" to reminisce. "It took me back to much happier days receiving your letter dear Mrs. Alexander," Catherine notes. "I have never forgotten the great kindness we received from your husband and yourself at Boston."[39]

38. ALS Catherine Dickens to Mrs. [Francis] Alexander, 22 August 1870, Department of Rare Books and Special Collections, University of Rochester Library.

39. Ibid.

With Dickens's death, Catherine emerged from what she characterized as "12 years of widowhood," feeling that "nobody [was] nearer to him than she." Her nostalgic reunion with Dickens formed a contrast to the divisions plaguing his other survivors, as Georgina and the children, with Forster and Ouvry, settled matters pertaining to the estate. While his mother, at Herne Bay in August, recovered from the illness triggered by Dickens's death, Charley outbid Georgina and Forster's agent at the auction of Gad's Hill Place, purchasing it for himself and his family for £8,647. Dickens's executors were furious with Charley, who, Forster complained to Thomas Carlyle, had not communicated with him beforehand and "represent[ed] his father alas! in no one particular but his name." Charley "showed himself prominently in the crowded sale-room," Forster wrote, which "very probably deterred many from bidding." But "believing (this is his own account apologetically made to us after) that the property was about to be sacrificed, [Charley] was induced to take up bidding himself...bidding only against the auctioneer representing *us,*—and had the whole knocked down to him at the next bidding above our reserved price."[40] Georgina suspected that Charley planned to resell Gad's Hill. "Unless he intends that his Brothers and Sisters should share in the profit," she told Ouvry, "I shall always consider it a dishonest transaction."[41] While Ouvry defended Charley's purchase, Georgina contended that her nephew had "taken an unfair advantage" and hoped he would fail to secure his bid.[42] Underlying Georgina's allegations against Charley was the bitter realization that "the dear old Home"[43] she had shared with Dickens and Mamie now belonged to the family member closest to Catherine, as did the volumes of its library, which Charley might—or might not—share. "After [Charley's] refusing to give me a book I asked for," Mamie complained to Alfred in October 1870, "I would never ask him anything again."[44]

Tensions over Charley's purchase of Gad's Hill deepened when he chose to sell the Swiss chalet on its grounds, a structure given to Dickens by Charles Fechter. Dickens had often worked in the chalet, writing the last pages of *Edwin Drood* there

40. John Forster to Thomas Carlyle, 9 August 1870, quoted in Adrian, *Georgina Hogarth and the Dickens Circle*, 158–59.

41. ALS Georgina Hogarth to Frederic Ouvry, 10 August 1870, Ouvry Papers, 14.2, Charles Dickens Museum, London.

42. ALS Georgina Hogarth to Frederic Ouvry, 16 August 1870, Ouvry Papers, 14.5, Charles Dickens Museum, London.

43. ALS Mamie Dickens to Annie Fields, 1 September 1870, FI 1233, Huntington Library, quoted in Adrian, *Georgina Hogarth and the Dickens Circle*, 157.

44. Mamie Dickens to Alfred Dickens, n.d. [October 1870], typescript, Charles Dickens Museum, London.

on 8 June 1870, the day before he died. Georgina and Mamie were especially disturbed that Charley had sold the chalet to the Crystal Palace Company, knowing that it would be publicly exhibited, "an indecent action" on his part, Georgina claimed. "*Legally,* of course, it was his own as he bought the property—but *morally,* he had no business to compromise *us all.* . . . [W]hen this dear sacred little place where his Father spent his last living day comes to be puffed and hawked about, *all* his family . . . will be disgraced by it."[45] Refusing to see Charley, as least for a time, Georgina removed him as an executor of her will and reduced by half her legacies to his daughters. What Mamie termed "the Chalet business"[46] was turned over to their lawyers and finally resolved in May 1871, when Charley accepted £250 for the chalet from Georgina and others she rallied to the cause. Mamie, Katey, Alfred, Henry, and Plorn contributed to the fund, while Frank and Sydney sided with Charley. Only "*three* of the six boys . . . have a proper respect and veneration for their Father's memory,"[47] Georgina alleged, altering her will once more, with the £1,200 she had divided equally among her six nephews now shared instead by Alfred, Henry, and Plorn.

In the midst of these divisions, Catherine remained a neutral figure and enabled family factions to converge, her welfare a concern shared by the antagonists and her home a place where they met, intentionally or not. By mid-July 1870 Mamie had called on her mother at Gloucester Crescent. Taking responsibility for her long silence, she "declared that the separation between them had resulted solely from her . . . own self-will." So Brooks noted in his diary, adding that "Miss H has also visited her—I will not write about this, but the affair is to the honour of Mrs. D's heart."[48] In September, Georgina told Mary Howitt, "You will be glad, I think, to hear that we all went to her immediately [after Dickens's death] and have seen her several times since."[49]

While Catherine remained in her home and Charley and his family moved to Gad's Hill, Georgina and Mamie rented 81 Gloucester Terrace, Hyde Park. On

45. ALS Georgina Hogarth to Annie Fields, 1 March 1871, FI 2698, Huntington Library, quoted in Adrian, *Georgina Hogarth and the Dickens Circle,* 167.

46. Mamie Dickens to Alfred Dickens, n.d. [October 1870], typescript, Charles Dickens Museum, London.

47. ALS Georgina Hogarth to Annie Fields, 20 April 1871, FI 2699, Huntington Library, quoted in Adrian, *Georgina Hogarth and the Dickens Circle,* 169.

48. Shirley Brooks, diary entry for 11 July 1870, the Morgan Library & Museum, New York. Transcription kindly provided by Patrick Leary, 2003.

49. ALS Georgina Hogarth to Mary Howitt, 27 September 1870, quoted in Adrian, *Georgina Hogarth and the Dickens Circle,* 145.

his breaks from Trinity Hall, Cambridge, Henry stayed with his aunt and eldest sister; on his leaves from naval service, Sydney stayed with his mother. But everyone made contact with Catherine. In varied groupings, Helen and Georgina, Catherine's children and grandchildren, could all be found at 70 Gloucester Crescent; her eldest grandchild, Mary Angela, happened to be there on 2 April 1871, the day the decennial census was taken. Catherine spent weeks at a time with Charley, Bessie, and their family at Gad's Hill, and Henry sometimes joined them—in the summer of 1873, for instance, when Catherine took refuge there after her housemaid triggered a gas explosion that damaged her home. "Charley has got another baby—a girl!! (seven girls & only one boy)," Henry told Plorn on 1 October. "I have been staying there for 5 weeks. Mother was there. She was very well & jolly. You have heard from her I suppose of the explosion in her house which might have been very serious indeed. Thank God, however, she was quite unharmed, and the damage has been made good by the Insurance Company, so no harm was done, though of course, she was very much shaken and frightened."[50]

As his will suggests, Dickens hoped to maintain the distance separating Catherine from some of their children after his death. To this end he made Georgina the guardian of those who were underage, "solemnly enjoin[ed]" the children "always to remember" their debt to their aunt "and never to be wanting in a grateful and affectionate attachment to her," and reminded them of their mother's alleged flaws. Nonetheless, Catherine strengthened her ties to Mamie, Katey, and Henry in her widowhood. Although Mamie cherished her father's memory, while Katey, years later, wished she "had been more kind" to her "poor mother" when she had the chance,[51] both she and Mamie were attentive to Catherine in the 1870s, especially after Catherine fell ill and was diagnosed with cervical cancer. "Mamie tells me" became a refrain in Catherine's letters during her last two years,[52] one measure of the time she and her eldest daughter spent together. If Katey's 1897 account to George Bernard Shaw is reliable, Catherine spent part of nearly every day with her younger daughter at Gloucester Crescent during the last eighteen months of her life, the two speaking of Dickens when they were alone and Katey trying, with partial success,

---

50. Henry Dickens to Plorn Dickens, 1 October 1873, typescript, Charles Dickens Museum, London. An account of the explosion in Catherine's home, caused when a tap in the dining-room gasolier had been left on overnight, appeared in "London Correspondence," *Belfast News-Letter*, 19 September 1873.

51. Storey, *Dickens and Daughter*, 212.

52. ALS Catherine Dickens to Alfred Dickens, 7 May 1879, MS 2563, by the permission of the National Library of Australia, Canberra.

"to soften [Catherine's] remembrance of him" when "her grievances against him came out."[53]

In the 1870s Henry followed his father's cue by sharing Georgina and Mamie's household until he married. But he was often at Gloucester Crescent "cheering" his mother, particularly after Sydney's death at sea in 1872 and the departure of Helen and May for Cheltenham. "Harry was with me nearly all day on Sunday," Catherine told Plorn in November 1873. "He was called to the Bar yesterday. I have cut the paragraph out of the 'Times' and will put it in this letter as you will be interested and happy I know to see the announcement."[54] "I very often see dear Harry," she wrote again in December. "He is so kind in coming to cheer me in my solitary life."[55] "Harry, I am happy to say, is going to Gad's Hill for Christmas," she wrote Plorn a year later, explaining that she, Henry, and Charley would spend the holiday together.[56] When Henry married Marie Roche in September 1876, Catherine was included in the wedding and thus delayed her usual fall visit to Helen and May, who had been staying with her beforehand. "They left last Wednesday and . . . I should have gone with them [to Cheltenham] but I have to be present at my son Henry's wedding which (to me) interesting event is to take place on Monday next the 25th," Catherine told Mary Chester. "He is going to marry a very charming girl. Her name is Marie Roche, and she is a granddaughter of the late celebrated [Ignaz] Moscheles, the composer and pianist."[57]

In conveying her information about Henry, Catherine tempered her happiness with news about her "poor Katey," who had "lost her little baby"—Catherine's second grandson—in July, "a great sorrow" to them all.[58] Two years earlier Catherine had written to Mrs. Chester about Katey in happier terms. Although her daughter had been widowed in April 1873, when Charles Collins died of stomach cancer, she remarried in 1874. "I know you will be interested and pleased to hear that my dear

53. ALS Katey Perugini to George Bernard Shaw, 31 December 1897, British Library, Add. 50546, ff. 34–35.

54. Catherine Dickens to Plorn Dickens, 18 November 1873, typescript, Charles Dickens Museum, London.

55. Catherine Dickens to Plorn Dickens, 16 December 1873, typescript, Charles Dickens Museum, London.

56. Catherine Dickens to Plorn Dickens, 11 December 1874, typescript, Charles Dickens Museum, London.

57. ALS Catherine Dickens to Mrs. Chester, n.d. [September 1876], D. Jacques Benoliel Collection of the Letters of Charles Dickens, 86-2754, Rare Book Department, Free Library of Philadelphia.

58. Ibid.

Katey is to be married early in June to Mr. Perugini," Catherine told her friend, trusting that her daughter had "every prospect of being very happy."[59]

Unlike Henry, Katey did not include Catherine in her wedding, though the event gave her a chance to make up for her mother's absence from her first. Katey's explanation was that she and Carlo did not want *his* mother and father to attend and so were excluding parents altogether. But Georgina, Mamie, and Forster were present at the church and the wedding breakfast. Katey may have felt that she was keeping faith with her father in making these arrangements, but she was worried enough about wounding Catherine's feelings to send her a note about the ceremony later that day. Although Gladys Storey claims that Catherine concurred with her daughter's arrangements and wrote to Plorn that she "quite understood,"[60] she was likely hurt by her exclusion. When Georgina and Mamie learned of Alfred's March 1873 wedding to Jessie Devlin before she did, Catherine voiced her disappointment to Plorn.[61] Yet Catherine went on to engage in an affectionate correspondence with the couple, thanking Alfred for a photograph he soon sent of himself with Jessie, responding to their family news, sending love to her "Australian granddaughters,"[62] and hosting Jessie's father, Captain Devlin, at Gloucester Crescent when he visited London in November 1873. Catherine was already suffering from cancer when Jessie died in a Melbourne carriage accident late in 1878. Confined to bed, her hand "very shaky," she wrote Alfred "half lying down" to explain that her delay in responding to news of his "awful bereavement" was solely due to the "painful and tedious illness [she had] suffered from for so many months" and that her "beloved son" and "darling granddaughters" were "constantly" in her thoughts. "I can only pray my own dear Alfred that God will support you and give you strength to bear the heavy affliction He has thought fit to inflict upon you[,] . . . but dearest Alfred thank God your two darlings are spared to be I trust a comfort and *in time* when your grief is softened a little, they will be a source of great happiness to you. . . . [K]iss your darlings for their Granny."[63]

59. ALS Catherine Dickens to Mrs. Chester, 27 April 1874, D. Jacques Benoliel Collection of the Letters of Charles Dickens, 86-2752, Rare Book Department, Free Library of Philadelphia.

60. Storey, *Dickens and Daughter*, 158.

61. Catherine Dickens to Plorn Dickens, 6 May 1873, typescript of H1324 (ALS), Gimbel Collection, Beineke Rare Book and Manuscript Library, Yale University.

62. ALS Catherine Dickens to Jessie Dickens, 17 May 1876, MS 2563, by permission of the National Library of Australia, Canberra.

63. ALS Catherine Dickens to Alfred Dickens, 7 May 1879, MS 2563, by permission of the National Library of Australia, Canberra.

For Georgina in the 1870s, no such "source of great happiness" countered grief. With Dickens's death she entered a state of bereavement that Arthur Adrian compares to Victoria's for Prince Albert.[64] By June 1870 Catherine had been "widowed" for twelve years, but life without Dickens was new to Georgina. Catherine felt closer to Dickens in 1870 than she had since their separation; Georgina, however, felt only the "blank...left in life."[65] So she told Mary Howitt in September. "I do not think the freshness of grief is the hardest to bear," she wrote Annie Fields three years later. "It is the continuance of living without *the* thing that made life interesting and *worth* living."[66]

Dickens's death made possible Catherine and Georgina's reconciliation, which seemed appropriate to all who knew them and provided some satisfaction to both, though without generating much happiness or warmth. "[Catherine] comes to dine with us, and we go to her, from time to time," Georgina told Annie Fields in 1872. "I cannot say we get much pleasure out of it, but it is better it should be so," she continued, the ambiguities of her syntax suggesting her mixed feelings.[67] If Catherine discussed Georgina or their renewed relationship in any of her correspondence, those letters have disappeared. In Georgina's remarks about Catherine, Dickens's voice continued to sound, particularly his claims in the "violated" letter. Writing to Annie Fields, Georgina regretted that Forster could not "comment on the peculiarities" of Catherine's character, and thereby do "proper justice...to Charles," when he published the third volume of his *Life of Dickens* in 1874.[68] And despite abundant evidence to the contrary, Georgina continued to describe Catherine as emotionally detached from her children, claiming that she recovered too quickly from the loss of Sydney. "She is a very curious person—unlike anyone else in the world," Georgina told Annie Fields in August 1872, three months after Sydney's death on board the *Malta*. "We dined with her on Saturday. She was very well, and seemed to be in very good spirits again."[69]

---

64. Adrian, *Georgina Hogarth and the Dickens Circle*, 250.

65. Georgina Hogarth to Mary Howitt, 27 September 1870, quoted ibid., 161.

66. ALS Georgina Hogarth to Annie Fields, 21 February 1873, FI 2711, Huntington Library, quoted ibid., 199.

67. ALS Georgina Hogarth to Annie Fields, 18 June 1872, FI 2707, Huntington Library, quoted ibid., 172.

68. ALS Georgina Hogarth to Annie Fields, 30 August 1873, FI 2715, Huntington Library, quoted ibid., 183–84. Adrian dates this letter 1874.

69. ALS Georgina Hogarth to Annie Fields, 5 August 1872, FI 2701, Huntington Library, quoted ibid., 172.

For years the distance between Catherine and Georgina had been magnified by their reactions to Sydney, who threatened to disgrace his father and knew "the misery of...debt and difficulty," as he acknowledged.[70] Georgina had little patience with Sydney's "folly,"[71] but Catherine loved him and placed her faith in him until—and even after—his death. In 1874 she was the defendant in *McGahey vs. Dickens,* a case argued in Portsmouth County Court, with Alexander McGahey, a Portsea bootmaker, seeking to recover £19.7.6 lent in December 1867 "to her son, Sidney Smith Dickens, deceased," whose effects she administered. After McGahey proved his case, Catherine's lawyer, Mr. Burbidge, declared that "Mrs. Dickens would have paid the money without troubling the court, but she wished the plaintiff to swear upon oath that the money had been lent," still believing the best of Sydney.[72]

Despite Georgina's allegation that Catherine failed to grieve properly for her sailor son, she felt sorrow enough for the loss but conveyed her feelings to those closer to her than her middle sister. Writing to Plorn soon after the first anniversary of Sydney's death—"a year on the 2nd since he died," she noted—Catherine told her youngest son that she "wished so much [she] could send [him] a photo of [her] poor darling" but that "Mr. Mayall ha[d] unfortunately lost the negative."[73] "I am a little better than when I saw you," she told Annie Thomas in June 1872, "but I need not tell you I am very miserable and depressed."[74] "I am going shortly down to Gad's Hill, and I am looking forward to the change," Catherine wrote to Mary Chester one month later, thanking her for her sympathy. "I need not tell you how depressed and ill I feel."[75] If there was any family member who responded in a "curious" way to Sydney's death, Georgina was that person. In light of Sydney's financial difficulties, she "fear[ed] we *must* feel that his being taken away early

70. ALS Sydney Dickens to Frederic Ouvry, 22 November 1870, Ouvry Papers, Charles Dickens Museum, London.

71. Georgina Hogarth to Annie Fields, 18 June 1872, FI 2707, Huntington Library, quoted in Adrian, *Georgina Hogarth and the Dickens Circle,* 172.

72. "Action Against the Widow of Charles Dickens," *Hampshire Telegraph and Sussex Chronicle,* 6 December 1873.

73. Catherine Dickens to Plorn Dickens, 6 May 1873, typescript of H1324 (ALS), Gimbel Collection, Beineke Rare Book and Manuscript Library, Yale University.

74. ALS Catherine Dickens to Annie [Thomas] Cudlip, 29 June 1872, D. Jacques Benoliel Collection of the Letters of Charles Dickens, 87-1906, Rare Book Department, Free Library of Philadelphia.

75. ALS Catherine Dickens to Mrs. Chester, 27 July 1872, D. Jacques Benoliel Collection of the Letters of Charles Dickens, 86-2750, Rare Book Department, Free Library of Philadelphia.

is the most merciful thing that could have happened to him," she assured Annie Fields.[76]

Georgina's comments on Sydney's "merciful" removal, like her remarks on Catherine's unnatural character, echo those of Dickens, who had wished his fifth son "were honestly dead" in May 1870 (Pilgrim 12:530). As these echoes suggest, Georgina served as Dickens's medium in the 1870s, a role she performed more systematically and publicly by co-editing, with Mamie, the first edition of Dickens's letters, published in two volumes by Chapman and Hall on 21 November 1879, the day before Catherine's death. To Georgina, the edition promised to revitalize Dickens and would be "a wonderful Book—like a new one from the dear dead Hand."[77] Writing to dozens of those in the Dickens circle or to their survivors, Georgina collected and heavily edited Dickens's letters, cutting, pasting, and rearranging their contents so as to safeguard his reputation. She suppressed passages in which he disparaged his parents, his brothers, and his sons and in which he tallied the profits made from his public readings. With each of the three successive editions Georgina published over the years, her pruning became more extensive. From first to last she omitted all mention of the marital breakdown.[78]

To Ouvry in 1879 Georgina noted that Catherine, though "very, *very* ill," had "taken the greatest interest and the greatest pleasure" in the forthcoming collection of letters. "I really think it has been of much...comfort to her," Georgina wrote. "Under the sad circumstances [of Catherine's final illness] this has been a real happiness to Mamie and me."[79] Catherine may have taken pleasure in the project, hearing and discussing her husband's letters as she lay ill and revisiting a past from which its most painful episode had been omitted. But she may also have felt that Georgina carried her excisions too far. Organized chronologically, the 1879 collection covers nearly four decades, from 1833 to 1870, its second volume beginning in 1857. Yet Georgina included only nineteen of the 136 letters written by Dickens to Catherine. Because the nineteen dated from 1835 to 1856, all appeared in the first volume, altered so as to obscure the intimacy as well as the difficulties of husband

76. ALS Georgina Hogarth to Annie Fields, 18 June 1872, FI 2707, Huntington Library, quoted in Adrian, *Georgina Hogarth and the Dickens Circle,* 171.

77. ALS Georgina Hogarth to Annie Fields, 11 August 1878, FI 2739, Huntington Library, quoted ibid., 208.

78. The last letter to Catherine that Georgina includes is dated 5 May 1856. For discussions of her editorial practices and aims in *The Letters of Charles Dickens,* see Pilgrim 1:ix–xi; and Adrian, *Georgina Hogarth and the Dickens Circle,* 206–25.

79. ALS Georgina Hogarth to Frederic Ouvry, 14 November [1879], Ouvry Papers, 11.30, Charles Dickens Museum, London.

and wife. More significant than any particular omission is the cumulative effect of Georgina's cuts, which make the marital relationship seem distant. Deleting passages in which Dickens gossiped with his wife as well as those in which he criticized her, Georgina obscured Catherine's role as her husband's confidante as well as her submission to his will. It may have been Catherine's perception of these limitations that led her to ask Katey to bring her *complete* collection of letters from Dickens to the British Museum after her death.

Like the medium at a Victorian séance, Georgina, writing for and as "the dear dead Hand," merges the roles of editor and author in her "careful selection" of letters and text,[80] repeating but also rearranging and suppressing Dickens's words to construct portraits of him, Catherine, and their marriage and lay claim to her own place in Dickens's life. While restricting Catherine to volume one of *The Letters of Charles Dickens,* Georgina figures prominently in both, with many dozens of letters to her included. Subdividing the two volumes into three books without explaining why, she structures the *Letters* according to her entrance into—and Catherine's departure from—the household, with book two opening in 1843 and book three in 1858. Because book one is less than one quarter the length of each that follows, and book three the longest of all, Georgina gives her role as Dickens's housekeeper and helpmeet undue prominence while minimizing that of Catherine. "Showing [Dickens] in his homely, domestic life,"[81] she prefaces each year's letters with a "narrative" in which she notes her importance to the children and points to the illnesses and injury that "incapacitated" Catherine and "prevented [her] . . . from being present" at certain events: her postpartum recovery after the birth of Sydney in 1847 and her miscarriage ("sudden illness") in Edinburgh later that year; the fall and sprain that kept her offstage during the 1850 theatricals; the "very bad health" that brought her to Malvern in 1851.[82] Although many of Dickens's letters to Catherine show a "joyous spontaneity of comic description," as Michael Slater notes, and demonstrate that when Dora was born, Dickens was still "quite as much in love" with his wife as most English husbands were with theirs, as George Bernard Shaw contends,[83] Georgina's edition of the letters pushes Catherine to the margins, suggests she was an ineffectual wife, and makes her disappear from Tavistock House in May 1856, two years before Dickens did so by means of the separation.

80. Georgina Hogarth and Mary Dickens, eds., *The Letters of Charles Dickens,* 2 vols. (London: Chapman and Hall, 1880), 1:vii.

81. Ibid., 1:ix.

82. Ibid., 1:170, 215, 239.

83. Michael Slater, *Dickens and Women* (London: J. M. Dent, 1983), 110; George Bernard Shaw, "A Letter from Bernard Shaw," *Time and Tide,* 27 July 1935, 1111.

In its textual manipulations, Georgina's edition of the letters largely confirms the accounts of Catherine and the marriage that Dickens related in his statements of 1858 and justifies his behavior and attitudes as a husband. Like Georgina, Catherine made use of Dickens's letters after the separation—but to challenge rather than confirm his allegations about her. In 1878 she retold their family history in a narrative of her own, providing a telling counterpoint to his and correcting the misrepresentations that both he and Georgina promoted. Characterized by its inclusiveness rather than by its exclusions, the history Catherine relates in her last will and testament positions her at the center of her family, not on its margins, and answers the will of her husband in its bequests.

In *Family Fortunes,* Davidoff and Hall observe that female patterns of property distribution within the English middle class differed markedly from male patterns in the Victorian period. Whereas men tended to consolidate property in their wills, women often did the reverse, leaving "personal effects and small parcels of money to named individuals, many of them wider kin or friends, a pattern which emphasizes both the dispersion and the personal nature of their property."[84] Unlike her husband, whose estate was worth more than £90,000 at the time of his death, Catherine did not have much property to leave. What she *did* possess, however, she distributed as *Family Fortunes* leads us to expect—among a wide range of kin and friends, with an emphasis on personal rather than financial value. Catherine includes not only her relatives and close friends in her will but also her servants at Gloucester Crescent, past and present. Matilda Butler, Sarah Slade, Emily Brooks, and Maria Bywaters are all mentioned by name: among the four, Catherine distributes brooches, sleeve studs, and a photograph, as well as her sewing machine.

In distributing her property widely, Catherine acted as a woman of the Victorian middle class but also as a wife and mother who had been exiled from her family, who was anxious to defend her kinship ties, and who had found portions of her husband's will inequitable and hurtful. Although Dickens left his copyrights to all his children in equal shares, his will privileged some family members over others—most pointedly Georgina over Catherine, but also Charley, the firstborn son, over the other children, and the unmarried Mamie over Katey. Of his nine surviving children, he named only three: Charley, Mamie, and Henry, the last appointed, with Charley, as Catherine's trustee. Dickens's choice of Henry might seem a practical one, since he was the "most accessible of [the] boys" (Pilgrim 12:344). Yet his very presence in England marked his favor as the son who modeled himself on his father and whose ambition and success brought tears to Dickens's eyes.

84. Davidoff and Hall, *Family Fortunes,* 276.

Catherine's will, unlike her husband's, acknowledges *each* of the children, regardless of success or failure. Aiming above all else to be loving, inclusive, and evenhanded, she organizes her bequests objectively, according to birth order. Gender, marital status, merits and demerits: these play no part in her testamentary scheme. Insofar as Catherine draws moral distinctions in her will, she does so implicitly and only in regard to the Hogarths: not by what she *leaves* to Georgina, an enamel snake ring, but by what she *doesn't* leave her—any mementoes or relics from the Hogarth family. The sketch of Mary, Mary's hair bracelet and album, Mrs. Hogarth's prayer book, a locket and gold brooch with photos and hair: these go to Helen and May Roney, and to William Hogarth, Catherine's "poor dear brother Edward" having died of tuberculosis in the spring of 1879.[85] In an otherwise well-ordered series of bequests that moves from one category of relation to another, Catherine places her legacy to Georgina among those to her daughters- and sons-in-law, conveying her sense of Georgina's anomalous behavior and position. At the same time, she concludes her will with a last bequest to Helen, acknowledging her youngest sister's fidelity: "the balance (if any)" of Catherine's estate is left to Helen "for her own absolute use and benefit."[86]

Among her descendants, Catherine strives for equity and feeling in making her bequests, naming each person and leaving objects with sentimental significance to all. After her children, she lists their spouses, her grandchildren, and her niece May, followed by her close friends and her servants. Catherine's will demonstrates her family connections and acknowledges her personal attachments. There are no sums of money to be had, no real estate to sell or profits to divide, only a varied assortment of objects received and collected over the years. "To my grandson Charles Walter Dickens[,] the bronze inkstand…brought me from Rome by his Uncle Sydney[;] the Ivory Elephant with Houdah sent me by his Uncle Walter.…To my Granddaughter Mary Angela Dickens[,] the Japanese Cabinet brought to me by her father from Japan."[87]

While the value of such objects is trifling compared to the sums and trusts Dickens left to his heirs, Catherine uses these objects to redefine the very idea of worth. Describing the origins or provenance of many of the items she bequeaths, she gives

85. ALS Catherine Dickens to Alfred Dickens, 7 May 1879, MS 2563, by permission of the National Library of Australia, Canberra. By 1853, one or both of the other Hogarth brothers had immigrated to Australia; Kate Horne reported to her husband that Robert or James was "a Postmaster, or some such thing" at Victoria. ALS Kate Horne to R. H. Horne, 1 May 1853, HM 37777, Huntington Library.

86. Catherine Dickens, "Last Will and Testament," 1878.

87. Ibid.

her heirs a sense of family history and interconnection, despite the far-flung travels of some. With several of her sons sent to the colonies by their father, Catherine distributes the curios they brought or sent to her among a new and more homebound generation, placing herself at a center to which some of her children never returned. Having experienced her own form of exile, she uses her bequests to position her descendants and herself in a nexus of family relations. Representing herself as a Hogarth daughter, sister, and aunt, and as the loving mother and grandmother of the Dickenses, Catherine reminds her relations of their ties to the woman her husband wished to forget.

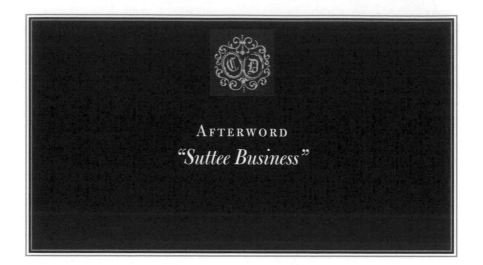

AFTERWORD
"Suttee Business"

*Stay home I shall, but I do not plan to go back to my old, idle ways. I almost
feel I have Alfred's blood running through my veins. I go to the little desk,
and pull a sheaf of paper towards me. I take up my pen. I hold it high up so
I don't dirty my fingers. I dip it in the ink. And I start to write.*
—Gaynor Arnold, *Girl in a Blue Dress* (2008)

Since the 1880s Catherine Dickens has been consigned to her grave prematurely,
her death assumed to coincide with her husband's in 1870—or with their separation
twelve years earlier. Invested in what Annie Thomas terms "the suttee business,"
Eleanor Christian, in her 1888 reminiscence, mistakenly claims that Catherine "did
not long survive her husband,"[1] and later writers usually agree, even when they
know that Catherine outlived her husband by nine years. In his play *Widow of
Charles Dickens* (1953), Norman Holland compresses Catherine's widowhood into
the single day following her husband's death, on which she meets and is quickly
reconciled with Ellen Ternan at Gad's Hill Place. "Better twenty-two years with
Charles Dickens than the happiest lifetime with any other man!" she exclaims.[2]
From Phyllis Rose's *Parallel Lives* (1983) and Jean Elliott's *My Dearest Kate* (1983)
to Claire Tomalin's *Invisible Woman* (1991), Catherine's days become "empty"

1. Annie Thomas, *The Two Widows: A Novel*, new ed. (1873; London: Chapman and Hall,
1875), 128; Eleanor E. Christian, "Recollections of Charles Dickens, His Family and Friends,"
Temple Bar 82 (April 1888): 506.

2. Norman Holland, *Widow of Charles Dickens: A Play in One Act* (London: Samuel
French, 1953), 18.

ones after 1858 and her widowhood a blank space,[3] the contents of a single paragraph or the events of a single day—her life without Dickens, as Rose puts it, a "living death."[4]

Catherine felt that at least *one* woman in her circle existed in such a state. In 1863 she applied Rose's very phrase to Elizabeth Dickens. Widowed in 1851, Catherine's mother-in-law believed that "to have an affectionate Husband to share pleasures and sorrows is the happiest state in the World" and eulogized John Dickens as "a most affectionate, kind Husband and Father."[5] Yet Catherine perceived Elizabeth as dead-in-life "for many years"[6] not because Elizabeth outlived her husband for over a decade, her life deprived of meaning without him, but because she had fallen into senility and thus lost contact with the world. To Catherine, more often struck by the divide between life and death than by their intersection, Elizabeth's state was as unusual as it was pitiable. Though an apt metaphor for senility, a "living death" was never emblematic of widowhood for Catherine, who knew its vitality at first hand.

A faithful Christian, Catherine believed in the resurrection, which promised to bridge life and death, and she conceived of her dead sister Mary as an "angel" in heaven.[7] But she also spoke persistently of the shock occasioned by the deaths of family members, for whom she felt a severe and "irreparable" sense of loss. Though death was "a blessed change" for Mary, Catherine found it "dreadful to think" that her sister had left them permanently, as she wrote in 1837,[8] a sentiment that recurred with other bereavements. "The loss of my beloved mother is indeed an irreparable one to us all," Catherine told Zenobia Cunningham in 1863, "and it came upon us suddenly, for although she had been ill for some months, yet no danger was apprehended."[9] "The shock was so sudden and unexpected," she wrote to

3. Claire Tomalin, *The Invisible Woman: The Story of Nelly Ternan and Charles Dickens* (New York: Knopf, 1991), 128.

4. Phyllis Rose, *Parallel Lives: Five Victorian Marriages* (New York: Vintage Books, 1984), 190.

5. Elizabeth Dickens to Samuel Haydon, n.d. [1851], typescript, Charles Dickens Museum, London.

6. ALS Catherine Dickens to Mrs. Cunningham, 17 September 1863, Special Collections and Digital Programs, Margaret I. King Library, University of Kentucky.

7. ALS Catherine Dickens to Mary Scott Hogarth, 30 May [1837], D. Jacques Benoliel Collection of the Letters of Charles Dickens, 86-2740, Rare Book Department, Free Library of Philadelphia.

8. Ibid.

9. ALS Catherine Dickens to Mrs. Cunningham, 17 September 1863, Special Collections and Digital Programs, Margaret I. King Library, University of Kentucky.

Miss Coutts the next year of Walter's death, "as I was looking forward with so much joy to the prospect of seeing [him]."[10] "After the great shock I sustained," she told a friend in August 1870, referring to her husband's death, "I was taken suddenly *very* ill."[11] When Catherine used ordinary rather than black-bordered mourning stationary to convey news of bereavements, she was hoping "not to give . . . a sudden shock."[12]

Catherine herself died of cervical cancer on 22 November 1879 after more than a year of intermittent but intense physical suffering.[13] As late as September 1878, she still had "good hopes of recovery," she told her cousin Robert, though she was generally "confined to the sofa" and had to cut short her visit to Gad's Hill in August of that year to be near her doctor.[14] By her life's close, she had survived by nearly a decade the famous husband from whom she was estranged. The very time of her death was recorded in her obituary notice, which observed that "Mrs. Dickens breathed her last . . . at half-past eight o'clock" in the morning, "passing away at the end rather suddenly."[15] Yet the shock that is suggested here, and that Catherine herself felt at the suddenness of such passings, has been lost to posterity in her case since she has been consigned to a "living death" by most of those writing about her, her life conflated with her death because of her marital history and the fame and power of her husband. To do justice to Catherine and her story, we need to rethink its ending and pluck her from the flames of her husband's funeral pyre.

In *Girl in a Blue Dress,* Gaynor Arnold suggests one way to do so—when she ends her novel with Dorothea Gibson, the Catherine Dickens figure, on the brink of authorship. Despite her similarities to the self-immolating Queen Victoria, whom she visits midway through the novel, Arnold's Dodo seems capable of returning from extinction. The queen admires Alfred Gibson's novels and regrets that he never finished his last; but his widow is poised to complete it for him. In Dodo Gibson, the widow become narrator and author, Arnold has "tried to give voice to

10. ALS Catherine Dickens to Angela Burdett Coutts, 8 March 1864, MA 1352, the Morgan Library & Museum, New York.

11. ALS Catherine Dickens to Mrs. [Francis] Alexander, 22 August 1870, Department of Rare Books and Special Collections, University of Rochester Library.

12. ALS Catherine Dickens to Alfred Dickens, 16 February 1870, MS 2563, by permission of the National Library of Australia, Canberra.

13. Her death certificate cites "scirrhus [hardness] of the cervix" as her terminal illness. I am indebted to Dr. Thomas F. Baskett, professor of Obstetrics and Gynaecology, Dalhousie University, for an explanation of this diagnosis.

14. ALS Catherine Dickens to Robert Hogarth, 26 September 1878, Arthur Adrian Dickens Collection, Kelvin Smith Library, Case Western Reserve University.

15. "Mrs. Charles Dickens," *Athenaeum,* 29 November 1879, 694.

the largely voiceless Catherine Dickens, who once requested that her letters from her husband be preserved so that 'the world may know he loved me once.'"[16]

Although the heroine of *Girl in a Blue Dress* is based largely on the stereotype of Mrs. Dickens, the insecure wife and incompetent mother who competes with her sisters for her husband's love, Arnold grants her more agency than others usually do in such depictions. Yet Catherine Dickens herself was not "voiceless." She took up her pen, as Dodo does, and wrote—as much to counter as to complete her husband's story. For the "real" Catherine Dickens, not simply for the figure imagined by the novelist, widowhood was a starting point and offered more than a chance for retrospection and nostalgia. Arnold leaves her readers wondering what Dodo has begun to write in the novel's last line. But we possess at least *some* of Catherine's own writings—among them the will in which she answered Dickens's own.

Catherine authored her last will and testament in 1878. Instead of dating her afterlife from 1856, when she drops from sight in her sister's collection of Dickens's letters, or from 1864, when Dickens imagines her as a "page" he has erased (Pilgrim 10:356), we need to recognize that it began on the morning of Saturday, 22 November 1879, when she died at Gloucester Crescent with her daughter Katey by her side. Only by rejecting the myths and metaphors of Catherine's live burial, immolation, or erasure can we see how animated her life was in the 1860s and 1870s and recover the sense of shock at her "rather sudden" passing that was felt by those who loved her to the end. In effect, we need to perceive her death through the eyes of Helen Roney rather than Georgina Hogarth or their brother-in-law. "Ah, dear Plorn, I miss your mother so very much, we were so much together, but it was impossible to see her suffer as we did, and wish her to live," Helen wrote to Catherine's youngest child in June 1880. "I never shall forget the shock."[17]

16. Gaynor Arnold, *Girl in a Blue Dress* (Birmingham: Tindal Street Press, 2008), 440.

17. Helen Roney to Plorn (Edward Bulwer Lytton) Dickens, 13 June 1880, typescript, Charles Dickens Museum, London.

Primary Sources

Manuscript Collections

LIBRARIES AND ARCHIVES

Beineke Rare Book and Manuscript Library, Yale University. Gimbel Collection.

Bodleian Library, University of Oxford. Bradbury and Evans Papers.

British Library. Add. 43689; Add. 50546; Add. 52351; Add. 52338; Add. 54316; Add. 60373.

Cambridge University Library. Add. 9178; Add. 9180; Add. 9184.

Charles Dickens Museum, London. Autograph and typescript letters; Ouvry Papers.

Chicago Historical Society. Charles Dickens Collection.

Congregational Libraries, London. II.a.49.

Dartmouth College Library. Special Collections. Ms. 870415.2.

Dunedin Public Libraries, Dunedin, New Zealand. Reed Collections.

Fales Library & Special Collections, New York University. Fales MSS folder 40:15.

Free Library of Philadelphia, Rare Book Department. D. Jacques Benoliel Collection of the Letters of Charles Dickens.

Harry Ransom Humanities Research Center, University of Texas at Austin. *Cornhill* Magazine Collection; Charles Dickens Collection; autograph letters.

Harvard University Archives, Pusey Library. UAI 15.890.2.

Henry E. Huntington Library, Art Collections, and Botanical Gardens, San Marino, Calif. FI 1233; FI 2698-2780; HM 18482-18483; HM 18524; 18553-18554; HM 28178; HM 28195-28217; HM 37741-37811.

Historical Society of Pennsylvania. Dreer Collection.

Jagiellonian Library, Jagiellonian University, Krakow, Poland. Varnhagen Sammlung 52.

John Rylands University Library, University of Manchester. ENG MS 725.

Kelvin Smith Library, Case Western Reserve University. Arthur Adrian Dickens Collection.

Leeper Library, Trinity College Archives, University of Melbourne. Rusden Manuscripts.

Lilly Library, Indiana University. Miscellaneous Mss.

Liverpool Record Office. Nicholson Papers.

London Metropolitan Archives, City of London. Foundling Hospital Collection. A/FH/M/02/004.

Margaret I. King Library, University of Kentucky. 63M16 Special Collections and Digital Programs.

Milton S. Eisenhower Library, Johns Hopkins University. Special Collections.

Morgan Library & Museum, New York. Diary of Shirley Brooks; MA 104; MA 1338 M. 14; MA 1352.

National Library of Australia, Canberra. MS 2563.

National Library of Scotland. Acc. 9089; MS 3914; MS 4027; MS 4029; MS 4033; MS 7198; MS 7223; MS 7225; MS 10371.

National Maritime Museum, Greenwich. STN/5/23.

New College Library, University of Oxford. New College Archives. PA/LAN 1, p. 35.

New York Public Library. The Henry W. and Albert A. Berg Collection of English and American Literature.

North London Collegiate School Archives. Admission book; journal of Septimus Buss.

Princeton University Library, Rare Books & Special Collections. Misc. Correspondence.

Rare Book and Manuscript Library, Columbia University. MS Coll Schang; Special Manuscript Collection, Jay Family.

Rosenbach Museum & Library. Ems 519/22.10.

Royal College of Surgeons of Edinburgh. James Young Simpson Papers.

Shakespeare Birthplace Trust, Records Office. DR 1136/1/5, fol. 135v; DR 1136/8/1, no. 19.

University of Rhode Island Libraries. Special Collections. Hale collection, Mss. Gr. 155.

University of Rochester Library. Department of Rare Books and Special Collections. Autograph letter.

Wadleigh Memorial Library, Milford, N.H. Ludlow Patton's Hutchinson Family Scrapbook.

William Andrews Clark Memorial Library, University of California, Los Angeles. D547L 1875 Feb. 12; H715L 1853 June 2.

PRIVATE COLLECTIONS

Adam Mills, Rare Books, Cambridge, England. Autograph letters.

Coutts & Co., London. Charles Dickens, Esq., account ledger.

Meynell Family Papers, Greatham, England. Autograph and typescript letters; diaries of Christiana Weller Thompson.

Published Letters and Diaries

CHARLES AND CATHERINE DICKENS

Arvin, Neil C. "Some Unpublished Letters to Eugène Scribe." *Sewanee Review* 33, no. 3 (July 1925): 259–65.

Dickens to His Oldest Friend: The Letters of a Lifetime from Charles Dickens to Thomas Beard. Ed. Walter Dexter. London: Putnam, 1932.

The Letters of Charles Dickens. Ed. Georgina Hogarth and Mary Dickens. 2 vols. London: Chapman and Hall, 1880.

Mr. & Mrs. Dickens: His Letters to Her. Ed. Walter Dexter. London: Constable, 1935.

The Pilgrim Edition of the Letters of Charles Dickens. Ed. Madeline House, Graham Storey, and Kathleen Tillotson. 12 vols. Oxford: Clarendon, 1965–2002.

Tomlin, E. W. F. "Newly Discovered Dickens Letters." *Times Literary Supplement,* 22 February 1974, 184.

Yeats-Brown, F. "Dickens in Genoa." *Spectator,* 22 September 1928, 358.

GEORGINA HOGARTH

Adrian, Arthur. "Georgina Hogarth to Percy Fitzgerald: Some Unpublished Letters." *Dickensian* 88, no. 1 (1992): 5–18.

WILKIE COLLINS

The Letters of Wilkie Collins. Ed. William Baker and William M. Clarke. 2 vols. New York: St. Martin's Press, 1999.

The Public Face of Wilkie Collins: The Collected Letters. Ed. William Baker, Andrew Gasson, Graham Law, and Paul Lewis. 4 vols. London: Pickering & Chatto, 2005.

WILLIAM HARDMAN

The Hardman Papers: A Further Selection (1865–1868). Ed. S. M. Ellis. London: Constable, 1930.

The Letters and Memoirs of Sir William Hardman. 2nd series. 1863–1865. Ed. S. M. Ellis. New York: George H. Doran, 1925.

A Mid-Victorian Pepys: The Letters and Memoirs of Sir William Hardman. Ed. S. M. Ellis. New York: George H. Doran, 1923.

CONTEMPORARY LETTERS, DIARIES, AND MEMOIRS

Carlyle, Jane Welsh. *Jane Welsh Carlyle: Letters to Her Family, 1839–1863.* Ed. Leonard Huxley. London: J. Murray, 1924.

Chorley, Henry Fothergill. *Autobiography, Memoir, and Letters.* Comp. Henry G. Hewlett. 2 vols. London: Richard Bentley, 1873.

[Christian, Eleanor E.] "Reminiscences of Charles Dickens: From a Young Lady's Diary. *Englishwoman's Domestic Magazine* (1871): 336–44.

Clowes, Alice A. *Charles Knight: A Sketch.* London: Richard Bentley, 1892.

Dickens: Interviews and Recollections. Ed. Phillip Collins. 2 vols. London: Macmillan, 1981.

Felton, Cornelius Conway. *Familiar Letters from Europe.* Boston: Ticknor and Fields, 1865.

Fielding, K. J. "Charles Dickens and His Wife." *Études Anglaises* 8, no. 3 (1955): 212–22.

Holman, L. E. *Lamb's 'Barbara S---': The Life of Frances Maria Kelly, Actress.* London: Methuen, 1935.

Jeffrey, Francis. *The Life of Lord Jeffrey.* Ed. Lord Cockburn. 2 vols. Edinburgh: Adam and Charles Black, 1852.

Macready, William Charles. *The Diaries of William Charles Macready.* Ed. William Toynbee. 2 vols. London: Chapman and Hall, 1912.

Martineau, Harriet. *Harriet Martineau's Letters to Fanny Wedgwood.* Ed. Elisabeth Sanders Arbuckle. Stanford: Stanford University Press, 1983.

Millais, John Everett. *The Life and Letters of Sir John Everett Millais.* Ed. John Guille Millais. 2 vols. New York: Frederick A. Stokes, 1899.

Morley, Henry. *The Life of Henry Morley, LL.D.* Ed. Henry Shaen Solly. London: Edward Arnold, 1898.

Priestley, Lady [Eliza]. *The Story of a Lifetime.* London: Kegan Paul, 1908.

Thackeray, William M. *The Letters and Private Papers of William Makepeace Thackeray.* 4 vols. Ed. Gordon N. Ray. Cambridge: Harvard University Press, 1945–46.

Index

Dickens, Charles *(cont.)*
—as champion of the oppressed, 18
—and Charles Dickens, Jr., 106,
121–23, 234, 245, 276–78, 281,
283, 320, 324–25, 335
—and Christiana Thompson, 120,
126, 135–37, 141–42
—as conjuror, 210–11
—and cooking, 187–88
—and Coutts bank account, 64–66,
101–2, 127, 130, 172–73, 184,
198–99, 207
—death of, 2, 208, *303,* 305–6, 308,
311, 315, 340
—and death of John Dickens,
180–81
—as domestic supervisor, 65–67,
101–2, 130
—and "dominating power," 57
—earnings of, 48, 52, 64, 98–99, 108
—and Edward Bulwer Lytton
("Plorn") Dickens, 283, 288,
317, 320
—and Ellen Ternan, 214, 240,
245–48, 254, 259–60, 268, 272,
275, 277, 281, 283, 295, 316,
319–21
—events constructed by, 89, 169–70,
192–93, 206, 213–14, 259, 263
—and failure of imagination, 123
—and "fallen women," 147–49
—and family size, 69, 151, 155–57,
160–61
—as father, 69–70, 106–7, 121–23,
155, 180, 183, 244–45, 249,
275–85
—flirtation of, 94, 175, 219–20
—and Francis Dickens, 281
—and gender: difference, 56, 58, 67,
71, 102–3, 117; norms and ideals,
68, 71, 93–95, 102–3, 110, 135,
137, 142, 146–47, 189; transgression, 94, 136, 141–42, 171
—and George Hogarth, 48–49,
259–63
—and Georgina Hogarth (mother-
in-law), 28–29, 92–93, 111, 127,
209, 258–63, 296, 319
—and Georgina Hogarth (sister-in-
law), 129, 190, 192–94, 198–206,
240, 242, 269, 316–21; allowance
to, 198, 243; as amanuensis and
auditor, 124, 201; criticism
of, 129, 196, 202; equivalence
with, 200–205, 240; praise for,
102, 240, 269, 305, 320; sexual
intimacy with, alleged, 259, 261,

265, 277; treatment of, in last will
and testament, 316–22, 325, 328;
in trio with Catherine Dickens,
194, 203–5, *204,* 209, 240, 242,
269; veneration by, 86–87, 259,
273, 327
—and Helen Roney, 87, 258–63,
319; antipathy toward, *3,* 298–99;
praise for, 298–99
—and Henry Dickens, 283, 320, 335
—and Hogarth sisters, *204,* 305;
appropriation of, 2, 79–80,
84–86, 129, 193; distinctions
among, perceived by, 83, 86, 201,
240, 269, 318–21, 335; intimacy
with, alleged, 78, 203, 259, 261,
265, 277
—as "the Inimitable," 1, 103
—and James Young Simpson, 165,
167–69
—and Kate Horne, 219–21
—and Katey Perugini, 7, 234, 248,
279, 317, 319, 330, 335
—and last will and testament, 238,
296, 305, 307, 316–22, 324–25,
328, 335–36; criticism of, 319
—and Lavinia Watson, 228–29
—letters of, 7, 9, 11, 15, 21–22, 58,
233, 295–96, 333–34
—and literary network, 48, 53, 105–6
—magnetic powers of, 2, 88–90,
116–18
—and male privilege and bonds,
102–3, 109, 180, 219, 226
—and Maria (Beadnell) Winter, 53,
214, 232–36, 242
—and marital disloyalty, 131–33,
213–14, 233–34, 239, 245–48
—and Mary Hogarth, 75, 83–84,
111, 201; appropriation of,
84–86, 129; dreams of, 127–29;
idealization of, 78, 85–87,
127–29, 152
—and Mary ("Mamie") Dickens,
234, 317, 319–20, 335
—and maternal neglect, 61
—and mesmerism, 95, 98; of Anna
Dickens, 90, 136, 196, 221; of
Augusta de la Rue, 88–89, 118,
120, 130–33, 174, 213; of Georgina Hogarth (sister-in-law), 118,
193, 197; resistance of William
Macready to, 89, 97, 193
—as micromanager, 66, 101–2, 185,
217–18
—mid-life crisis of, 14, 214,
232–35, 239, 245

—and "Personal" statement, 262–66,
275, 277
—physical appearance of, 49, *236*
—portraits of, *13, 98, 99,* 203, *204,*
236, 237, 242, 308
—and prostitutes, 68, 146, 239
—and racism, 18
—and self-justification, 11, 59, 132,
192, 206, 213–14, 233, 263, 321
—and sexual difference, 30, 67, 70,
181, 218–19, 236
—and sexuality, 68–70, 124, 146,
157–59, 206, 239–40
—and social discipline, 18, 141,
148–49
—and sons: colonial plans for,
281–85; failings of, 279–83
—and spiritualism, 231–32
—and Staplehurst rail crash, 295–96
—and Sydney Dickens, 280–81,
332–33
—and Urania Cottage, 141, 147–49
—and the "violated" letter, 177,
192–93, 206, 268–72, 316
—and Walter Dickens, 245, 282
—and the Weller sisters, 135–37,
146, 148, 221–22
—and William Makepeace Thackeray, 277
—and women: concerns of, as trivial,
21, 151; middle-class, as parasitic,
237
—working habits of, 65
—works: *American Notes,* 107–8,
125; "Appeal to Fallen Women,"
149; *Barnaby Rudge,* 67, 99,
107–8; *The Battle of Life,*
140–42; "The Black Veil," 67;
Bleak House, 183; *The Chimes,*
130; *A Christmas Carol,* 69, 235,
246; *The Cricket on the Hearth,*
137, 308, 323; *David Copperfield,* 173, 183, 201; *Dombey and
Son,* 140–41, 144; *The Frozen
Deep,* 240, 242–44, 246–47;
Great Expectations, 295; *Hard
Times,* 228, 238; *Household
Words,* 183–84, 189, 217–18,
232, 247; *Little Dorrit,* 228,
241; *Martin Chuzzlewit,* 107,
125; *Master Humphrey's Clock,*
98–100, 107–8; *The Mystery of
Edwin Drood,* 295, 321, 326–27;
Nicholas Nickleby, 98, 151; *Old
Curiosity Shop,* 102, 105, 107;
Oliver Twist, 64, 67; *Our Mu-
tual Friend,* 295; *The Pickwick*

divorce, Victorian, 251, 254
Dobson, Helen. *See* Dickens, Helen
Dolby, Charlotte, 297
Drury, Major William Price, 292
Duke, Sir James, 140, 143
Duncan, Ian, 49

Edinburgh, 24–25, 27; as "Athens of the North," 24; and New Town, 24, 34–35, 38, 42; and Old Town, 42; and Scottish Enlightenment, 24–25. *See also under* travel and residence abroad
Edinburgh Review, 25, 31
education, women and, 30–31, 34–35
Egg, Augustus, 132, 185, 190, 218, 293; and Georgina Hogarth, 205–6
Eliot, George, *Middlemarch,* 150
Elliotson, John, 95, 97–98, 116–21, 139–40, 144
Elliott, Jean, *My Dearest Kate,* 15–16, 338
Emerson, Ralph Waldo, 68
Evans, Bessie. *See* Dickens, Bessie
Evans, Frederick, 100, 270, 291
—and Catherine Dickens: separation of, 259, 266, 277–78, 299; as trustee of, 255, 323
Evans, Frederick, Jr., 277
Evans, Margaret Moule. *See* Orridge, Margaret
Exeter, 41; and cholera, 44–45

Farren, William, 12–14, 323
Fechter, Charles, 326
Felton, Cornelius C., 124, 202, 231–32
fertility, attitudes toward, 69; and sexual activity, 157, 159. *See also under* pregnancies and childbearing
Fields, Annie (Mrs. James), 306, 331, 333
Fisher, Anne (Mrs. William), 25, 27
Fletcher, Angus, 105–6, 112, 127
Forster, Eliza (Mrs. John), 229
Forster, John, 112, 116–17, 125, 132, 143–45, 172, 208, 216, 218, 330
—and Catherine Dickens, 180–81, 218, 229, 325; as "Beloved," 114–15; marriage of, 241–42; report on, 180; separation of, 263, 267–69

—and Charles Dickens, 66, 120, 127–29, 143, 180–81, 196, 210; confidences of, 232–34, 242; last will and testament of, 320, 325; as reader and editor for, 102
—and Charles Dickens, Jr., 326
—and *Life of Charles Dickens,* 321, 324, 331
—marriage of, 229
—needs of, as editor, 225–26
Foster, Caroline. *See* Hullah, Caroline
Frampton, Miss (neighbor), 20, 40, 48, 80
Frampton, Stephen, 20, 48
Franklin, Eliza, 41, 71, 93, 100
Franklin, George, 41, 100
Franklin, Sir John, 228
Free Library of Philadelphia, The, 21
French Revolution, 43–44
Friendly Dickens, The (Norrie Epstein), 12
Frith, Isabella (Mrs. W. P.), 270, 272, 278, 285–86
Frith, W. P., 286

Gale, Mrs. (servant), 6, 293–94
Garnett, Robert, 254
Gartland, Mary, 173
Gaskell, Elizabeth, 172, 294
gender: and equity and inequity, 2, 17, 23, 30–33, 50–51, 90, 179, 251, 258, 312–13; nineteenth-century conceptions of, 7, 29–32, 34, 40, 57–58, 60, 68, 73, 77–78, 110, 162–63, 226, 238; and relations, roles, and transgressions, 7, 54–55, 58–60, 64–65, 90, 189, 232, 313
gender identity and roles of Catherine Dickens
—and Charles Dickens: amanuensis for, 67, 111, 115, 223, 225; feminine ideal of, 61
—and domestic management, 60, 63–66, 83, 98, 101–2, 152, 173, 185–88, 224, 238–39, 241–43
—and Eve, 29, 161
—and "fallen women," 147–48
—and female competition, 80–81
—and hostessing, 64–65, 76, 98–100, 137–38, 146–48, 150–51, 172, 175, 185, 188, 190, 238, 244
—and ideals and inversions, 29, 79, 81–83, 92, 109–10, 114–15, 120, 133, 142, 148

—and male authority, responses to, 81, 98, 108–10, 170
—and male networks, 49, 162, 169, 180
—and norms, equities, and inequities, 2, 20–21, 29, 36, 39–40, 51, 54–61, 63–67, 71, 79, 81–82, 91–92, 125, 218–19, 226
—and objectification, 58, 103, 168–69, 180, 187
—and propriety, 10, 92, 143–44, 147–48, 171, 202, 266–67
—and sexual virtue, 147–48
—*See also* marriage. *See also under* selfhood
Genesis, 29, 162–63, 189
Gibson, Reverend Matthew, 245
Gillies, Mary, 220–21
Gimbel Collection, Beineke Library, 226–27, 308–9
Gore, Catherine, 155–56, 263
Graham, Angelique (Mrs. Selwyn), 300–301, 303
Graham, Selwyn, 300–301, 303
Grant, Anne, 25, 32–33
Gream, G. T., 163–65
Gregory, George, 224–25
Griffin, James, 96
Gruner, Elizabeth, 86

Halifax Guardian, 34, 44, 46
Hall, Basil, 110
Hall, Catherine, 315, 335
Hall, William, 98–100, 108
Halliday, Andrew, 294, 323
Hardman, Mary Anne (Mrs. William), 291
Hardman, William, 236, 256, 291
Harvey, Helen, 161, 235
Hatfield, Sarah, 257
Hawthorne, Nathaniel: "The Birthmark," 50; *English Notebooks,* 65
Hogarth, Christian. *See* Ballantyne, Christian
Hogarth, Edward, 21, 48, 144, 194–95, 259, 298–99, 302; and amateur theatricals, 243–44, 259; baptism of, 46; birth of, 27–28, 46, 67, 157; career of, 230–31; death of, 336
Hogarth, George, 53, 62, 100, 105, 111, 126, 133, 136, 143–44, 172, 231, 289, 298–99, 302, 308; birth of, 27; and Catherine Dickens, separation of, 240, 259–62; character and values of, 33, 37–38, 49; and Charles

Hogarth, Mary (sister) *(cont.)*
—and Georgina Hogarth (sister), 86–87, 194–95
—and Helen Roney, 194; perceived tie to, 87, 297–98
—as irreplaceable, 85–86, 91
—letters of, 80–81
—objects associated with, 80, *336*
—sources on, 80
—*See also* sisterhood, Hogarth
Hogarth, Mary Scott (cousin), 2, 19–22, 36, 49, 63, 70, 72, 75–76, 80–85, 87, 91, 176, 195; and camaraderie with Hogarth sisters, 81, 129, 142, 299–300; as proxy for Mary Hogarth, 85–87, 91–92
Hogarth, Mary Scott (grandmother), 27
Hogarth, Robert (brother), 54, 79, 84; birth of, 27; employment of, 195
Hogarth, Robert (cousin), 340
Hogarth, Robert (grandfather), 25, 27, 39–40
Hogarth, William: birth of, 27; and Catherine Dickens, bequests of, *336*; education of, 36, 195
Holland, Norman, *Widow of Charles Dickens,* 338
Holskamp, Margaret, 139
homes of Catherine Dickens: in Edinburgh, 24, 38, 105; in Halifax, 46; in London, 47–48, 52, 63–64, 98–99, 125, 144, 184–85, 206, 241, 250, 256–57. *See also* travel and residence abroad
Horne, Kate (Mrs. R. H.), 185, 219–21, 235; and marriage, 220–22
Horne, R. H., 185, 219–21
Hotten, John Camden, 324
Howell, Edward, 300–301
Howitt, Mary, 240, 322, 327, 331
Hugo, Adèle (Mme. Victor), 143
Hugo, Victor, 143; *Hernani,* 146
Hullah, Caroline (Mrs. John), 96, 100
Hullah, John, 95–96, 100
Hunt, Leigh, 146, 236, 294
Hunt, William Holman, 265
Hutchinson, Abby, 138–39

Ibsen, Henrik, 7–8, 17
identities of Catherine Dickens, 2, 9–10, 17, 91, 103, 105, 152, 188–89; as "the Beloved," 103, 115–16; and the body, 152, 236;

as Catherine Hogarth, 1, 98, 103, 111, 139, 231–32, 235, *337*; and conflicting duties and allegiances, 108–9, 121; as Mrs. Charles Dickens, 1, 9, 49, 62, 91, 98, 103, 107, 152, 236, 295; multiplicity of, 235–36; as Scotswoman, 105–6, 188–89; and separation, 250. *See also* class identity and class relations; gender identity and roles

Jeffrey, Francis, 25, 105, 108, 145, 150–51, 153–54, 160, 165–66; death of, 153; and *Edinburgh Review,* 25; as godfather, 125
Jerrold, Douglas, 138, 146, 185, 202, 294; death of, 246
Joachim, Amalie (Mrs. Joseph), 302
Joachim, Joseph, 302
Johnson, Edgar, 11, 14, 171; *Charles Dickens: His Tragedy and Triumph,* 11
Johnson, Samuel, *Life of Mr. Richard Savage,* 60–61

Keeley, Mary Ann, 293
Kelly, Frances ("Fanny"), 137, 175–77
King, Joseph, 144, 147
Knight, Charles, 190, 202

Ladies' Guild, 220–21
Lady Maria Clutterbuck: as pen name for Catherine Dickens, 186; as role of Catherine Dickens, 175
Lane, Margaret, 187
Lankester, Phebe (Mrs. Edwin), 172, 270
last will and testament of Catherine Dickens, 35, 43, 87, 207, 297–98, 305, 308, 310, 321, 335–37, 341
Laurence, Samuel, 98, 236, 308
Lawrence, Miss (acquaintance), 216
Lee, Henry, 190
Leech, Annie (Mrs. John), 146–47, 172, 176
Leech, John, 146–47, 176, 202, 276, 290
Lehmann, Frederick, 282, 285
Lehmann, John, 285
Lehmann, Nina (Mrs. Frederick), 282
Lemon, Mark, 146, 181, 185, 188–90, 257, 259, 277, 290, 294

—and Catherine Dickens: separation of, 251, 263, 266–67, 299; trustee of, 255, 257–58, 260, 323
—*Falstaff,* 289
Lemon, Nelly (Mrs. Mark), 146, 154, 161, 172, 176, 185, 188, 190
Leon, May (Mrs. William H.), 209, 304–6
—birth of, 302
—as bridge among Hogarths, 306
—career of, 307
—and Catherine Dickens: bequests of, 308, *336*; feelings for, 308–10; portrait of, by Samuel Laurence, 308
—and death of William H. Leon, 308
—and financial difficulties, 308
—and Georgina Hogarth (aunt), 307
—marriage of, 307
Leon, William H., 307–8
letters of Catherine Dickens, 6, 9–10, 15, 19–22, 52–53, 58, 80–81, 89, 142–43, 217, 223–31, 243, 267, 290, 328
—and Charles Dickens: destruction by, 6, 10, 58; intervention in, by, 228–30; misattributions to, 214, 223–25; postscripts of, 21, 223, 225–28; texts provided by, 148, 212–13; view of, by, 226
—disappearance of, 21, 223, 226–28
life stories of Catherine Dickens: plotlines and parameters of, 2–3, 61, 89, 235; and postmodern theory, 17; problem of sources for, 89, 169, 189; rationale for, 1–2, 16–17; and "suttee business," 338–39
Lind, Jenny, 146
Lockhart, J. G., 25, 40, 46, 48–49
Lockhart, Sophia (Mrs. J. G.), 48–49
Locock, Charles, 145
Lord Lyndhurst's Act, 86
Loudon, Jane, 201
Lovell, Harriet. *See* Dickens, Harriet
Lytton, Rosina Bulwer, 10, 17, 170–71, 256, 267; *Cheveley, or the Man of Honour,* 10; as mother, 171
Lytton, Sir Edward Bulwer, 10, 170–71, 175, 177, 182, 184, 256, 293; *Not So Bad As We Seem,* 170, 180, 183–84

Maclise, Daniel, 68, 93–94, 100, 103, 111, 113, 115, 117, 121,

125, 132, 193, 196, 243; and Catherine Dickens, portrait of, 103, *104;* and Dickens children, drawing of, 111–13, *114;* and Georgina Hogarth, Catherine Dickens, and Charles Dickens, drawing of, 203–5, *204*

Macready, Catherine ("Kitty"; Mrs. William Charles), 93, 95, 109, 111, 113, 129–30, 138–39, 145–46, 172, 176, 184; and childbearing, 97, 154–55; death of, 97, 154, 190; marriage of, 96–97, 109

Macready, Cecilia: birth of, 155; christening of, 146

Macready, Letitia, 97, 109

Macready, Nina, 211; death of, 173

Macready, William Charles, 90, 93, 95, 100, 109–15, 117–18, 120–21, 128–30, 138, 146, 155, 166–68, 172–73, 176–77, 184, 218, 225–28, 238, 244, 263, 279; and gender norms, 92; marriage of, 95–97, 109; and mesmerism by Charles Dickens, 89, 97, 193; and persuasion of Catherine Dickens, 98, 109–10; and powers of influence, 98

Macrone, Eliza (Mrs. John), 71–72, 317

Macrone, John, 60, 62, 71, 82, 325

Malthus, Thomas, 69, 154, 161

marriage, Victorian: and birth control, 69, 154, 159; and coverture, 2, 11, 90, 220, 251, 312–13; and female surrogacy, 85–86; and gender inequities, 17, 58, 251, 258, 312–13; and husband as master, 65; and male network, 48–49; and married women's property rights, 10, 17, 90, 312–13, 315; and middle-class conventions, 52, 64–65; as partnership, 102; and sexuality, 10, 68–69; and wifely ideal, 32, 110. *See also* Deceased Wife's Sister Bill; child custody rights

marriage of Catherine Dickens, 208

—and autonomy, 213–16, 219, 229, 231

—and Charles Dickens: as author of, 61, 134, 149; last will and testament of, 316–17; letters of, characterizing, 7, 9, 15, 333–34

—as companionate, 49, 53–54, 61, 63, 68–70, 83, 107, 160, 181, 239–40, 316, 324, 334

—and constraints, social and legal, 22–23, 58, 63–64, 70–72, 75, 149, 258

—and coverture, 90, 103, 107, 117, 203, 235

—deterioration of, 234–35, 239–42, 248

—dissatisfaction with, 119–20, 131–32, 171

—and engagement, 52–63, 79, 134

—fundamental flaws with, alleged, 240, 263, 268–69

—and Georgina Hogarth (mother), counterpoint with, 92–93

—and Georgina Hogarth (sister), trio with, 194, 203–5, *204,* 209, 240, 242, 269

—and honeymoon, 63

—and jealousy, alleged, 11, 16, 259–60, 263

—and mesmerism, 90, 116–17

—and "mind reading," 212–16

—revisionist history of, 206, 240, 263, 268–69

—and sexual difference, 236 and wedding and anniversaries, 62, 81, 116–17, 125, 139, 144, 172, 180, 242.

—*See also under* Dickens, Catherine; Dickens, Charles; gender identity and roles; pregnancies and childbearing; sexuality

Matrimonial Causes Act (1857), 251

medical treatment of Catherine Dickens, 150, 162, 165–70, 177–80, 183, 247; and cervical cancer, 340; and chloroform for labor and delivery, 128, 155, 162, 165–70, 173, 179, 190; gender dynamics of, 162, 169, 180; and migraine headaches, 174–75, 177; and postpartum depression, 72–73, 75, 84, 129, 144, 160, 174–75; and "tendency of blood to the head," 176–79; and water cure, 177–80, 192

medicine, Victorian: and breastfeeding, 73; and "determination theory," 178; and female sexuality, 67, 73–74, 149, 178–80; gender dynamics of, 165–66, 169, 179; and miscarriage, 149–52; and mourning, 183; and obstetrical anesthesia, 155, 162–65; and

postpartum depression, 73–74; and pregnancy and childbirth, 70–72, 145, 178; and teething, 181; and vascular ailments, 176, 178; and water cure, 178–79

Mendelssohn, Felix, 36, 301

mesmerism, 90–91, 94–95, 97–98, 117–20; of Anna Dickens by Charles Dickens, 90, 136, 196, 221; of Augusta de la Rue by Charles Dickens, 88, 118, 120, 130–33, 174, 213; of Catherine Dickens by Charles Dickens, 88–91, 95, 116–20, 130–31, 133, 148, 212; and chloroform, 169–70; of Christiana Thompson by Émile de la Rue, 133; of Georgina Hogarth (sister) by Charles Dickens, 118, 193; and marriage, 90, 116–17; of William Charles Macready by Charles Dickens, attempted, 89, 97, 193

Meynell, Alice, 136, 221; birth of, 146

Mill, John Stuart, 102

Millais, Effie (Mrs. John Everett), 177, 290

Millais, John Everett, 290

Miller, Katherine. *See* Thomson, Katherine

Milton, John, *Poetical Works,* 62, 325

mind and body of Catherine Dickens: and agency, 118, 169–71, 214–15, 266; and appetite, 186–87, 236–37; connection between, perceived, 171; and consciousness, suspended, 166–70; and consent to separation, 251, 266; and corporeality, 11–12, 152, 162, 168, 186–87, 190, 236–38; and disentrancement, 118–20; and dreams, 128, 170, 185; and mental illness, alleged, 11–12, 16, 171–75, 177–79, 182–83, 186, 260, 269–70; and mesmerism by Charles Dickens, 88–91, 95, 116–20, 130–31, 133, 148, 212; and "mind reading," 211–16; and obesity, 236–38; and physical appearance and activity, 48, 131, 187, 201–2, 236–38; and self-assertion, 120; and sexual difference, 236; and the subconscious, 166, 169. *See also* medical treatment; pregnancies and childbearing; sexuality. *See also under* motherhood